Violence in the Black Imagination

Essays and Documents

Violence in the Black Imagination

Essays and Documents
Expanded Edition

Ronald T. Takaki

New York   Oxford
Oxford University Press
1993

Oxford University Press

Oxford   New York   Toronto
Delhi   Bombay   Calcutta   Madras   Karachi
Kuala Lumpur   Singapore   Hong Kong   Tokyo
Nairobi   Dar es Salaam   Cape Town
Melbourne   Auckland   Madrid

and associated companies in
Berlin   Ibadan

Revised and expanded edition first published by Oxford University Press, Inc.,
200 Madison Avenue, New York, New York 10016

Oxford is a registered trademark of Oxford University Press

Library of Congress Cataloging-in-Publication Data
Takaki, Ronald T., 1939–
Violence in the Black Imagination : essays and documents / Ronald T. Takaki.
p. cm.   Includes bibliographical references (p.   ).
ISBN 0-19-508249-4
1. American fiction—Afro-American authors—History and criticism.
2. American fiction—Afro-American authors.
3. American fiction—19th century.
4. Afro-Americans in literature.
5. Violence in literature.
I. Title.
PS374.N4T3   1993   813.009′896073—dc20
92-33493

9 8 7 6 5 4 3 2 1

Printed in the United States of America
on acid-free paper

A Note of Appreciation

Several people were involved in the process of writing these essays. Richard J. Wolfe, director of the rare book room at the Countway Library of Harvard Medical School, provided the kind of assistance I would ordinarily expect only from a friend. Raymond Wolters read the manuscript and offered important suggestions for revisions. Lawrence Friedman and Carol Takaki gave the drafts their critical and creative as well as repeated attention and influenced my interpretations in many crucial ways. As an editor and friend, Herbert Hill gave me the confidence and support I needed to overcome the difficulties I encountered in the writing of *Violence in the Black Imagination*.

Contents

Preface

A VIEW FROM 1992 LOS ANGELES:
VIOLENCE AND THE RACIAL CRISIS IN AMERICA

One of the crucial moments of the civil rights movement occurred when hundreds of thousands of people gathered at the 1963 March on Washington. "Five score years ago, a great American, in whose symbolic shadow we stand, signed the Emancipation Proclamation," Martin Luther King, Jr., reminded them. Now, a hundred years later, blacks were still not free. King described his vision of a brighter future for America: "I say to you today, my friends, that in spite of the difficulties and frustrations of the moment I still have a dream. It is a dream deeply rooted in the American dream. I have a dream that one day this nation will rise up and live out the true meaning of its creed: 'We hold these truths to be self-evident; that all men are created equal.' "[1]

"Black and white together," the marchers sang, "we shall overcome someday." The way to overcome, King had been insisting, was through nonviolence. Eight years before the March on Washington, King had been catapulted into the leadership of the Montgomery bus boycott. In the crucible of that struggle, he had forged his philosophy and strategy of non-violence. King told the boycotters: "There comes a time when people get tired. We are here this evening to say to those who have mistreated us so long that we are tired—tired of being segregated and humiliated; tired of being kicked about by the brutal feet of oppression." What should be the course of resistance? "Our actions must be guided by the deepest principles of our Christian faith," King declared. "Love must be our regulating ideal.

1

Once again we must hear the words of Jesus echoing across the centuries: 'Love your enemies, bless them that curse you, and pray for them that despitefully use you.' " In the struggle for freedom, King fused this Christian doctrine of love with Mahatma Gandhi's tactic of nonviolence. The boycott ended more than a year later when the court ordered the desegregation of the bus system. The victory affirmed the power of blacks to transform the conditions of their lives through nonviolent protest. Their courageous action inspired an inner transformation—a hard-won sense of self-esteem. "We got our heads up now," exclaimed a black janitor proudly, "and we won't ever bow down again—no, sir—except before God."[2]

The civil rights movement, composed of blacks and whites fighting together against discrimination, led to successes. In 1964, Congress prohibited discrimination in public accommodations and employment and established the Fair Employment Opportunity Commission. A year later, the lawmakers authorized federal examiners to register qualified voters and abolished devices like literacy tests designed to deny voting rights to blacks. These major laws, it was hoped, would help blacks overcome discrimination.

But the civil rights revolution was not able to correct the structural economic foundations of racial inequality. While the laws and court orders prohibited discrimination, they failed to abolish poverty among blacks. African-Americans had won the right to sit at a lunch counter and order a hamburger, but many of them did not have the money to pay for their meal. Blacks were told that the law now prohibited discrimination in employment, but they also saw that jobs for them were scarce. The desperation was especially acute in the inner cities of the North. "You know the average young person out here don't have a job, man, they don't have anything to do," a black in Harlem explained angrily in the early 1960s. "You go down to the employment agency and you can't get a job. They have you waiting all day, but you can't get a job." Young blacks of the inner cities knew that the playing field was not an even one. "Those who are required to live in congested and rat-infested homes," scholar Kenneth Clark noted in *Dark Ghetto,* "are aware that others are not so dehumanized. Young people in the ghetto are aware that other young people have been taught to read, that they have been prepared for college, and can compete successfully for white-collar, managerial, and executive jobs." One of these alienated blacks predicted in 1962: "When the time comes, it is going to be too late. Everything will explode because the people they live under tension now; they going to a point where they can't stand it no more." This point was dramatically reached in Los Angeles during the long hot summer of 1965.[3]

"The fire bombs of Watts blasted the civil rights movement into a new phase," declared Martin Luther King. Ultimately, the struggle to realize the American dream had to advance beyond antidiscrimination laws and confront what King called the "airtight cage of poverty." The underlying economic basis of racial inequality was a far more elusive and formidable foe than lynch mobs and police attack dogs. "Jobs are harder and costlier to create than voting rolls," King explained. 'The eradication of slums housing millions is complex far beyond integrating buses and lunch counters." This harsh reality of urban squalor and despair was reflected in the jagged mirrors of every northern ghetto. "I see a young Negro boy," King wrote in 1963. "He is sitting on a stoop in front of a vermin-infested apartment house in Harlem. The stench of garbage is in the halls. The drunks, the jobless, the junkies are shadow figures of his everyday world."[4]

This impoverished and depressing world was familiar to Malcolm X. "I don't see any American dream," he declared in 1964; "I see an American nightmare." Growing up in the ghettos of the North, Malcolm Little had entered a life of drugs and crime. Arrested and found guilty of burglary, he was sentenced to eight years in prison. As Malcolm X later explained, his "high school" had been the "black ghetto of Roxbury" in Boston; his "college," the "streets of Harlem"; and his graduate school, the "prison." In prison, he was converted to Elijah Muhammad's Nation of Islam. As a leader of the Black Muslims, he advanced a separatist ideology and mocked King's philosophy of nonviolence. As the struggle for racial justice shifted from the South to the urban North, Malcolm X's message exposed the failure of the civil rights movement to address the problems of joblessness and poverty. Even Martin Luther King began to feel the despair. Four years after he described his "dream" in his famous Washington speech, he confessed: "I watched that dream turn into a nightmare as I moved through the ghettos of the nation and saw black brothers and sisters perishing on a lonely island of poverty in the midst of a vast ocean of material prosperity, and saw the nation doing nothing to grapple with the Negroes' problem of poverty." After the Watts riot and his encounter with the "other America" of ghettoized poor blacks, King more clearly and painfully understood "something of the world that created Malcolm X."[5]

Twenty-seven years later, on April 29, 1992, racial violence suddenly exploded again, rudely waking America like a fireball in the night. Immediately after four Los Angeles police officers were found not guilty of brutality against Rodney King, rage swept through the streets of Los Angeles. During the nightmarish rampage, scores of people were killed, over 2,000 injured, 12,000 arrested, and property worth almost $1 billion destroyed. The live televised images mesmerized all of America. The rioting and the murderous melee on the streets resembled the strife in Beirut or on the West Bank. The thousands of fires burning out of control and the dark smoke filling the skies brought back images of the burning oil fields of Kuwait during Desert Storm. Entire sections of Los Angeles looked like bombed cities. "Is this America?" many shocked viewers asked.

"I don't feel like I'm in America anymore,' said Denisse Bustamente, a child who watched police protecting firefighters. "I feel like I am far away." Indeed, Americans are witnessing ethnic strife erupting around the world—India, South Africa, Guyana, Northern Ireland, Lebanon, and what had been the Soviet Union and Yugoslavia. Is the situation here different, we are nervously wondering, or do ethnic conflicts elsewhere represent a prologue for America?[6]

"It took a brutal beating, an unexpected jury verdict, and the sudden rampage of rioting, looting, and indiscriminate violence to bring this crisis [of urban America] back to the forefront," *Business Week* reported. "Racism surely explains some of the carnage in Los Angeles. But the day-to-day living conditions with which many of America's urban poor must contend is an equally compelling story—a tale of economic injustice." This usually conservative magazine pointed out that "the poverty rate, which fell as low as 11% in the 1970s, moved higher in the Reagan years and jumped during the last couple of years. Last year, an estimated 36 million people—or about 14.7% of the total population—were living in poverty."[7]

South Central Los Angeles has come to symbolize the plight of poor blacks trapped in inner cities. "South central Los Angeles is a Third World country," declared Krashaun Scott, a former member of the Los Angeles Crips gang. "There's a south central in every city, in every state." Describing the desperate conditions in his community, he continued: "What we got is inadequate housing and inferior education. I wish someone would tell me the difference between Guatemala and south central." The comparison graphically illustrates the squalor and poverty present within one of America's wealthiest and most modern cities. Like a Third World country, South Central Los Angeles is also extremely volatile. A gang member known as Bone explained that recent violence was "not a riot—it was a class struggle. When Rodney King asked, 'Can we get along?' it ain't just about Rodney King. He was the lighter and it blew up."[8]

What exploded was anguish born of despair. Factories have been moving out of central Los Angeles into the suburbs as well as across the border into Mexico and even overseas to countries like South Korea. The Firestone factory, which had employed many of the parents of these young blacks, is now boarded up, like a tomb. In terms of manufacturing jobs, South Central Los Angeles has become a wasteland. Many young black men and women nervously peer down the corridor of their futures and do not see the possibility of full-time employment paying above the minimum wage, or any jobs at all. The unemployment rate in this area is 50 percent—higher than the national rate during the Great Depression.

"Once again, young blacks are taking to the streets to express their outrage at perceived injustice," *Newsweek* reported, "and once again, whites are fearful that The Fire Next Time will consume them." But this time, the magazine noticed, the situation was different: the conflict was no longer between only blacks and whites. "The nation is rapidly moving toward a multiethnic future," *Newsweek* reported, "in which Asians, Hispanics, Caribbean islanders, and many other immigrant groups compose a diverse and changing social mosaic that cannot be described by the old vocabulary of race relations in America." The terms "black" and "white," *Newsweek* concluded, no longer "depict the American social reality."[9]

One of the lessons of the Los Angeles explosion is the recognition of the fact that we are a multiracial society and that race can no longer be defined in binary terms of white and black. Hispanics and Asians will have to be included. While blacks currently constitute 13 percent of the Los Angeles population, Hispanics represent 40 percent. The 1990 Census showed that South Central Los Angeles, which was predominantly black in 1965 when the Watts rebellion occurred, is now 45 percent Hispanic. A majority of the first 5,438 people arrested were Hispanic, while 37 percent were black. Of the fifty-eight people who died in the riot, more than 30 percent were Hispanic, and about 40 percent of the businesses destroyed were Hispanic-owned. Most of the other shops and stores were Korean-owned. The dreams of many Korean immigrants went up in smoke during the riot: 2,000 Korean-owned businesses were damaged or destroyed, totaling about $400 million in losses. There is evidence indicating that they were targeted. "After all," explained a black gang member, "we didn't burn our community, just *their* stores."[10]

At the street level, black community organizer Ted Watkins observed: "This riot was deeper, and more dangerous [than the 1965 riot]. More ethnic groups were involved." Watkins had witnessed the Watts rebellion, an expression of black fury; since then, he has watched the influx of Hispanics and Koreans into South Central Los Angeles. Shortly after the 1992 explosion, social critic Richard Rodriguez reflected on the significance of these changes: "The Rodney King riots were appropriately multiracial in this multicultural capital of America. We cannot settle for black and white conclusions when one of the most important conflicts the riots revealed was the tension between Koreans and African Americans." He also noted that "the majority of looters who were arrested . . . turned out to be Hispanic." Out of the Los Angeles conflict came a sense of connectedness. "Here was a race riot that had no border," Rodriguez wrote, "a race riot without nationality. And, for the first time, everyone in the city realized— if only in fear—that they were related to one another."[11]

Beyond the awareness of our connectedness to one another was another lesson: the need to become listeners. "A riot," Martin Luther King had stated, "is the language of the unheard." The cry of the ghetto could be heard in the suburbs. "I think good will come of [the riot]," stated a chaplain at Central Juvenile Hall. "People need to take off their rose-colored glasses," Harris added, "and take a hard look at what they've been doing. They've been living in invisible cages. And they've shut out that world. And maybe the world came crashing in on them and now people will be moved to do something."[12]

"Please, we can get along here," pleaded Rodney King, urging everyone to calm down. "We all can get along. I mean, we're all stuck here for a while. Let's try to work it out."[13]

How did we get to this point? Americans everywhere are anxiously asking. What does our diversity mean, and where is it leading us? *How* do we work it out in the post–Rodney King era?

But answers have been limited. Television media have been broadcasting reports that are little more than strings of thirty-second sound bites. Newspapers have been bombarding readers with descriptions of racial antagonisms and the current urban malaise. What is lacking is a historical perspective, and, consequently, we are left feeling bewildered. More than ever before, we must examine our past in order to understand the roots of racism and its legacy of racial conflict and violence.

FOOTNOTES

1. Martin Luther King, Jr., "I Have A Dream," in Francis L. Broderick and August Meier, eds., *Negro Protest Thought in the Twentieth Century* (New York, 1965), pp. 400–405.
2. Martin Luther King, Jr., *Stride Toward Freedom: The Montgomery Story* (New York, 1958), pp. 47–48; Stephen B. Oates, *Let the Trumpet Sound: The Life of Martin Luther King, Jr.* (New York, 1982), p. 112. See Gloria Steinem, *Revolution from Within* (Boston, 1992).
3. Kenneth B. Clark, *Dark Ghetto: Dilemmas of Social Power* (New York, 1965), pp. 1, 12, 10.
4. James H. Cone, *Martin & Malcolm & America: A Dream or a Nightmare* (Maryknoll, New York, 1991), p. 223; Martin Luther King, Jr., *Why We Can't Wait* (New York, 1964), pp. 80, ix; Martin Luther King, Jr., *Where Do We Go From Here: Chaos or Community?* (New York, 1967), p. 6.
5. Cone, *Martin & Malcolm & America*, pp. 1, 42, 213, 222.
6. Rick DelVecchio, Suzanne Espinosa, and Carl Nolte, "Bradley Ready to Lift Curfew," *San Francisco Chronicle*, May 4, 1992, p. A1.
7. "The Economic Crisis of Urban America," *Business Week*, May 18, 1992, pp. 38, 40, 43.
8. Gregory Lewis, "L.A. Riot Area Likened to Third World Nation," *San Francisco Examiner*, May 31, 1992, p. B1; April Lynch, "Southland's Hopes Turn to Ashes: Promise Eroded by Recession, Ethnic Tensions," *San Francisco Chronicle*, May 22, 1992, p. A6.
9. "Beyond Black and White," *Newsweek*, May 18, 1992, p. 28.
10. Tim Rutten, "A New Kind of Riot," *New York Review of Books*, June 11, 1992, pp. 52–53; Maria Newman, "Riots Bring Attention to Growing Hispanic Presence in South-Central Area," *New York Times*, May 11, 1992, p. A10; Mike Davis, "In L.A. Burning All Illusions," *The Nation*, June 1, 1992, pp. 744–45; Jack Viets and Peter Fimrite, "S.F. Mayor Visits Riot-Torn Area to Buoy Businesses," *San Francisco Chronicle*, May 6, 1992, p. A6.
11. Sara Rimer, "Watts Organizer Feels Weight of Riots, and History," *New York Times*, June 24, 1992, p. A9; Richard Rodriguez, "Horizontal City", *San Francisco Chronicle*, May 24, 1992, p. 16.
12. Martin Luther King, Jr., quoted in Willie L. Brown, "Riots Echo Decades-Old Anguish of Dispossessed," *San Francisco Examiner*, May 3, 1992, p. A13; interview with Sister Janet Harris, in *Los Angeles Times*, May 13, 1992, p. T11.
13. Rodney King's statement to the press, in *The New York Times*, May 2, 1992, p. 6.

Introduction

> I am an invisible man. No, I am not a spook like those who haunted Edgar Allan Poe; nor am I one of your Hollywood-movie ectoplasms. I am a man of substance, of flesh and bone, fiber and liquids—and I might even be said to possess a mind. I am invisible, understand, simply because people refuse to see me. . . . That invisibility to which I refer occurs because of a peculiar disposition of the eyes of those with whom I come in contact. A matter of the construction of their *inner* eyes, those eyes with which they look through their physical eyes upon reality.
>
> Ralph Ellison, *Invisible Man*[1]

THE invisibility Ralph Ellison so eloquently denounces has tragically influenced the ways many scholars have interpreted the history of antebellum black America. Historians have in many cases been able to see blacks only as they wished to see them—only as servile, lazy, and happy, or only as defiant, discontented, and rebellious. The invisibility may, however, be the result of something more pernicious and less obvious than ideological or racial biases. It may be not merely "a matter of the construction of their *inner* eyes" but also a matter of methodology.

Clearly most studies of antebellum black America have been based on an institutional approach: They have analyzed blacks collectively in relationship to slavery in the South or segregation in the North. To be sure, this method has contributed greatly to our understanding of the black past, but it does not encourage or allow historians to give attention to blacks as individuals, as whole and complex persons; and it tends to preclude an appreciation of human uniqueness. Stanley Elkins illustrates this tendency. In his book *Slavery: A Problem in American Institutional & Intellectual Life*, Elkins assumed that "there are certain problems in social psychology which require that this 'uniqueness' aspect be for the moment taken for granted and *set to one side*, so that under specified conditions one may deal with whatever patterns and continuities are observable in group behavior." But in his very methodology, Elkins severely limited his attempt to deal with his most puzzling problem, the contradictory emotions a slave and even a group of slaves may have felt, or what Elkins called "the existence of a broad belt of indeterminacy between 'mere acting' and the 'true self.' "[2]

The difficulty Elkins was unable to resolve had been pointed out earlier by Kenneth Stampp in his book *The Peculiar Institution*. How do we really know, Stampp asked, what slaves thought and felt? It was relatively easy to discover what masters felt about slaves since they wrote diaries, letters, and books. Slaves not only wrote a good deal less; "most of them seemed determined that no white man should ever know their thoughts." Stampp realized he could not be too certain about what was happening within the minds of slaves and concluded that "slaves did not have one uniform attitude toward whites, but a whole range of attitudes," including love, hate, and fear.[3]

All of this indicates that what is needed at this point in the historiography of the antebellum black experience is an analysis of individual blacks and their relationships to the institutions in which they lived. Studies based on a biographical approach, such as Richard Hofstadter's *The American Political Tradition*, Christopher Lasch's *The New Radicalism in America*, and Lawrence Friedman's *The White Savage*, have helped to deepen our understanding of American culture and society.[4] The biographical approach seems to be a useful but rarely used method for historians of black America to grapple with the problem of human complexity and to explore the ways blacks as individuals perceived and experienced their oppression.

The potential of the biographical approach to open fresh possibilities can be seen to some degree in Eugene Genovese's discussion of the slave Annica. As a house slave on a Mississippi plantation, Annica lived in the big house with another slave woman and her two slaveholding mistresses, Aunt Olivia and Eliza Magruder. Using the diary of Eliza Magruder, Genovese followed Annica's life for an eleven-year period, beginning in 1846. On July 11, 1855, Eliza wrote: "I whipt Annica." Again, on September 4, 1856, she jotted in her diary: "Annica was very impertinent, and I boxed her ears." But there were also moments of kindness. Occasionally Eliza wrote letters for Annica and sent them to Annica's mother, living in Jackson. On December 29, 1856, Eliza stayed up to nurse her. A few months later, on April 23, Annica gave Eliza a white bonnet she had made, but three days later she was punished for making trouble. What all of this illustrated for Genovese was the complicated feelings Annica, thrown into an intimate and day-to-day relationship with Eliza, had toward her oppressor. In his mind's eye, Genovese imagined Annica marching off to the federal lines during the war, but doing this with mixed feelings. "We should not," he argued, "be too quick to assume that she would easily have left the only home she had known as an adult and the woman who wrote letters to her mamma, exchanged confidences with her, and stayed up with her on feverish nights." But then he reminded us that "the only thing we can be sure of is that she remained impudent to the day she died."[5] In Genovese's provocative attempt to understand Annica's inner emotions and thoughts, Annica became human: She became complicated, multidimensional.

But Genovese's discussion also implicitly reveals one of the frustrations historians experience: the comparative scarcity of black written documents for the period before the Civil War. This fact underscores the need to use as fully and creatively as possible the available documents. While historians have combed through newspapers, slave narratives, and letters, they have generally ignored or overlooked black fiction as source material deserving their serious attention and analysis. Here is an unexamined genre of evidence. *The Heroic Slave* by Frederick Douglass, the most widely known black abolitionist, *Blake; or, the Huts of America* by Martin Delany, the father of black nationalism in America, and *Clotelle: A Tale of the Southern States* by William Wells Brown, the first black novelist in

America, are almost never mentioned, much less analyzed, in even the major studies of antebellum black America. Only recently have a few specialists appreciated the fictional writings of Brown and Delany, while Douglass' *The Heroic Slave* has been long forgotten.[6] (It is here republished for the first time since 1853.)

The neglect of black fiction has been unfortunate, for black fiction not only adds to our already limited number of antebellum black written documents but also represents a particularly important genre of evidence. Much more than editorials, letters, or autobiographies, fiction reflects the imagination or fantasy of its creator. It permits the writer to express the dreams and the deeply felt emotions he may not have been able or willing to articulate in his speeches or nonfictional writings. Under the guise of fiction, blacks like Douglass, Delany, and Brown may have felt less intimidated in telling the truth, especially to whites and perhaps even to themselves. Delany's *Blake*, for example, seems to reveal more about the father of black nationalism than all of his political essays and tracts. Thus fiction analyzed as a social document rather than a work of art offers a unique way to gain insight into the feelings blacks had toward their experiences within the peculiar institution and/or north of slavery, the whites around them, the selves within them, and the violence they wished to bring down upon their oppressors.

Violence against the oppressor is a dominant concern in the fiction of Douglass, Delany, and Brown. The theme of violence provides a provocative angle from which to probe the complexity of their lives and the intricacies of their thoughts on racial integration, black separatism, and the destiny of blacks in America. Unlike Nat Turner's rebellion, theirs is fantasized violence. Here, then, is an opportunity to study not so much the violence that had taken place in history but the violence that had occurred in the black imagination. Yet, unless it is assumed fantasy and reality have no relationship to each other and unless it is claimed the line between them has always been clear, it is quite possible that an analysis of fantasy can reveal much about what has happened in the real world.

Thus *Violence in the Black Imagination* focuses on blacks— Douglass, Delany, and Brown—as individuals, complex and human, and analyzes oppression as they uniquely experienced it in their often chaotic and always terrible social realities and as they interpreted and pondered over it in the fantasies of their plays and novels about slave violence and rebellion in order to help move our understanding of the black past closer to the point beyond which all is mystery.

Hull, Massachusetts   R. T. T.

FOOTNOTES

1. Ralph Ellison, *Invisible Man* (New York, Signet, 1952), p. 7.
2. Stanley M. Elkins, *Slavery: A Problem in American Institutional & Intellectual Life* (New York, Grosset & Dunlap, 1963), pp. 227-28. Italics added.
3. Kenneth M. Stampp, *The Peculiar Institution: Slavery in the Antebellum South* (New York, Vintage, 1956), pp. 377-81.
4. Richard Hofstadter, *The American Political Tradition* (New York, Vintage, 1960); Christopher Lasch, *The New Radicalism in America, 1889-1963* (New York, Vintage, 1965); Lawrence Friedman, *The White Savage: Racial Fantasies in the Postbellum South* (Englewood Cliffs, N.J., Prentice-Hall, 1970).
5. Eugene D. Genovese, "American Slaves and Their History," *New York Review of Books*, December 3, 1970.
6. See Floyd Miller, "Introduction," in Martin R. Delany, *Blake; or, the Huts of America* (New York, Beacon, 1970); William Farrison, *William Wells Brown: Author and Reformer* (Chicago, University of Chicago Press, 1969). Robert Bone, in *The Negro Novel in America* (New Haven, Yale University Press, 1968), devotes only two brief paragraphs to Brown and one to Delany, pp. 30-31.

The literature created by Negroes is not only a protest against the irrational racial situation, not only an attempt to explain the unique status of American Negroes to white society and to the world, but, most significantly, the literature of American Negroes is an attempt to explain the racial situation to themselves.

Herbert Hill, *Anger, And Beyond*

Part I
Not Afraid to Die:

Frederick Douglass and Violence

He murdered Mary Dalton, accidentally, without thinking, without plan, without conscious motive. But, after he murdered, he accepted the crime. And that's the important thing. It was the first full act of his life; it was the most meaningful, exciting and stirring thing that had ever happened to him. He accepted it because it made him free, gave him the possibility of choice, of action, the opportunity to act and to feel that his actions carried weight.

* * *

I ain't trying to forgive nobody, said Bigger Thomas, and I ain't asking for nobody to forgive me. I ain't going to cry. They wouldn't let me live and I killed. Maybe it ain't fair to kill, and I reckon I really didn't want to kill. But when I think of why all the killing was, I begin to feel what I wanted, what I am. . . .

Richard Wright, Native Son

They would do well to read Fanon; for he shows clearly that this irrepressible violence [of the colonized against the colonizer] is neither sound and fury, nor the resurrection of savage instincts, nor even the effect of resentment: it is man re-creating himself. I think we understood this truth at one time, but we have forgotten it—that no gentleness can efface the marks of violence; only violence itself can destroy them. The native cures himself of colonial neurosis by

17

thrusting out the settler through force of arms. When his rage boils over, he rediscovers his lost innocence and he comes to know himself in that he himself creates his self. . . . When the peasant takes a gun in his hands, the old myths grow dim and the prohibitions are one by one forgotten. The rebel's weapon is the proof of his humanity.

Jean Paul Sartre, in Preface to
Wretched of the Earth by Frantz Fanon

There, then, is the heart of the matter: There are no masculine and feminine virtues. There are only human virtues.

Theodore Roszak, "The Hard and the
Soft: The Force of Feminism in
Modern Times."[1]

VIOLENCE against the oppressor was a question Frederick Douglass faced with profound ambivalence. Committed to Garrisonian abolitionism during the 1840's, Douglass sincerely hoped the abolitionist movement could successfully appeal to men's sense of right and emancipation could be achieved nonviolently. "Slavery is one of those monsters of darkness," he argued, "to whom the light of truth is death. . . . I would have condemnation blaze down upon him [the slaveholder] in every direction, till, stunned and overwhelmed with shame and confusion, he is compelled to let go the grasp he holds upon the persons of his victims, and restore them to their long lost rights." As a moral suasionist, Douglass denounced Henry Highland Garnet's bold address to the slaves advocating a war to the knife against the slaveholding class. "There was," Douglass protested, "too much physical force both in the address and remarks of Garnet."[2] But at the same time Douglass believed slave violence against the master class could have crucial psychological and political meaning for the wretched, for the oppressed. The ambivalence Douglass felt toward violence was very personal: It was deeply rooted in his years of childhood and early manhood, in his relationships with gentlewomen like his slaveholding mistress Sophia Auld and his grandmother Betsey Bailey and with hardened men like Hugh and Thomas Auld and Edward Covey, and in his very mulattoness—his racial ties to both white and black.

II

As a young slave living on the eastern shore of Maryland, Douglass could not really see how the tragic situation in the South could be overcome without violence against the oppressor. He thought that slaveholders were too insensitive and too selfish to be moved morally and that violent resistance was important for the psychological liberation of the slave.

All of this had been made unforgettably clear to him during his fight with the slave-breaker Edward Covey. At the age of sixteen, Douglass had been placed under Covey's supervision for one year. Master Thomas Auld's instructions to Covey were simple and clear: He wanted young Douglass "to be broken."[3] Slavery had failed to reduce Douglass into a Sambo, a docile and happy slave. "To make a contented slave," Douglass later explained, "you must make a thoughtless one. . . . He must be able to detect no inconsistencies in slavery. The man who takes his earnings must be able to convince him that he has a perfect right to do so. It must not depend on mere force—the slave must know no higher law than his master's will. The whole relationship must not only demonstrate to his mind its necessity, but its absolute rightfulness."[4] Douglass was too intelligent and too thoughtful not to see the inconsistencies of slavery, and he had too great a sense of self-worth, even in his slavery, not to feel wretched and discontent.

In trying to explain Douglass' unhappiness and impudence, Master Thomas Auld complained that "city life" had affected Douglass "perniciously."[5] Here Master Auld was echoing a widespread Southern white anxiety: Slavery did not work well in an urban context. "The city is no place for niggers," one distressed white Southerner declared. "They get strange notions in their heads, and grow discontented. They ought, everyone of them, be sent back on to the plantations."[6]

As a young boy, Douglass had been sent to live with Hugh Auld and his wife, Sophia, in Baltimore. There he quickly discovered that the urban slavery of Baltimore was not as coercive and closed as the rural slavery of the plantation. There he was exposed to influences subversive to slavery. In the city, which had a large population of free blacks, he could easily see that not all blacks were slaves. Their very presence refuted the

Southern racist claim that slavery was the black's natural condition. "I was living among freemen, and was in all respects equal to them by nature and attainments. Why should I be a slave?" On the wharves of Baltimore Douglass met two Irishmen who told him about the free society of the North, and he went home with thoughts of escape and freedom pounding in his head. The city also offered Douglass educational opportunities. Once Douglass realized knowledge was a path to freedom, he was determined to learn to read. He carried a copy of *Webster's Spelling Book* in his pocket when he went outside to play and took spelling lessons from his white playmates in the streets of Baltimore. Douglass blacked boots to earn money to buy *The Columbian Orator* from a shop on Thames Street. He drank deeply from this antislavery book, and the thought of being a slave for life pressed more heavily upon his heart. Compared to his life on the plantation, Douglass felt he was almost free in Baltimore, for he had greater freedom of movement and contact with a wider variety of people and ideas. All of this intensified his awareness of the terrible contradiction he was living as an enslaved human being. Thus his transfer to Baltimore was a highly significant event in his life. "It is quite probable," Douglass speculated, "that but for the mere circumstance of being thus removed [to Baltimore], before the rigors of slavery had fully fastened upon me, before my young spirit had been crushed under the iron control of the slave-driver, I might have continued in slavery until emancipated by the war." Clearly Baltimore had a "pernicious" influence on Douglass as a slave.[7]

Actually Douglass had developed a sense of selfhood and a consciousness of freedom long before his experience in Baltimore. During the crucial years of early childhood, Douglass had lived with his grandmother and grandfather, Betsey and Isaac Bailey. Grandmother Bailey was in charge of the children of the younger slave women. The Bailey cabin was isolated, located twelve miles away from Colonel Lloyd's plantation and far away psychologically from the reality of slavery. Young Frederick had almost no contact with whites; moreover, he did not directly experience the brutality of the "peculiar institution." "I had always lived with my grandmother on the outskirts of the plantation," Douglass observed. "I had therefore been, until now, out of the way of the bloody scenes that often occurred on the plantation."[8]

Douglass' childhood years at Grandmother Bailey's home were happy and secure. A skillful fisherwoman and gardener, Grandmother Bailey made certain young Frederick never went hungry. She was also somewhat permissive: Frederick was allowed to play and grow up free from restraints, free to run wild and to be joyous and even roguish. More important, Grandmother Bailey gave him love and affection. "Living here, with my dear old grandmother and grandfather," Douglass recalled, "it was a long time before I knew myself to be a *slave*. . . . Grandmother and grandfather were the greatest people in the world to me; and being with them so smugly in their own little cabin—I supposed it to be their own—knowing no higher authority over me . . . than the authority of grandmamma, for a time there was nothing to disturb me."[9] This was a critical period in his character formation. In the sheltered home of Grandmother Bailey the child Frederick discovered that he was a person; only later, after he was taken away to the plantation, would he learn he was a slave, a piece of property. But, by then, it would be quite late.

Master Thomas Auld hoped it was not too late and sent the sixteen-year-old Douglass to Edward Covey to be broken. Reduced to a field hand for the first time in his life, Douglass was so brutally whipped and overworked that he felt Covey had succeeded in breaking him. "My natural elasticity was crushed; my intellect languished; the disposition to read departed; the cheerful spark that lingered about my eye died out; the dark night of slavery closed in upon me, and behold a man transformed to a brute!" But Douglass did not realize how greatly Grandmother Bailey and Baltimore had unfitted him to be a slave. Thus, though he found himself in a "sort of beast-like stupor between sleeping and waking," he could still gaze at the sailboats skimming across the waters of the Chesapeake Bay and exclaim: "You are loosed from your moorings, and free. I am fast in my chains, and am a slave! . . . O, that I were free! O, that I were on one of your gallant decks, and under your protecting wing! . . . I will run away. . . . I had as well be killed running as die standing."[10] Beaten and cuffed, kept hungry and spiritless, still Douglass did not follow his master like a dog, still thoughts of freedom intruded in his anguished mind.

Covey sensed this and was determined to stamp out those thoughts completely. While working in the treading yard during a hot August day, Douglass collapsed from heat and exhaustion. He was too ill to respond to Covey's order to get up and work, and he was savagely kicked and beaten. Bleeding profusely, Douglass managed to crawl to Master Auld, pleading for protection from the inhuman slave-breaker. Master Auld scolded him and ordered him to return to Covey. Douglass felt his "last hope had been extinguished": His master, whom Douglass did not hope would protect him *"as a man,"* had now refused to protect him *"as his property."*[11]

Hungry and bloodstained, Douglass walked back to Covey's farm, hating himself and thinking life itself had become almost burdensome. A terrifying but perhaps redemptive loneliness and isolation enveloped him. "I was in the wood, buried in its somber gloom and hushed in its solemn silence, hidden from all human eyes, shut in with nature and with nature's God, and absent from all human contrivances. Here was a good place to pray, to pray for help, for deliverance—a prayer I had often made before. But how could I pray?"[12] Alienated from his master, himself, his God, Douglass in the darkness of the woods was now willing to exchange his manhood for the bestiality of an ox.

But his feelings of wretchedness had not completely overwhelmed his sense of selfhood. Douglass walked back to Covey's farm, determined to defend himself. When Covey tried to tie and whip him, Douglass fought violently. "The fighting madness had come upon me, and I found my strong fingers firmly attached to the throat of the tyrant, as heedless of consequences, at the moment, as if we stood as equals before the law. The very color of the man was forgotten. . . . I held him so firmly by the throat that his blood followed my nails."[13] Clearly, as Douglass choked his oppressor, he forgot Covey was white and everything that that whiteness implied and he experienced a moment of equality. No longer sinking into the stupor of bestiality, he now felt intensely alive.

Douglass' act of violence liberated him psychologically. It completed his rebellion against his slavish hatred of himself and his slavish fear of the white oppressor. It enabled him to repudiate the definition of property imposed on him by the master class and to affirm his identity as a human being and his right to be free. The supreme moment of physical confrontation with Covey was a turning point in Douglass' life. "I was a changed being after that fight. I was nothing before—I was a man now. . . . I had reached the point at which I was *not afraid to die*. This spirit made me a freeman in *fact*, though I still remained a slave in form." In the process of violent struggle against the oppressor, Douglass had not merely "drawn blood from him": He had overthrown his fear of death and suddenly realized more deeply than ever before the sense of selfhood and consciousness of freedom that the love of Grandmother Bailey and the openness of Baltimore had given him.[14]

Douglass' fight with Covey taught him a lesson he would always remember: "A man without force is without the essential dignity of humanity."[15] This belief was one of the key reasons why Douglass broke from the nonviolent approach of Garrison and moved toward the violent strategy of John Brown. After his meeting with Brown in 1847, Douglass became less confident in the peaceful abolition of slavery. "My utterances became more and more tinged by the color of this man's strong impressions." Soon Douglass sounded a lot like Henry Highland Garnet. In 1849 Douglass announced he would welcome the news that the slaves had risen and that "the sable arms which have been engaged in beautifying and adorning the South were engaged in spreading death and devastation there." Ten years later Douglass eloquently justified Brown's attack on Harpers Ferry. Referring to Garrisonian abolitionism, he argued that moral considerations had long since been exhausted on slaveholders and that it was vain to reason with them. Then, perhaps remembering his fight with Covey, he charged that slavery was a system of brute force and had to be met with its own weapons. "Capt. Brown has initiated a new mode of carrying on the crusade of freedom, and his blow has sent dread and terror throughout the entire ranks of the piratical army of slavery."[16]

Actually Brown's influence on Douglass was not as important as Douglass himself thought it was. Brown simply helped him to understand more clearly what he had already sensed—the necessity of violence to destroy the institution of slavery.

Moreover, violence against the oppressor had a far greater meaning for Douglass than it did for Brown: Violence as Douglass viewed it was a way for blacks to assert their humanity. In his condemnation of the Fugitive Slave Law, Douglass insisted that the only way to make the law a "dead letter" was to make half a dozen or more "dead kidnappers," and that every dead slave hunter was "an argument in favor of the manhood of our race." The killing of slave catchers had more than a political meaning. All of these thoughts on violence against the oppressor came to a climax in Douglass' famous 1863 editorial "Men of Color, To Arms!" Urging black men to enlist in the Union Army, Douglass declared: "The chance is now given you to end in a day the bondage of centuries, and to rise in one bound from social degradation to the place of common equality with all other varieties of man."[17] For Douglass, black violence against white Southerners during the Civil War would do more than destroy the slave system: The sable arm of the black soldier would also wipe out racist claims of black submissiveness and inferiority and restore black manhood.

During the early 1850's, while Douglass increasingly called for the violent abolition of slavery, he wrote *The Heroic Slave*, a fictional narrative based on the 1841 mutiny on board the slave ship *Creole*. Douglass knew little about Madison Washington, the leader of the slave rebellion. "Curiously, earnestly, anxiously we peer into the dark," Douglass informed his reader in the introduction, "and wish even for the blinding flash, or the light of northern skies to reveal him. But alas! he is still enveloped in darkness. . . ." Thus Douglass used his imagination, relied on "possibles" and "probabilities," and even projected himself onto the black protagonist to create his heroic slave.

In *The Heroic Slave*, Madison Washington is desperately trying to deal with a dehumanizing system. Like the slave Douglass, Washington fully realizes the contradiction he must live. "What, then, is life to me?" he cries. "It is aimless and worthless. . . . *I am a slave.* . . . How mean a thing am I. . . . But here am I, *a man,*—yes, a man!" Washington feels he must have his liberty or die in the attempt to gain it. He is not afraid to die. And at that moment he discovers, as did Douglass during his fight with Covey, that he is free, "at least in spirit." But all efforts—moral suasion, political action (Gerrit Smith), and even escape and emigration—fail to free him completely. The most wretched moment of his agony occurs when his wife is shot to death. In the end, the heroic slave, in his bitterness and rage, leads a rebellion; and in this supreme act of violence he liberates himself and his fellow slaves and refutes racist notions of black servility (". . . a nigger's a nigger, on sea or land," argues a white sailor, "and is a coward, find him where you will; a drop of blood from one on 'em will skeer a hundred"). In defense of his bloody deed Washington denies he is a "*black murderer*" and invokes the American Revolution to justify his violence. "We have struck for our freedom," he shouts at a white sailor, "and if a true man's heart be in you, you will honor us for the deed. We have done that which you applaud your fathers for doing, and if we are murderers, *so were they.*"[18] Thus Douglass' heroic slave gives his act explicit meaning: He has killed for freedom.

III

Yet violence against the white oppressor was not easy for Douglass to accept. This was probably a crucial reason why he did not join John Brown and strike actual terror in the hearts of white Southerners. "The fact remains," Professor Willie Lee Rose has recently reminded us, "that Douglass, though a man of great physical courage, was never *personally* engaged in the kind of violence that results in death to others."[19] No doubt Douglass thought the Brown strategy was suicidal, and he also believed every man should work for the abolition of slavery in his own way—"the tools to those who can use them." But it is not certain whether these were the real or only reasons why he refused to go with Brown. "Come with me, Douglass," Brown pleaded shortly before his fateful raid on Harpers Ferry. "When I strike, the bees will begin to swarm, and I shall want you to help hive them." Killing for freedom, however, was no simple matter for Douglass. Unlike Shields Green, he could not coolly say: "I b'leve I'll go wid de ole man."[20] Douglass knew the raised knife of revolt would not be pointed merely at blank-faced white oppressors. It would be aimed at people tragically ensnared in a vicious system, people he cared for—his slaveholding mistress, Sophia Auld, and perhaps even his own father.

As a slave Douglass had been forced into close and intimate relationships with whites, and he had come to know many of them as persons as well as masters. He had come to understand the travail of slavery for many members of the master class. They had to view the slave as both person and property. Bondage as Douglass experienced it enabled him to regard white Southerners as fellow human beings trapped like himself in a tragic and absurd system.

His relationship with his slaveholding mistress, Sophia Auld, revealed to him the destructive impact the slave system had on whites. At first the "kind" and "gentle" Sophia, who had never before been a slaveholder, regarded Douglass as "a child, like any other." Her own son, Tommy, and Frederick "got on swimmingly together." She made Douglass something like Tommy's half brother in her affections. "Nor did the slave-boy lack the caressing strokes of her gentle hand, soothing him into the consciousness that, though motherless, he was not friendless." [21] Sophia was, he thought, like a mother to him. Douglass had been unable to feel a deep closeness to his own mother; separated from her during infancy, he had had only a few moments of her love and affection. "Never having enjoyed, to any considerable extent, her soothing presence, her tender and watchful care," he recalled, "I received the tidings of her death with much the same emotions I should have probably felt at the death of a stranger."[22] In a sense, Sophia offered Douglass what he was unable as a slave child to get from his own mother. He soon came to regard Sophia as something more like a "mother" than a "slaveholding mistress."[23] Under her care Douglass was, as he put it, "well-off." His physical wants were satisfied. He had a straw bed with a cover, plenty of food, and clean clothes. More important, he felt like a human being rather than a slave in her presence. "Why should I hang down my head, and speak with bated breath, when there was no pride to scorn me, no coldness to repel me, and no hatred to inspire me with fear?" Sophia seemed to say to young Frederick: "Look up, child; don't be afraid."[24]

But the slave system soon came down on both of them. Shortly after Douglass had joined the Auld household in Baltimore, he had a strong desire to learn how to read, and

Sophia gladly consented to teach him. Douglass was extremely precocious and learned very quickly. Sophia seemed almost as proud of his progress as if he had been "her own child" and told her husband about her new pupil. Hugh Auld was shocked. He scolded her severely, forbidding her to give Douglass any further instruction. "If you give a nigger an inch he will take an ell," he angrily lectured his wife. "Learning will spoil the best nigger in the world." Master Auld's fury had a damaging effect on Sophia. She was forced to repress her feelings of love for Douglass and her concern for him as a human being; she had to oppress him and degrade him into property. Her husband's "iron sentences, cold and harsh," disciplined her, and like "an obedient wife," she set her face like a "flint" against Douglass' education. But she could not do this without a sense of guilt. And she could only seek to mitigate this awesome guilt by aggressively denying Douglass' humanity. "In ceasing to instruct me," Douglass observed, "my mistress had to seek to justify herself *to* herself. . . . She finally became even more violent in her opposition to my learning to read than Mr. Auld himself." She spied on him and even interrogated him to find out about all his movements. Whenever she caught Douglass reading a book, she would angrily snatch it away from him. The system of slavery was cruelly transforming Sophia into something she was not and did not want to be. One thing was clear in his mind: He could not censure her harshly.[25]

Still the system could not completely crush Sophia's personal feelings toward Douglass. A few years after the reading incident, Douglass went to work as an apprentice in the Baltimore shipyards and was horribly beaten by white workers. When Sophia saw his puffed-out eye and his bloodstained face, she was moved to tears. She gently washed the blood from his face and covered his wounded eye with a piece of fresh beef. Sophia's kindness deeply consoled the hurt Douglass. "No mother's hand could have been more tender than hers. . . . Her affectionate heart was not yet dead, though much hardened by time and circumstances."[26]

Sophia's friendship made it impossible for Douglass to feel an unambiguous and violent hatred for Southern whites. Had his masters been uniformly cruel Douglass might have had a different attitude toward whites. Had Douglass felt only the hard whip of Covey and not the soft hands of Sophia he might have been able to categorize all whites as brutes and make war against them. Slavery as Douglass experienced it was too complicated and too contradictory for him to have a single and clear set of emotions toward whites.

Southern slavery, Douglass felt, had made white Southerners what they were. Told his father was a white man and possibly his master, Douglass bitterly condemned slavery as a system which cruelly alienated white fathers from their mulatto children. "Slavery had no recognition of fathers, as none of families. That the mother was a slave was enough for its deadly purpose. . . . The father might be a white man, glorying in the purity of his Anglo-Saxon blood, and the child ranked with the blackest slaves." Slavery had forced the slaveholder to reject his slave child. "Men do not love those who remind them of their sins . . . and the mulatto child's face is a standing accusation against him who is master and father to the child." Douglass was never entirely certain about his own paternity. "In regard to the *time* of my birth, I cannot be as definite as I have been respecting the *place*. Nor, indeed, can I impart much knowledge concerning my parents." But he did think, at least for a time, that his father may have been Master Thomas Auld. "I was given away by my father [Thomas Auld], or the man who was called my father, to his own brother [Hugh Auld]."[27] Years later, after the Civil War and emancipation, Douglass visited Thomas Auld, and as he stood at Auld's bedside, he felt a certain closeness to his former master. Douglass insisted that Auld call him "Frederick," "as formerly," and asked, perhaps significantly, his former master to satisfy an old, lingering, and anxious curiosity—his birth date. The date of his birth and his paternity were puzzling questions Douglass had linked together in his mind. Reminiscing about his escape, Douglass assured Auld that he did not run away from him but from slavery. The two men had a warm meeting. "He was to me no longer a slaveholder either in fact or in spirit, and I regarded him as I did myself, a victim of the circumstances of birth, education, and custom."[28] In Douglass' judgment, slavery had sadly and grotesquely victimized both white and black in Southern society.

For Douglass, violence against the oppressor meant warring against his white kinsfolk. Douglass never denied his black ancestry, and his relationship with Grandmother Bailey provided a strong basis for an identity with blacks. He was "not ashamed to be numbered with this race," and he abhorred the "cowardly meanness" which led any man to repudiate his connection with his race. No wonder Douglass had little feeling for Alexander Dumas. As he stood in front of Dumas' statue in Paris, he "remembered how this son of a negress had never spoken a word or written a line in defense of his mother's race."[29] But throughout his life Douglass also had a consciousness of his white ancestry and identity with whites—a consciousness which was certainly reinforced by Sophia's friendship.

This sense of kinship with whites was apparent. Angry over the racial exclusion of his daughter from a private school for girls, Douglass told one of the parents responsible for the injustice: "She had not been excluded from Seward Seminary five hours, before she was gladly welcomed into another quite as respectable, and *equally* christian to the one from which she was excluded. She now sits in a school among children as pure, and as white as you or yours. . . . We differ in color, it is true, (and *not much in that respect*). . . ." Time and again in his antislavery lectures he claimed he was "the child of a white man" and "the son of a slaveholder." During his antislavery tour abroad, Douglass described England as "the land of my paternal ancestors." In his speech on the Dred Scott Decision, Douglass referred to himself as a "colored man of both Anglo-Saxon and African descent." Years later, after the death of his wife Anna, he married Helen Pitts. In defense of his second marriage he remarked that his first wife "was the color of my mother, and the second, the color of my father," and that "no one ever complained of my marriage to my former wife, though contrast of color was more decided and pronounced than in the present instance. . . ." In the first edition of his autobiography (1846) he pointed out the great increase of mulattoes in the South. "A very different-looking people are now springing up at the South, and are now held in slavery, from those originally brought to this country from Africa; and if their increase will do no other good, it will do away the force of the argument, that God cursed Ham, and therefore American slavery is right. If the lineal descendants of Ham are alone to be scripturally enslaved, it is certain that slavery at the south must soon become unscriptural; for thousands are ushered into this world, annually, who, like myself, owe their existence to white fathers, and those fathers most frequently their own masters."[30]

A descendant of white and black, Douglass hoped for a racially integrated America. Time and again, in his opposition to black emigration and separatism, Douglass insisted that blacks were Americans and did not wish to return to Africa or form "a separate nation" in America. He wanted to stay precisely where he was—in the land of his birth. In a letter to Harriet Beecher Stowe, Douglass wrote: "The black man (unlike the Indian) loves civilization. . . . The truth is, dear madam, we are *here*, and here we are likely to remain. . . . We have grown up with this republic, and I see nothing in her character, or even in the character of the American people as yet, which compels the belief that we must leave the United States." In his editorial on "Horace Greeley and Colonization," Douglass argued "that contact with the white race, even under the many unjust and painful restrictions to which we are subjected, does more toward our elevation and improvement, than the mere circumstance of being separated from them could do." He did not think blacks, if they remained in America, could survive and flourish as a distinct and separate race. As he later explained in his essay on "The Future of the Colored Race," he believed the blacks would be "absorbed, assimilated, and will only appear as the Phoenicians now appear on the shores of the Shannon in the features of a blended race."[31] Thus Douglass wanted to become a part of America, and he wanted American society to become racially like him. But violence against the white oppressor could blast his hope for racial integration and amalgamation: A bloody war to the knife could forever drive apart black and white in America.

Douglass thought he had a possible way out of his dilemma. If black violence could be placed within the tradition of the American Revolution, as it had been in *The Heroic Slave*, then it could help to confirm the identity of blacks as Americans and bring them into American society. Thus, during the Civil War, Douglass saw that the war could have far greater significance than the abolition of slavery. If black men were allowed to participate in the war to save the Union, they could help seal their oneness with the nation. Black men in blue would then be "on the battlefield mingling their blood with that of white men in one common effort to save the country."[32] Hence the violence of war could unite black and white in a common cause and give both a claim to "the mystic cords of memory" stretching from the battlefields of the American Revolution to the battlefields of the Civil War.

Yet the ambivalence Douglass felt toward violence could not be overcome easily. For Douglass, a contradiction seemed to be inherent in violence: It enabled him to preserve his humanity and at the same time it forced him to deny an important basis of his humanity. Linked to this dilemma was a conflict in his mind between the gentleness and love of feminine influences and the harshness and violence of masculine influences.[33]

The feminine-masculine division seems to have made a profound impression on Douglass as a slave and helped to create within him a tension between nonviolence and violence. His own feelings of selfhood and humanity were largely derived from his experiences with certain women—his affectionate and loving Grandmother Bailey and the kind and motherly Sophia. Both of them regarded young Douglass with great "tenderness." They sheltered him from the cruelties and the "rigid training" of the plantation and helped him to become "sensitive."[34] They taught him he was a person, a human being. But then Douglass had to confront masculine oppressors—the cold and insensitive Hugh and Thomas Auld and the violent and vicious Edward Covey. They were "hard," "rigid," "malicious," and "ambitious"; they represented the antithesis of what Grandmother Bailey and Sophia were. Master Hugh Auld, for example, "knew more of the world and was more a part of the world, than his wife." He was a man with ambition, determined to become a successful and wealthy shipbuilder. "This was his ambition, and it fully occupied him." Sometimes he smiled upon young Douglass, but "the smile was borrowed from his lovely wife, and like borrowed light, was transient, and vanished with the source whence it was derived." Thus Douglass tended to see his oppressors as masculine and slavery as a white male-dominated institution. Armed with the whip and the gun, symbols of violence and masculine power, white men had tried to reduce him into property. They had cruelly denied him his mother and separated him from his grandmother. They had made Sophia become like them—tyrannical and harsh; her face once "lighted with the kindliest emotions" had become hard like "flint."[35]

These feelings about men and women may be seen clearly in Douglass' advocacy of female suffrage. "War, slavery, injustice, and oppression, and the idea that might makes right," Douglass later observed in his *Life and Times*, "have been uppermost in all such [male] governments. . . . The slayers of thousands have been exalted into heroes, and the worship of mere physical force has been considered glorious. Nations have been and still are but armed camps, expending their wealth and strength and ingenuity in forging weapons of destruction against each other. . . . [M]any reasons can be given to show that woman's influence would greatly tend to check and modify this barbarous and destructive tendency. At any rate, seeing that the male governments of the world have failed, it can do no harm to try the experiment of a government by man and woman united."[36] Thus, in Douglass' mind, men and women had different qualities.

Deep within himself, however, Douglass did not set up a rigid feminine-masculine division. He thought kindness was a human rather than a feminine quality. He believed men, too, could be compassionate. After his escape from the ferocious Covey, the bloodstained Douglass stood before his master, as he had stood before Sophia after his beating in the shipyard, and he noticed that Thomas Auld "seemed somewhat affected by the story of my wrongs." But Master Thomas "soon *repressed* whatever feeling he may have had, and became as cold and hard as iron." Douglass distinctly saw Auld's "human nature asserting its conviction against the slave system," but his master's humanity collapsed under the systematic tyranny of slavery.[37] This recognition of Southern white male repression made Douglass feel violence was inevitable. "To talk to these imps about justice or mercy [moral suasion] would have been as absurd as to reason with bears and tigers." They could appreciate only *hard* arguments—"lead and steel" and the "iron hand" of John Brown.[38] Yet, as Douglass appealed to his master for protection from Covey, he could see that Master Thomas, like Sophia, had a certain kindness or softness and that this softness reflected a human quality common to both Sophia and Master Thomas and transcended the mere division between women and men.

All of this deepened the paradox of violence. In order to

protect himself and redeem his humanity and in order to bring an end to a world of might and slavery and usher in a world of softness and freedom, Douglass was compelled to act masculinely, to use violence against his male oppressors. In a sense he had been forced to act like his heroic slave, Madison Washington. But the violence Douglass advocated and accepted as a means to be *free* involved not only the possible destruction of white kinsfolk and friends trapped in a masculine system and the possible widening of the division between black and white in America but also the abandonment of the virtues of gentleness and love Douglass admired in women like Grandmother Bailey and Sophia and needed to be *human*.

FOOTNOTES

1. The quotes are from Richard Wright, *Native Son* (New York, Harper & Row, 1940), pp. 364, 391; Jean Paul Sartre, Preface in Frantz Fanon, *Wretched of the Earth* (New York, Grove Press, 1966), p. 18; Theodore Roszak, "The Hard and the Soft: The Force of Feminism in Modern Times," in Betty Roszak and Theodore Roszak, *Masculine/Feminine: Readings in Sexual Mythology and the Liberation of Women* (New York, Harper & Row, 1969), p. 102.

2. Douglass, quoted in W. Brewer, "Henry Highland Garnet," *Journal of Negro History,* XIII (1929), p. 44; Douglass, in Boston *Liberator,* February 5, 1847, September 22, 1848; Douglass, *Life and Times of Frederick Douglass* (New York, Collier Books, 1962), originally published in 1884 and 1892, pp. 213, 260; Douglass, Speech at Finsbury Chapel, in Philip S. Foner, ed., *The Life and Writings of Frederick Douglass,* 4 vols. (New York, International Publishers, 1950), Vol. 1, pp. 164-65; Douglass to William Lloyd Garrison, in Boston *Liberator,* February 27, 1846.

3. Douglass, *Life and Times,* p. 113.

4. *Ibid.,* p. 186.

5. *Ibid.,* p. 112.

6. Quoted in Richard Wade, *Slavery in the Cities: The South, 1820-1860* (New York, Oxford, 1964), pp. 245-46.

7. Douglass, *Life and Times,* pp. 75-94.

8. Douglass, *Narrative of the Life of Frederick Douglass* (New York, New American Library, 1968), originally published in 1845, p. 26.

9. Douglass, *My Bondage and My Freedom* (New York, Dover Publications, 1969), originally published in 1855, pp. 36, 38, 40-41; Douglass, in Boston *Liberator,* September 22, 1848; Douglass, *Life and Times,* pp. 27-30.

10. Douglass, *Life and Times,* pp. 124-25.

11. *Ibid.,* pp. 125-34.

12. *Ibid.,* p. 135.

13. *Ibid.,* p. 140.

14. *Ibid.,* p. 142-43.

15. *Ibid.*

16. *Ibid.,* pp. 271-75; Douglass, in Boston *Liberator,* June 8, 1849; *Douglass' Monthly,* November, 1859; Douglass, letter to John Brown, in Boston *Liberator,* November 11, 1859.

17. Douglass, "The Fugitive Slave Law," in Foner, *op. cit.,* Vol. II, p. 207; *Douglass' Paper,* June 2, 1854, and March 2, 1863; Douglass, *Life and Times,* pp. 339-41.

18. Douglass, *The Heroic Slave,* text, p. 75.

19. Willie Lee Rose, in "An Exchange on John Brown," *New York Review of Books,* February 11, 1971, p. 44; see also Rose, "Killing for Freedom," *ibid.,* December 3, 1970.

20. Douglass, in Boston *Liberator,* November 11, 1859; Douglass, *Life and Times,* pp. 314-20.

21. Douglass, *Life and Times,* pp. 75-82; Douglass, *My Bondage,* pp. 142-44; Douglass, *Narrative,* pp. 46-48.

22. Douglass, *Narrative,* pp. 22-23.

23. Douglass, *My Bondage,* p. 142.

24. Douglass, *Life and Times,* pp. 76-78.

25. *Ibid.,* pp. 78-82.

26. Douglass, *My Bondage,* pp. 315-16.

27. Douglass, *Life and Times*, p. 29; Douglass, *My Bondage*, pp. 34, 51, 52, 58, 59; Douglass, *Narrative*, pp. 21-22, 24; Douglass, in Rochester *North Star*, September 15, 1848; Douglass, "Farewell Speech to the British People," in Foner, *op. cit.*, Vol. I, p. 224. Douglass had been transferred from Thomas Auld to Hugh Auld.

28. Douglass, *Life and Times*, pp. 440-52.

29. Douglass, "The Present Condition and Future Prospects of the Negro People," in *Annual Report of the American and Foreign Anti-Slavery Society for 1853* (New York, American & Foreign Anti-Slavery Society, 1853), p. 184; Theodore Stanton, "Frederick Douglass in Paris," *Open Court,* I (April 28, 1887), p. 151; Rochester *North Star*, September 29, 1848.

30. Douglass, letter to H. G. Warner, in Boston *Liberator* October 6, 1848; Douglass, in Foner, *op. cit.*, Vol I, p. 423; Rochester *North Star*, September 15, 1848; Douglass, quoted in Benjamin Quarles, *Frederick Douglass* (New York, Atheneum, 1968), p. 35; Douglass, in Foner, *op. cit.*, Vol. II, p. 421; Douglass, in Foner, *op. cit.*, Vol. IV, pp. 116, 427; Douglass, *Life and Times*, p. 534; Douglass, *Narrative*, p. 24; Douglass to Francis Jackson, January 29, 1846, Anti-Slavery Collection, Boston Public Library. Italics added.

31. Douglass to Stowe, March 8, 1853, in Douglass, *Life and Times*, pp. 284-90; *Douglass' Paper*, February 26, 1852; Douglass, in Boston *Liberator*, June 8, 1849; Rochester *North Star*, November 16, 1849; Douglass, "The Future of the Colored Race," *The North American Review*, in Foner, *op. cit.*, Vol. IV, pp. 193-96.

32. Douglass, *Life and Times*, pp. 335-36, 365.

33. For a brilliant discussion on this masculine/feminine dichotomy, see Theodore Roszak, "The Hard and the Soft: The Force of Feminism in Modern Times," in Betty Roszak and Theodore Roszak, eds., *Masculine/Feminine: Readings in Sexual Mythology and the Liberation of Women* (New York, Harper & Row, 1969), pp. 87-106.

34. Douglass, *Life and Times*, pp. 27-29, 31, 75-81; Douglass, *Narrative*, pp. 26, 46-48; Douglass, *My Bondage*, pp. 38-41, 142-46.

35. Douglass, *Life and Times*, pp. 77, 79, 81, 86, 115, 118, 123, 143.

36. *Ibid.*, pp. 473-74.

37. *Ibid.*, pp. 131-32.

38. *Ibid.*, pp. 174-75, 302-3, 312; Douglass, in Boston *Liberator*, July 27, 1860; *Douglass' Monthly*, November, 1859.

The Heroic Slave

BY FREDERICK DOUGLASS*

Part I

Oh! child of grief, why weepest thou?
Why droops thy sad and mournful brow?
Why is thy look so like despair?
What deep, sad sorrow lingers there?

THE State of Virginia is famous in American annals for the multitudinous array of her statesmen and heroes. She has been dignified by some the mother of statesmen. History has not been sparing in recording their names, or in blazoning their deeds. Her high position in this respect, has given her an enviable distinction among her sister States. With Virginia for his birth-place, even a man of ordinary parts, on account of the general partiality for her sons, easily rises to eminent stations. Men, not great enough to attract special attention in their native States, have, like a certain distinguished citizen in the State of New York, sighed and repined that they were not born in Virginia. Yet not all the great ones of the Old Dominion have, by the fact of their birth-place, escaped undeserved obscurity. By some strange neglect, *one* of the truest, manliest, and bravest of her children,—one who, in after years, will, I think, command the pen of genius to set his merits forth, holds now no higher place in the records of that grand old Commonwealth than is held by a horse or an ox. Let those account for it who can, but there stands the fact, that a man who loved liberty as well as did

*Frederick Douglass, *The Heroic Slave*, in *Douglass' Paper*, March, 1853; also in Julia Griffiths, ed., *Autographs For Freedom* (Boston, Jewett, 1853).

Patrick Henry,—who deserved it as much as Thomas Jefferson,—and who fought for it with a valor as high, an arm as strong, and against odds as great, as he who led all the armies of the American colonies through the great war for freedom and independence, lives now only in the chattel records of his native State.

Glimpses of this great character are all that can now be presented. He is brought to view only by a few transient incidents, and these afford but partial satisfaction. Like a guiding star on a stormy night, he is seen through the parted clouds and the howling tempests; or, like the gray peak of a menacing rock on a perilous coast, he is seen by the quivering flash of angry lightning, and he again disappears covered with mystery.

Curiously, earnestly, anxiously we peer into the dark, and wish even for the blinding flash, or the light of northern skies to reveal him. But alas! he is still enveloped in darkness, and we return from the pursuit like a wearied and disheartened mother, (after a tedious and unsuccessful search for a lost child,) who returns weighed down with disappointment and sorrow. Speaking of marks, traces, possibles, and probabilities, we come before our readers.

In the spring of 1835, on a Sabbath morning, within hearing of the solemn peals of the church bells at a distant village, a Northern traveller through the State of Virginia drew up his horse to drink at a sparkling brook, near the edge of a dark pine forest. While his weary and thirsty steed drew in the grateful water, the rider caught the sound of a human voice, apparently engaged in earnest conversation.

Following the direction of the sound, he descried, among the tall pines, the man whose voice had arrested his attention. "To whom can he be speaking?" thought the traveller. "He seems to be alone." The circumstance interested him much, and he became intensely curious to know what thoughts and feelings, or, it might be, high aspirations, guided those rich and mellow accents. Tieing his horse at a short distance from the brook, he stealthily drew near the solitary speaker; and, concealing himself by the side of a huge fallen tree, he distinctly heard the following soliloquy:—

"What, then, is life to me? it is aimless and worthless, and worse than worthless. Those birds, perched on yon swinging boughs, in friendly conclave, sounding forth their merry notes in seeming worship of the rising sun, though liable to the sportsman's fowling-piece, are still my superiors. They *live free,* though they may die slaves. They fly where they list by day, and retire in freedom at night. But what is freedom to me, or I to it? I am a *slave,*—born a slave, an abject slave,—even before I made part of this breathing world, the scourge was platted for my back; the fetters were forged for my limbs. How mean a thing am I. That accursed and crawling snake, that miserable reptile, that has just glided into its slimy home, is freer and better off than I. He escaped my blow, and is safe. But here am I, a man,—yes, *a man!*—with thoughts and wishes, with powers and faculties as far as angel's flight above that hated reptile, —yet he is my superior, and scorns to own me as his master, or to stop to take my blows. When he saw my uplifted arm, he darted beyond my reach, and turned to give me battle. I dare not do as much as that. I neither run nor fight, but do meanly stand, answering each heavy blow of a cruel master with doleful wails and piteous cries. I am galled with irons; but even these are more tolerable than the consciousness, the *galling* consciousness of cowardice and indecision. Can it be that I *dare* not run away? *Perish the thought,* I *dare* do any thing which may be done by another. When that young man struggled with the waves *for life,* and others stood back appalled in helpless horror, did I not plunge in, forgetful of life, to save his? The raging bull from whom all others fled, pale with fright, did I not keep at bay with a single pitchfork? Could a coward do that? *No,—no,—*I wrong myself,—I am no coward. *Liberty* I will have, or die in the attempt to gain it. This working that others may live in idleness! This cringing submission to insolence and curses! This living under the constant dread and apprehension of being sold and transferred, like a mere brute, is *too* much for me. I will stand it no longer. What others have done, I will do. These trusty legs, or these sinewy arms shall place me among the free. Tom escaped; so can I. The North Star will not be less kind to me than to him. I will follow it. I will at least make the trial. I have nothing to lose. If I am caught, I shall only be a slave. If I am shot, I shall only lose a life which is a burden and a curse. If

I get clear, (as something tells me I shall,) liberty, the inalienable birth-right of every man, precious and priceless, will be mine. My resolution is fixed. *I shall be free.*"

At these words the traveller raised his head cautiously and noiselessly, and caught, from his hiding-place, a full view of the unsuspecting speaker. Madison (for that was the name of our hero) was standing erect, a smile of satisfaction rippled upon his expressive countenance, like that which plays upon the face of one who has but just solved a difficult problem, or vanquished a malignant foe; for at that moment he was free, at least in spirit. The future gleamed brightly before him, and his fetters lay broken at his feet. His air was triumphant.

Madison was of manly form. Tall, symmetrical, round, and strong. In his movements he seemed to combine, with the strength of the lion, a lion's elasticity. His torn sleeves disclosed arms like polished iron. His face was "black, but comely." His eye, lit with emotion, kept guard under a brow as dark and as glossy as the raven's wing. His whole appearance betokened Herculean strength; yet there was nothing savage or forbidding in his aspect. A child might play in his arms, or dance on his shoulders. A giant's strength, but not a giant's heart was in him. His broad mouth and nose spoke only of good nature and kindness. But his voice, that unfailing index of the soul, though full and melodious, had that in it which could terrify as well as charm. He was just the man you would choose when hardships were to be endured, or danger to be encountered,—intelligent and brave. He had the head to conceive, and the hand to execute. In a word, he was one to be sought as a friend, but to be dreaded as an enemy.

As our traveller gazed upon him, he almost trembled at the thought of his dangerous intrusion. Still he could not quit the place. He had long desired to sound the mysterious depths of the thoughts and feelings of a slave. He was not, therefore, disposed to allow so providential an opportunity to pass unimproved. He resolved to hear more; so he listened again for those mellow and mournful accents which, he says, made such an impression upon him as can never be erased. He did not have to wait long. There came another gush from the same full fountain; now bitter, and now sweet. Scathing denunciations of the cruelty and injustice of slavery; heart-touching narrations of his own personal suffering, intermingled with prayers to the God of the oppressed for help and deliverance, were followed by presentations of the dangers and difficulties of escape, and formed the burden of his eloquent utterances; but his high resolution clung to him,—for he ended each speech by an emphatic declaration of his purpose to be free. It seemed that the very repetition of this, imparted a glow to his countenance. The hope of freedom seemed to sweeten, for a season, the bitter cup of slavery, and to make it, for a time, tolerable; for when in the very whirlwind of anguish,—when his heart's cord seemed screwed up to snapping tension, hope sprung up and soothed his troubled spirit. Fitfully he would exclaim, "How can I leave her? Poor thing! what can she do when I am gone? Oh! oh! 'tis impossible that I can leave poor Susan!"

A brief pause intervened. Our traveller raised his head, and saw again the sorrow-smitten slave. His eye was fixed upon the ground. The strong man staggered under a heavy load. Recovering himself, he argued thus aloud: "All is uncertain here. To-morrow's sun may not rise before I am sold, and separated from her I love. What, then, could I do for her? I should be in more hopeless slavery, and she no nearer to liberty,—whereas if I were free,—my arms my own,—I might devise the means to rescue her."

This said, Madison cast around a searching glance, as if the thought of being overheard had flashed across his mind. He said no more, but, with measured steps, walked away, and was lost to the eye of our traveller amidst the wildering woods.

Long after Madison had left the ground, Mr. Listwell (our traveller) remained in motionless silence, meditating on the extraordinary revelations to which he had listened. He seemed fastened to the spot, and stood half hoping, half fearing the return of the sable preacher to his solitary temple. The speech of Madison rung through the chambers of his soul, and vibrated through his entire frame. "Here is indeed a man," thought he, "of rare endowments,—a child of God,—guilty of no crime but the color of his skin,—hiding away from the face of humanity, and pouring out his thoughts and feelings, his hopes and resolutions to the lonely woods; to him those distant church bells have no grateful music. He shuns the church, the altar, and the great congregation of christian worshippers, and wanders away to the gloomy forest, to utter in the vacant air complaints and griefs, which the religion of his times and his country can neither console nor relieve. Goaded almost to madness by the sense of the injustice done him, he resorts hither to give vent to his pent up feelings, and to debate with himself the feasibility of plans, plans of his own invention, for his own deliverance. From this hour I am an abolitionist. I have seen enough and heard enough, and I shall go to my home in Ohio resolved to atone for my past indifference to this ill-starred race, by making such exertions as I shall be able to do, for the speedy emancipation of every slave in the land."

Part II

"The gaudy, blabbling and remorseful day
  Is crept into the bosom of the sea;
  And now loud-howling wolves arouse the jades
  That drag the tragic melancholy night;
  Who with their drowsy, slow, and flagging wings
  Clip dead men's graves, and from their misty jaws
  Breathe foul contagions, darkness in the air."

Shakspeare

Five years after the foregoing singular occurrence, in the winter of 1840, Mr. and Mrs. Listwell sat together by the fireside of their own happy home, in the State of Ohio. The children were all gone to bed. A single lamp burnt brightly on the centre-table. All was still and comfortable within; but the night was cold and dark; a heavy wind sighed and moaned sorrowfully around the house and barn, occasionally bringing against the clattering windows a stray leaf from the large oak trees that embowered their dwelling. It was a night for strange noises and for strange fancies. A whole wilderness of thought might pass through one's mind during such an evening. The smouldering embers, partaking of the spirit of the restless night, became fruitful of varied and fantastic pictures, and revived many bygone scenes and old impressions. The happy pair seemed to sit in silent fascination, gazing on the fire. Suddenly this *reverie* was interrupted by a heavy growl. Ordinarily such an occurrence would have scarcely provoked a single word, or excited the least apprehension. But there are certain seasons when the slightest sound sends a jar through all the subtle chambers of the mind; and such a season was this. The happy pair started up, as if some sudden danger had come upon them. The growl was from their trusty watch-dog.

"What can it mean? certainly no one can be out on such a night as this," said Mrs. Listwell.

"The wind has deceived the dog, my dear; he has mistaken the noise of falling branches, brought down by the wind, for that of the footsteps of persons coming to the house. I have several times to-night thought that I heard the sound of footsteps. I am sure, however, that it was but the wind. Friends would not be likely to come out at such an hour, or such a night; and thieves are too lazy and self-indulgent to expose themselves to this biting frost; but should there be any one about, our brave old Monte, who is on the lookout, will not be slow in sounding the alarm."

Saying this they quietly left the window, whither they had gone to learn the cause of the menacing growl, and re-seated themselves by the fire, as if reluctant to leave the slowly expiring embers, although the hour was late. A few minutes only intervened after resuming their seats, when again their sober meditations were disturbed. Their faithful dog now growled and barked furiously, as if assailed by an advancing foe. Simultaneously the good couple arose, and stood in mute expectation. The contest without seemed fierce and violent. It was, however, soon over,—the barking ceased, for, with true canine instinct, Monte quickly discovered that a friend, not an enemy of the family, was coming to the house, and instead of rushing to repel the supposed intruder, he was now at the door, whimpering and dancing for the admission of himself and his newly made friend.

Mr. Listwell knew by this movement that all was well; he advanced and opened the door, and saw by the light that streamed out into the darkness, a tall man advancing slowly towards the house, with a stick in one hand, and a small bundle in the other. "It is a traveller," thought he, "who has missed his way, and is coming to inquire the road. I am glad we did not go to bed earlier,—I have felt all the evening as if somebody would be here to-night."

The man had now halted a short distance from the door, and looked prepared alike for flight or battle. "Come in, sir, don't be alarmed, you have probably lost your way."

Slightly hesitating, the traveller walked in; not, however, without regarding his host with a scrutinizing glance. "No, sir," said he, "I have come to ask you a greater favor."

Instantly Mr. Listwell exclaimed, (as the recollection of the Virginia forest scene flashed upon him,) "Oh, sir, I know not your name, but I have seen your face, and heard your voice before. I am glad to see you. *I know all.* You are flying for your liberty,—be seated,—be seated,—banish all fear. You are safe under my roof."

This recognition, so unexpected, rather disconcerted and disquieted the noble fugitive. The timidity and suspicion of persons escaping from slavery are easily awakened, and often what is intended to dispel the one, and to allay the other, has precisely the opposite effect. It was so in this case. Quickly observing the unhappy impression made by his words and action, Mr. Listwell assumed a more quiet and inquiring aspect, and finally succeeded in removing the apprehensions which his very natural and generous salutation had aroused.

Thus assured, the stranger said, "Sir, you have rightly guessed, I am, indeed, a fugitive from slavery. My name is Madison,— Madison Washington my mother used to call me. I am on my way to Canada, where I learn that persons of my color are protected in all the rights of men; and my object in calling upon you was, to beg the privilege of resting my weary limbs for the night in your barn. It was my purpose to have continued my journey till morning; but the piercing cold, and the frowning darkness compelled me to seek shelter; and, seeing a light through the lattice of your window, I was encouraged to come here to beg the privilege named. You will do me a great favor by affording me shelter for the night."

"A resting-place, indeed, sir, you shall have; not, however, in my barn, but in the best room of my house. Consider yourself, if you please, under the roof of a friend; for such I am to you, and to all your deeply injured race."

While this introductory conversation was going on, the kind lady had revived the fire, and was diligently preparing supper; for she, not less than her husband, felt for the sorrows of the oppressed and hunted ones of earth, and was always glad of an opportunity to do them a service. A bountiful repast was quickly prepared, and the hungry and toil-worn bondman was cordially invited to partake thereof. Gratefully he acknowledged the favor of his benevolent benefactress; but appeared scarcely to understand what such hospitality could mean. It was the first time in his life that he had met so humane and friendly a greeting at the hands of persons whose color was unlike his own; yet it was impossible for him to doubt the charitableness of his new friends, or the genuineness of the welcome so freely given; and he therefore, with many thanks, took his seat at the table with Mr. and Mrs. Listwell, who, desirous to make him feel at home, took a cup of tea themselves, while urging upon Madison the best that the house could afford.

Supper over, all doubts and apprehensions banished, the three drew around the blazing fire, and a conversation commenced which lasted till long after midnight.

"Now," said Madison to Mr. Listwell, "I was a little surprised and alarmed when I came in, by what you said; do tell me, sir, *why* you thought you had seen my face before, and by what you knew me to be a fugitive from slavery; for I am sure that I never was before in this neighborhood, and I certainly sought to conceal what I supposed to be the manner of a fugitive slave."

Mr. Listwell at once frankly disclosed the secret, describing the place where he first saw him; rehearsing the language which he (Madison) had used; referring to the effect which his manner and speech had made upon him; declaring the resolution he there formed to be an abolitionist; telling how often he had spoken of the circumstance, and the deep concern he had ever since felt to know what had become of him; and whether he had carried out the purpose to make his escape, as in the woods he declared he would do.

"Ever since that morning," said Mr. Listwell, "you have seldom been absent from my mind, and though now I did not dare to hope that I should ever see you again, I have often wished that such might be my fortune; for, from that hour, your face seemed to be daguerreotyped on my memory."

Madison looked quite astonished, and felt amazed at the narration to which he had listened. After recovering himself he said, "I well remember that morning, and the bitter anguish that wrung my heart; I will state the occasion of it. I had, on the previous Saturday, suffered a cruel lashing; had been tied up to the limb of a tree, with my feet chained together, and a heavy iron bar placed between my ankles. Thus suspended, I received on my naked back forty stripes, and was kept in this distressing position three or four hours, and was then let down, only to have my torture increased; for my bleeding back, gashed by the cow-skin, was washed by the overseer with old brine, partly to augment my suffering, and partly, as he said, to prevent inflammation. My crime was that I had stayed longer at the mill, the day previous, than it was thought I ought to have done, which, I assured my master and the overseer, was no fault of mine; but no excuses were allowed. 'Hold your tongue, you impudent rascal,' met my every explanation. Slave-holders are so imperious when their passions are excited, as to construe every word of the slave into insolence. I could do nothing but submit to the agonizing infliction. Smarting still from the wounds, as well as from the consciousness of being whipt for no cause, I took advantage of the absence of my master, who had gone to church, to spend the time in the woods, and brood over my wretched lot. Oh, sir, I remember it well,—and can never forget it."

"But this was five years ago; where have you been since?"

"I will try to tell you," said Madison. "Just four weeks after that Sabbath morning, I gathered up the few rags of clothing I had, and started, as I supposed, for the North and for freedom. I must not stop to describe my feelings on taking this step. It seemed like taking a leap into the dark. The thought of leaving my poor wife and two little children caused me indescribable anguish; but consoling myself with the reflection that once free, I could, possibly, devise ways and means to gain their freedom also, I nerved myself up to make the attempt. I started, but ill-luck attended me; for after being out a whole week, strange to say, I still found myself on my master's grounds; the third night after being out, a season of clouds and rain set in, wholly preventing me from seeing the North Star, which I had trusted as my guide, not dreaming that clouds might intervene between us.

"This circumstance was fatal to my project, for in losing my star, I lost my way; so when I supposed I was far towards the North, and had almost gained my freedom, I discovered myself at the very point from which I had started. It was a severe trial, for I arrived at home in great destitution; my feet were sore, and in travelling in the dark, I had dashed my foot against a stump, and started a nail, and lamed myself. I was wet and cold; one week had exhausted all my stores; and when I landed on my master's plantation, with all my work to do over again,—hungry, tired, lame, and bewildered,—I almost cursed the day that I was born. In this extremity I approached the quarters. I did so stealthily, although in my desperation I hardly cared whether I was discovered or not. Peeping through the rents of the quarters, I saw my fellow-slaves seated by a warm fire, merrily passing away the time, as though their hearts knew no sorrow. Although I envied their seeming contentment, all wretched as I was, I despised the cowardly acquiescence in their own degradation which it implied, and felt a kind of pride and glory in my own desperate lot. I dared not enter the quarters,—for where there is seeming contentment with slavery, there is certain treachery to freedom. I proceeded towards the great house, in the hope of catching a glimpse of my poor wife, whom I knew might be trusted with my secrets even on the scaffold. Just as I reached the fence which divided the field from the garden, I saw a woman in the yard, who in the darkness I took to be my wife; but a nearer approach told me it was not she. I was about to speak; had I done so, I would not have been here this night; for an alarm would have been sounded, and the hunters been put on my track. Here were hunger, cold, thirst, disappointment, and chagrin, confronted only by the dim hope of liberty. I tremble to think of that dreadful hour. To face the deadly cannon's mouth in warm blood unterrified, is, I think, a small achievement, compared with a conflict like this with gaunt starvation. The gnawings of hunger conquers by degrees, till all that a man has he would give in exchange for a single crust of bread. Thank God, I was not quite reduced to this extremity.

"Happily for me, before the fatal moment of utter despair, my good wife made her appearance in the yard. It was she; I knew her step. All was well now. I was, however, afraid to speak, lest I should frighten her. Yet speak I did; and, to my great joy, my voice was known. Our meeting can be more easily imagined than described. For a time hunger, thirst, weariness, and lameness were forgotten. But it was soon necessary for her to return to the house. She being a house-servant, her absence from the kitchen, if discovered, might have excited suspicion. Our parting was like tearing the flesh from my bones; yet it was the part of wisdom for her to go. She left me with the purpose of meeting me at midnight in the very forest where you last saw me. She knew the place well, as one of my melancholy resorts, and could easily find it, though the night was dark.

"I hastened away, therefore, and concealed myself, to await the arrival of my good angel. As I lay there among the leaves, I was strongly tempted to return again to the house of my master and give myself up; but remembering my solemn pledge on that memorable Sunday morning, I was able to linger out the two long hours between ten and midnight. I may well call them long hours. I have endured much hardship; I have encountered many perils; but the anxiety of those two hours, was the bitterest I ever experienced. True to her word, my wife came laden with provisions, and we sat down on the side of a log, at that dark and lonesome hour of the night. I cannot say we talked; our feelings were too great for that; yet we came to an understanding that I should make the woods my home, for if I gave myself up, I should be whipped and sold away; and if I started for the North, I should leave a wife doubly dear to me. We mutually determined, therefore, that I should remain in the vicinity. In the dismal swamps I lived, sir, five long years,—a cave for my home during the day. I wandered about at night with the wolf and the bear,—sustained by the promise that my good Susan would meet me in the pine woods at least once a week. This promise was redeemed, I assure you, to the letter, greatly to my relief. I had partly become contented with my mode of life, and had made up my mind to spend my days there; but the wilderness that sheltered me thus long took fire, and refused longer to be my hiding-place.

"I will not harrow up your feelings by portraying the terrific scene of this awful conflagration. There is nothing to which I can liken it. It was horribly and indescribably grand. The whole world seemed on fire, and it appeared to me that the day of judgment had come; that the burning bowels of the earth had burst forth, and that the end of all things was at hand. Bears and wolves, scorched from their mysterious hiding-places in the earth, and all the wild inhabitants of the untrodden forest, filled with a common dismay, ran forth, yelling, howling, bewildered amidst the smoke and flame. The very heavens seemed to rain down fire through the towering trees; it was by the merest chance that I escaped the devouring element. Running before it, and stopping occasionally to take breath, I looked back to behold its frightful ravages, and to drink in its savage magnificence. It was awful, thrilling, solemn, beyond compare. When aided by the fitful wind, the merciless tempest of fire swept on, sparkling, creaking, cracking, curling, roaring, out-doing in its dreadful splendor a thousand thunderstorms at once. From tree to tree it leaped, swallowing them up in its lurid, baleful glare; and leaving them leafless, limbless, charred, and lifeless behind. The scene was overwhelming, stunning,—nothing was spared,— cattle, tame and wild, herds of swine and of deer, wild beasts of every name and kind,—huge night-birds, bats, and owls, that had retired to their homes in lofty tree-tops to rest, perished in that fiery storm. The long-winged buzzard and croaking raven mingled their dismal cries with those of the countless myriads of small birds that rose up to the skies, and were lost to the sight in clouds of smoke and flame. Oh, I shudder when I think of it! Many a poor wandering fugitive, who, like myself, had sought among wild beasts the mercy denied by our fellow men, saw, in helpless consternation, his dwelling-place and city of refuge reduced to ashes forever. It was this grand conflagration that drove me hither; I ran alike from fire and from slavery."

After a slight pause, (for both speaker and hearers were deeply moved by the above recital,) Mr. Listwell, addressing Madison, said, "If it does not weary you too much, do tell us something of your journeyings since this disastrous burning,—we are deeply interested in everything which can throw light on the hardships of persons escaping from slavery; we could hear you talk all night; are there no incidents that you could relate of your travels hither? or are they such that you do not like to mention them."

"For the most part, sir, my course has been uninterrupted; and, considering the circumstances, at times even pleasant. I have suffered little for want of food; but I need not tell you how I got it. Your moral code may differ from mine, as your customs and usages are different. The fact is, sir, during my flight, I felt myself robbed by society of all my just rights; that I was in an enemy's land, who sought both my life and my liberty. They had transformed me into a brute; made merchandise of my body, and, for all the purposes of my flight, turned day into night,—and guided by my own necessities, and in contempt of their conventionalities, I did not scruple to take bread where I could get it."

"And just there you were right," said Mr. Listwell; "I once had doubts on this point myself, but a conversation with Gerrit Smith, (a man, by the way, that I wish you could see, for he is a devoted friend of your race, and I know he would receive you gladly,) put an end to all my doubts on this point. But do not let me interrupt you."

"I had but one narrow escape during my whole journey," said Madison.

"Do let us hear of it," said Mr. Listwell.

"Two weeks ago," continued Madison, "after travelling all night, I was overtaken by daybreak, in what seemed to me an almost interminable wood. I deemed it unsafe to go farther, and, as usual, I looked around for a suitable tree in which to spend the day. I liked one with a bushy top, and found one just to my mind. Up I climbed, and hiding myself as well as I could, I, with this strap, (pulling one out of his old coat-pocket,) lashed myself to a bough, and flattered myself that I should get a *good night's* sleep that day; but in this I was soon disappointed. I had scarcely got fastened to my natural hammock, when I heard the voices of a number of persons, apparently approaching the part of the woods where I was. Upon my word, sir, I dreaded more these human voices than I should have done those of wild beasts. I was at a loss to know what to do. If I descended, I should probably be discovered by the men; and if they had dogs I should, doubtless, be *'treed.'* It was an anxious moment, but hardships and dangers have been the accompaniments of my life; and have, perhaps, imparted to me a certain hardness of character, which, to some extent, adapts me to them. In my present predicament, I decided to hold my place in the tree-top, and abide the consequences. But here I must disappoint you; for the men, who were all colored, halted at least a hundred yards from me, and began with their axes, in right good earnest, to attack the trees. The sound of their laughing axes was like the report of as many well-charged pistols. By and by there came down at least a dozen trees with a terrible crash. They leaped upon the fallen trees with an air of victory. I could see no dog with them, and felt myself comparatively safe, though I could not forget the possibility that some freak or fancy might bring the axe a little nearer my dwelling than comported with my safety.

"There was no sleep for me that day, and I wished for night. You may imagine that the thought of having the tree attacked under me was far from agreeable, and that it very easily kept me on the look-out. The day was not without diversion. The men at work seemed to be a gay set; and they would often make 'the woods resound with that uncontrolled laughter for which we, as a race, are remarkable. I held my place in the tree till sunset,—saw the men put on their jackets to be off. I observed that all left the ground except one, whom I saw sitting on the side of a stump, with his head bowed, and his eyes apparently fixed on the ground. I became interested in him. After sitting in the position to which I have alluded ten or fifteen minutes, he left the stump, walked directly towards the tree in which I was secreted, and halted almost under the same. He stood for a moment and looked around, deliberately and reverently took off his hat, by which I saw that he was a man in the evening of life, slightly bald and quite gray. After laying down his hat carefully, he knelt and prayed aloud, and such a prayer, the most fervent, earnest, and solemn, to which I think I ever listened. After reverently addressing the Almighty, as the all-wise, all-good, and the common Father of all mankind, he besought God for grace, for strength, to bear up under, and to endure, as a good soldier, all the hardships and trials which beset the journey of life, and to enable him to live in a manner which accorded with the gospel of Christ. His soul now broke out in humble supplication for deliverance from bondage. 'O thou,' said he, 'that hearest the raven's cry, take pity on poor me! O deliver me! O deliver me! in mercy, O God, deliver me from the chains and manifold hardships of slavery! With thee, O Father, all things are possible. Thou canst stand and measure the earth. Thou hast beheld and drove asunder the nations,—all power is in thy hand,—thou didst say of old, "I have seen the affliction of my people, and am come to deliver them,"—Oh look down upon our afflictions, and have mercy upon us.' But I cannot repeat his prayer, nor can I give you an idea of its deep pathos. I had given but little attention to religion, and had but little faith in it; yet, as the old man prayed, I felt almost like coming down and kneel by his side, and mingle my broken complaint with his.

"He had already gained my confidence; as how could it be otherwise? I knew enough of religion to know that the man who prays in secret is far more likely to be sincere than he who loves to pray standing in the street, or in the great congregation. When he arose from his knees, like another Zacheus, I came down from the tree. He seemed a little alarmed at first, but I told him my story, and the good man embraced me in his arms, and assured me of his sympathy.

"I was now about out of provisions, and thought I might safely ask him to help me replenish my store. He said he had no money; but if he had, he would freely give it me. I told him I had *one dollar;* it was all the money I had in the world. I gave it to him, and asked him to purchase some crackers and cheese, and to kindly bring me the balance; that I would remain in or near that place, and would come to him on his return, if he would whistle. He was gone only about an hour. Meanwhile, from some cause or other, I know not what, (but as you shall see very wisely,) I changed my place. On his return I started to meet him; but it seemed as if the shadow of approaching danger fell upon my spirit, and checked my progress. In a very few minutes, closely on the heels of the old man, I distinctly saw *fourteen men,* with something like guns in their hands."

"Oh! the old wretch!" exclaimed Mrs. Listwell, "he had betrayed you, had he?"

"I think not," said Madison, "I cannot believe that the old man was to blame. He probably went into a store, asked for the articles for which I sent, and presented the bill I gave him; and it is so unusual for slaves in the country to have money, that fact, doubtless, excited suspicion, and gave rise to inquiry. I can easily believe that the truthfulness of the old man's character compelled him to disclose the facts; and thus were these bloodthirsty men put on my track. Of course I did not present myself; but hugged my hiding-place securely. If discovered and attacked, I resolved to sell my life as dearly as possible.

"After searching about the woods silently for a time, the whole company gathered around the old man; one charged him with lying, and called him an old villain; said he was a thief; charged him with stealing money; said if he did not instantly tell where he got it, they would take the shirt from his old back, and give him thirty-nine lashes.

" 'I did *not* steal the money,' said the old man, 'it was given me, as I told you at the store; and if the man who gave it me is not here, it is not my fault.'

" 'Hush! you lying old rascal; we'll make you smart for it. You shall not leave this spot until you have told where you got that money.'

"They now took hold of him, and began to strip him; while others went to get sticks with which to beat him. I felt, at the moment, like rushing out in the midst of them; but considering that the old man would be whipped the more for having aided a fugitive slave, and that, perhaps, in the *melée* he might be killed outright, I disobeyed this impulse. They tied him to a tree, and began to whip him. My own flesh crept at every blow, and I seem to hear the old man's piteous cries even now. They laid thirty-nine lashes on his bare back, and were going to repeat that number, when one of the company besought his comrades to desist. 'You'll kill the d——d old scoundrel! You've already whipt a dollar's worth out of him, even if he stole it!' 'O yes,' said another, 'let him down. He'll never tell us another lie, I'll warrant ye!' With this, one of the company untied the old man, and bid him go about his business.

"The old man left, but the company remained as much as an hour, scouring the woods. Round and round they went, turning up the underbrush, and peering about like so many blood-hounds. Two or three times they came within six feet of where I lay. I tell you I held my stick with a firmer grasp than I did in coming up to your house tonight. I expected to level one of them at least. Fortunately, however, I eluded their pursuit, and they left me alone in the woods.

"My last dollar was now gone, and you may well suppose I felt the loss of it; but the thought of being once again free to pursue my journey, prevented that depression which a sense of destitution causes; so swinging my little bundle on my back, I caught a glimpse of the *Great Bear* (which ever points the way to my beloved star,) and I started again on my journey. What I lost in money I made up at a hen-roost that same night, upon which I fortunately came."

"But you did'nt eat you food raw? How did you cook it?" said Mrs. Listwell.

"O no, Madam," said Madison, turning to his little bundle;—"I had the means of cooking." Here he took out of his bundle an old-fashioned tinder-box, and taking up a piece of a file, which he brought with him, he struck it with a heavy flint, and brought out at least a dozen sparks at once. "I have had this old box," said he, "more than five years. It is the *only* property saved from the fire in the dismal swamp. It has done me good service. It has given me the means of broiling many a chicken!"

It seemed quite a relief to Mrs. Listwell to know that Madison had, at least, lived upon cooked food. Women have a perfect horror of eating uncooked food.

By this time thoughts of what was best to be done about getting Madison to Canada, began to trouble Mr. Listwell; for the laws of Ohio were very stringent against any one who should aid, or who were found aiding a slave to escape through that State. A citizen, for the simple act of taking a fugitive slave in his carriage, had just been stripped of all his property, and thrown penniless upon the world. Notwithstanding this, Mr. Listwell was determined to see Madison safely on his way to Canada. "Give yourself no uneasiness," said he to Madison, "for if it cost my farm, I shall see you safely out of the States, and on your way to a land of liberty. Thank God that there is *such* a land so near us! You will spend to-morrow with us, and to-morrow night I will take you in my carriage to the Lake. Once upon that, and you are safe."

"Thank you! thank you," said the fugitive; "I will commit myself to your care."

For the *first* time during *five* years, Madison enjoyed the luxury of resting his limbs on a comfortable bed, and inside a human habitation. Looking at the white sheets, he said to Mr. Listwell, "What, sir! you don't mean that I shall sleep in that bed?"

"Oh yes, oh yes."

After Mr. Listwell left the room, Madison said he really hesitated whether or not he should lie on the floor; for that was *far* more comfortable and inviting than any bed to which he had been used.

We pass over the thoughts and feelings, the hopes and fears, the plans and purposes, that revolved in the mind of Madison during the day that he was secreted at the house of Mr. Listwell. The reader will be content to know that nothing occurred to endanger his liberty, or to excite alarm. Many were the little attentions bestowed upon him in his quiet retreat and hiding-place. In the evening, Mr. Listwell, after treating Madison to a new suit of winter clothes, and replenishing his exhausted purse with five dollars, all in silver, brought out his two-horse wagon, well provided with buffaloes, and silently started off with him to Cleveland. They arrived there without interruption, a few minutes before sunrise the next morning. Fortunately the steamer Admiral lay at the wharf, and was to start for Canada at nine o'clock. Here the last anticipated danger was surmounted. It was feared that just at this point the hunters of men might be on the look-out, and, possibly, pounce upon their victim. Mr. Listwell saw the captain of the boat; cautiously sounded him on the matter of carrying liberty-loving passengers, before he introduced his precious charge. This done, Madison was conducted on board. With usual generosity this true subject of the emancipating queen welcomed Madison, and assured him that he should be safely landed in Canada, free of charge. Madison now felt himself no more a piece of merchandise, but a passenger, and, like any other passenger, going about his business, carrying with him what belonged to him, and nothing which rightfully belonged to anybody else.

Wrapped in his new winter suit, snug and comfortable, a pocket full of silver, safe from his pursuers, embarked for a free country, Madison gave every sign of sincere gratitude, and bade his kind benefactor farewell, with such a grip of the hand as bespoke a heart full of honest manliness, and a soul that knew how to appreciate kindness. It need scarcely be said that Mr. Listwell was deeply moved by the gratitude and friendship he had excited in a nature so noble as that of the fugitive. He went to his home that day with a joy and gratification which knew no bounds. He had done something "to deliver the spoiled out of the hands of the spoiler," he had given bread to the hungry, and clothes to the naked; he had befriended a man to whom the laws of his country forbade all friendship,—and in proportion to the odds against his righteous deed, was the delightful satisfaction that gladdened his heart. On reaching home, he exclaimed, *"He is safe,—he is safe,—he is safe,"*—and the cup of his joy was shared by his excellent lady. The following letter was received from Madison a few days after.

"WINDSOR, CANADA WEST, DEC. 16, 1840.

My dear Friend,—for such you truly are:—
   Madison is out of the woods at last; I nestle in the mane of the British lion, protected by his mighty paw from the talons and the beak of the American eagle. I AM FREE, and breathe an atmosphere too pure for *slaves,* slave-hunters, or slave-holders. My heart is full. As many thanks to you, sir, and to your kind lady, as there are pebbles on the shores of Lake Erie; and may the blessing of God rest upon you both. You will never be forgotten by your profoundly grateful friend,

MADISON WASHINGTON."

Part III

————His head was with his heart,
And that was far away!

Childe Harold.

JUST upon the edge of the great road from Petersburg, Virginia, to Richmond, and only about fifteen miles from the latter place, there stands a somewhat ancient and famous public tavern, quite notorious in its better days, as being the grand resort for most of the leading gamblers, horse-racers, cock-fighters, and slave-traders from all the country round about. This old rookery, the nucleus of all sorts of birds, mostly those of ill omen, has, like everything else peculiar to Virginia, lost much of its ancient consequence and splendor; yet it keeps up some appearance of gaiety and high life, and is still frequented, even by respectable travellers, who are unacquainted with its past history and present condition. Its fine old portico looks well at a distance, and gives the building an air of grandeur. A nearer view, however, does little to sustain this pretension. The house is large, and its style imposing, but time and dissipation, unfailing in their results, have made ineffaceable marks upon it, and it must, in the common course of events, soon be numbered with the things that were. The gloomy mantle of ruin is, already, outspread to envelop it, and its remains, even but now remind one of a human skull, after the flesh has mingled with the earth. Old hats and rags fill the places in the upper windows once occupied by large panes of glass, and the moulding boards along the roofing have dropped off from their places, leaving holes and crevices in the rented wall for bats and swallows to build their nests in. The platform of the portico, which fronts the highway is a rickety affair, its planks are loose, and in some places entirely gone, leaving effective man-traps in their stead for nocturnal ramblers. The wooden pillars, which once supported it, but which now hang as encumbrances, are all rotten, and tremble with the touch. A part of the stable, a fine old structure in its day, which has given comfortable shelter to hundreds of the noblest steeds of "the Old Dominion" at once, was blown down many years ago, and never has been, and probably never will be, rebuilt. The doors of the barn are in wretched condition; they will shut with a little human strength to help their worn out hinges, but not otherwise. The side of the great building seen from the road is much discolored in sundry places by slops poured from the upper windows, rendering it unsightly and offensive in other respects. Three or four great dogs, looking as dull and gloomy as the mansion itself, lie stretched out along the door-sills under the portico; and double the number of loafers, some of them completely rum-ripe, and others ripening, dispose themselves like so many sentinels about the front of the house. These latter understand the science of scraping acquaintance to perfection. They know every-body, and almost every-body knows them. Of course, as their title implies, they have no regular employment. They are (to use an expressive phrase) *hangers on,* or still better, they are what sailors would denominate *holders-on to the slack, in every-body's mess, and in nobody's watch.* They are, however, as good as the newspaper for the events of the day, and they sell their knowledge almost as cheap. Money they seldom have; yet they always have capital the most reliable. They make their way with a succeeding traveller by intelligence gained from a preceding one. All the great names of Virginia they know by heart, and have seen their owners often. The history of the house is folded in their lips, and they rattle off stories in connection with it, equal to the guides at Dryburgh Abbey. He must be a shrewd man, and well skilled in the art of evasion, who gets out of the hands of these fellows without being at the expense of a treat.

It was at this old tavern, while on a second visit to the State of Virginia in 1841, that Mr. Listwell, unacquainted with the fame of the place, turned aside, about sunset, to pass the night. Riding up to the house, he had scarcely dismounted, when one of the half dozen bar-room fraternity met and addressed him in a manner exceedingly bland and accommodating.

"Fine evening, sir."

"Very fine," said Mr. Listwell. "This is a tavern, I believe?"

"O yes, sir, yes; although you may think it looks a little the worse for wear, it was once as good a house as any in Virginy. I make no doubt if ye spend the night here, you'll think it a good house yet; for there aint a more accommodating man in the country than you'll find the landlord."

Listwell. "The most I want is a good bed for myself, and a full manger for my horse. If I get these, I shall be quite satisfied."

Loafer. "Well, I alloys like to hear a gentleman talk for his horse; and just becase the horse can't talk for itself. A man that don't care about his beast, and don't look arter it when he's travelling, aint much in my eye anyhow. Now, sir, I likes a horse, and I'll guarantee your horse will be taken good care on here. That old stable, for all you see it looks so shabby now, once sheltered the great *Eclipse,* when he run here agin *Batchelor* and *Jumping Jemmy.* Them was fast horses, but he beat 'em both."

Listwell. "Indeed."

Loafer. "Well, I rather reckon you've travelled a right smart distance to-day, from the look of your horse?"

Listwell. "Forty miles only."

Loafer. "Well! I'll be darned if that aint a pretty good *only.* Mister, that beast of yours is a singed cat, I warrant you. I never see'd a creature like that that wasn't good on the road. You've come about forty miles, then?"

Listwell. "Yes, yes, and a pretty good pace at that."

Loafer. "You're somewhat in a hurry, then, I make no doubt? I reckon I could guess if I would, what you're going to Richmond for? It would'nt be much of a guess either; for it's rumored hereabouts, that there's to be the greatest sale of niggers at Richmond to-morrow that has taken place there in a long time; and I'll be bound you're a going there to have a hand in it."

Listwell. "Why, you must think, then, that there's money to be made at that business?"

Loafer. "Well, 'pon my honor, sir, I never made any that way myself; but it stands to reason that it's a money making business; for almost all other business in Virginia is dropped to engage in this. One thing is sartain, I never see'd a nigger-buyer yet that had'nt a plenty of money, and he was'nt as free with it as water. I has known one on 'em to treat as high as twenty times in a night; and, ginerally speaking, they's men of edication, and knows all about the government. The fact is, sir, I alloys like to hear 'em talk, bekase I alloys can learn something from them."

Listwell. "What may I call your name, sir?"

Loafer. "Well, now, they calls me Wilkes. I'm known all around by the gentlemen that comes here. They all knows old Wilkes."

Listwell. "Well, Wilkes, you seem to be acquainted here, and I see you have a strong liking for a horse. Be so good as to speak a kind word for mine to the hostler to-night, and you'll not lose anything by it."

Loafer. "Well, sir, I see you don't say much, but you've got an insight into things. It's alloys wise to get the good will of them that's acquainted about a tavern; for a man don't know when he goes into a house what may happen, or how much he may need a friend." Here the loafer gave Mr. Listwell a significant grin, which expressed a sort of triumphant pleasure at having, as he supposed, by his tact succeeded in placing so fine appearing a gentleman under obligations to him.

The pleasure, however, was mutual; for there was something so insinuating in the glance of this loquacious customer, that Mr. Listwell was very glad to get quit of him, and to do so more successfully, he ordered his supper to be brought to him in his private room, private to the eye, but not to the ear. This room was directly over the bar, and the plastering being off, nothing but pine boards and naked laths separated him from the disagreeable company below,—he could easily hear what was said in the bar-room, and was rather glad of the advantage it afforded, for, as you shall see, it furnished him important hints as to the manner and deportment he should assume during his stay at that tavern.

Mr. Listwell says he had got into his room but a few moments, when he heard the officious Wilkes below, in a tone of disappointment, exclaim, "Whar's that gentleman?" Wilkes was evidently expecting to meet with his friend at the bar-room, on his return, and had no doubt of his doing the handsome thing. "He has gone to his room," answered the landlord, "and has ordered his supper to be brought to him."

Here some shouted out, "Who is he, Wilkes? Where's he going?"

"Well, now, I'll be hanged if I know; but I'm willing to make any man a bet of this old hat agin a five dollar bill, that that gent is as full of money as a dog is of fleas. He's going down to Richmond to buy niggers, I make no doubt. He's no fool, I warrant ye."

"Well, he acts d——d strange," said another, "anyhow. I likes to see a man, when he comes up to a tavern, to come straight into the bar-room, and show that he's a man among men. Nobody was going to bite him."

"Now, I don't blame him a bit for not coming in here. That man knows his business, and means to take care on his money," answered Wilkes.

"Wilkes, you're a fool. You only say that, becase you hope to get a few coppers out on him."

"You only measure my corn by your half-bushel, I won't say that you're only mad becase I got the chance of speaking to him first."

"O Wilkes! you're known here. You'll praise up any body that will give you a copper; besides, 't is my opinion that that fellow who took his long slab-sides up stairs, for all the world just like a half-scared woman, afraid to look honest men in the face, is a *Northerner,* and as mean as dish-water."

"Now what will you bet of that," said Wilkes.

The speaker said, "I make no bets with you, 'kase you can get that fellow up stairs there to say anything."

"Well," said Wilkes, "I am willing to bet any man in the company that *that* gentleman is a *nigger*-buyer. He did'nt tell me so right down, but I reckon I knows enough about men to give a pretty clean guess as to what they are arter."

The dispute as to *who* Mr. Listwell was, what his business, where he was going, etc., was kept up with much animation for some time, and more than once threatened a serious disturbance of the peace. Wilkes had his friends as well as his opponents. After this sharp debate, the company amused themselves by drinking whiskey, and telling stories. The latter consisting of quarrels, fights, *rencontres,* and duels, in which distinguished persons of that neighborhood, and frequenters of that house, had been actors. Some of these stories were frightful enough, and were told, too, with a relish which bespoke the pleasure of the parties with the horrid scenes they portrayed. It would not be proper here to give the reader any idea of the vulgarity and dark profanity which rolled, as "a sweet morsel," under these corrupt tongues. A more brutal set of creatures, perhaps, never congregated.

Disgusted, and a little alarmed withal, Mr. Listwell, who was not accustomed to such entertainment, at length retired, but not to sleep. He was *too* much wrought upon by what he had heard to rest quietly, and what snatches of sleep he got, were interrupted by dreams which were anything than pleasant. At eleven o'clock, there seemed to be several hundreds of persons crowding into the house. A loud and confused clamour, cursing and cracking of whips, and the noise of chains startled him from his bed; for a moment he would have given the half of his farm in Ohio to have been at home. This uproar was kept up with undulating course, till near morning. There was loud laughing,— loud singing,—loud cursing,—and yet there seemed to be weeping and mourning in the midst of all. Mr. Listwell said he had heard enough during the forepart of the night to convince him that a buyer of men and women stood the best chance of being respected. And he, therefore, thought it best to say nothing which might undo the favorable opinion that had been formed of him in the bar-room by at least one of the fraternity that swarmed about it. While he would not avow himself a purchaser of slaves, he deemed it not prudent to disavow it. He felt that he might, properly, refuse to cast such a pearl before parties which, to him, were worse than swine. To reveal himself, and to impart a knowledge of his real character and sentiments would, to say the least, be imparting intelligence with the certainty of seeing it and himself both abused. Mr. Listwell confesses, that this reasoning did not altogether satisfy his conscience, for, hating slavery as he did, and regarding it to be the immediate duty of every man to cry out against it, "without compromise and without concealment," it was hard for him to admit to himself the possibility of circumstances wherein a man might, properly, hold his tongue on the subject. Having as little of the spirit of a martyr as Erasmus, he concluded, like the latter, that it was wiser to trust the mercy of God for his soul, than the humanity of slave-traders for his body. Bodily fear, not conscientious scruples, prevailed.

In this spirit he rose early in the morning, manifesting no

surprise at what he had heard during the night. His quondam friend was soon at his elbow, boring him with all sorts of questions. All, however, directed to find out his character, business, residence, purposes, and destination. With the most perfect appearance of good nature and carelessness, Mr. Listwell evaded these meddlesome inquiries, and turned conversation to general topics, leaving himself and all that specially pertained to him, out of discussion. Disengaging himself from their troublesome companionship, he made his way towards an old bowling-alley, which was connected with the house, and which, like all the rest, was in very bad repair.

On reaching the alley Mr. Listwell saw, for the first time in his life, a slave-gang on their way to market. A sad sight truly. Here were one hundred and thirty human beings,—children of a common Creator—guilty of no crime—men and women, with hearts, minds, and deathless spirits, chained and fettered, and bound for the market, in a christian country,—in a country boasting of its liberty, independence, and high civilization! Humanity converted into merchandise, and linked in iron bands, with no regard to decency or humanity! All sizes, ages, and sexes, mothers, fathers, daughters, brothers, sisters,—all huddled together, on their way to market to be sold and separated from home, and from each other *forever*. And all to fill the pockets of men too lazy to work for an honest living, and who gain their fortune by plundering the helpless, and trafficking in the souls and sinews of men. As he gazed upon this revolting and heart-rending scene, our informant said he almost doubted the existence of a God of justice! And he stood wondering that the earth did not open and swallow up such wickedness.

In the midst of these reflections, and while running his eye up and down the fettered ranks, he met the glance of one whose face he thought he had seen before. To be resolved, he moved towards the spot. It was MADISON WASHINGTON! Here was a scene for the pencil! Had Mr. Listwell been confronted by one risen from the dead, he could not have been more appalled. He was completely stunned. A thunderbolt could not have struck him more dumb. He stood, for a few moments, as motionless as one petrified; collecting himself, he at length exclaimed, *"Madison! is that you?"*

The noble fugitive, but little less astonished than himself, answered cheerily, "O yes, sir, they've got me again."

Thoughtless of consequences for the moment, Mr. Listwell ran up to his old friend, placing his hands upon his shoulders, and looked him in the face! Speechless they stood gazing at each other as if to be doubly resolved that there was no mistake about the matter, till Madison motioned his friend away, intimating a fear lest the keepers should find him there, and suspect him of tampering with the slaves.

"They will soon be out to look after us. You can come when they go to breakfast, and I will tell you all."

Pleased with this arrangement, Mr. Listwell passed out of the alley; but only just in time to save himself, for, while near the door, he observed three men making their way to the alley. The thought occurred to him to await their arrival, as the best means of diverting the ever ready suspicions of the guilty.

While the scene between Mr. Listwell and his friend Madison was going on, the other slaves stood as mute spectators,—at a loss to know what all this could mean. As he left, he heard the man chained to Madison ask, "Who is that gentleman?"

"He is a friend of mine. I cannot tell you now. Suffice it to say he is a friend. You shall hear more of him before long, but mark me! whatever shall pass between that gentleman and me, in your hearing, I pray you will say nothing about it. We are all chained here together,—ours is a common lot; and that gentleman is not less *your* friend than *mine*." At these words, all mysterious as they were, the unhappy company gave signs of satisfaction and hope. It seems that Madison, by that mesmeric power which is the invariable accompaniment of genius, had already won the confidence of the gang, and was a sort of general-in-chief among them.

By this time the keepers arrived. A horrid trio, well fitted for their demoniacal work. Their uncombed hair came down over foreheads *"villainously low,"* and with eyes, mouths, and noses to match. "Hallo! hallo!" they growled out as they entered. "Are you all there!"

"All here," said Madison.

"Well, well, that's right! your journey will soon be over. You'll be in Richmond by eleven to-day, and then you'll have an easy time on it."

"I say, gal, what in the devil are you crying about?" said one of them. "I'll give you something to cry about, if you don't mind." This was said to a girl, apparently not more than twelve years old, who had been weeping bitterly. She had, probably, left behind her a loving mother, affectionate sisters, brothers, and friends, and her tears were but the natural expression of her sorrow, and the only solace. But the dealers in human flesh have *no* respect for such sorrow. They look upon it as a protest against their cruel injustice, and they are prompt to punish it.

This is a puzzle not easily solved. *How* came he here? what can I do for him? may I not even now be in some way compromised in this affair? were thoughts that troubled Mr. Listwell, and made him eager for the promised opportunity of speaking to Madison.

The bell now sounded for breakfast, and keepers and drivers, with pistols and bowie-knives gleaming from their belts, hurried in, as if to get the best places. Taking the chance now afforded, Mr. Listwell hastened back to the bowling-alley. Reaching Madison, he said, "Now *do* tell me all about the matter. Do you know me?"

"Oh, yes," said Madison, "I know you well, and shall never forget you nor that cold and dreary night you gave me shelter. I must be short," he continued, "for they'll soon be out again. This, then, is the story in brief. On reaching Canada, and getting over the excitement of making my escape, sir, my thoughts turned to my poor wife, who had well deserved my love by her virtuous fidelity and undying affection for me. I could not bear the thought of leaving her in the cruel jaws of slavery, without making an effort to rescue her. First, I tried to get money to buy her; but oh! the process was *too slow*. I despaired of accomplishing it. She was in all my thoughts by day, and my dreams by night. At times I could almost hear her voice, saying, 'O Madison! Madison! will you then leave me here? can you leave me here to die? No! no! you will come! you will come!' I was wretched. I lost my appetite. I could neither work, eat, nor sleep, till I resolved to hazard my own liberty, to gain that of my wife! But I must be short. Six weeks ago I reached my old master's place. I laid about the neighborhood nearly a week, watching my chance, and, finally, I ventured upon the desperate attempt to reach my poor wife's room by means of a ladder. I reached the window, but the noise in raising it frightened my wife, and she screamed and fainted. I took her in my arms, and was descending the ladder, when the dogs began to bark furiously, and before I could get to the woods the white folks were roused. The cool night air soon restored my wife, and she readily recognized me. We made the best of our way to the woods, but it was now *too* late,—the dogs were after us as though they would have torn us to pieces. It was all over with me now! My old master and his two sons ran out with loaded rifles, and before we were out of gunshot, our ears were assailed with *'Stop! stop! or be shot down.'* Nevertheless we ran on. Seeing that we gave no heed to their calls, they fired, and my poor wife fell by my side dead, while I received but a slight flesh wound. I now became desperate, and stood my ground, and awaited their attack over her dead body. They rushed upon me, with their rifles in hand. I parried their blows, and fought them 'till I was knocked down and overpowered."

"Oh! it was madness to have returned," said Mr. Listwell.

"Sir, I could not be free with the galling thought that my poor wife was still a slave. With her in slavery, my body, not my spirit, was free. I was taken to the house,—chained to a ring-bolt,—my wounds dressed. I was kept there three days. All the slaves, for miles around, were brought to see me. Many slave-holders came with their slaves, using me as proof of the completeness of their power, and of the impossibility of slaves getting away. I was taunted, jeered at, and berated by them, in a manner that pierced me to the soul. Thank God, I was able to smother my rage, and to bear it all with seeming composure. After my wounds were nearly healed, I was taken to a tree and stripped, and I received sixty lashes on my naked back. A few days after, I was sold to a slave-trader, and placed in this gang for the New Orleans market."

"Do you think your master would sell you to me?"

"O no, sir! I was sold on condition of my being taken South. Their motive is revenge."

"Then, then," said Mr. Listwell, "I fear I can do nothing for you. Put your trust in God, and bear your sad lot with the manly fortitude which becomes a man. I shall see you at Richmond, but don't recognize me." Saying this, Mr. Listwell handed Madison ten dollars; said a few words to the other slaves; received their hearty "God bless you," and made his way to the house.

Fearful of exciting suspicion by too long delay, our friend went to the breakfast table, with the air of one who half reproved the greediness of those who rushed in at the sound of the bell. A cup of coffee was all that he could manage. His feelings were too bitter and excited, and his heart was too full with the fate of poor Madison (whom he loved as well as admired) to relish his breakfast; and although he sat long after the company had left the table, he really did little more than change the position of his knife and fork. The strangeness of meeting again one whom he had met on two several occasions before, under extraordinary circumstances, was well calculated to suggest the idea that a supernatural power, a wakeful providence, or an inexorable fate, had linked their destiny together; and that no efforts of his could disentangle him from the mysterious web of circumstances which enfolded him.

On leaving the table, Mr. Listwell nerved himself up and walked firmly into the bar-room. He was at once greeted again by that talkative chatter-box, Mr. Wilkes.

"Them's a likely set of niggers in the alley there," said Wilkes.

"Yes, they're fine looking fellows, one of them I should like to purchase and for him I would be willing to give a handsome sum."

Turning to one of his comrades, and with a grin of victory, Wilkes said, "Aha, Bill, did you hear that? I told you I know'd that gentleman wanted to buy niggers, and would bid as high as any purchaser in the market."

"Come, come," said Listwell, "don't be too loud in your praise, you are old enough to know that prices rise when purchasers are plenty."

"That's a fact," said Wilkes, "I see you knows the ropes—and there's not a man in old Virginy whom I'd rather help to make a good bargain than you, sir."

Mr. Listwell here threw a dollar at Wilkes, (which the latter caught with a dexterous hand,) saying, "Take that for your kind good will." Wilkes held up the dollar to his right eye, with a grin of victory, and turned to the morose grumbler in the corner who had questioned the liberality of a man of whom he knew nothing.

Mr. Listwell now stood as well with the company as any other occupant of the bar-room.

We pass over the hurry and bustle, the brutal vociferations of the slave-drivers in getting their unhappy gang in motion for Richmond; and we need not narrate every application of the lash to those who faltered in the journey. Mr. Listwell followed the train at a long distance, with a sad heart; and on reaching Richmond, left his horse at a hotel, and made his way to the wharf in the direction of which he saw the slave-coffle driven. He was just in time to see the whole company embark for New Orleans. The thought struck him that, while mixing with the multitude, he might do his friend Madison one last service, and he stept into a hardware store and purchased three strong *files*. These he took with him, and standing near the small boat, which lay in waiting to bear the company by parcels to the side of the brig that lay in the stream, he managed, as Madison passed him, to slip the files into his pocket, and at once darted back among the crowd.

All the company now on board, the imperious voice of the captain sounded, and instantly a dozen hardy seamen were in the rigging, hurrying aloft to unfurl the broad canvas of our Baltimore built American Slaver. The sailors hung about the ropes, like so many black cats, now in the round-tops, now in the cross-trees, now on the yard-arms; all was bluster and activity. Soon the broad fore topsail, the royal and top gallant sail were spread to the breeze. Round went the heavy windlass, clank, clank went the fall-bit,—the anchors weighed,—jibs, mainsails, and topsails hauled to the wind, and the long, low, black slaver, with her cargo of human flesh, careened and moved forward to the sea.

Mr. Listwell stood on the shore, and watched the slaver till the last speck of her upper sails faded from sight, and announced the limit of human vision. "Farewell! farewell! brave and true man! God grant that brighter skies may smile upon your future than have yet looked down upon your thorny pathway."

Saying this to himself, our friend lost no time in completing his business, and in making his way homewards, gladly shaking off from his feet the dust of Old Virginia.

Part IV

Oh, where's the slave so lowly
Condemn'd to chains unholy,
    Who could he burst
    His bonds at first
Would pine beneath them slowly?

Moore.

————Know ye not
Who would be free, *themselves* must strike the blow.

Childe Harold.

WHAT a world of inconsistency, as well as of wickedness, is suggested by the smooth and gliding phrase, AMERICAN SLAVE TRADE; and how strange and perverse is that moral sentiment which loathes, execrates, and brands as piracy and as deserving of death the carrying away into captivity men, women, and children from the *African coast;* but which is neither shocked nor disturbed by a similar traffic, carried on with the same motives and purposes, and characterized by even *more* odious peculiarities on the coast of our MODEL REPUB-LIC. We execrate and hang the wretch guilty of this crime on the coast of Guinea, while we respect and applaud the guilty participators in this murderous business on the enlightened shores of the Chesapeake. The inconsistency is so flagrant and glaring, that it would seem to cast a doubt on the doctrine of the innate moral sense of mankind.

Just two months after the sailing of the Virginia slave brig, which the reader has seen move off to sea so proudly with her human cargo for the New Orleans market, there chanced to meet, in the Marine Coffee-house at Richmond, a company of *ocean birds,* when the following conversation, which throws some light on the subsequent history, not only of Madison Washington, but of the hundred and thirty human beings with whom we last saw him chained.

"I say, shipmate, you had rather rough weather on your late passage to Orleans?" said Jack Williams, a regular old salt, tauntingly, to a trim, compact, manly looking person, who proved to be the first mate of the slave brig in question.

"Foul play, as well as foul weather," replied the firmly knit personage, evidently but little inclined to enter upon a subject which terminated so ingloriously to the captain and officers of the American slaver.

"Well, betwixt you and me," said Williams, "that whole affair on board of the Creole was miserably and disgracefully managed. Those black rascals got the upper hand of ye altogether; and, in my opinion, the whole disaster was the result of ignorance of the real character of *darkies* in general. With half a dozen *resolute* white men, (I say it not boastingly,) I could have had the rascals in irons in ten minutes, not because I'm so strong, but I know how to manage 'em. With my back against the *caboose*, I could, myself, have flogged a dozen of them; and had I been on board, by every monster of the deep, every black devil of 'em all would have had his neck stretched from the yard-arm. Ye made a mistake in yer manner of fighting 'em. All that is needed in dealing with a set of rebellious *darkies,* is to show that yer not afraid of 'em. For my own part, I would not honor a dozen niggers by pointing a gun at one on 'em,—a good stout whip, or a stiff rope's end, is better than all the guns at Old Point to quell a *nigger* insurrection. Why, sir, to take a gun to a *nigger* is the best way you can select to tell him you are afraid of him, and the best way of inviting his attack."

This speech made quite a sensation among the company, and a part of them indicated solicitude for the answer which might be made to it. Our first mate replied, "Mr. Williams, all that you've now said sounds very well *here* on shore, where, perhaps, you have studied negro character. I do not profess to understand the subject as well as yourself; but it strikes me, you apply the same rule in dissimilar cases. It is quite easy to talk of flogging niggers here on land, where you have the sympathy of the community, and the whole physical force of the government, State and national, at your command; and where, if a negro shall lift his hand against a white man, the whole community, with one accord, are ready to unite in shooting him down. I say, in such circumstances, it's easy to talk of flogging negroes and of negro cowardice; but, sir, I deny that the negro is, naturally, a coward, or that your theory of managing slaves will stand the test of *salt* water. It may do very well for an overseer, a contemptible hireling, to take advantage of fears already in existence, and which his presence has no power to inspire; to swagger about whip in hand, and discourse on the timidity and cowardice of negroes; for they have a smooth sea and a fair wind. It is one thing to manage a company of slaves on a Virginia plantation, and quite another thing to quell an insurrection on the lonely billows of the Atlantic, where every breeze speaks of courage and liberty. For the negro to act cowardly on shore, may be to act wisely; and I've some doubts whether *you*, Mr. Williams, would find it very convenient were you a slave in Algiers, to raise your hand against the bayonets of a whole government."

"By George, shipmate," said Williams, "you're coming rather *too* near. Either I've fallen very low in your estimation, or your notions of negro courage have got up a button-hole too high. Now I more than ever wish I'd been on board of that luckless craft. I'd have given ye practical evidence of the truth of my theory. I don't doubt there's some difference in being at sea. But a nigger's a nigger, on sea or land; and is a coward, find him where you will; a drop of blood from one on 'em will skeer a hundred. A knock on the nose, or a kick on the shin, will tame the wildest *'darkey'* you can fetch me. I say again, and will stand by it, I could, with half a dozen good men, put the whole nineteen on 'em in irons, and have carried them safe to New Orleans too. Mind, I don't blame you, but I do say, and every gentleman here will bear me out in it, that the fault was somewhere, or them niggers would never have got off as they have done. For my part I feel ashamed to have the idea go abroad, that a ship load of slaves can't be safely taken from Richmond to New Orleans. I should like, merely to redeem the character of Virginia sailors, to take charge of a ship load on 'em to-morrow."

Williams went on in this strain, occasionally casting an imploring glance at the company for applause for his wit, and sympathy for his contempt of negro courage. He had, evidently however, waked up the wrong passenger; for besides being in the right, his opponent carried that in his eye which marked him a man not to be trifled with.

"Well, sir," said the sturdy mate, "you can select your own method for distinguishing yourself;—the path of ambition in this direction is quite open to you in Virginia, and I've no doubt that you will be highly appreciated and compensated for all your valiant achievements in that line; but for myself, while I do not profess to be a giant, I have resolved never to set my foot on the deck of a slave ship, either as officer, or common sailor again; I have got enough of it."

"Indeed! indeed!" exclaimed Williams, derisively.

"Yes, *indeed*," echoed the mate; "but don't misunderstand me. It is not the high value that I set upon my life that makes me say what I have said; yet I'm resolved never to endanger my life again in a cause which my conscience does not approve. I dare say *here* what many men *feel*, but *dare not speak*, that this whole slave-trading business is a disgrace and scandal to Old Virginia."

"Hold! hold on! shipmate," said Williams, "I hardly thought you'd have shown your colors so soon,—I'll be hanged if you're not as good an abolitionist as Garrison himself."

The mate now rose from his chair, manifesting some excitement. "What do you mean, sir," said he, in a commanding tone. *"That man does not live who shall offer me an insult with impunity."*

The effect of these words was marked; and the company clustered around. Williams, in an apologetic tone, said, "Shipmate! keep your temper. I meant no insult. We all know that Tom Grant is no coward, and what I said about your being an abolitionist was simply this: you *might* have put down them black mutineers and murderers, but your conscience held you back."

"In that, too," said Grant, "you were mistaken. I did all that any man with equal strength and presence of mind could have done. The fact is, Mr. Williams, you underrate the courage as well as the skill of these negroes, and further, you do not seem to have been correctly informed about the case in hand at all."

"All I know about it is," said Williams, "that on the ninth day after you left Richmond, a dozen or two of the niggers ye had on board, came on deck and took the ship from you;—had her steered into a British port, where, by the by, every woolly head of them went ashore and was free. Now I take this to be a discreditable piece of business, and one demanding explanation."

"There are a great many discreditable things in the world," said Grant. "For a ship to go down under a calm sky is, upon the first flush of it, disgraceful either to sailors or caulkers. But when we learn, that by some mysterious disturbance in nature the waters parted beneath, and swallowed the ship up, we lose our indignation and disgust in lamentation of the disaster, and in awe of the Power which controls the elements."

"Very true, very true," said Williams, "I should be very glad to have an explanation which would relieve the affair of its present discreditable features. I have desired to see you ever since you got home, and to learn from you a full statement of the facts in the case. To me the whole thing seems unaccountable. I cannot see how a dozen or two of ignorant negroes, not one of whom had ever been to sea before, and all of them were closely ironed between decks, should be able to get their fetters off, rush out of the hatchway in open daylight, kill two white men, the one the captain and the other their master, and then carry the ship into a British port, where every *'darkey'* of them was set free. There must have been great carelessness, or cowardice somewhere!"

The company which had listened in silence during most of this discussion, now became much excited. One said, I agree with Williams; and several said the thing looks black enough. After the temporary tumultous exclamations had subsided,—

"I see," said Grant, "how you regard this case, and how difficult it will be for me to render our ship's company blameless in your eyes. Nevertheless, I will state the fact precisely as they came under my own observation. Mr. Williams speaks of 'ignorant negroes,' and, as a general rule, they are ignorant; but had he been on board the *Creole* as I was, he would have seen cause to admit that there are exceptions to this general rule. The leader of the mutiny in question was just as shrewd a fellow as ever I met in my life, and was as well fitted to lead in a dangerous enterprise as any one white man in ten thousand. The name of this man, strange to say, (ominous of greatness,) was MADISON WASHINGTON. In the short time he had been on board, he had secured the confidence of every officer. The negroes fairly worshipped him. His manner and bearing were such, that no one could suspect him of a murderous purpose. The only feeling with which we regarded him was, that he was a powerful, good-disposed negro. He seldom spake to any one, and when he did speak, it was with the utmost propriety. His words were well chosen, and his pronunciation equal to that of any schoolmaster. It was a mystery to us *where* he got his knowledge of language; but as little was said to him, none of us knew the extent of his intelligence and ability till it was too late. It seems he brought three files with him on board, and must have gone to work upon his fetters the first night out; and he must have worked well at that; for on the day of the rising, he got the irons *off eighteen* besides himself.

"The attack began just about twilight in the evening. Apprehending a squall, I had commanded the second mate to order all hands on deck, to take in sail. A few minutes before this I had seen Madison's head above the hatchway, looking out upon the white-capped waves at the leeward. I think I never saw him look more good-natured. I stood just about midship, on the larboard side. The captain was pacing the quarter-deck on the starboard side, in company with Mr. Jameson, the owner of most of the slaves on board. Both were armed. I had just told the men to lay aloft, and was looking to see my orders obeyed, when I heard the discharge of a pistol on the starboard side; and turning suddenly around, the very deck seemed covered with fiends from the pit. The nineteen negroes were all on deck, with their broken fetters in their hands, rushing in all directions. I put my hand quickly in my pocket to draw out my jack-knife; but before I could draw it, I was knocked senseless to the deck. When I came to myself, (which I did in a few minutes, I suppose, for it was yet quite light,) there was not a white man on deck. The sailors were all aloft in the rigging, and dared not come down. Captain Clarke and Mr. Jameson lay stretched on the quarter-deck,—both dying,—while Madison himself stood at the helm unhurt.

"I was completely weakened by the loss of blood, and had not recovered from the stunning blow which felled me to the deck; but it was a little too much for me, even in my prostrate condition, to see our good brig commanded by a *black murderer*. So I called out to the men to come down and take the ship, or die in the attempt. Suiting the action to the word, I started aft. You murderous villain, said I, to the imp at the helm, and rushed upon him to deal him a blow, when he pushed me back with his strong, black arm, as though I had been a boy of twelve. I looked around for the men. They were still in the rigging. Not one had come down. I started towards Madison again. The rascal now told me to stand back. 'Sir,' said he, 'your life is in my hands. I could have killed you a dozen times over during this last half hour, and could kill you now. You call me a *black murderer.* I am not a murderer. God is my witness that LIBERTY, not *malice,* is the motive for this night's work. I have done no more to those dead men yonder, than they would have done to me in like circumstances. We have struck for our freedom, and if a true man's heart be in you, you will honor us for the deed. We have done that which you applaud your fathers for doing, and if we are murderers, *so were they.*'

"I felt little disposition to reply to this impudent speech. By heaven, it disarmed me. The fellow loomed up before me. I forgot his blackness in the dignity of his manner, and the eloquence of his speech. It seemed as if the souls of both the great dead (whose names he bore) had entered him. To the sailors in the rigging he said: 'Men! the battle is over, your captain is dead. I have complete command of this vessel. All resistance to my authority will be in vain. My men have won their liberty, with no other weapons but their own BROKEN FETTERS. We are nineteen in number. We do not thirst for your blood, we demand only our rightful freedom. Do not flatter yourselves that I am ignorant of chart or compass. I know both. We are now only about sixty miles from Nassau. Come down, and do your duty. Land us in Nassau, and not a hair of your heads shall be hurt.'

"I shouted, *Stay where you are, men,*—when a sturdy black fellow ran at me with a handspike, and would have split my head open, but for the interference of Madison, who darted between me and the blow. 'I know what you are up to,' said the latter to me. 'You want to navigate this brig into a slave port, where you would have us all hanged; but you'll miss it; before this brig shall touch a slave-cursed shore while I am on board, I will myself put a match to the magazine, and blow her, and be blown with her, into a thousand fragments. Now I have saved your life twice within these last twenty minutes,—for, when you lay helpless on deck, my men were about to kill you. I held them in check. And if you now (seeing I am your friend and not your enemy) persist in your resistance to my authority, I give you fair warning, YOU SHALL DIE.'

"Saying this to me, he cast a glance into the rigging where the terror-stricken sailors were clinging, like so many frightened monkeys, and commanded them to come down, in a tone from which there was no appeal; for four men stood by with muskets in hand, ready at the word of command to shoot them down.

"I now became satisfied that resistance was out of the question; that my best policy was to put the brig into Nassau, and secure the assistance of the American consul at that port. I felt sure that the authorities would enable us to secure the murderers, and bring them to trial.

"By this time the apprehended squall had burst upon us. The wind howled furiously,—the ocean was white with foam, which, on account of the darkness, we could see only by the quick flashes of lightning that darted occasionally from the angry sky. All was alarm and confusion. Hideous cries came up from the slave women. Above the roaring billows a succession of heavy thunder rolled along, swelling the terrific din. Owing to the great darkness, and a sudden shift of the wind, we found ourselves in the trough of the sea. When shipping a heavy sea over the starboard bow, the bodies of the captain and Mr. Jameson were washed overboard. For awhile we had dearer interests to look after than slave property. A more savage thunder-gust never swept the ocean. Our brig rolled and creaked as if every bolt would be started, and every thread of oakum would be pressed out of the seams. To the pumps! to the pumps! I cried, but not a sailor would quit his grasp. Fortunately this squall soon passed over, or we must have been food for sharks.

"During all the storm, Madison stood firmly at the helm,—his keen eye fixed upon the binnacle. He was not indifferent to the dreadful hurricane; yet he met it with the equanimity of an old sailor. He was silent but not agitated. The first words he uttered after the storm had slightly subsided, were characteristic of the man. 'Mr. mate, you cannot write the bloody laws of slavery on those restless billows. The ocean, if not the land, is free.' I confess, gentlemen, I felt myself in the presence of a superior man; one who, had he been a white man, I would have followed willingly and gladly in any honorable enterprise. Our difference of color was the only ground for difference of action. It was not that his principles were wrong in the abstract; for they are the principles of 1776. But I could not bring myself to recognize their application to one whom I deemed my inferior.

"But to my story. What happened now is soon told. Two hours after the frightful tempest had spent itself, we were plump at the wharf in Nassau. I sent two of our men immediately to our consul with a statement of facts, requesting his interference in our behalf. What he did, or whither he did anything, I don't know; but, by order of the authorities, a company of *black* soldiers came on board, for the purpose, as they said, of protecting the property. These impudent rascals, when I called on them to assist me in keeping the slaves on board, sheltered themselves adroitly under their instructions only to protect property,—and said they did not recognize *persons* as *property*. I told them that by the laws of Virginia and the laws of the United States, the slaves on board were as much property as the barrels of flour in the hold. At this the stupid blockheads showed their *ivory*, rolled up their white eyes in horror, as if the idea of putting men on a footing with merchandise were revolting to their humanity. When these instructions were understood among the negroes, it was impossible for us to keep them on board. They deliberately gathered up their baggage before our eyes, and, against our remonstrances, poured through the gangway,—formed themselves into a procession on the wharf,—bid farewell to all on board, and uttering the wildest shouts of exultation, they marched, amidst the deafening cheers of a multitude of sympathizing spectators, under the triumphant leadership of their heroic chief and deliverer, MADISON WASHINGTON."

Part II
War upon the Whites

BLACK RAGE IN THE FICTION
OF MARTIN DELANY

Yes; strike again that sounding string,
  And let the wildest numbers roll;
Thy song of fiercest passion sing,
  It breathes responsive to my soul!
A soul whose gentlest hours were nursed
  In stern adversity's dark way,
And o'er whose pathway never burst
  One gleam of hope's enlivening ray.

If thou wilt soothe my burning brain,
  Sing not to me of joy and gladness;
'Twill but increase the raging pain,
  And turn the fever into madness!
Sing not to me of landscapes bright,
  Of fragrant flowers and fruitful trees,
Of azure skies and mellow light,
  Or whisperings of the gentle breeze.

But tell me of the tempest roaring
  Across the angry foaming deep,
Of torrents from the mountains pouring
  Down precipices dark and deep.
Sing of the lightning's lurid flash,
  The ocean's roar, the howling storm,
The earthquake's shock, the thunder's crash,
  Where ghastly terrors teeming swarm.

Sing of the battle's deadly strife,
  The ruthless march of war and pillage;
The awful waste of human life,
  The plunder'd town, the burning village
Of streets with human gore made red,
  Of priests under the altar slain,
The scenes of rapine, woe and dread,
  That fill the warrior's horrid train.
Thy song may then an echo wake,
  Deep in this soul, long crush'd and sad,
The direful impressions shake,
  Which threaten now to drive me mad.

Martin Delany, *Blake; or, the Huts of America*

"If you want white man to love you, you must fight im!"

Indian Chief to Blake,
in *Blake: or, the Huts of America*[1]

IN one of his insightful comparisons, Frederick Douglass summed up the essential difference between himself and Martin Delany. "I thank God for making me a man simply," he observed, "but Delany always thanks him for making him a *black* man."[2] Unlike Douglass, Delany viewed revolutionary violence in relation to black separation and emigration to Africa rather than integration in America. As an abolitionist, Delany believed violence was necessary in the struggle for black liberation. "Shall the American slave," he asked in the newspaper *North Star* in 1849, "remain in abject bondage, waiting patiently, toiling on and suffering on, having nothing in prospect but the hope of his heartless relentless master's good will? Never. Let him be taught that he dare strike for liberty,—let him know this, and he at once rises up disenthralled—a captive redeemed from the portals of infamy to the true dignity of his nature—an elevated freeman." At the 1854 National Emigration Convention, Delany again advocated resistance. "Our submission does not gain for us an increase of friends nor respectability," he declared, "as the white race will only respect those who oppose their usurpation, and acknowledge as equals those who

will not submit to their oppression."[3] Yet as Delany called for
violence against the oppressor in his political writings and in his
novel *Blake; or, the Huts of America,* and as he urged blacks to
develop an African basis for their identity and freedom, he also
realized his deep attachment to America.

The conflicting emotions he felt toward Africa and America
had a profound impact on Delany during his 1859 visit to the
Niger Valley. In his *Report* on his expedition he recorded a
remarkable and revealing account of his personal encounter
with the land of his ancestry, the place he as a child living in
Virginia had heard described in the chants of his Mandingo
grandmother, and the country he as a black emigrationist of the
1850's had chosen for the redemption of black people.

The first sight and impressions of the coast of Africa
are always inspiring, producing the most pleasant emotions. These pleasing sensations continue for several days,
more or less, until they gradually merge into feelings of
almost intense excitement, not only mentally, but the
entire physical system share largely in it, so that it might
be termed a hilarity of feeling almost akin to approaching intoxication. . . . The first symptoms are succeeded
by a relaxity of feelings in which there is a disposition to
stretch, gape, and yawn, with fatigue.

The second may or may not be succeeded by actual
febril attacks, with nausea, chills, or violent headache;
but whether or not such symptoms ensue, there is one
most remarkable, as almost (and I think quite) a necessary affection, attendant upon the acclimation at this
incipient stage: *a feeling of regret that you left your
native country for a strange one; an almost frantic desire
to see friends and nativity; a despondency and loss of the
hope of ever seeing those you love at home again.*

These feelings, of course, must be resisted, and *regarded as a mere morbid affection of the mind* at the
time, arising from an approaching disease. . . . When an
entire recovery takes place, the love of the country is
most ardent and abiding.[4]

In a crucial sense, Delany's visit to Africa was a psychological journey. Africa inspired him and evoked within him pleasant and intense emotions, "a hilarity of feeling." But then the African intoxication subsided, and a weariness and despondency swept over him. Delany still regarded America as his "native country," his "home," a place where friends and loved ones lived; and he referred to Africa as a "strange" land. In his struggle against depression, Delany thought his feeling of regret was unreal, *"a mere morbid affection of the mind"* due to illness. Clearly an emotional storm was raging within Delany. He was finally in the land of his grandparents, making arrangements for the settlement of American blacks in order to usher in a new era of African greatness and pride and to affirm his blackness in African nationhood. Yet, as he stood on the soil of his ancestral country, Delany experienced mysterious despondency and sensed the depth of the ambivalence he felt toward Africa and America.

II

Delany's passionate interest in Africa reflected his most striking personal quality—his pride in his blackness. *"Africa for the African race,"* he asserted, *"and black men to rule them.* By black men I mean, men of African descent who claim an identity with the race." Delany clearly had a high regard for himself as a "black" man, and he gave his children distinctively black names such as Toussaint L'Ouverture, Rameses Placido, and Ethiopia Halle Amelia. Indeed, he so fiercely and defiantly claimed his racial identity that his contemporaries described him as "unadulterated in race and proud of his complexion" and as "the intensest embodiment of black Nationality to be met with outside the valley of the Niger."[5]

Delany's identity with the race was influenced by his parentage. He was born in 1812 in Charles Town, (West) Virginia, the son of a slave father and a free mother—Samuel and Pati Delany. His mother's father was a Mandingo prince, Shango, who had been captured as a youth during intertribal hostilities and brought to America with his betrothed Graci. Shango was given his freedom because of his noble birth and returned to

Africa; Graci was also freed but remained in America with her daughter, Pati. During his childhood, Martin had an intimate contact with Africa—his Mandingo grandmother (who died at the age of 107) and her chants about her homeland. Samuel Delany, the son of a Golah chieftain, managed to purchase his freedom when Martin was about ten years old. On his face Martin's father bore a mark of his terrible slavery as well as his heroic resistance—a scar from a wound inflicted upon him as he resisted arrest for striking his master.[6] Thus Martin's closeness to Africa and his father's courage gave him a basis for racial pride and identity.

During these early years, Martin realized how his very membership in the race made him an object of white scorn and how deeply white America despised him. A bitter incident, which took place when Martin was ten years old, dramatized the hatred whites had toward him. While teaching Martin and her other children how to read and write, Pati Delany aroused angry opposition from white neighbors anxious to keep their fantasy of black intellectual inferiority intact and to suppress educated black rebels like Denmark Vesey. White resentment against Martin's education was so intense that his mother felt compelled to move with her children to Chambersburg, Pennsylvania. Yet, as Delany was to discover painfully, the North was hardly the land of promise for blacks. As a young man studying in Pittsburgh during the 1830's, he experienced the brutality of anti-black riots. Blacks in Pittsburgh, like their brethren in Cincinnati, New York, and Philadelphia, were the victims of white mobs composed of insecure and jealous workers. Not all oppression happened in the streets, however. Delany married Catherine Richards, the mulatto daughter of a man of wealth, and she became the heir of property worth nearly $250,000 in 1847. Although Delany was the respected editor of the Pittsburgh *Mystery* at the time, he was unable to claim the inherited property. The property was lost reportedly because attorneys were unwilling to litigate the large claim in favor of a black family against white families.[7]

The depth of racism in Northern society became clear to Delany during the late 1840's while he helped Douglass edit the *North Star*. As a reporter for the newspaper and as an anti-slavery lecturer, Delany traveled widely throughout the North and met racial hostility and violence almost everywhere he went. On one occasion, a white mob in Marseilles, Ohio, threatened to tar and feather him and burn him alive. In a letter to Douglass, he complained: "Leesburg is the first and only town that I have been in Ohio, where the miserable effort at disparagement was not attempted toward me."[8] But what disturbed Delany most profoundly was the abuse he suffered from white children. In his essay "American Civilization—Treatment of the Colored People in the United States," Delany analyzed the manners of white children in this country. "As the deportment of individuals is a characteristic evidence of their breeding," he pointed out, "so is the conduct of children generally observed as an evidence of the character of their parents. . . ." Thus the persecution blacks experienced from white children was distressingly significant. "And though at times this abuse may not be corporeal or physical, yet it is at all times an abuse of the feelings, which in itself is a blasting outrage on humanity, and insufferable to the better senses of man and womanhood." Even while involved in their sports and play, white children were never too busy to notice a black passing by and scream "nigger."[9] In Delany's judgment, the attitude and behavior of white children toward blacks indicated the pervasiveness, the vulgarity, and meanness of racism in American culture.

His bitterness toward Northern society was sharpened by an admissions controversy at Harvard Medical School. In 1850, Delany along with two other blacks had been admitted to the school, an institution traditionally reserved for white men only. The admission of black students in 1850 was hardly an indication of enlightened racial views. It was understood by the faculty that the black students would emigrate and practice medicine in Africa. The faculty probably would have denied their application for admission had the black students wished to remain in America. Oliver Wendell Holmes, dean of the Harvard Medical School, asked Dr. H. H. Childs of the Pittsfield Medical School for advice on the admission of black students. In his reply, Dr. Childs stated that he was willing to train blacks sponsored by the American Colonization Society. He added: "We have had applications to educate colored students to practice medicine in this country, which have been uniformly refused."[10]

The admission of Delany and his fellow blacks provoked a storm of student indignation and hostility. At a meeting of Harvard medical students held on December 10, the angry men demanded the dismissal of the blacks. In their resolutions against the blacks, they voiced a concern for academic standards: The admission of blacks would lower the "reputation" of Harvard and "lessen the value of a diploma from it." They also declared their refusal to be identified as fellow students with a people they considered socially repulsive, insisting they could not attend classes with blacks, "whose company we would not keep in the streets, and whose society as associates we would not tolerate in our houses." Expressing a kind of racial domino theory, they warned that their grievance was "but the beginning of an Evil, which, if not checked will increase, and that the number of respectable *white* students will, in future, be in an inverse ratio, to that of *blacks*." Finally, the students attached a threat to their protest: The faculty must heed their demands or they would complete their medical studies elsewhere.[11]

The Harvard Medical School faculty quickly capitulated. The professors ignored a student counterpetition favoring the admission of the blacks. There was little reason for the faculty to give the counterpetition serious consideration. In their argument that Harvard should not refuse to offer educational privileges to "this unfortunate class," the dissenting students had admitted that "their prejudices would perhaps lead them to wish that no occasion had occurred for the agitation of this question."[12] Meeting at the home of Dean Holmes on December 26, the faculty deemed it "inexpedient" to allow blacks to attend the lectures. In defense of their position, they argued that their commitment to teaching and academic excellence required the exclusion of blacks from the school. The "intermixing" of the white and black races in the lecture room, they declared, was "distasteful" to a large portion of the class and "injurious" to the interests of the school. Thus the presence of blacks was a "source of irritation and distraction" and interfered with the "success of their teaching."[13]

One can easily imagine the intense humiliation and rage

Delany felt. He was fully qualified for admission to Harvard Medical School. The letters of recommendation from his private instructors, Dr. Joseph Gazzam and Dr. Julius Le Moyne, indicate he had shown impressive competence in the study of medicine.[14] But protesting Harvard white students refused to acknowledge that black men like Delany could compete with them intellectually. "For the reputation of the school," they chided the faculty, "it is to be hoped that the professors will not graduate their instructions according to their estimation of the intellectual abilities of the negro race; at least, not until the number of blacks preponderate!" Notions of black intellectual inferiority were ubiquitous in mid-nineteenth-century American society. Racial theorists like Dr. Samuel G. Morton of Philadelphia were diligently and "scientifically" measuring the cranial capacities of skulls belonging to the different races and informing Harvard students and others that blacks were intellectually inferior to whites. Morton's well-known *Crania Americana* (1839) was in the private libraries of Harvard medical professors. Dean Holmes had such a high regard for the writings of Dr. Morton that he considered Morton's research "permanent data for all future students of Ethnology. . . ."[15] The presence of Delany and the other black students in the lecture room was a standing contradiction to a belief in white intellectual superiority. In their demand for the exclusion of blacks and in their very defense of academic excellence, Harvard white men were affirming in their own minds their claims to membership in a race of superior intelligence.

Clearly, in the eyes of anxious Harvard white students black men like Delany threatened white supremacy and had to be segregated from the temples of knowledge and power. This need to separate themselves from blacks, however, did not preclude the possibility or even the desire for integration, if the integration could be on a hierarchical basis—white over black. Frederick Douglass, an astute analyst of the white psychology, understood the reality of this hierarchical integration. "While we are servants," he explained, "we are never offensive to the whites. . . . On the very day we were brutally assaulted in New York for riding down Broadway in company with ladies, we saw several white ladies riding with *black servants.*"[16] White Harvard students were upset because Delany had been permitted to attend lectures as a fellow student. They would not have objected to Delany's presence had he been a janitor.

After leaving Harvard in 1851, Delany tried to secure a patent for an invention designed to facilitate the movement of a locomotive over mountainous terrain. But he learned from his lawyer that the Patent Office in Washington would issue patents only to United States citizens. Presumably Delany was not, in the judgment of the Patent Office, an American citizen. Thus, even before the Supreme Court had declared that Dred Scott and hence all blacks were not citizens, Delany could clearly see that this was indeed a white man's country.[17]

III

Two years after the Harvard School admissions controversy, Delany issued his manifesto for black emigration—*The Condition, Elevation, Emigration and Destiny of the Colored People of the United States,* including an appendix on "A Project for an Expedition of Adventure, to the Eastern Coast of Africa." In 1854 Delany spearheaded the organization of the National Emigration Convention meeting in Cleveland and read at this convention his paper on "Political Destiny of the Colored Race on the American Continent." Five years later Delany, under a commission from the National Emigration Convention, led an expedition to explore the Niger Valley. His stated purpose was to gather scientific and general information: The commission explicitly denied any reference to emigration to Africa. But it also allowed Delany the right to negotiate in his own behalf for the organization of territory in Africa. In Liberia the black educator and Pan-Africanist Edward Blyden welcomed Delany as "the far-famed champion of the elevation of colored men" and as the Moses appointed to lead the black exodus from the house of bondage. During his visit Delany and fellow commissioner Robert Campbell signed treaties with native chiefs for land grants to settle educated and skilled blacks from America in the Abbeokuta area. At the end of his *Official Report of the Niger Valley Exploring Party,* published in 1861, Delany wrote: "I return, of course, to Africa, with my family."[18] This, however, he never did.

Delany had been only a young man of nineteen years when he "formed the design of going to Africa, the land of my ancestry." He had entered into "a solemn promise" with his friend Molliston Madison Clark to complete an education and go to Africa, Clark as a clergyman and Delany as a physician. Shortly after making this promise, Delany laid out a plan for the settlement of American blacks on the coast of eastern Africa.[19] As Delany developed his thoughts on emigration in the 1840's, he made a crucial distinction between emigration and the program of the American Colonization Society. Unlike colonization, emigration involved a radical break from black dependence on and deference to whites. He had nothing but scorn for the American Colonization Society, a white-controlled organization seeking to transport American blacks to Liberia. In 1849, as coeditor of the *North Star*, Delany hailed the independence of Liberia as "a new field of action" and potentially "a place of note and interest." But then he quickly denounced the American Colonization Society as a "degrading, expatriating, insolent, slaveholding scheme" and condemned the new Liberian president, J. J. Roberts, as "a white man's Negro." In Delany's judgment, Roberts represented the despicable colonizationist mentality. Shortly after the independence of Liberia, Delany pointed out, Roberts had been appointed envoy extraordinary to negotiate with England, France, and Prussia for recognition of his country. But "like the slave, 'cap in hand, obedient to the commands of the dons who employ them,' bidden on an errand of his master, President Roberts, no sooner concludes the business of his mission, a knowledge and official account which was alone due to his own government, but he writes to A. G. Phelps, a Colonizationist of the United States, giving him an official report of his proceedings as the Minister of Liberia, an independent nation!"[20] In 1850, the year the insulting incident at Harvard took place, Delany "fully matured a plan for an adventure" to Africa.[21] His program for the settlement of blacks in Africa was quite different from that of Roberts and the American Colonization Society: It was to be black inspired and controlled and to serve black interests.

In his call for black emigration during the 1850's, Delany presented a detailed analysis of the degradation and despair blacks experienced in Northern society. Blacks in the North, he charged, were simply "slaves in the midst of freedom," for the Fugitive Slave Law of 1850 had given every white man power to claim any black as his slave and had in effect reduced all Northern blacks to a condition of slavery. The new law represented "the crowning act of infamy on the part of the general government towards the colored inhabitants of the United States—an act so vile in its nature, that rebellion against its demands should be promptly made in every attempt to enforce its infernal provisions."[22] But the problem of racial oppression in the North was more profound and subtle than the Fugitive Slave Law. The inferior and dependent economic and social position blacks occupied in the North not only reinforced white prejudice but also created among blacks feelings of inferiority and self-hatred. "Caste our eyes about us and reflect for a moment," Delany sadly declared, "and what do we behold! every thing that presents to view gives evidence of the skill of the white man. Should we purchase a pound of groceries, a yard of linen, a vessel of crockeryware, a piece of furniture, the very provisions that we eat,—all, all are the products of the white man." This condition of dependency and the constant social and economic reminders of their subordinate status in America had a disastrous impact on the black psychology. Black children, born under oppression and unfavorable circumstances, could not "be raised in this country, without being stooped shouldered." Black men and women, moreover, appeared to be satisfied as menial workers. They seemed to have become "accustomed" to being maids and cooks and to lack a sense of "self-respect." The pernicious psychological consequences of black dependence on whites, Delany argued, could be seen in the slave personality. "The slave may become a lover of his master, and learn to forgive him for continual deeds of maltreatment and abuse; just as the Spaniel would couch and fondle at the feet that kick him; because he has been taught to reverence them, and consequently, becomes adapted in body and mind to his condition. . . . It has been so with us in our position among our oppressors; we have been so prone to such positions, that we have learned to love them."[23] In Delany's judgment, blacks had been so broken by white oppression that they were actually helping to perpetuate their sad and tragic condition.

Blacks would never be elevated in America and whites would never abandon their racial prejudice, Delany contended, unless blacks changed their condition and became in a sense like whites—"a business, money-making people," educated for "the Store and Counting House." Black liberation depended upon entrepreneurial success. Blacks must strive to have what enabled whites to elevate themselves—"a knowledge of all the various business enterprises, trades, professions, and sciences." They must acquire "a good business practical Education" rather than a "Classical" education. "What did John Jacob Astor, Stephen Girard, or do the millionaires and the greater part of the merchant princes, and mariners, know about Latin and Greek, and the Classics?"[24] In his emphasis on enterprise and in his admiration of the economic achievements and values of men like Astor, Delany was a forerunner of Booker T. Washington.

"What is necessary to be done," Delany explained, "in order to attain an equality, is to change the condition, and the person is at once changed." Such a change in condition, however, was unlikely in America. Racism in American culture and institutions was so widespread and virulent that the elevation and equality of blacks were impossible, unless the "identity" of their "former condition" was entirely destroyed. "Even were this desirable, which we by no means admit," Delany argued, blacks would have to contend with prejudices so deep that "ages incalculable might reasonably be expected to roll around before this could be honorably accomplished; otherwise, we should encourage, and at once commence, an indiscriminate concubinage and immoral commerce of our mothers, sisters, wives, and daughters, revolting to think of, and a physical curse to humanity." Delany rejected amalgamation as a proposed solution to racial conflict in America; unlike Douglass, he did not want blacks to lose their "identity as a distinct race." "The truth is," Delany declared, "we are not identical with the Anglo-Saxon . . . and the sooner we know and acknowledge this truth, the better for ourselves and posterity." Blacks should be proud, for they had "the highest traits of civilization" and would yet instruct the world in the true principles of morals, religion, and law.[25] Furthermore, the oppression of blacks as Delany viewed it was essentially based on caste, not class. Were the interests of the common people identical with ours, he observed, blacks might then succeed because they would be numerically superior as a class. "But this is not a question of the rich against the poor . . . but a question of white against black."26 Aware of the anti-black hatred among the white workers of Pittsburgh, Delany ruled out class struggle as a possible strategy for black liberation.

To be redeemed blacks had to emigrate, to separate themselves from their white oppressors. "Were we content to remain as we are," Delany warned, "sparsely interspersed among our white fellow-countrymen, we might never be expected to equal them in any honorable or respectable competition for a livelihood." Thus American blacks should direct their attention toward those places where blacks comprise by population and constitute by necessity of numbers the *"ruling element"* of the body politic. "No people can be free who themselves do not constitute an essential part of the *ruling element* of the country in which they live." If blacks could establish themselves within the context of a black nation, elevate themselves socially and economically, and demonstrate their achievements to the world, they would claim respectability for blacks everywhere and hasten the emancipation of slaves in the Americas. "The claims of no people, according to established policy and usage," Delany insisted, "are respected by any nation, until they are presented in a national capacity."27

But where should American blacks go? Delany, who moved to Chatham, Ontario, in 1856, considered Canada only a place of "temporary relief," not a country "to fix our destiny." Canada had too large a white population and was destined to be annexed by the United States.28 Instead Delany saw Central and South America as the future home of American blacks in the New World. In Nicaragua and New Granada, he pointed out, blacks had full opportunity to realize their manhood. "Remember this fact, that in these countries, colored men now fill the highest places in the country; and colored people have the same chances there, that white people have in the United States. All that is necessary to do, is to go, and the moment your foot touches the soil, you have all the opportunities for elevating yourselves as the highest, according to your industry and merits."29 American blacks must seek their freedom south of American slavery.

Delany's deepest emigrationist emotions, however, reached out toward Africa. He believed the redemption of blacks ultimately depended on the commercial development and regeneration of Africa, the land of his ancestry. Africa possessed the potential for a great black nationality—land, natural resources, and a black population. If "civilized" blacks from America could create a self-reliant and economically powerful nation in Africa, they would enrich themselves and win respect for the race. Thus Africa "must someday rise, in the majesty of ancient grandeur, and vindicate the rights and claims of her own children, against the incalculable wrongs perpetrated through the period of sixty ages by professedly enlightened Christians, against them." Clearly, to Delany, all black emigrationist roads eventually led to Africa. Africa, not South America, was the "fatherland" of all blacks. All of this helps to explain why he appended his plan for an expedition to the eastern coast of Africa to his book on emigration to South America and why the 1854 National Emigration Convention meeting to consider black claims to Central and South America agreed in "secret sessions" to hold Africa *"in reserve."*[30]

Still Delany could not deny his identity with and love for America. This may be seen in his advocacy of black emigration to South America, for emigration southward rather than to Africa allowed him to satisfy both his desire for a black nation and his wish to remain in America. "We must not leave this continent [the Americas]," he instructed his fellow blacks in his book on emigration. "America is our destination and our home." America had been designed by Providence to be "an asylum for all the nations of the earth," especially for the African race.[31]

In his very rush to embrace Africa, Delany was looking backward at America, claiming he was an American and had birthright to citizenship. His book on the condition, elevation, and emigration of blacks reflected this tension. It was "sincerely dedicated to the American people, North and South. By their most devout, and patriotic fellow-citizen, the author." In his book Delany not only advocated emigrationism but also set forth a strong case for black citizenship in the United States. He pointed out the immense contributions to America blacks had made as workers and as businessmen, and he reminded his readers about the black patriots of the American Revolution. "Among the highest claims that an inhabitant has upon his country," he argued, "is that of serving in its cause, and assisting to fight its battles." Under Delany's leadership, the 1854 National Emigration Convention declared "that as men and equals, we demand every political right, privilege and position to which whites are eligible in the United States. . . ." Some twenty years earlier, Delany had not only entered into "a solemn promise" to go to Africa but had also demanded black equality with whites within America. "Here is our nativity," Delany wrote in his book on emigration, "and here have we the natural right to abide and be elevated through the measure of our own efforts. . . . Our common country is the United States. Here were we born, here raised and educated, here are the scenes of childhood . . . the sacred graves of our departed fathers and mothers." But here, too, Delany had encountered the abuse of white children, the violence of white mobs in Ohio, and the scorn of white students at Harvard. Thus Delany cried out: "We love our country, dearly love her, but she don't love us—she despises us. . . ."[32] In a letter to William Lloyd Garrison, dated May 14, 1852, Delany described the contradictory emotions exploding within him.

I am not in favor of caste, nor a separation of the brotherhood of mankind, and would as willingly live among white men as black, if I had an *equal possession and enjoyment* of privileges; but shall never be reconciled to live among them, subservient to their will—existing by mere *sufferance*, as we, the colored people, do, in this country. The majority of white men cannot see why colored men cannot be satisfied with their condition in Massachusetts—what they desire [is] more than the *granted* right of citizenship. Blind selfishness on the one hand, and deep prejudice on the other, will not permit them to understand that we desire the *exercise* and *enjoyment* of these rights, as well as the *name* of their possession. If there were any probability of this, I should be willing to remain in the country, fighting and struggling on, the good fight of faith. But I must admit, that I have no hopes in this country—no confidence in the American people—with a *few* excellent exceptions—therefore, I have written as I have done. Heathenism and Liberty, before Christianity and Slavery.[33]

Thus Delany chose emigration to Africa. Yet, as an emigrationist, Delany wanted to "civilize" Africa. Many of Delany's social views were influenced by the American culture in which he lived. Like most white Americans of the age of Jackson, he valued economic success and entrepreneurial activity. Delany observed regretfully that young American blacks generally did not appear to have "an ambition above a private-house, hotel-table, or a body-servant," and that they "must sink inevitably down into *barbarism*" unless they became ambitious and "a *business, money-making* people."[34] In his quest to "regenerate" Africa, Delany wanted to develop the great trade potential of Africa, to clear away the mangrove swamps of Liberia, and to erect "cesspools" in African towns. "Every family," he remarked, "as in civilized countries, should have such conveniences." He wanted to clothe Africans and to uplift them from what he considered a primitive way of life.

> If all persons who settle among the natives [Delany advised missionaries] would . . . induce, by making it a rule of their house or family, every native servant to sit on a stool or chair; eat at a table instead of on the ground; eat with a knife and fork . . . instead of with their fingers; eat in the house instead of going out in the yard, garden, or somewhere else under a tree or shed; and sleep on a bed, instead of on a bare mat on the ground; and have them to wear some sort of garment to cover the entire person above the knees, should it be but a single shirt or chemise, instead of a loose native cloth thrown around them, to be dropped at pleasure, at any moment exposing the entire upper part of the person—or as in Liberia, where that part of the person is entirely uncovered—I am certain that it would go far toward impressing them with some of the habits of civilized life, as being adapted to them as well as the 'white man.' . . .[35]

Delany's black separatism and emigrationism were essentially reactions to racial oppression in America. His black separatism was born out of rejection: Had he had *"an equal possession and enjoyment"* of privileges in this country, he would have been willing to live among whites as well as blacks. His black emigrationism expressed not so much his longing for the land of his Mandingo and Golah grandparents as his angry protest against an America that was driving him from "her embraces" and compelling him to leave the country he "dearly" loved. The oppression Delany encountered in America trapped him in a paradox. He wanted the "liberty" he could not find in America, the land of "slavery"; yet at the same time he actually accepted its "Christianity" as well as its commercialism and hoped to bring them to Africa, the land of "heathenism."

IV

Beneath Delany's defiant blackness lay an ambivalence—an attachment to America and an allegiance to Africa. This tension in his mind intensified the rage he felt toward whites for the painful humiliations he had experienced at Charles Town, Pittsburgh, Marseilles, and Cambridge and the need he had to redeem himself not only in passionate African nationalism but also in violence against the white oppressor. Black violence in the struggle for liberation could, *in turn*, help Delany reduce and even possibly eliminate this tension. Violence could destroy all hope of racial harmony in America, complete his alienation from the land of his birth, and thus commit him clearly, irrevocably, and unambiguously to "Afraka."

> I'm a goin' to Afraka
> Where de white man dare not stay;
> I ketch 'im by de collar
> Den de white man holler,
> I hit 'im on de pate,
> Den I make 'im blate,
> I seize 'im by de throat—
> Laud!—he beller like a goat![36]

So sings a black sailor on board the slave ship *The Vulture* in

Delany's novel *Blake; or, the Huts of America* (1859-62). The song brings together the two important themes of the novel: black emigration to Africa and black violence against whites.

In the novel the protagonist, Henry Blake (Holland), has many of the qualities Delany identified with himself. Blake is "a black—a pure negro—handsome and intelligent . . . a man of good literary attainments."[37] Born in Cuba the son of a merchant, he had as a young man been decoyed away and sold to Mississippi planter Colonel Franks. Blake then married Maggie and had a son whom they named Little Joe. In the opening of the story, the relationship between Blake and Maggie is cruelly broken by Master Franks: She is sold and sent to Cuba. Outraged by his master's barbarism, Blake runs away and organizes slave insurrections in the South and in Cuba.

But Blake has no reason to hope that the destruction of slavery will signify freedom for blacks. Using Judge Ballard as the spokesman of the white North, Delany clearly reveals the depth of racial hatred and oppression in the states where slavery had been long abolished. In a conversation between Ballard and his white Southern friends, the judge endorses the Fugitive Slave Law and the Dred Scott Decision as he explains that free blacks everywhere may be enslaved by any white person. "It was a just decision of the Supreme Court. . . ," he comments, "that persons of African descent have no rights that white men are bound to respect." Judge Ballard also offers assurances that blacks in the North have no political rights. "Well, Judge," one of the white Southerners remarks, "I'm compelled to admit that you are a very good southerner, upon the whole, you are severe upon the negroes; you seem to allow them no chance." And the judge replies: "I like negroes well enough in their place!"[38] Thus racism is widespread in America, and blacks can never realize their freedom and manhood unless they emigrate.

Canada holds forth no promise to American blacks. After Blake and his fellow fugitive slaves arrive in Canada, they experience a sense of relief and joy. As he kneels to kiss the earth, Andy exclaims: "Is dis free gound'? De lan' whar black folks is free! Thang God a' mighty for dis privilege!"[39] But Andy does not yet know the prejudice white Canadians have toward blacks and the segregation and discrimination aimed at blacks in Canada. His search for freedom in Canada would soon be blasted, and "an emotion of unutterable indignation would swell the heart of the determined slave, and almost compel him to curse the country of his adoption."

The land of black redemption is Africa. Thus the revolutionary struggle of Blake and his friends focuses ultimately on the fatherland. An important element of the revolution as Blake defines it is the accumulation of money. Thus he tells his fellow black revolutionaries that they must have money in order to obtain their freedom. "With money you may effect your escape almost at any time. Your most difficult point is an elevated obstruction, a mighty hill, a mountain; but through that hill there is a gap; and *money* is the passport through that *White Gap* to freedom. . . . Money alone will carry you through the White mountains or across the White river to liberty."[40] Later in the novel, it becomes clear that the *"White Gap"* is related to the regeneration of Africa. In a conversation between two of Blake's fellow revolutionaries in Cuba, Madame Cordora and Placido, the significance of black enterprise in Africa as a basis of black redemption is made explicit. Placido, the thoughtful poet of the revolution, explains that images of Africa as a land of lazy and savage people have buttressed notions of black inferiority and have allowed whites to regard blacks as incapable of civilization and fit only to be slaves. Once blacks prove that in "Africa their native land, they are among the most industrious people in the world, highly cultivating the lands, and that ere long they and their country must hold the balance of commercial power by supplying . . . the greatest staple commodities in demand," they would be respected in the world. There are, Placido adds, "undoubted probabilities" that Africa could become a great commercial country. And Madame Cordora, a wealthy mulatto lady involved in Blake's revolution, suddenly realizes the meaning of the struggle and its relationship to African nationalism. "I never before felt as proud of my black as I did of my white blood," she joyfully exlaims. "I can readily see that the blacks compose an important element in the commercial and social relations of the world."[41] Clearly black psychological as well as political liberation depends on the success of black economic enterprise within the framework of building a black nation in Africa, the "native land" of blacks everywhere.

In Blake's judgment, black redemption requires not only economic enterprise and African nationalism but also violence against the white oppressor. Blake is committed to revolutionary violence in order to destroy slavery, avenge the wrongs inflicted on blacks, and force whites to fear and respect blacks. "If you want white man to love you," the Indian chief tells Blake, "you must fight im!" Driven by a need for revenge and a burning, pure hatred for whites, Blake's friend Gofer Gondolier is determined to use violence against whites. "I do hate them reptiles so!" exclaims Gondolier, the cook armed with a huge carving knife. "Let me into the streets and give me but a half a chance and I'll unjoint them faster than ever I did a roast pig for the palace dinner table." Gondolier sums up his unambiguous feeling toward whites when he cries: "Woe be unto those devils of whites, I say!"[42]

Unlike Gondolier, Blake seems to be ambivalent toward anti-white violence. Clearly Blake has suffered greatly at the cruel hands of Colonel Franks, yet he does not kill his oppressor. "Had I dealt with Franks as he deserved," Blake confides in his fellow revolutionaries, "for doing that for which he would have taken the life of any man had it been his case—tearing my wife from my bosom—the most I could take courage directly to do, was to leave him, and take as many from him as I could induce to go. But maturer reflection drove me to the expedient of avenging the general wrongs of our people, by inducing the slave, in his might, to scatter red ruin throughout the region of the South. But still, I cannot find it in my heart to injure an individual, except in personal conflict."[43] Blake's relationship with Franks and thus possibly America is complicated and contradictory: Maggie is the slave daughter of Colonel Franks. Like Delany's own wife and children, Blake's wife and his son, Little Joe, have white blood flowing through them. Blake is unable to bring himself to kill Franks and feels a wide range of clashing emotions concerning violence, but he decides he must prepare for rebellion and revenge against whites. His commitment to revolution seems to help him resolve his ambivalence. In a revolutionary council in Cuba Blake declares in unambiguous terms: "I am for war—war upon the whites."[44]

In Blake's call for "war upon the whites" we have a clue to help us understand the relationship between Delany's thoughts on violence against the white oppressor and the tension between America and Africa raging within Delany. Clearly this ambivalence could not be overcome easily. America was his birthplace and the land he "deeply" loved. His own wife and children had blood ties with white America: Catherine was the daughter of white and black parents. As he advocated black separation and emigration from the land where he had heard white children screaming "nigger" and Harvard white students clamoring for his exclusion and where he encountered the violence of anti-black urban riots and lynch mobs, Delany still felt a sense of regret and a closeness to America impinging heavily on his African nationalism. And as he traveled in the Niger Valley in 1859, he experienced an almost inexplicable illness, a mixture of intoxication and despondency.

Violence against the white oppressor as Delany advocated and imagined it in his novel seemed to have had greater significance than revenge, the destruction of slavery, and the restoration of black manhood and respect. Violence was, in a crucial sense, an expression of rage. But the rage was complicated: It was based on alienation from an America to which Delany was attached. Revolutionary violence, even the violence happening in the fantasy of fiction, offered Delany a means to free himself from the anguish of ambivalence he felt toward America and Africa and affirm clearly and simply his blackness and his identity with the land of his ancestry and his Mandingo grandmother's chants. A declaration of "war upon the whites," like Gondolier's shout of "woe be unto those devils of whites," would not only assert the absence of contradictory emotions Delany had but also help him to resolve the tension and possibly experience the peace Henry Blake was seeking.

FOOTNOTES

1. Martin Delany, *Blake: or, the Huts of America*, published in serial form in New York *Weekly Anglo-African*, April 5, 1862; Indian chief quote, text, p. 163.
2. Douglass, quoted in Frank A. Rollin, *Life and Public Services of Martin R. Delany* (Boston, Lee and Shepard, 1883), p. 19.
3. Delany, "Annexation of Cuba," Rochester *North Star*, April 27, 1849; Delany, "The Redemption of Cuba," Rochester *North Star*, July 20, 1849; Delany, "Domestic Economy," Rochester *North Star*, April 13, 1849; Delany, "Political Destiny of the Colored Race on the American Continent," in Appendix, Rollin, *Delany*, p. 336.
4. Delany, *Official Report of the Niger Valley Exploring Party*, reprinted in Howard H. Bell, *Search for a Place: Black Separatism and Africa, 1860* (Ann Arbor, University of Michigan Press, 1969), p. 64.
5. *Ibid.*, p. 121; Rollin, *Delany*, pp. 28-29; William Wells Brown, *The Black Man, His Antecedents, His Genius, and His Achievements* (New York, Thomas Hamilton, 1863), p. 175; *Douglass' Monthly*, August, 1862.
6. Rollin, *Delany*, pp. 14-16, 18, 25, 26, 36; W. Montague Cobb, "Martin Robinson Delany," *Journal of the National Medical Association*, XLIV (May, 1952), p. 233.
7. Rollin, *Delany*, pp. 28, 35-36, 48; Floyd J. Miller, "Introduction," in Delany, *Blake: or, the Huts of America* (Boston, Beacon, 1970), p. xiii; Cobb, "Delany," pp. 233, 237; Theodore Draper, "Martin Delany: The Father of American Black Nationalism," *New York Review of Books*, March 12, 1970, p. 33; Victor Ullman, *Martin R. Delany: The Beginnings of Black Nationalism* (Boston, Beacon, 1971), p. 45; Dorothy Sterling, *The Making of an Afro-American: Martin Robinson Delany, 1812-1885* (Garden City, New York, Doubleday, 1971), pp. 79-80.
8. Delany, Rochester *North Star*, April 28, 1848; Delany, Rochester *North Star*, July 14, 1848.
9. Delany, "American Civilization—Treatment of the Colored People in the United States," Rochester *North Star*, March 30, 1849; see also Delany, Rochester *North Star*, April 7, 1848.
10. Childs to Holmes, December 12, 1850, file on Delany, Countway Library of Harvard Medical School, Boston; Records of the Medical Faculty of Harvard University, Vol. 2, Minutes for November 4 and 23, 1850, Countway Library.
11. Student petition to the faculty, December 10, 1850, Countway Library.
12. Student petition, December 11, 1850, Countway Library.
13. Records of the Medical Faculty, Vol. 2, Minutes for December 26, 1850; drafts of letters to the Massachusetts Colonization Society and to Abraham R. Thompson, Countway Library.
14. Gazzam and Le Moyne, letters, in Delany file, Countway Library.
15. Student petition, December 10, 1850, Countway Library; letter signed "Common Sense," published in the Boston *Journal*, clipping on file in Delany folder, Countway Library; Holmes to Morton, November 27, 1849, quoted in Thomas F. Gossett, *Race: The History of an Idea in America* (Dallas, Southern Methodist University Press, 1963), p. 59.
16. Douglass, Rochester *North Star*, June 13, 1850.
17. Cobb, "Delany," p. 235; Rollin, *Delany*, pp. 77-78.
18. Delany, *The Condition, Elevation, Emigration and Destiny of the Colored People of the United States* (New York, Arno Press, 1969); Delany, "Political Destiny," in Appendix, Rollin, *Delany*, pp. 327-67; Delany, *Report*, pp. 31-32, 39, 77, 148; Hollis R. Lynch, *Edward Wilmot Blyden: Pan-Negro Patriot* (New York, Oxford University Press, 1970), p. 24.

19. Delany, *Report*, p. 32; Delany, *Condition, Elevation, Emigration*, Appendix.
20. Delany, "Liberia," Rochester *North Star*, March 2, 1849.
21. Delany, *Report*, pp. 32-33.
22. Delany, *Condition, Elevation, Emigration*, pp. 155-59; Delany, "Political Destiny," in Rollin, *Delany*, p. 358.
23. Delany, *Condition, Elevation, Emigration*, pp. 42, 47-48, 190, 197-98, 207-8; Delany, "Southern Customs—Madame Chevalier," Rochester *North Star*, June 22, 1849.
24. Delany, "Domestic Economy," Rochester *North Star*, March 23, 1849; Delany, Rochester *North Star*, April 28, 1848; Delany, *Condition, Elevation, Emigration*, pp. 44-46, 192-95.
25. Delany, *Condition, Elevation, Emigration*, p. 44; "Political Destiny," in Rollin, *Delany*, pp. 330-35.
26. Delany, "Political Destiny," in Rollin, *Delany*, p. 355.
27. *Ibid.*, pp. 329-34; Delany, *Condition, Elevation, Emigration*, pp. 183, 191, 205, 210.
28. Delany, *"Political Destiny,"* in Rollin, *Delany*, p. 332; Delany, *Condition, Elevation, Emigration*, pp. 174-76.
29. Delany, *Condition, Elevation, Emigration*, pp. 171-89; Delany, "Political Destiny," in Rollin, *Delany*, pp. 352-53.
30. Delany, *Condition, Elevation, Emigration*, pp. 87, 162; Delany, *Report*, pp. 28-38, 110, 112, 118, 120; Delany, "A Project," in Appendix, Delany, *Condition, Elevation, Emigration;* Delany, Rochester *North Star*, December 15, 1848.
31. Delany, *Condition, Elevation, Emigration*, pp. 171-72, 173, 178, 179, 183-84, 187.
32. *Ibid.*, pp. 48, 49, 67-84, 109, 196, 203; "Platform: or Declaration of Sentiments of the Cleveland Convention," in Herbert Aptheker, ed., *A Documentary History of the Negro People in the United States*, 2 vols. (New York, Citadel Press, 1967), Vol. 1, p. 365; Delany, *Report*, p. 32.
33. Delany, Letter to Garrison, in Boston *Liberator*, May 21, 1852.
34. Delany, "Domestic Economy," Rochester *North Star*, March 23, 1849; Delany, Rochester *North Star*, April 28, 1848. Italics added.
35. Delany, *Report*, pp. 66, 101, 105-6, 131; Delany, "A Project," Appendix, Delany, *Condition, Elevation, Emigration*, pp. 213-15.
36. Delany, *Blake, or, the Huts of America*, in New York *Weekly Anglo African*, February 8, 1862.
37. Delany, *Blake*, text, p. 113.
38. *Ibid.*, p. 140.
39. *Ibid.*, p. 209.
40. *Ibid.*, p. 160.
41. Delany, *Blake*, in New York *Weekly Anglo-African*, March 15, 1862.
42. *Ibid.*, April 26, 1862.
43. Delany, *Blake*, text, pp. 184-85.
44. Delany, *Blake*, in New York *Weekly Anglo-African*, April 12, 1862.

Blake; or, the Huts of America

A Tale of the Mississippi Valley, the Southern United States, and Cuba.

BY MARTIN DELANY*

I. The Project

On one of those exciting occasions, during a contest for the Presidency of the United States, a number of gentlemen met in the city of Baltimore. They were few in number, and appeared little concerned about the affairs of the general government. Though men of intelligence, their time and attention appeared to be entirely absorbed in an adventure of self interest. They met for the purpose of completing arrangements for refitting the old ship 'Merchantman,' which then lay in the harbor near Fell's Point. Colonel Stephen Franks, Major James Armsted, Captain Richard Paul and Captain George Royer, composed those who represented the American side—Captain Juan Garcia and Captain Jose Castello, those of Cuban interest.

Here a conversation ensued upon what seemed a point of vital importance to the company; it related to the place best suited for the completion of their arrangements. The Americans

Blake: or, the Huts of America, by Martin Delany, Part I, from the New York *Anglo-African Magazine,* January-July, 1859. The entire novel has two parts and some eighty chapters. Floyd Miller recently discovered Part II, which deals with the revolution in Cuba, in the New York *Weekly Anglo-African* of 1862. The final six chapters, however, seem to be still missing. Chapter XXXIV, which belongs to Part I, has not been included here because it is primarily a connection to Part II. Two chapters were originally numbered XXVIII; thus chapters 28-33 have been renumbered to correct this mistake. Chapters 24-28, 32-33 are from the New York *Weekly Anglo-African*, December 28, 1861; January 4, 1862; and January 18, 1862.

insisted on Baltimore as affording the greatest facilities, and having done more for the encouragement and protection of the trade, than any other known place. Whilst the Cubans on the other side, urged their objections on the ground that the continual increase of liberal principles in the various political parties, which were fast ushering into existence, made the objection beyond a controversy. Havana was contended for as a point best suited for adjusting their arrangements, and that too with many apparent reasons; but for some cause, the preference for Baltimore prevailed.

Subsequently to the adjustment of their affairs by the most complete arrangement for refitting the vessel, Col. Franks took leave of the party for his home in the distant State of Mississippi.

II. Colonel Franks at Home

On the return of Col. Stephen Franks to his home at Natchez, he met there Mrs. Arabella, the wife of Judge Ballard, an eminent jurist of one of the Northern States. She had arrived but a day before him, on a visit to some relatives, of whom Mrs. Franks was one. The conversation, as is customary on the meeting of Americans residing in such distant latitudes, readily turned on the general policy of the country.

Mrs. Ballard possessed the highest intelligence, and Mrs. Maria Franks was among the most accomplished of Southern ladies.

'Tell me, Madam Ballard, how will the North go in the present issue?' enquired Franks.

'Give yourself no concern about that, Colonel,' replied Mrs. Ballard, 'you will find the North true to the country.'

'What you consider true, may be false—that is, it might be true to you, and false to us,' continued he.

'You do not understand me, Colonel,' she rejoined, 'we can have no interests separate from yours; you know the time-honored motto, 'united we stand,' and so forth, must apply to the American people under every policy in every section of the Union.'

'So it should, but amidst the general clamor in the contest for ascendency, may you not lose sight of this important point?'

'How can we? You, I'm sure, Colonel, know very well that in our country commercial interests have taken precedence of all others, which is a sufficient guarantee of our fidelity to the South.'

'That may be, madam, but we are still apprehensive.'

'Well sir, we certainly do not know what more to do to give you assurance of our sincerity. We have as a plight of faith yielded Boston, New York, and Philadelphia—the intelligence and wealth of the North in carrying out the Compromise measures for the interests of the South; can we do more?'

'True, Madam Ballard, true! I yield the controversy. You have already done more than we of the South expected. I now remember that the Judge himself, tried the first case under the Act, in your city, by which the measures were tested.'

'He did, sir, and if you will not consider me unwomanly by telling you, desired me, on coming here, to seek every opportunity to give the fullest assurance that the judiciary are sound on that question. Indeed, so far as an individual might be concerned, his interests in another direction as you know, place him beyond suspicion,' concluded Mrs. Ballard.

'I am satisfied, madam, and by your permission, arrest the conversation. My acknowledgments, madam!' bowed the Colonel, with true southern courtesy.

'Maria, my dear, you look careworn; are you indisposed?' inquired Franks of his wife, who during conversation sat silent.

'Not physically, Colonel,' replied she, 'but—'

Just at this moment a servant throwing open the door announced dinner.

Besides a sprightly black boy of some ten years of age, there was in attendance a prepossessing, handsome maid-servant, who generally kept, as much as the occasion would permit, behind the chair of her mistress. A mutual attachment appeared to exist between them, the maid apparently disinclined to leave the mistress, who seemed to keep her as near her person as possible.

Now and again the fat cook, mammy Judy, would appear at

the door of the dining room bearing a fresh supply for the table, who with a slight nod of the head, accompanied with an affectionate smile and the word "Maggie," indicated a tie much closer than that of mere fellow-servants.

Maggie had long been the favorite maid-servant of her mistress, having attained the position through merit. She was also nurse and foster-mother to the two last children of Mrs. Franks, and loved them, to all appearance, as her own. The children reciprocated this affection, calling her 'mammy.'

Mammy Judy, who for years had occupied this position, ceded it to her daughter, she preferring, in consequence of age, the less active life of the culinary department.

The boy Tony would frequently cast a comic look upon Mrs. Ballard, then imploringly gaze in the face of his mistress. So intent was he in this, that twice did his master admonish him by a nod of the head.

'My dear,' said the Colonel, 'you are dull to day; pray tell me what makes you sad?'

'I am not bodily afflicted, colonel Franks, but my spirit is heavy,' she replied.

'How so? What is the matter?'

'That will best be answered at another time and place, colonel.'

Giving his head an unconscious scratch accompanied with a slight twitch of the corner of the mouth, Franks seemed to comprehend the whole of it.

On one of her Northern tours to the watering places, during a summer season some two years previous, having with her Maggie the favorite, Mrs. Franks visited the family of the Judge, at which time Mrs. Ballard first saw the maid. She was a dark mulatto of a rich, yellow, autumn-like complexion, with a matchless, cushion-like head of hair, neither straight nor curly, but handsomer than either.

Mrs. Franks was herself a handsome lady of some thirty five summers, but ten years less in appearance, a little above medium height, between the majestic and graceful, raven black hair, and dark, expressive eyes. Yet it often had been whispered that in beauty the maid equalled if not excelled the mistress. Her age was twenty-eight.

The conduct of Mrs. Franks toward her servant was more like that of an elder sister than a mistress, and the mistress and maid sometimes wore dresses cut from the same web of cloth. Mrs. Franks would frequently adjust the dress and see that the hair of her maid was properly arranged. This to Mrs. Ballard was as unusual as it was an objectionable sight, especially as she imagined there was an air of hauteur in her demeanor. It was then she determined to subdue her spirit.

Acting from this impulse, several times in her absence, Mrs. Ballard took occasion to administer to the maid severities she had never experienced at the hands of her mistress, giving her at one time a severe slap on the cheek, calling her an 'impudent jade.'

At this, Mrs. Franks, on learning, was quite surprised, but on finding that the maid gave no just cause for it, took no further notice of it, designedly evading the matter. But before leaving, Mrs. Ballard gave her no rest until she gave her the most positive assurance that she would part with the maid on her next visit at Natchez. And thus she is found pressing her suit at the residence of the Mississippi planter.

III. The Fate of Maggie

After dinner colonel Franks again pressed the inquiry concerning the disposition of his lady. At this time the maid was in the culinary department taking her dinner. The children having been served, she preferred the company of her old mother whom she loved, the children hanging around, and upon her lap. There was no servant save the boy Tony present in the parlor.

'I can't, I won't let her go! she's a dear good girl!' replied Mrs. Franks. 'The children are attached to her, and so am I; let Minny or any other of them go—but do not, for Heaven's sake, tear Maggie from me!'

'Maria, my dear, you've certainly lost your balance of mind! Do try and compose yourself,' admonished the Colonel. 'There's certainly no disposition to do contrary to your desires; try and be a little reasonable.'

'I'm sure cousin, I see no cause for your importunity. No one that I know of designs to hurt the negro girl. I'm sure it's not me!' impatiently remarked Mrs. Ballard.

During this, the boy had several times gone into the hall, looking toward the kitchen, then meaningly into the parlor as if something unusual were going on.

Mammy Judy becoming suspicious, went into the hall and stood close beside the parlor door, listening at the conversation.

'Cousin, if you will listen for a moment, I wish to say a word to you,' said Mrs. Ballard. 'The Judge, as you know, has a country seat in Cuba near the city of Havana, where we design making every year our winter retreat. As we cannot take with us either free negroes or white servants, on account of the existing restrictions, I must have a slave, and of course I prefer a well-trained one, as I know all of yours to be. The price will be no object; as I know it will be none to you, it shall be none to me.'

'I will not consent to part with her, cousin Arabella, and it is useless to press the matter any further!' emphatically replied Mrs. Franks.

'I am sure cousin Maria, it was well understood between the Colonel and the Judge, that I was to have one of your best-trained maid servants!' continued Mrs. Ballard.

'The Colonel and the Judge! If any such understanding exist, it is without my knowledge and consent, and—'

'It is true, my dear,' interposed the Colonel, 'but—'

'Then,' replied she, 'heaven grant that I may go too! from—'

'Pah, pah! cousin Maria Franks, I'm really astonished at you to take on so about a negro girl! You really appear to have lost your reason. I would not behave so for all the negroes in Mississippi.'

'My dear,' said Franks, 'I have been watching the conduct of that girl for some time past; she is becoming both disobedient and unruly, and as I have made it a rule of my life never to keep a disobedient servant, the sooner we part with her the better. As I never whip my servants, I do not want to depart from my rule in her case.'

Maggie was true to her womanhood, and loyal to her mistress, having more than once communicated to her ears facts the sound of which reflected no credit in his. For several repulses, such as this, it was that she became obnoxious to her master.

'Cousin Maria, you certainly have forgotten, I'm sure, when last at the North, you promised in presence of the girl, that I was to have her, and I'm certain she's expecting it,' explained Mrs. Ballard.

'This I admit,' replied Mrs. Franks, 'but you very well know, cousin Arabella, that that promise was a mere *ruse,* to reconcile an uneasiness which you informed me you discovered in her, after overhearing a conversation between her and some free negroes, at Saratoga Springs.'

'Well, cousin, you can do as you please,' concluded Mrs. Ballard.

'Colonel, I'm weary of this conversation. What am I to expect?' inquired Mrs. Franks.

'It's a settled point, my dear, she must be sold!' decisively replied Franks.

'Then I must hereafter be disrespected by our own slaves! You know, Colonel, that I gave my word to Henry, her husband, your most worthy servant, that his wife should be here on his return. He had some misgiving that she was to be taken to Cuba before his return, when I assured him that she should be here. How can I bear to meet this poor creature, who places every confidence in what we tell him? He'll surely be frantic.'

'Nonsense, cousin, nonsense,' sneered Mrs. Ballard; 'frantic, indeed! Why you speak of your negro slaves as if speaking of equals. Make him know that whatever you order, he must be contented with.'

'I'll soon settle the matter with him, should he dare show any feelings about it!' interposed Franks; 'when do you look for him, Maria?'

'I'm sure, Colonel, you know more about the matter than I do. Immediately after you left, he took the horses to Baton Rouge, where at the last accounts, he was waiting the conclusion of the races. Judge Dilbreath had entered them according to your request one horse for each day's races. I look for him every day. Then there are more than him to reconcile. There's old mammy Judy, who will run mad about her. You know, Colonel, she thought so much of her, that she might be treated tenderly the old creature gave up her situation in the house as nurse and foster-mother to our children, going into the kitchen to do the harder work.'

'Well, my dear, we'll detain your cousin till he comes. I'll telegraph the Judge that if not yet left, to start him home immediately.'

'Colonel that will be still worse, to let him witness her departure; I would much rather she'd leave before his return. Poor thing!' she sighed.

'Then she may go!' replied he.

'And what of poor old mammy and his boy?'

'I'll soon settle the matter with old Judy.'

Mrs. Franks looking him imploringly in the face, let drop her head, burying her face in the palms of her hands. Soon it was found necessary to place her under the care of a physician.

Old mammy Judy had long since beckoned her daughter, where both stood in breathless silence catching every word that passed.

At the conclusion, Maggie clasping her hands, exclaimed in suppressed tones,—

'O mammy, O mammy! what shall I do? O, is there no hope for me? Can't you beg master—can't you save me!'

'Look to de Laud, my chile! him ony able to bring yeh out mo' nah conkeh!' was the prayerful advice of the woe-stricken old mother; both hastening into the kitchen, falling upon their knees, invoked aloud the God of the oppressed.

Hearing in that direction an unusual noise, Franks hastened past the kitchen door, dropping his head, and clearing his throat as he went along. This brought the slaves to an ordinary mood, who trembled at his approach.

* * *

(Editor's note: In chapters 4 and 5 Maggie is taken away and Mrs. Franks, Daddy Joe, and Mammy Judy weep over the loss of Maggie.)

VI. Henry's Return

Early on Monday morning, a steamer was heard puffing up the Mississippi. Many who reside near the river, by custom can tell the name of every approaching boat by the peculiar sound of the steam-pipe, the one in the present instance being the Sultana.

Daddy Joe had risen and just leaving for the plantation, but stopped a moment to be certain.

'Hush!' admonished mammy Judy, 'hush! sho chile, do'n yeh heah how she hollah? Sholy dat's de wat's name! wat dat yeh call eh? "Suckana," wat not; sho! I ain' gwine bautha my head long so—sho! See, ole man see! dah she come! See dat now! I tole yeh so, but yeh uden bleve me!' and the old man and woman stood for some minutes in breathless silence, although the boat must have been some five miles distant, as the escape of steam can be heard on the western waters a great way off.

The approach toward sunrise, admonished daddy Joe of demands for him at the cotton farm, when after bidding 'good monin' ole umin,' he hurried to the daily task which lie before him.

Mammy Judy had learned by the boy Tony, that Henry was expected on the Sultana, and at the approach of every steamer, her head had been thrust out of the door or window to catch a distinct sound. In motionless attitude after the departure of her husband this morning, the old woman stood awaiting the steamer, when presently the boat arrived. But then to be certain that it was the expected vessel—now came the suspense.

The old woman was soon relieved from this most disagreeable of all emotions, by the cry of news boys returning from the wharf—

' 'Ere's the Picayune, Atlas, Delta! lates' news from New Orleans by the swift steamer Sultana!'

'Dah now!' exclaimed mammy Judy in soliloquy; 'dah now! I tole yeh so!—de wat's name come!' Hurrying into the kitchen, she waited with anxiety the arrival of Henry.

Busying about the breakfast for herself and other servants about the house—the white members of the family all being absent—mammy Judy for a time lost sight of the expected arrival. Soon however, a hasty footstep arrested her attention, when on looking around it proved to be Henry who came smiling up the yard.

'How'd you do mammy! how's Mag' and the boy?' inquired he, grasping the old woman by the hand.

She burst into a flood of tears, throwing herself upon him.

'What is the matter!' exclaimed Henry, 'is Maggie dead?'

'No chile,' with increased sobs she replied, 'much betteh she wah.'

'My God! has she disgraced herself?'

'No chile, may be betteh she dun so, den she bin heah now an' not sole. Maus Stephen sell eh case she!—I dun'o, reckon dat's da reason!'

'What!—Do you tell me mammy she had better disgraced herself than been sold! By the—!'

'So, Henry! yeh ain' gwine swah! hope yeh ain' gwine lose yeh 'ligion? Do'n do so; put yeh trus' in de Laud, he is suffishen fah all!'

'Don't tell me about religion! What's religion to me? My wife is sold away from me by a man who is one of the leading members of the very church to which both she and I belong! Put my trust in the Lord! I have done so all my life nearly, and of what use is it to me? My wife is sold from me just the same as if I didn't. I'll—'

'Come, come, Henry, yeh mus'n talk so; we is po' weak an' bline cretehs, an' cah see de way uh da Laud. He move' in a mystus way, his wundahs to puhfaum.'

'So he may, and what is all that to me? I don't gain anything by it, and—'

'Stop, Henry, stop! ain' de Laud bless yo' soul? ain' he take yeh foot out de miah an' clay, an' gib yeh hope da uddah side dis vale ub teahs?'

'I'm tired looking the other side; I want a hope this side of the vale of tears. I want something on this earth as well as a promise of things in another world. I and my wife have been both robbed of our liberty, and you want me to be satisfied with a hope of heaven. I won't do any such thing; I have waited long enough on heavenly promises; I'll wait no longer. I—'

'Henry, wat de mauttah wid yeh? I neveh heah yeh talk so fo'—yeh sin in de sight ub God; yeh gone clean back, I reckon.

De good Book tell us, a tousan' yeahs wid man, am but a day wid de Laud. Boy, yeh got wait de Laud own pinted time.'

'Well mammy, it is useless for me to stand here and have the same gospel preached into my ears by you, that I have all my life time heard from my enslavers. My mind is made up, my course is laid out, and if life last, I'll carry it out. I'll go out to the place to-day, and let them know that I have returned.'

'Sho boy! what yeh gwine do, bun house down? Bettah put yeh trus' in de Laud!' concluded the old woman.

'You have too much religion mammy for me to tell you what I intend doing,' said Henry in conclusion.

After taking up his little son, impressing on his lips and cheeks kisses for himself and tears for his mother, the intelligent slave left the abode of the care-worn old woman, for that of his master at the cotton place.

Henry was a black—a pure negro—handsome, manly and intelligent, in size comparing well with his master, but neither so fleshy nor heavy built in person. A man of good literary attainments—unknown to Col. Franks, though he was aware he could read and write—having been educated in the West Indies, and decoyed away when young. His affection for wife and child was not excelled by colonel Franks for his. He was bold, determined and courageous, but always mild, gentle and courteous, though impulsive when an occasion demanded his opposition.

Going immediately to the place, he presented himself before his master. Much conversation ensued concerning the business which had been entrusted to his charge, all of which was satisfactorily transacted, and full explanations concerning the horses, but not a word was uttered concerning the fate of Maggie, the Colonel barely remarking 'your mistress is unwell.'

After conversing till a late hour, Henry was assigned a bed in the great house, but sleep was far from his eyes. He turned and changed upon his bed with restlessness and anxiety, impatiently awaiting a return of the morning.

VII. Master and Slave

Early on Tuesday morning in obedience to his master's orders, Henry was on his way to the city, to get the house in readiness for the reception of his mistress, Mrs. Franks having much improved in three or four days. Mammy Judy had not yet risen when he knocked at the door.

'Hi Henry! yeh heah ready! huccum yeh git up so soon; arter some mischif I reckon? Do'n reckon yeh arter any good!' saluted mammy Judy.

'No mammy,' replied he; 'no mischief, but like a good slave such as you wish me to be, come to obey my master's will, just what you like to see.'

'Sho boy! none yeh nonsens'; huccum I want yeh bey maus Stephen? Git dat nonsens' in yeh head las' night long so, I reckon! Wat dat yeh gwine do now?'

'I have come to dust and air the mansion for their reception. They have sold my wife away from me, and who else would do her work?' This reply excited the apprehension of mammy Judy.

'Wat yeh gwine do Henry? yeh arter no good; yeh ain' gwine 'tack maus Stephen is yeh?'

'What do you mean mammy, strike him?'

'Yes! reckon yeh ain' gwine hit 'im?'

'Curse—!'

'Henry, Henry, membeh wat ye 'fess! fah de Laud sake, yeh ain gwine take to swahin?' interrupted the old woman.

'I make no profession mammy. I once did believe in religion, but now I have no confidence in it. My faith has been wrecked on the stony hearts of such pretended christians as Stephen Franks, while passing through the stormy sea of trouble and oppression! and—'

'Hay, boy! yeh is gittin high! yeh call maussa "Stephen?" '

'Yes, and I'll never call him "master" again, except when compelled to do so.'

'Bettah g'long ten' t' de house fo' wite folks come, an' nebeh mine talkin' 'bout fightin' 'long wid maus Stephen. Wat yeh gwine do wid white folks? Sho!'

'I don't intend to fight him, mammy Judy, but I'll attack him concerning my wife, if the words be my last! Yes, I'll—!' and pressing his lips to suppress the words, the outraged man turned away from the old slave mother, with such feelings as only an intelligent slave could realize.

The orders of the morning were barely executed, when the carriage came to the door. The bright eyes of the foot boy Tony sparkled when he saw Henry approaching the carriage.

'Well Henry! ready for us?' enquired his master.

'Yes sir,' was the simple reply. 'Mistress!' he saluted, politely bowing as he took her hand to assist her from the carriage.

'Come Henry, my man, get out the riding horses,' ordered Franks after a little rest.

'Yes sir.'

A horse for the Colonel and lady each, was soon in readiness at the door, but none for himself, it always having been the custom in their morning rides, for the maid and man-servant to accompany the mistress and master.

'Ready did you say?' enquired Franks on seeing but two horses standing at the stile.

'Yes sir.'

'Where's the other horse?'

'What for sir?'

'What for? yourself to be sure!'

'Colonel Franks!' said Henry, looking him sternly in the face, 'when I last rode that horse in company with you and lady, *my wife* was at my side, and I will not now go without her! Pardon me—my life for it, I won't go!'

'Not another word you black imp!' exclaimed Franks, with an uplifted staff in a rage, 'or I'll strike you down in an instant!'

'Strike away if you will sir, I dont care—I wont go without my wife!'

'You impudent scoundrel! I'll soon put an end to your conduct! I'll put you on the auction block, and sell you to the negro traders.'

'Just as soon as you please sir, the sooner the better, as I dont want to live with you any longer!'

'Hold your tongue sir, or I'll cut it out of your head! you ungrateful black dog! Really things have come to a pretty pass, when I must take impudence off my own negro! By gracious!—

God forgive me for the expression—I'll sell every negro I have first! I'll dispose of him to the hardest negro trader I can find!' said Franks in a rage.

'You may do your mightiest, colonel Franks. I'm not your slave, nor never was, and you know it! and but for my wife and her people, I never would have staid with you till now. I was decoyed away when young, and then became entangled in such domestic relations as to induce me to remain with you; but now the tie is broken! I know that the odds are against me, but never mind!'

'Do you threaten me, sir! Hold your tongue, or I'll take your life instantly, you villain!'

'No sir, I dont threaten you, colonel Franks, but I do say that I wont be treated like a dog. You sold my wife away from me, after always promising that she should be free. And more than that, you sold her because——! and now you talk about whipping me. Shoot me, sell me, or do anything else you please, but dont lay your hands on me, as I will not suffer you to whip me!'

Running up to his chamber, colonel Franks seized a revolver, when Mrs. Franks grasping hold of his arm exclaimed—

'Colonel! what does all this mean?'

'Mean, my dear? It's rebellion! a plot—this is but the shadow of a cloud that's fast gathering around us! I see it plainly, I see it!' responded the Colonel, starting for the stairs.

'Stop Colonel!' admonished his lady, 'I hope you'll not be rash. For Heaven's sake, do not stain your hands in blood!'

'I do not mean to, my dear! I take this for protection!' Franks hastening down stairs, when Henry had gone into the back part of the premises.

'Dah now! dah now!' exclaimed mammy Judy as Henry entered the kitchen, 'see wat dis gwine back done foh yeh! Bettah put yo' trus' in de Laud! Henry, yeh gone clean back t'de wuhl ghin, yeh knows it!'

'You're mistaken mammy, I do trust the Lord as much as ever, but I now understand him better than I use to, that's all. I dont intend to be made a fool of any longer by false preaching.'

'Henry!' interrogated Daddy Joe, who apprehending difficulties in the case, had managed to get back to the house, 'yeh gwine lose all yo' ligion? Wat yeh mean boy!'

'Religion!' replied Henry rebukingly, 'that's always the cry with black people. Tell me nothing about religion when the very man who hands you the bread at communion, has sold your daughter away from you!'

'Den yeh 'fen' God case man 'fen' yeh! Take cah Henry, take cah! mine wat yeh 'bout; God is lookin' at yeh, an' if yeh no' willin' trus' 'im, yeh need'n call on 'im in time o' trouble.'

'I dont intend, unless He does more for me then than he has done before. "Time of need!" If ever man needed his assistance, I'm sure I need it now.'

'Yeh do'n know wat yeh need; de Laud knows bes.' On'y trus' in 'im, an' 'e bring yeh out mo' nah conkah. By de help o' God I's heah dis day, to gib yeh cumfut!'

'I have trusted in Him daddy Joe, all my life, as I told mammy Judy this morning, but—'

'Ah boy, yeh's gwine back! Dat on't do Henry, dat on't do!'

'Going back from what? my oppressor's religion! If I could only get rid of his inflictions as easily as I can his religion, I would be this day a free man, when you might then talk to me about "trusting." '

'Dis Henry, am one uh de ways ob de Laud; 'e fus 'flicks us an' den he bless us.'

'Then it's a way I dont like.'

'Mine how yeh talk, boy!'

> 'God moves in a myst'us way
> His wundahs to pehfaum,' an—'

'He moves too slow for me daddy Joe; I'm tired waiting so—'

'Come Henry, I hab no sich talk like dat! yeh is gittin' rale weaked; yeh gwine let de debil take full 'session on yeh! Take cah boy, mine how yeh talk!'

'It is not wickedness, daddy Joe; you dont understand these things at all. If a thousand years with us is but a day with God, do you think that I am required to wait all that time?'

'Dont Henry, dont! de wud say "Stan' still an' see de salbation." '

'That's no talk for me daddy Joe, I've been "standing still" long enough; I'll "stand still" no longer.'

'Den yeh no call t' bey God wud? Take cah boy, take cah!'

'Yes I have, and I intend to obey it, but that part was intended for the Jews, a people long since dead. I'll obey that intended for me.'

'How yeh gwine bey it?'

' "Now is the accepted time, to-day is the day of salvation." So you see, daddy Joe, this is very different to standing still.'

'Ah boy, I's feahd yeh's losen yeh 'ligion!'

'I tell you once for all daddy Joe, that I'm not only "losing," but I have altogether lost my faith in the religion of my oppressors. As they are our religious teachers, my estimate of the thing they give, is no greater than it is for those who give it.'

With elbows upon his knees, and face resting in the palms of his hands, daddy Joe for some time sat with his eyes steadily fixed on the floor, whilst Ailcey who for a part of the time had been an auditor to the conversation, went into the house about her domestic duties.

'Never mind Henry! I hope it will not always be so with you. You have been kind and faithful to me and the Colonel, and I'll do anything I can for you!' sympathetically said Mrs. Franks, who having been a concealed spectator of the interview between Henry and the old people, had just appeared before them.

Wiping away the emblems of grief which stole down his face, with a deep toned voice, upgushing from the recesses of a more than iron-pierced soul, he enquired—

'Madam, what can you do! Where is my wife?' To this, Mrs. Franks gave a deep sigh. 'Never mind, never mind!' continued he, 'yes, I will mind, and by—!'

'O! Henry, I hope you've not taken to swearing! I do hope you will not give over to wickedness! Our afflictions should only make our faith the stronger.'

' "Wickedness!" Let the righteous correct the wicked, and the Christian condemn the sinner!'

'That is uncharitable in you Henry! as you know I have always treated you kindly, and God forbid that I should consider myself any less than a Christian! and I claim as much at least for the Colonel, though like frail mortals he is liable to err at times.'

'Madam!' said he with suppressed emotion—starting back a pace or two—'do you think there is anything either in or out of hell so wicked, as that which colonel Franks has done to my wife, and now about to do to me? For myself I care not—my wife!'

'Henry!' said Mrs. Franks, gently placing her hand upon his shoulder, 'there is yet a hope left for you, and you will be faithful enough I know, not to implicate any person; it is this: Mrs. Van Winter, a true friend of your race, is shortly going to Cuba on a visit, and I will arrange with her to purchase you through an agent on the day of your sale, and by that means you can get to Cuba, where probably you may be fortunate enough to get the master of your wife to become your purchaser.'

'Then I have two chances!' replied Henry.

Just then Ailcey thrusting her head in the door, requested the presence of her mistress in the parlor.

VIII. The Sale

'Dah now, dah now!' exclaimed mammy Judy; 'jis wat ole man been tellin' on yeh! Yeh go out yandah, yeh kick up yeh heel, git yeh head clean full proclamation an' sich like dat, an' let debil fool yeh, den go fool long wid wite folks long so, sho! Bettah go 'bout yeh bisness; been sahvin' God right, yeh no call t'do so eh reckon!'

'I dont care what comes! my course is laid out and my determination fixed, and nothing they can do can alter it. So you and daddy Joe, mammy, had just as well quit your preaching to me the religion you have got from your oppressors.'

'Soul-driveh git yeh, yeh cah git way fom dem eh doh recken! Sho chile, yeh, ain' dat mighty!' admonished mammy Judy.

'Henry my chile, look to de Laud! look to de Laud? case 'e 'lone am able t' bah us up in ouah trouble! an—'

'Go directly sir, to captain John Harris' office and ask him to call immediately to see me at my house!' ordered Franks.

Politely bowing, Henry immediately left the premises on his errand.

'Laud a' messy maus Stephen!' exclaimed mammy Judy, on

hearing the name of John Harris the negro-trader; 'hope yeh arteh no haum! gwine sell all on us to de tradehs?'

'Hoot-toot, hoot-toot! Judy, give yourself no uneasiness about that, till you have some cause for it. So you and Joe may rest contented Judy,' admonished Franks.

'Tank'e maus Stephen! case ah heahn yeh tell Henry dat yeh sell de las' nig—'

'Hush! ole umin, hush! yeh tongue too long! Put yeh trus' in de Laud!' interrupted daddy Joe.

'I treat my black folks well,' replied Franks; 'and all they have to—'

Here the door bell having been rung, he was interrupted with a message from Ailcey, that a gentleman awaited his presence in the parlor.

At the moment which the Colonel left the kitchen, Henry stepped over the style into the yard, which at once disclosed who the gentleman was to whom the master had been summoned. Henry passed directly around and behind the house.

'See, ole man, see! reckon 'e gwine dah now!' whispered mammy Judy, on seeing Henry pass through the yard without going into the kitchen.

'Whah?' enquired daddy Joe.

'Dun'o out yandah, whah 'e gwine way from wite folks!' she replied.

The interview between Franks and the trader Harris was not over half an hour duration, the trader retiring, Franks being prompt and decisive in all of his transactions, making little ceremony.

So soon as the front door was closed, Ailcey smiling bore into the kitchen a half pint glass of brandy, saying that her master had sent it to the old people.

The old man received it with compliments to his master, pouring it into a black jug in which there was both tansy and garlic, highly recommending it as a 'bitters' and certain antidote for worms, for which purpose he and the old woman took of it as long as it lasted, though neither had been troubled with that particular disease since the days of their childhood.

'Wat de gwine do wid yeh meh son?' enquired mammy Judy as Henry entered the kitchen.

'Sell me to the soul-drivers! what else would they do?'

'Yeh gwin 'tay 'bout till de git yeh?'

'I shant move a step! and let them do their—!'

'Maus wants to see yeh in da front house Henry,' interrupted Ailcey, he immediately obeying the summons.

'Heah dat now!' said mammy Judy, as Henry followed the maid out of the kitchen.

'Carry this note sir, directly to captain Jack Harris!' ordered Franks, handing to Henry a sealed note. Receiving it, he bowed politely, going out of the front door, directly to the slave prison of Harris.

'Eh heh! I see,' said Harris on opening the note; 'colonel Frank's boy; walk in here;' passing through the office into a room which proved to be the first department of the slave-prison. 'No common negro I see! you're a shade higher. A pretty deep shade too! Can read, write cipher; a good religious fellow, and has a Christian and sir name. The devil you say! Who's your father? Can you preach?'

'I have never tried,' was the only reply.

'Have you ever been a member of Congress?' continued Harris with ridicule.

To this Henry made no reply.

'Wont answer hey! beneath your dignity. I understand that you're of that class of gentry who dont speak to common folks! You're not quite well enough dressed for a gentleman of your cloth. Here! Mr. Henry, I'll present you with a set of ruffles: give yourself no trouble sir, as I'll dress you! I'm here for that purpose,' said Harris, fastening upon the wrists of the manly bondman, a heavy pair of handcuffs.

'You hurt my wrist!' admonished Henry.

'New clothing will be a little tight when first put on. Now sir!' continued the trader, taking him to the back door and pointing into the yard at the slave gang there confined; 'as you have been respectably dressed, walk out and enjoy yourself among the ladies and gentleman there; you'll find them quite a select company.'

Shortly after this the sound of the bell-ringer's voice was heard—a sound which usually spread terror among the slaves: 'Will be sold this afternoon at three o'clock by public outcry, at the slave-prison of captain John Harris, a likely choice negro-fellow, the best trained body servant in the state, trained to the business by the most accomplished lady and gentleman negro-trainers in the Mississippi Valley. Sale positive without a proviso.'

'Dah, dah! did'n eh tell yeh so? Ole man, ole man! heah dat now! Come heah. Dat jis what I been tellin on im, but 'e uden blieve me!' ejaculated old mammy Judy on hearing the bell ring and the hand bill read.

Falling upon their knees, the two old slaves prayed fervently to God, thanking him that it was as 'well with them' as it was.

'Bless de Laud! my soul is happy!' cried out mammy Judy being overcome with devotion, clapping her hands.

'Tang God, fah wat I feels in my soul!' responded daddy Joe.

Rising from their knees with tears trickling down their cheeks, the old slaves endeavored to ease their troubled souls by singing—

'Oh, when shall my sorrows subside,
And when shall my troubles be ended;
And when to the bosom of Christ be conveyed,
To the mansions of joy and bliss;
To the mansions of joy and bliss!'

'Wuhthy to be praise! blessed be de name uh de Laud! Po' black folks, de Laud o'ny knows wats t' come ob us!' exclaimed mammy Judy.

'Look to de Laud ole umin, 'e's able t' bah us out mo' neh conkeh. Keep de monin stah in sight!' advised daddy Joe.

'Yes ole man yes, dat I is done dis many long day, an' ah ain' gwine lose sight uh it now! No, God bein' my helpeh, I is gwine keep my eyes right on it, dat I is!'

As the hour of three drew near, many there were going in the direction of the slave-prison, a large number of persons having assembled at the sale.

'Draw near, gentlemen! draw near!' cried Harris; 'the hour of sale is arrived: a positive sale with no proviso, cash down, or no sale at all!' A general laugh succeeded the introduction of the auctioneer.

'Come up here my lad!' continued the auctioneer, wielding a long red rawhide; 'mount this block, stand beside me, an' let's see which is the best looking man! We have met before, but I never had the pleasure of introducing you. Gentlemen one and all, I take pleasure in introducing to you Henry—pardon me sir—Mr. Henry Holland, I believe—am I right sir?—Mr. Henry Holland, a good looking fellow you will admit.

'I am offered one thousand dollars; one thousand dollars for the best looking negro in all Mississippi! If all the negro boys in the state was as good looking as him, I'd give two thousand dollars for 'em all myself!' This caused another laugh. 'Who'll give me one thousand five—'

Just then a shower of rain came on.

'Gentlemen!' exclaimed the auctioneer; 'without a place can be obtained large enough to shelter the people here assembled, the sale will have to be postponed. This is a proviso we could'nt foresee, an' therefore is not responsible for it.' There was another hearty laugh.

A whisper went through the crowd, when presently a gentleman came forward saying, that those concerned had kindly tendered the use of the Church which stood near by, in which to continue the sale.

'Here we are again, gentlemen! Who bids five hundred more for the likely negro fellow? I am offered fifteen hundred dollars for the finest negro servant in the state! Come my boy bestir yourself an' dont stan' there like a statue; cant you give us a jig? whistle us a song! I forgot, the negro fellow is religious; by the by, an excellent recommendation gentlemen. Perhaps he'll give us a sermon. Say, git up there old fellow, an' hold forth. Cant you give us a sermon on Abolition? I'm only offered fifteen hundred dollars for the likely negro boy! Fifteen, sixteen, sixteen hundred dollars, seventeen hundred, just agoing at—eighteen, eighteen, nineteen hundred, nineteen nineteen! Just agoing at nineteen hundred dollars for the best body servant in the State; just agoing at nineteen and without a better bid, I'll—going! going! go—!'

Just at this point a note was passed up the aisle to the auctioneer, who after reading it said:

'Gentlemen! circumstances beyond my control, make it necessary that the sale be postponed until one day next week; the time of continuance will be duly announced,' when bowing he left the stand.

'That's another proviso not in the original bill!' exclaimed a voice as the auctioneer left the stand, at which there were peals of laughter.

To secure himself against contingency, Harris immediately delivered Henry over to Franks.

There were present at the sale, Crow, Slider, Walker, Borbridge, Simpson, Hurst, Spangler and Williams, all noted slave traders, eager to purchase, some on their return home, and some with their gangs *en route* for the southern markets.

The note handed the auctioneer read thus:

'CAPT. HARRIS:—Having learned that there are private individuals at the sale, who design purchasing my negro man, Harry, for his own *personal advantage*, you will peremptorily postpone the sale—making such apology as the occasion demands—and effect a private sale with Richard Crow, Esq., who offers me two thousand dollars for him. Let the boy return to me. Believe me to be,

Very Respectfully,
STEPHEN FRANKS.

Capt. John Harris.
Natchez, Nov. 29th, 1852.'

'Now sir,' said Franks to Henry, who had barely reached the house from the auction block; 'take this pass and go to Jackson and Woodville, or anywhere else you wish to see your friends, so that you be back against Monday afternoon. I ordered a postponement of the sale, thinking that I would try you awhile longer, as I never had cause before to part with you. Now see if you can't be a better boy!'

Eagerly taking the note, thanking him with a low bow, turning away, Henry opened the paper, which read:

'Permit the bearer my boy Henry, sometimes calling himself Henry Holland—a kind of negro pride he has—to pass and repass wherever he wants to go, he behaving himself properly.

STEPHEN FRANKS.

To all whom it may concern.
Natchez, Nov. 29th 1952.'

Carefully depositing the *charte volante* in his pocket wallet, Henry quietly entered the hut of mammy Judy and daddy Joe.

IX. The Runaway

'De Laud's good—bless his name!' exclaimed mammy Judy wringing her hands as Henry entered their hut, ' 'e heahs de prahs ob 'is chilen. Yeh hab reason t' tang God yeh is heah dis day!'

'Yes Henry, see wat de Laud's done fah yeh. Tis true's I's heah dis day! Tang God fah dat!' added daddy Joe.

'I think,' replied he after listening with patience to the old people, 'I have reason to thank our Ailcey and Van Winter's Biddy; they, it seems to me should have some credit in the matter.'

'Sho boy, g' long whah yeh gwine! Yo' backslidin, gwine git yeh in trouble ghin eh reckon?' replied mammy Judy.

Having heard the conversation between her mistress and Henry, Ailcey as a secret, informed Van Winter's Derba, who informed her fellow servant Biddy, who imparted it to her acquaintance Nelly, the slave of esquire Potter, Nelly informing her mistress, who told the 'Squire, who led Franks into the secret of the whole matter.

'Mus'n blame me, Henry!' said Ailcey in an undertone, 'I did'n mean de wite folks to know wat I tole Derba, nor she di'n mean it nuther, but dat devil, Pottah's Nell! us gals mean da fus time we ketch uh out, to duck uh in da rivah! She's rale wite folk's nigga, dat's jus' wat she is. Nevah mine, we'll ketch her yit!'

'I dont blame you Ailcey, nor either of Mrs. Van Winter's girls, as I know that you are my friends, neither of whom would do anything knowingly to injure me. I know Ailcey that you are a good girl, and believe you would tell me—'

'Yes Henry, I is yo' fren' an' come to tell yeh now wat da wite folks goin' to do.'

'What is it Ailcey; what do you know?'

'Wy dat ugly ole devil Dick Crow—God fah gim me! but I hate 'im so, case he nothin' but po' wite man, no how—I know 'im he come from Fagina on—'

'Never mind his origin, Ailcey, tell me what you know concerning his visit in the house.'

'I is goin' to, but da ugly ole devil, I hates 'im so! Maus Stephen had 'im in da pahla, an' 'e sole yeh to 'im, dat ugly ole po' wite devil, fah—God knows how much—a hole heap a money; "two" somethin.'

'I know what it was, two thousand dollars, for that was his selling price to Jack Harris.'

'Yes, dat was da sum, Henry.'

'I am satisfied as to how much he can be relied on. Even was I to take the advice of the old people here, and become reconciled to drag out a miserable life of degradation and bondage under them, I would not be permitted to do so by this man, who seeks every opportunity to crush out my lingering manhood, and reduce my free spirit to the submission of a slave. He cannot do it, I will not submit to it, and I defy his power to make me submit.'

'Laus a messy, Henry, yeh free man! huccum yeh not tell me long'o? Sho boy, bettah go long whah yeh gwine, out yandah, an' not fool long wid wite folks!' said mammy Judy with surprise, 'wat bring yeh heah anyhow?'

'That's best known to myself, mammy.'

'Wat make yeh keep heah so long den, dat yeh ain' gone fo' dis?'

'Your questions become rather pressing mammy; I cant tell you that either.'

'Laud, Laud, Laud! So yeh free man? Well, well, well!'

'Once for all, I now tell you old people, what I never told you before, nor never expected to tell you under such circumstances; that I never intend to serve any white man again. I'll die first!'

'De Laud a' messy on my po' soul! An' huccum yeh not gone befo'?'

'Carrying out the principles and advice of you old people "standing still, to see the salvation." But with me, "now is the accepted time, to-day is the day of salvation." '

'Well, well, well!' sighed mammy Judy.

'I am satisfied that I am sold, and the wretch who did it, seeks to conceal his perfidy by deception. Now if ever you old people did anything in your lives, you must do it now.'

'Wat dat yeh want wid us?'

'Why, if you'll go, I'll take you on Saturday night, and make our escape to a free country.'

'Wat place yeh call dat?'

'Canada!' replied Henry, with emotion.

'How fah yeh gwine take me?' earnestly enquired the old woman.

'I cant just now tell the distance, probably some two or three thousand miles from here, the way we'd have to go.'

'De Laus a messy on me! an' wat yeh gwine do wid little Joe; ain gwine leave 'im behine?'

'No, mammy Judy, I'd bury him in the bottom of the river first! I intend carrying him in a bundle on my back, as the Indians carry their babies.'

'Wat yeh gwine do fah money; yeh ain' gwine rob folks on de road?'

'No mammy, I'll starve first. Have you and daddy Joe saved nothing from your black-eye peas and poultry selling for many years?'

'Ole man, how much in dat pot undeh de flo' dah; how long since yeh count it?'

'Don'o,' replied daddy Joe, 'las' time ah count it, da wah faughty guinea* uh sich a mauttah, an' ah put in some six-seven guinea mo' since dat.'

'Then you have some two hundred and fifty dollars in money.'

'Dat do yeh?' enquired mammy Judy.

'Yes, that of itself is enough, but—'

'Den take it an' go long whah yeh gwine; we ole folks too ole fah gwine headlong out yandah an' don'o whah we gwine. Sho boy! take de money an' g'long!' decisively replied the old woman after all her inquisitiveness.

'If you dont know, I do mammy, and that will answer for all.'

'Dat ain' gwine do us. We ole folks ain' politishon an' undehstan' de graumma uh dese places, an' w'en we git dah den maybe do'n like it an cahn' git back. Sho chile, go long whah yeh gwine!'

'What do you say, daddy Joe? Whatever you have to say, must be said quick, as time with me is precious.'

'We is too ole dis time a-day chile, t'go way out yauah de Laud knows whah; bettah whah we is.'

'You'll not be too old to go if these whites once take a notion to sell you. What will you do then?'

* 'Guinea' with the slave, is a five dollar gold piece.

'Trus' to de Laud!'

'Yes, the same old slave song—"Trust to the Lord." Then I must go, and—'

'Ain' yeh gwine take de money Henry?' interrupted the old woman.

'No mammy, since you will not go, I leave it for you and daddy Joe, as you may yet have use for it, or those may desire to use it, who better understand what use to make of it than you and daddy Joe seem willing to be instructed in.'

'Den yeh 'ont have de money?'

'I thank you and daddy most kindly, mammy Judy, for your offer, and only refuse because I have two hundred guineas about me.'

'Sho boy, yeh got all dat, yeh no call t'want dat little we got. Whah yeh git all dat money? Do'n reckon yeh gwine tell me! Did'n steal from maus Stephen, do'n reckon?'

'No mammy I'm incapable of stealing from any one, but I have, from time to time, taken by littles, some of the earnings due me for more than eighteen years' service to this man Franks, which at the low rate of two hundred dollars a year, would amount to sixteen hundred dollars more than I secured, exclusive of the interest, which would have more than supplied my clothing, to say nothing of the injury done me by degrading me as a slave. "Steal" indeed! I would that when I had an opportunity, I had taken fifty thousand instead of two. I am to understand you old people as positively declining to go, am I?'

'No no, chile, we cahn go! We put ouh trus' in de Laud, he bring us out mo' nah konkah.'

'Then from this time hence, I become a runaway. Take care of my poor boy while he's with you. When I leave the swamps, or where I'll go, will never be known to you. Should my boy be suddenly missed, and you find three notches cut in the bark of the big willow tree, on the side away from your hut, then give yourself no uneasiness; but if you don't find these notches in the tree, then I know nothing about him. Good bye!' and Henry strode directly for the road to Woodville.

'Fahwell me son, fahwell, an' may God a'mighty go wid you! May de Laud guide an' 'tect yeh on de way!'

The child, contrary to his custom, commenced crying, desiring to see mama Maggie and dadda Henry. Every effort to quiet him was unavailing. This brought sorrow to the old people's hearts and tears to their eyes, which they endeavored to soothe in a touching lamentation:

'See wives and husbands torn apart,
Their children's screams, they grieve my heart.
   They are torn away to Georgia!
   Come and go along with me—
   They are torn away to Georgia!
   Go sound the Jubilee!'

* * *

(Editor's note: In Chapter 10 the slaves on the Franks plantation have a holiday festival.)

XI. A Shadow

'Ah, boys! here you are, true to your promise,' said Henry, as he entered a covert in the thicket adjacent the cotton place, late on Sunday evening, 'have you been waiting long?'

'Not very,' replied Andy, 'not mo' dan two—three ouahs.'

'I was fearful you would not come, or if you did before me, that you would grow weary, and leave.'

'Yeh no call to doubt us Henry, case yeh fine us true as ole steel!'

'I know it,' answered he, 'but you know Andy, that when a slave is once sold at auction, all respect for him—'

'O pshaw! we ain' goin' to heah nothin' like dat a tall! case—'

'No!' interrupted Charles, 'all you got to do Henry, is to tell we boys what you want, an' we're your men.'

'That's the talk for me!'

'Well, what you doin' here?' enquired Charles.

'W'at brought yeh back fom Jackson so soon?' farther enquired Andy.

'How did you get word to meet me here?'

'By Ailcey; she give me the stone, an' I give it to Andy, an' we both sent one apiece back. Did'nt you git 'em?'

'Yes, that's the way I knew you intended to meet me,' replied Henry.

'So we thought,' said Charles, 'but tell us Henry, what you want us to do.'

'I suppose you know all about the sale, that they had me on the auction block, but ordered a postponement, and—'

'That's the very pint we cant understand, although I'm in the same family with you,' interrupted Charles.

'But tell us Henry, what yeh doin' here?' impatiently enquired Andy.

'Yes,' added Charles, 'we want to know.'

'Well, I'm a *runaway*, and from this time forth, I swear—I do it religiously—that I'll never again serve any white man living!'

That's the pint I wanted to git at before,' explained Charles, 'as I cant understan' why you run away, after your release from Jack Harris, an'—'

'Nah I, nuthah!' interrupted Andy.

'It seems to me,' continued Charles, 'that I'd 'ave went before they 'tempted to sell me, an' that you're safer now than before they had you on the block.'

'Dat's da way I look at it,' responded Andy.

'The stopping of the sale was to deceive his wife, mammy, and daddy Joe, as he had privately disposed of me to a regular soul-driver by the name of Crow.'

'I knows Dick Crow,' said Andy, ' 'e come f'om Faginy, whah I did, da same town.'

'So Ailcey said of him. Then you know him without any description from me,' replied Henry.

'Yes 'n deed! an' I knows 'im to be a inhuman, mean, dead-po' white man, dat's wat I does!'

'Well, I was privately sold to him for two thousand dollars, then ordered back to Franks, as though I was still his slave, and by him given a pass, and requested to go to Woodville where there were arrangements to seize me and hold me, till Crow ordered me, which was to have been on Tuesday evening. Crow is not aware of me having been given a pass; Franks gave it to deceive his wife; in case of my not returning, to make the impression that I had run away, when in reality I was sold to the trader.'

'Then our people had their merry-making all for nothin',' said Charles, 'an' Franks got what 'e didn't deserve—their praise.'

'No, the merry-making was only to deceive Franks, that I might have time to get away. Daddy Joe, mammy Judy, and Ailcey, knew all about it, and proposed the feast to deceive him.'

'Dat's good! sarve 'im right, da 'sarned ole scamp!' rejoined Andy.

'It couldn't be better!' responded Charles.

'Henry uh wish we was in yo' place an' you none da wus by it,' said Andy.

'Never mind, boys, give yourselves no uneasiness, as it wont be long before we'll all be together.'

'You think so, Henry?' asked Charles.

'Well uh hope so, but den body can haudly 'spect it,' responded Andy.

'Boys,' said Henry, with great caution, and much emotion, 'I am now about to approach an important subject, and as I have always found you true to me—and you can only be true to me by being true to yourselves—I shall not hesitate to impart it! But for Heaven's sake!—perhaps I had better not!'

'Keep nothin' back, Henry,' said Charles, 'as you know that we boys 'll die by our principles, that's settled!'

'Yes, I wants to die right now by mine; right heah, now!' sanctioned Andy.

'Well it is this—close boys! close!' when they gathered in a huddle beneath an underbush, upon their knees, 'you both go with me, but not now. I '

'Why not now?' anxiously enquired Charles.

'Dat's wat I like to know!' responded Andy.

'Stop boys, till I explain. The plans are mine and you must allow me to know more about them than you. Just here, for once, the slave-holding preacher's advice to the black man is appropriate, "Stand still and see the salvation." '

'Then let us hear it, Henry,' asked Charles.

'Fah God sake!' said Andy, 'let us heah w'at it is, anyhow, Henry; yeh keep a body in 'spence so long, till I's mose crazy to heah it. Dat's no way!'

'You shall have it, but I approach it with caution! Nay, with fear and trembling, at the thought of what has been the fate of all previous matters of this kind. I approach it with religious

fear, and hardly think us fit for the task; at least, I know I am
not. But as no one has ever originated, or given us anything of
the kind, I suppose I may venture.'

'Tell it! tell it!' urged both in a whisper.

'Andy,' said Henry, 'let us have a word of prayer first!' when
they bowed low, with their heads to the ground, Andy, who
was a preacher of the Baptist pursuasion among his slave
brethren, offering a solemn and affecting prayer, in whispers to
the Most High, to give them knowledge and courage in the
undertaking, and success in the effort.

Rising from their knees, Andy commenced an anthem, by
which he appeared to be much affected, in the following words:

> 'About our future destiny,
> There need be none debate—
> Whilst we ride on the tide,
> With our Captain and his mate.'

Clasping each other by the hand, standing in a band together,
as a plight of their union and fidelity to each other, Henry
said—

'I now impart to you the secret, it is this: I have laid a scheme,
and matured a plan for a general insurrection of the slaves in
every State, and the successful overthrow of slavery!'

'Amen!' exclaimed Charles.

'God grant it!' responded Andy.

'Tell us, Henry, how's dis to be carried out?' enquired Andy.

'That's the thing which most concerns me, as it seems that it
would be hard to do in the present ignorant state of our people
in the slave States,' replied Charles.

'Dat's jis wat I feah!' said Andy.

'This difficulty is obviated. It is so simple that the most stupid
among the slaves will understand it as well as if he had been
instructed for a year.'

'What!' exclaimed Charles.

'Let's heah dat aghin!' asked Andy.

'It is so just as I told you! So simple is it that the trees of the
forest or an orchard illustrate it; flocks of birds or domestic
cattle, fields of corn hemp or sugar cane; tobacco rice or cotton,
the whistling of the wind, rustling of the leaves, flashing of
lightning, roaring of thunder, and running of streams all keep it

constantly before their eyes and in their memory, so that they cant forget it if they would.'

'Are we to know it now?' enquired Charles.

'I'm boun' to know it dis night befo' I goes home, 'case I been longin' fah ole Pottah dis many day, an' uh mos' think uh got 'im now!'

'Yes boys, you've to know it before we part, but—'

'That's the talk!' said Charles.

'Good nuff talk fah me!' responded Andy.

'As I was about to say, such is the character of this organization, that punishment and misery are made the instruments for its propagation, so—'

'I cant understan' that part—'

'You know nothing at all about it Charles, and you must—'

'Stan' still an' see da salvation!' interrupted Andy.

'Amen!' responded Charles.

'God help you so to do, brethren!' admonished Henry.

'Go on Henry tell us! give it to us!' they urged.

'Every blow you receive from the oppressor impresses the organization upon your mind, making it so clear that even Whitehead's Jack could understand it as well as his master.'

'We are satisfied! The secret, the secret!' they importuned.

'Well then, first to prayer, and then to the organization. Andy!' said Henry, nodding to him, when they again bowed low with their heads to the ground, whilst each breathed a silent prayer, which was ended with 'Amen' by Andy.

Whilst yet upon their knees, Henry imparted to them the secrets of his organization.

'O, dat's da thing!' exclaimed Andy.

'Capital, capital!' responded Charles, 'what fools we was that we didn't know it long ago!'

'I is mad wid myse'f now!' said Andy.

'Well, well, well! Surely God must be in the work,' continued Charles.

' 'E's heah; Heaven's nigh! Ah feels it! it's right heah!' responded Andy, placing his hand upon his chest, the tears trickling down his cheeks.

'Brethren,' asked Henry, 'do you understand it?'

'Understand it? Why a child could understand, it's so easy!' replied Charles.

'Yes,' added Andy, 'ah not only undehstan' myse'f, but wid da knowledge I has uv it, ah could make Whitehead's Jack a Moses!'

'Stand still, then, and see!' said he.

'Dat's good Bible talk!' responded Andy.

'Well, what is we to do?' enquired Charles.

'You must now go on and organize continually. It makes no difference when, nor where you are, so that the slaves are true and trustworthy, as the scheme is adapted to all times and places.'

'How we gwine do Henry, 'bout gittin' da things 'mong da boys?' enquired Andy.

'All you have to do, is to find one good man or woman—I dont care which, so that they prove to be the right person—on a single plantation, and hold a seclusion and impart the secret to them, and make them the organizers for their own plantation, and they in like manner impart it to some other next to them, and so on. In this way it will spread like smallpox among them.'

'Henry, you is fit fah leadah ah see,' complimentingly said Andy.

'I greatly mistrust myself, brethren, but if I cant command, I can at least plan.'

'Is they anything else for us to do Henry?' enquired Charles.

'Yes, a very important part of your duties has yet to be stated. I now go as a runaway, and will be suspected of lurking about in the thickets, swamps and caves; then to make the ruse complete, just as often as you think it necessary, to make a good impression, you must kill a shoat, take a lamb, pig, turkey, goose, chickens, ham of bacon from the smoke house, a loaf of bread or crock of butter from the spring house, and throw them down into the old waste well at the back of the old quarters, always leaving the heads of the fowls lying about and the blood of the larger animals. Everything that is missed do not hesitate to lay it upon me, as a runaway, it will only cause them to have the less suspicion of your having such a design.'

'That's it,—the very thing!' said Charles, 'an it so happens that they's an ole waste well on both Franks' and Potter's places, one for both of us.'

'I hope Andy, you have no religious objections to this?'

'It's a paut ah my 'ligion Henry, to do whateveh I bleve right, an' shall sholy do dis, God being my helpah!'

'Now he's talkin'!' said Charles.

'You must make your religion subserve your interests, as your oppressors do theirs!' advised Henry. 'They use the Scriptures to make you submit, by preaching to you the texts of "obedience to your masters" and "standing still to see the salvation," and we must now begin to understand the Bible so as to make it of interest to us.'

'Dat's gospel talk' sanctioned Andy. 'Is da anything else yeh want tell us boss—I calls 'im *boss*, 'case 'e aint nothing else but "boss"—so we can make 'ase an' git to wuck? 'case I feels like goin' at 'em now, me!'

'Having accomplished our object, I think I have done, and must leave you to-morrow.'

'When shall we hear from you Henry?' enquired Charles.

'Not until you shall see me again; when that will be, I dont know. You may see me in six months, and might not not in eighteen. I am determined, now that I am driven to it, to complete an organization in every slave state before I return, and have fixed two years as my utmost limit.'

'Henry, tell me before we part, do you know anything about little Joe?' enquired Charles.

'I do!'

'Wha's da chile?' enquired Andy.

'He's safe enough, on his way to Canada!' at which Charles and Andy laughed.

'Little Joe on 'is way to Canada?' said Andy, 'mighty young travelah!'

'Yes,' replied Henry with a smile.

'You're a joking Henry?' said Charles, enquiringly.

'I am serious, brethren,' replied he, 'I do not joke in matters of this kind. I smiled because of Andy's surprise.'

'How did 'e go?' farther enquired Andy.

'In company with his "mother" who was waiting on her "mistress!" ' replied he quaintly.

'Eh heh!' exclaimed Andy, 'I knows all 'bout it now; but whah'd da "mammy" come f'om?'

'I found one!'

'Aint 'e high!' said Andy.

'Well brethren, my time is drawing to a close,' said Henry, rising to his feet.

'O!' exclaimed Andy, 'ah like to forgot, has yeh any money Henry?'

'Have either of you any?'

'We has?'

'How much?'

'I got two-three hundred dollahs!' replied Andy.

'An' so has I, Henry!' added Charles.

'Then keep it, as I have two thousand dollars now around my waist, and you'll find use for all you've got, and more, as you will before long have an opportunity of testing. Keep this studiously in mind and impress it as an important part of the scheme of organization, that they must have money, if they want to get free. Money will obtain them every thing necessary by which to obtain their liberty. The money is within all of their reach if they only knew it was right to take it. God told the Egyptian slaves to "borrow from their neighbors"—meaning their oppressors—"all their jewels;" meaning to take their money and wealth wherever they could lay hands upon it, and depart from Egypt. So you must teach them to take all the money they can get from their masters, to enable them to make the strike without a failure. I'll show you when we leave for the North, what money will do for you, right here in Mississippi. Bear this in mind; it is your certain *passport* through the *white gap,* as I term it.'

'I means to take all ah can git; I bin doin' dat dis some time. Ev'ry time ole Pottah leave 'is money pus, I borrys some, an' 'e all'as lays it on Miss Mary, but 'e think so much uh huh, dat anything she do is right wid 'im. Ef 'e 'spected me, an' Miss Mary say 'twant me, dat would be 'nough fah 'im.'

'That's right!' said Henry, 'I see you have been putting your own interpretation on the Scriptures, Andy, and as Charles will now have to take my place, he'll have still a much better opportunity than you, to "borrow from his master." '

'You needn't fear, I'll make good use of my time!' replied Charles.

The slaves now fell upon their knees in silent communion, all being affected to the shedding of tears, a period being put to their devotion by a sorrowful trembling of Henry's voice singing to the following touching words:

> 'Farewell, farewell, farewell!
> My loving friends farewell!
> Farewell old comrades in the cause,
> I leave you here, and journey on;
> And if I never more return,
> Farewell, I'm bound to meet you there!'

'One word before we part' said Charles. 'If we never should see you again, I suppose you intend to push on this scheme?'

'Yes!

> Insurrection shall be my theme!
> My watchword "Freedom or the grave!"
> Until from Rappahannock's stream,
> To where the Cuato waters lave,
> One simultaneous war cry
> Shall burst upon the midnight air!
> And rouse the tyrant but to sigh—
> Mid sadness, wailing, and dispair!'

Grasping each eagerly by the hand, the tears gushing from his eyes, with an humble bow, he bid them finally 'farewell!' and the runaway was off through the forest.

* * *

(Editor's note: In chapters 12-14 Colonel Franks discovers that Henry Blake and Little Joe are missing and organizes a search for the fugitives.)

XV. Interchange of Opinion

The landing of a steamer on her downward trip, brought Judge Ballard and Major Armsted to Natchez. The Judge had come to examine the country, purchase a cotton farm, and complete the arrangements of an interest in the 'Merchantman.' Already the proprietor of a large estate in Cuba, he was desirous of possessing a Mississippi cotton place. Disappointed by the absence of his wife abroad, he was satisfied to know that her object was accomplished.

Major Armsted was a man of ripe intelligence, acquired by years of rigid experience and close observation, rather than literary culture; though his educational attainments as a business man, were quite respectable. He for years had been the partner in business with Colonel Stephen Franks. In Baltimore, Washington City, Annapolis, Richmond, Norfolk, Charlestown, and Winchester, Va., a prison or receptacle for Coffle Gangs of Slaves purchased and sold in the market, comprised their principal places of business in the slave growing states of the Union.

The major was a great jester, full of humor, and fond of a good joke, ever ready to give and take such even from a slave. A great common sense man, by strict attention to men and things, and general observation, had become a philosopher among his fellows.

'Quite happy to meet you Judge, in these parts!' greeted Franks; 'wonder you could find your way so far south, especially at such a period, these being election times!'

'Don't matter a bit, as he's not up for anything I believe just now, except for negro trading! and in that he is quite a proselyte, and heretic to the teachings of his northern faith!' jocosely remarked Armsted.

'Don't mistake me gentlemen, because it was the incident of my life to be born in a non-slaveholding state. I'm certain that I am not at all understood as I should be on this question!' earnestly replied the Judge.

'The North has rather given you a bad name Judge, and it's difficult to separate yourself now from it, holding the position that you do, as one of her ablest jurists,' said Armsted.

'Well gentlemen!' seriously replied the Judge; 'as regards my opinion of negro slavery, the circumstances which brought me here, my large interest and responsibility in the slave-labor products of Cuba, should be I think sufficient evidence of my fidelity to southern principles, to say nothing of my official records, which modesty should forbid my reference to.'

'Certainly, certainly, Judge! The Colonel is at fault. He has lost sight of the fact that you it was, who seized the first runaway negro by the throat and held him by the compromise grasp, until we southern gentlemen sent for him and had him brought back!'

'Good, good, by hookie!' replied the Colonel rubbing his hands together.

'I hope I'm understood gentlemen!' seriously remarked the Judge.

'I think so Judge, I think so!' replied Armsted, evidently designing a full commitment on the part of the Judge; 'and if not, a little explanation will set us right.'

'It is true that I have not before been engaged in the slave trade, because until recently I had conscientious scruples about the thing—and I suppose I'm allowed the right of conscience as well as other folks'—smilingly said the Judge; 'never having purchased but for peopling my own plantation. But a little sober reflection set me right on that point. It is plain that the right to buy implies the right to hold, also to sell; and if there be right in the one, there is in the other; the premise being right the conclusion follows as a matter of course. I have therefore determined, not only to buy and hold, but buy and sell also. As I have heretofore been interested *for* the trade I will become interested *in* it.'

'Capital, capital, by George!—that's conclusive. Charles! a pitcher of cool water here; Judge, take another glass of brandy.'

'Good, very good!' said Armsted; 'so far, but there is such a thing as feeding out of two cribs—present company you know, and so—ahem!—therefore we should like to hear the Judge's opinion of equality, what it means anyhow. I'm anxious to learn some of the doctrines of human rights, not knowing how soon I may be called upon to practice them, as I may yet marry some little Yankee girl, full of her Puritan notions. And I'm told an old bachelor "cant come it" up that way, except he has a "pocket full of rocks," and can talk philanthropy like old Wilberforce.'

'Here gentlemen, I beg to make an episode, before replying to major Armsted,' suggested the Judge. 'His jest concerning the Yankee girl, reminds me—and I hope it may not be amiss in saying so—that my lady is the daughter of a clergyman, brought up amidst the sand of New England, and I think I'll not have to go from the present company, to prove her a good slaveholder. So the major may see that we northerners are not all alike.'

'How about the Compromise measures Judge? Stand up to the thing all through, and no flinching.'

'My opinion sir, is a matter of record, being the first judge, before whom a case was tested, which resulted in favor of the South. And I go farther than this; I hold as a just construction of the law, that not only has the slaveholder a right to reclaim his slave when and wherever found, but by its provision every free black in the Country north and south, are liable to enslavement by any white person. They are freemen by sufferance or slaves at large, whom any white person may claim at discretion. It was a just decision of the Supreme Court—though I was in advance of it by action—that persons of African descent have no rights that white men are bound to respect!'

'Judge Ballard, with this explanation, I am satisfied; indeed as a southern man I would say, that you've conceeded all that I could ask, and more than we expected. But this is a legal disquisition; what is your private opinion respecting the justice of the measures?'

'I think them right sir, according to our system of government.'

'But how will you get away from your representative system Judge? In this your blacks are either voters, or reckoned among the inhabitants.'

'Very well sir, they stand in the same relation as your negroes. In some of the states they are permitted to vote, but can't be voted for, and this leaves them without any political rights at all. Suffrage sir, is one thing, franchisement another; the one a mere privilege—a thing permitted—the other a right inherent, that which is inviolable—cannot be interfered with. And my good sir, enumeration is a national measure, for which we are not sectionally responsible.'

'Well Judge, I'm compelled to admit that you are a very good southerner, upon the whole, you are severe upon the negroes; you seem to allow them no chance.'

'I like negroes well enough in their place!'

'How can you reconcile yourself to the state of things in Cuba, where the blacks enter largely into the social system?'

'I don't like it at all, and never could become reconciled to the state of things there. I consider that Colony as it now stands, a moral pestilence, a blighting curse, and it is useless to endeavour to disguise the fact: Cuba must cease to be a Spanish Colony, and become American Territory. Those mongrel Creoles are incapable of self-government, and should be compelled to submit to the United States.'

'Well Judge admit the latter part of that, as I rather guess we are all of the same way of thinking—how do you manage to get on with society when you are there?'

'I cannot for a moment tolerate it! One of the hateful customs of the place is, that you must exchange civilities with whomsoever solicits it, consequently, the most stupid and ugly negro you meet in the street, may ask for a 'light' from your cigar.'

'I know it, and I invariably comply with the request. How do you act in such cases?'

'I invariably comply, but as invariably throw away my cigar! If this were all, it would not be so bad, but then the idea of meeting negroes and mulattoes at the Levees of the Captain General is intolerable! It will never do to permit this state of things so near our own shores.'

'Why throw away the cigar, Judge? What objection could there be to it, because a negro took a light from it?'

'Because they are certain to take hold of it with their black fingers!'

'Just as I've always heard Judge Ballard. You northerners are a great deal more fastidious about negroes than we of the south, and you'll pardon me if I add, "more nice than wise," to use a homily. Did ever it occur to you that black fingers made that cigar, before it entered your white lips!—all tobacco preparations being worked by negro hands in Cuba—and very frequently in closing up the wrapper, they draw it through their lips to give it tenacity.'

'The deuce! Is that a fact major!'

'Does that surprise you Judge? I'm sure the victuals you eat is cooked by black hands, the bread kneaded and made by black hands, and the sugar and molasses you use, all pass through black hands, or rather the hands of negroes pass through them, at least you could not refrain from thinking so, had you seen them as I have frequently, with arms full length immersed in molasses.'

'Well major, truly there are some things we are obliged to swallow, and I suppose these are among them.'

'Though a Judge, your honor, you perceive that there' are some things you have not learned.'

'True major, true; and I like the negro well enough in his place, but there is a disposition peculiar to the race, to shove themselves into the notice of the whites.'

'Not peculiar to them Judge, but common to mankind. The black man desires association with the white, because the latter is regarded his superior. In the south it is the poor white man with the wealthy, and in Europe the common with the gentle-folks. In the north you have not made these distinctions among the whites, which prevents you from noticing this trait among yourselves.'

'Tell me major, as you seem so well to understand them, why a negro swells so soon into importance?'

'Simply because he's just like you Judge, and I! It is simply a manifestation of human nature in an humble position, the same as that developed in the breast of a conqueror. Our strictures are not just on this unfortunate race, as we condemn in them, that which we approve in ourselves. Southerner as I am, I can joke with a slave just because he is a man; some of them indeed, fine warm hearted fellows, and intelligent, as was the Colonel's Henry.'

'I can't swallow that major! Joking with a negro; is rather too large a dose for me!'

'Let me give you an idea of my feeling about these things: I have on my place two good natured black fellows, full of pranks and jokes—Bob and Jef. Passing along one morning Jef was approaching me, when just as we met and I was about to give him the time of day, he made a sudden halt, placing himself in the attitude of a pugilist, grasping the muscle of his left arm, looking me full in the eyes exclaimed: "Maus Army, my arm aches for you!" when stepping aside he gave the path for me to pass by.'

'Did you not rebuke him for the impudence?'

'I laid my hand upon his shoulders as we passed, and gave him a laugh instead. At another time, passing along in company, Bob was righting up a section of fence, when Jef came along. "How is yeh, Jef?" saluted Bob, without a response. Supposing he had not seen me, I halloed out: "How are you Jef!" but to this, he made no reply. A gentleman in company with me who enjoyed the joke, said: "Why Jef, you appear to be above speaking to your old friends!" Throwing his head slightly down with a rocking motion in his walk, elongating his mouth after the manner of a sausage—which by the way needed no improvement in that direction—in a tone of importance; still looking down he exclaimed, "I totes a meat!" He had indeed, a fine gammon on his shoulder from which that evening, he doubtless intended a good supper with his wife, which made him feel important, just as Judge Ballard feels, when he receives the news that "sugar is up," and contemplates large profits from his crop of that season.'

'I'll be plagued, major, if your love of the ludicrous dont induce you to give the freest possible license to your negroes! I wonder they respect you!'

'One thing Judge, I have learned by my intercourse with men, that pleasantry is the life and soul of the social system; and good treatment begets more labor from the slave than bad. A smile from the master, is better than cross looks, and one crack of a joke with him, is worth a hundred cracks of the whip. Only confide in him, and let him be satisfied that you respect him as a man, he'll work himself to death to prove his worthiness.'

'After all major, you still hold them as slaves, though you claim for them the common rights of other people!'

'Certainly! and I would just as readily hold a white as a black in slavery, were it the custom and policy of the country to do so. It is all a matter of self interest with me; and though I am morally opposed to slavery, yet while the thing exists, I may as well profit by it, as others.'

'Well major,' concluded the Judge; 'let us drop the subject, and I hope that the free interchange of opinion, will prove no detriment to our future prospects and continued friendship.'

'Not at all sir, not at all!' concluded the major with a smile.

* * *

(Editor's note: In Chapter 16 Colonel Franks and his fellow white Southerners brutally whip a slave to amuse themselves. The whipping upsets Judge Ballard, and Franks remarks: "Not quite a Southerner yet Judge, if you can't stand that!")

XVII. Henry at Large

On leaving the plantation carrying them hanging upon his arm, thrown across his shoulders, and in his hands Henry had a bridle, halter, blanket, girt, and horsewhip, the emblems of a faithful servant in discharge of his master's business.

By shrewdness and discretion such was his management as he passed along, that he could tell the name of each place and proprietor, long before he reached them. Being a scholar, he carefully kept a record of the plantations he had passed, that when accosted by a white, as an overseer or patrol, he invariably pretended to belong to a back estate, in search of his master's race horse. If crossing a field, he was taking a near cut; but if met in a wood, the animal was in the forest, as being a great leaper no fence could debar him, though the forest was fenced and posted. The blanket a substitute for a saddle, was in reality carried for a bed.

With speed unfaltering and spirits unflinching, his first great strive was to reach the Red River, to escape from his own state as quickly as possible. Proceeding on in the direction of the Red River country, he met with no obstruction, except in one instance, when he left his assailant quietly upon the earth. A few days after an inquest was held upon the body of a deceased overseer—verdict of the Jury, 'By hands unknown.'

On approaching the river, after crossing a number of streams, as the Yazoo, Ouchita, and such, he was brought to sad reflections. A dread came over him, difficulties lie before him, dangers stood staring him in the face at every step he took. Here for the first time since his maturity of manhood responsibilities rose up in a shape of which he had no conception. A mighty undertaking, such as had never before been ventured upon, and the duty devolving upon him, was too much for a slave with no other aid than the aspirations of his soul panting for liberty. Reflecting upon the peaceful hours he once enjoyed as a professing Christian, and the distance which slavery had driven him from its peaceful portals, here in the wilderness, determining to renew his faith and dependence upon Divine aid, when falling upon his knees, he opened his heart to God, as a tenement of the Holy Spirit.

'Arm of the Lord awake! renew my faith, confirm my hope,

perfect me in love. Give strength, give courage, guide and protect my pathway, and direct me in my course!' Springing to his feet as if a weight had fallen from him, he stood up a new man.

The river is narrow, the water red as if colored by iron rust, the channel winding. Beyond this river lies his hopes, the broad plains of Louisiana with a hundred thousand bondsmen, seeming anxiously to await him.

Standing upon a high bank of the stream, contemplating his mission, a feeling of humbleness, and a sensibility of unworthiness impressed him, and that religious sentiment which once gave comfort to his soul now inspiring anew his breast, Henry raised in solemn tones amidst the lonely wilderness:

> 'Could I but climb where Moses stood,
> And view the landscape o'er;
> Not Jordan's streams, nor death's cold flood,
> Could drive me from the shore!'

To the right of where he stood was a cove, formed by the washing of the stream at high water, which ran quite into the thicket, into which the sun shone through a space among the high trees.

While thus standing and contemplating his position, the water being too deep to wade, and on account of numerous sharks and alligators, too dangerous to swim, his attention was attracted by the sound of a steamer coming up the channel. Running into the cove to shield himself, a singular noise disturbed him, when to his terror he found himself amidst a squad of huge alligators, which sought the advantages of the sunshine.

His first impulse was to surrender himself to his fate and be devoured, as in the rear and either side, the bank was perpendicular, escape being impossible except by the way he entered, to do which would have exposed him to the view of the boat, which could not have been avoided. Meantime the frightful animals were crawling over and among each other, at a fearful rate.

Seizing the fragment of a limb which lay in the cove, beating upon the ground and yelling like a madman, giving them all possible space, the beasts were frightened at such a rate, that they reached the water in less time than Henry reached the bank. Receding into the forest, he thus escaped the observation of the passing steamer, his escape serving to strengthen his fate in a renewed determination of spiritual dependence.

While gazing upon the stream in solemn reflection for Divine aid to direct him, logs came floating down, which suggested a proximity to the raft with which sections of that stream is filled, when going but a short distance up, he crossed in safety to the Louisiana side. His faith was now fully established, and thenceforth, Henry was full of hope and confident of success.

Reaching Alexandria with no obstruction, his first secret meeting was held in the hut of aunt Dilly. Here he found them all ready for an issue.

'An dis you chile?' said the old woman, stooping with age, sitting on a low stool in the chimney corner; 'dis many day, I heahn on yeh!' though Henry had just entered on his mission. From Alexandria he passed rapidly on to Latuer's making no immediate stops, preferring to organize at the more prominent places.

This is a mulatto planter, said to have come from the isle of Guadaloupe. Riding down the road upon a pony at a quick gallop, was a mulatto youth a son of the planter, an old black man on foot keeping close to the horse's heels.

'Whose boy are you?' enquired the young mulatto, who had just dismounted, the old servant holding his pony.

'I'm in search of master's race horse.'

'What is your name?' farther enquired the young mulatto.

'Gilbert sir.'

'What do you want?'

'I am hungry sir.'

'Dolly,' said he to an old black woman at the woodpile; 'show this man into the negro quarter, and give him something to eat; give him a cup of milk. Do you like milk my man?'

'Yes sir, I have no choice when hungry; anything will do.'

'Da is none heah but claubah, maus Eugene,' replied the old cook.

'Give him that,' said the young master. 'You people like that kind of stuff I believe; our negroes like it.'

'Yes sir,' replied Henry, when the lad left.

'God knows'e needn' talk 'bout wat we po' black folks eat, case da don' ghin us nothin' else but dat an' caun bread,' muttered the old woman.

'Dont they treat you well, aunty?' enquired Henry.

'God on'y knows my chile, wat we suffeh.'

'Who was that old man who ran behind your master's horse?'

'Dat Nathan, my husban'.'

'Do they treat him well, aunty?'

'No chile, wus an' any dog, da beat 'im foh little an nothin'.'

'Is uncle Nathan religious?'

'Yes chile ole man an' I's been sahvin' God dis many day, fo yeh baun! Wen any on 'em in de house git sick, den da sen foh "uncle Nathan" come pray foh dem; "uncle Nathan" mighty good den!'

'Do you know that the Latuers are colored people?'

'Yes, chile; God bless yeh soul yes! Case huh mammy ony dead two-three yehs, an' she black as me.'

'How did they treat her?'

'Not berry well; she nus da childen; an eat in a house arter all done.'

'What did Latuer's children call her?'

'Da call huh "mammy," same like wite folks childen call de nus.'

'Can you tell me aunty why they treat you people so badly, knowing themselves to be colored, and some of the slaves related to them?'

'God bless yeh hunny, de wite folks, dese plantehs make 'em so; da run heah, an' tell 'em da mus'n treat deh niggehs well, case da spile 'em.'

'Do the white planters frequently visit here?'

'Yes, hunny, yes, da heah some on' em all de time eatin' an' drinkin' long wid de old man; da on'y tryin' git wat little 'e got, dat all! Da 'tend to be great frien' de ole man; but laws a massy hunny, I doh mine dese wite folks no how!'

'Does your master ever go to their houses and eat with them?'

'Yes chile, some time'e go, but den half on 'em got nothin' fit to eat; da hab fat poke an' bean, caun cake an' sich like, dat all da got, some on 'em.'

'Does Mr. Latuer give them better at his table?'

'Laws hunny, yes; yes'n deed chile? 'E got mutton—some time

whole sheep mos'—fowl, pig, an' ebery tum ting a nuddeh, 'e got so much ting dah, I haudly know wat cook fus.'

'Do the white planters associate with the family of Latuer?'

'One on 'em, ten 'e coatin de dahta; I dont recon 'e gwine hab heh. Da cah fool long wid 'Toyeh's gals dat way.'

'Whose girls, Metoyers?'

'Yes chile.'

'Do you mean the wealthy planters of that name?'

'Dat same chile.'

'Well, I want to understand you: You don't mean to say that they are colored people.'

'Yes, hunny, yes; da good culed folks any body. Some five-six boys' an five-six gals on 'em; da all rich.'

'How do they treat their slaves?'

'Da boys all mighty haud maustas, da gals all mighty good; sahvants all like em.'

'You seem to understand these people very well aunty. Now please tell me what kind of masters there are generally in the Red river country.'

'Haud 'nough chile, haud 'nough, God on'y knows!'

'Do the colored masters treat theirs generally worse than the whites?'

'No hunny, 'bout da same.'

'That's just what I want to know. What are the usual allowances for slaves?'

'Da 'low de fiel' han' two snit a yeah foh umin one long linen coat,* make suit, an' foh man, pantaloon an' jacket.'

'How about eating?'

'Half peck meal ah day foh family uh fo!'

'What about weekly privileges? Do you have Saturday to yourselves?'

'Laud hunny, no! no chile, no! Da do'n 'low us no time, 'tall. Da 'low us ebery uddeh Sunday wash ouh close; dat all de time we git.'

'Then you don't get to sell anything for yourselves?'

'No, hunny, no? Da don' 'low pig, chicken, tucky, goose, bean, pea, tateh, nothin' else.'

'Well aunty, I'm glad to meet you, and as evening's drawing nigh, I must see your husband a little, then go.'

---

* Coat—a term used by slaves for frock.

'God bless yeh chile whah ebeh yeh go! Yeh ain' arteh no race-hos, dat yeh aint.'

'You got something to eat my man, did you?' enquired the lad Eugene, at the conclusion of his interview with uncle Nathan.

'I did sir, and feasted well!' replied Henry in conclusion; 'Good bye!' and he left for the next plantation suited to his objects.

'God bless de baby!' said old aunt Dolly as uncle Nathan entered the hut, referring to Henry.

'Ah, chile!' replied the old man with tears in his eyes; 'my yeahs has heahn dis day!'

XVIII. Fleeting Shadows

In high spirits Henry left the plantation of Latuer, after sowing seeds from which in due season, he anticipated an abundant harvest. He found the old man Nathan all that could be desired, and equal to the task of propagating the scheme. His soul swelled with exultation on receiving the tidings, declaring that though nearly eighty years of age, he never felt before an implied meaning, in the promise of the Lord.

'Now Laud!' with uplifted hand exclaimed he at the conclusion of the interview; 'my eyes has seen, and meh yeahs heahn, an' now Laud! I's willin' to stan' still an' see dy salvation!'

On went Henry to Metoyers, visiting the places of four brothers, having taken those of the white planters intervening, all without detection or suspicion of being a stranger.

Stopping among the people of Col. Hopkins at Grantico summit, here as at Latuer's and all intermediate places he found the people patiently looking for a promised redemption. Here a pet female slave, Silva, espied him and gave the alarm that a strange black was lurking among the negro quarters, which compelled him to retirement sooner than intended.

Among the people of Dickson at Pine Bluff, he found the best of spirits. There was Newman, a young slave man born without arms, who was ready any moment for a strike.

'How could you fight?' said Henry; 'you have no arms!'

'I am compelled to pick with my toes, a hundred pound of cotton a day, and I can sit on a stool and touch off a cannon!'

said this promising young man whose heart panted with an unsuppressed throb for liberty.

Heeley's, Harrison's and Hickman's slaves, were fearfully and pitiably dejected. Much effort was required to effect a seclusion, and more to stimulate them to action. The continual dread 'that maus wont let us!' seemed as immovably fixed as the words were constantly repeated; and it was not until an occasion for another subject of inquest in the person of a pest of an old black slave man, that an organization was effected.

Approaching Crane's on Little River, the slaves were returning from the field to the gin. Many being females some of whom were very handsome, had just emptied their baskets. So little clothing had they, and so loosely hung the tattered fragments about them, that they covered themselves behind the large empty baskets tilted over on the side, to shield their person from exposure.

The overseer engaged in another direction, the master absent, and the family at the great house, a good opportunity presented for an inspection of affairs.

'How do you do young woman?' saluted Henry.

'How de do sir!' replied a sprightly, comely young mulatto girl, who stood behind her basket with not three yards of cloth in the tattered relic of the only garment she had on.

'Who owns this place?'

'Mr. Crane sir,' she politely replied with a smile.

'How many slaves has he?'

'I don'o some say five 'a six hunded.'

'Do they all work on this place?'

'No sir, he got two-three places.'

'How many on this place?'

'Oveh a hundred an' fifty.'

'What allowances have you?'

'None sir.'

'What! no Saturday to yourselves?'

'No sir.'

'They allow you Sundays, I suppose.'

'No sir, we work all day ev'ry Sunday.'

'How late do you work?'

'Till we can' see to pick no mo' cotton; but w'en its moon light, we pick till ten o'clock at night.'

'What time do you get to wash your clothes?'

'None sir; da on'y 'low us one suit ev'ry New Yehs day, an' us gals take it off every Satady night aftah de men all gone to bed and wash it fah Sunday.'

'Why do you want clean clothes on Sunday, if you have to work on that day?'

'It's de Laud's day, an' we want to be clean, and we feel betteh.'

'How do the men do for clean clothes?'

'We wash de men's clothes afteh da go to bed.'

'And you say you are only allowed one suit a year? Now young woman; I don't know your name but—'

'Nancy, sir.'

'Well Nancy, speak plainly, and dont be backward; what does your one suit consist of?'

'A frock sir, made out er coarse tow linen.'

'Only one piece, and no underclothes at all?'

'Dat's all sir!' replied she modestly looking down and drawing the basket which sufficiently screened her, still closer to her person.

'Is that which you have on a sample of the goods your clothes are made of?'

'Yes sir, dis is da kine.'

'I would like to see some other of your girls.'

'Stop sir, I go call Susan!' when gathering up, and drawing around and before her, a surplus of the back section, the only remaining sound remnant of the narrow tattered garment that she wore, off she ran behind the gin, where lay in the sun, a number of girls to rest themselves during their hour of 'spell.'

'Susan!' she exclaimed rather loudly; 'I do'n want you gals!' she pleasantly admonished, as the whole twelve or fifteen rose from their resting place, and came hurriedly around the building, Nancy and Susan in the lead. They instinctively as did Nancy, drew their garments around and about them, on coming in sight of the stranger. Standing on the outside of the fence, Henry politely bowed as they approached.

'Dis is Susan sir!' said Nancy, introducing her friend with bland simplicity.

'How de do sir!' saluted she, a modest and intelligent, very pretty young black girl, of good address.

'Well Susan!' replied Henry; 'I dont want any thing but to see you girls; but I will ask you this question: how many suit of clothes do they give you a year?'

'One sir.'

'How many pieces make a suit?'

'Jus' one frock;' and they simultaneously commenced drawing still closer before, the remnant of coarse garment, which hung in tatters about them.

'Dont you have shoes and stockings in winter?'

'We no call foh shoes, case 'taint cole much; on'y some time little fros'.'

'How late in the evening do you work?'

'Da fiel' han's dah;' pointing to those returning to the field; 'da work till bed time, but we gals heah, we work in de gin, and spell each other ev'ey twelve ouahs.'

'You're at leisure now; who fills your places?'

'Nutha set a' han's go to work, fo' you come.'

'How much cotton do they pick for a task?'

'Each one mus' pick big basket full, an' fetch it in f'om da fiel' to de gin, else da git thirty lashes.'

'How much must the women pick as a task?'

'De same as de men.'

'That can't be possible!' said Henry, looking over the fence down upon their baskets; 'how much do they hold?'

'I dis membeh sir, but good, 'eal.'

'I see on each basket marked 225 lbs; is that the quantity they hold?'

'Yes sir, dat's it.'

'All mus' be in ghin certain ouah else da git whipped; sometime de men help 'em.'

'How can they do this when they have their own to carry?'

'Da put derse on de head, an' ketch holt one side de women basket. Sometimes they leave part in de fiel, an' go back afteh it.'

'Do yo get plenty to eat?'

'No sir, da feeds us po'ly; sometime, we do'n have mo'n half nough!'

'Did you girls ever work in the field?'

'O yes sir! all uv us, on'y we wan't strong nough to fetch in ouh cotton, den da put us in de gin.'

'Where would you rather; in the gin or in the field?'

'If 'twant foh carryin' cotton, we'a rather work in de fiel'.'

'Why so girls?'

'Case den da would'n be so many ole wite plantehs come an' look at us, like we was show!'

'Who sees that the tasks are all done in the field?'

'Da Driveh.'

'Is he a white man?'

'No sir, black.'

'Is he a free man?'

'No sir, slave.'

'Have you no white overseer?'

'Yes sir, Mr. Dorman.'

'Where is Dorman when you are at work?'

'He out at de fiel too.'

'What is he doing there?'

'He watch Jesse, da drivah.'

'Is Jesse a pretty good fellow?'

'No sir, he treat black folks like dog, he all de time beat 'em, when da no call to do it.'

'How did he treat you girls when you worked in the field?'

'He beat us if we jist git little behind de rest in pickin'! Da wite folks make 'im bad.'

'Point him out to me and after to-night, he'll never whip another.

'Now girls, I see that you are smart intelligent young women, and I want you to tell me why it is, that your master keeps you all here at work in the gin, when he could get high prices for you, and supply your places with common cheap hands at half the money?'

'Case we gals won' go! Da been mo'n a dozen plantehs heah lookin' at us, an' want to buy us foh house keepehs, an' we wont go; we die fus!' said Susan with a shudder.

'Yes,' repeated Nancy, with equal emotion; 'we die fus!'

'How can you prevent it girls; wont your master sell you against your will?'

'Yes sir, he would, but da plantehs da dont want us widout we willin' to go.'

'I see! Well girls, I believe I'm done with you; but before leaving let me ask you, is there among your men, a real clever good trusty man? I dont care either old or young, though I prefer an old or middle aged man.'

'O yes sir,' replied Nancy; 'da is some mong 'em.'

'Give me the name of one,' said Henry, at which request Nancy and Susan looked hesitatingly at each other.

'Dont be backward,' admonished he; 'as I sha'nt make a bad use of it.' But they still hesitated, when after an other admonition Nancy said—

'Dare's uncle Joe—'

'No, uncle Moses, uncle Moses!' in a suppressed tone interrupted the other girls.

'Who is uncle Moses!' enquired Henry.

'He' my fatha!' replied Susan; 'an—'

'My uncle!' interrupted Nancy.

'Then you two are cousins?'

'Yes sir, huh fatha an my motha is brotha an sisteh,' replied Nancy.

'Is he a religious man, girls?'

'Yes sir, he used to preach but'e do'n preach now,' explained Susan.

'Why?'

'Case da 'ligions people wo'n heah im now.'

'Who colored people?'

'Yes sir?'

'When did they stop hearing him preach?'

'Good while ago.'

'Where at?'

'Down in da bush meetin', at da Baptism.'

'He's a Baptist then—what did he do?'

Again became Susan and Nancy more perplexed than before, the other girls in this instance failing to come to their relief.

'What did he do girls, let me know it quick, as I must be off?'

'Da say—da say—I do'n want tell you!' replied Susan hesitating with much feeling.

'What is it girls, cant some of you tell me?' earnestly enquired Henry.

'Da say befo' 'e come heah way down in Fagina, he kill a man, ole po' wite ovehseeah!'

'Is that it girls?' enquired he.

'Yes sir!' they simultaneously replied.

'Then *he's* the very man I want to see!' said Henry. 'Now don't forget what I say to you; tell him that a man will meet him to-night below here on the river side, just where the carcass of an ox lies in the verge of the thicket. Tell him to listen, and when I'm ready, I'll give the signal of the runaway—the screech of the panther—when he must immediately obey the summons. One word more, and I'll leave you. Every one of you as you have so praiseworthily concluded, die before surrendering to such base purposes as that for which this man who holds you wishes to dispose of you. Girls, you will see me no more. Fare—'

'Yo' name sir, yo' name!' they all exclaimed.

'My name is—Farewell, girls, farewell!'—when Henry darted in the thickest of the forest, leaving the squad of young maiden slaves in a state of bewildering inquiry concerning the singular black man.

The next day Jesse the driver was missed, and never after heard of. On inquiry being made of the old man Moses concerning the stranger, all that could be elicited was—

'Stan' still child'en, and see da salvation uv da Laud!'

XIX. Come What Will

Leaving the plantation of Crane with high hopes and great confidence in the integrity of uncle Moses and the maiden gang of cotton girls, Henry turned his course in a retrograde direction so as again to take the stream of Red River. Little River where he then was, being but a branch of that water.

Just below its confluence with the larger stream, at the moment when he reached the junction, a steam cotton trader hove in view. There was no alternative but to stand like a freeman, or suddenly escape into the forest, thus creating suspicions and fears, as but a few days previous a French planter of the neighborhood lost a desperate slave, who became a terror to the country around. The master was compelled to go continually armed, as also other white neighbors, and all were afraid after nightfall, to pass out the threshold of their own doors. Permission was given to every white man to shoot him if ever seen within rifle shot, which facts having learned the evening before, Henry was armed with this precaution.

His dress being that of a race-groom—small leather cap with long front piece, neat fitting roundabout, high boots drawn over the pantaloon legs, with blanket, girth, halter, whip and bridle— Henry stood upon the shore awaiting the vessel.

'Well boy!' hailed the captain as the line was thrown out, which he caught making fast at the root of a tree; 'do you wish to come aboard!'

'Good man!' approvingly cried the mate, at the expert manner which he caught the line and tied the sailor knot.

'Have you ever steamboated my man?' continued the captain.

'Yes sir,' replied Henry.

'Where?'

'On the Upper and Lower Mississippi sir.'

'Whom do you know as masters of steamers on the Upper Mississippi?'

'Captains Thogmorton, Price, Swan, and—'

'Stop, stop! that'll do,' interrupted the captain; 'you know the master of every steamer in the trade I believe. Now who in the Lower trade?'

'Captains Scott, Hart, and—'

'What's Captain Hart's Christian name?' interrupted the captain.

'Jesse, sir.'

'That'll do; be George you know every body! do you want to ship?'

'No sir.'

'What are you doing here?'

'I hunting master's stray race horse.'

'Your "master's" race horse! Are you a slave boy?'

'Yes sir.'

'How did you come to be on the Mississippi River?'

'I hired my time sir.'

'Yes, yes, boy, I see!'

'Who is your master?'

'Colonel Sheldon; I used to belong to Major Gilmire.'

'Are you the boy Nepp, the great horse trainer the Major used to own?'

'No sir, I'm his son.'

'Are you as good at training horses as the old chap?'

'They call me better, sir.'

'Then you're worth your weight in gold. Will your master sell you?'

'I dont know sir.'

'How did your horse come to get away?'

'He was bought from the major by Colonel Sheldon to run at the great Green Wood Races, Texas, and while training he managed to get away, leaping the fences, and taking to the forest.'

'Then you're major Tom's race rider Gilbert! eh heh, yes, yes! You're a valuable boy; I wonder the major parted with you.'

The bell having rung for dinner, the captain left, Henry going to the deck.

Among those on deck was a bright mulatto young man, who immediately recognized Henry as having seen him on the Upper Mississippi, he being a free man. On going up to him, Henry observed that he was laden with heavy manacles.

'Have I not seen you somewhere before?' enquired he.

'Yes; my name is Lewis Grimes, you saw me on the Upper Mississippi,' replied the young man; 'your name is Henry Holland!'

'What have you been doing?' enquired Henry, on seeing the handcuffs.

'Nothing at all!' replied he with eyes flashing resentment and suffused with tears.

'What does this mean?' continued he, pointing at the hand-cuffs.

'I am stolen and now being taken to Texas, where I am to be enslaved for life!' replied Lewis sobbing aloud.

'Who did this vile deed?' continued Henry in a low tone of voice, pressing his lips to suppress his feelings.

'One Dr. Johns of Texas, now a passenger on this boat!'

'Was that the person who placed a glass to your lips which you refused, just as I came aboard?'

'Yes, that's the man.'

'Why dont you leave him instantly?' said Henry, his breast heaving with emotion.

'Because he always handcuffs me before the boat lands, keeping me so during the time she lies ashore.'

'Why don't you jump overboard when the boat is under way?'

'Because he guards me with a heavy loaded rifle, and I can't get a chance.'

'He "guards" you! "you cant get a chance!" Are there no nights, and does he never sleep?'

'Yes, but he makes me sleep in the state room with him, keeping his rifle at his bedside.'

'Are you never awake when he's asleep?'

'Often, but I'm afraid to stir lest he wakens.'

'Well dont you submit, die first if thereby you must take another into eternity with you! Were it my case and he ever went to sleep where I was, he'd never waken in this world!'

'I never thought of that before, I shall take your advice the first opportunity. Good by sir!' hastily said the young man, as the bell tapped a signal to start, and Henry stepped on shore.

'Let go that line!' sternly commanded the captain, Henry obeying orders on the shore, when the boat glided steadily up the stream, seemingly in unison with the lively though rude and sorrowful song of the black firemen—

I'm a goin to Texas—O! O-O-O!
I'm a goin to Texas, O! O-O-O!'

Having in consequence of the scarcity of spring houses and larders along his way in so level and thinly settled country, Henry took in his pouch from the cook of the boat, an ample supply of provisions for the succeeding four or five days. Thus provided for, standing upon the bank for a few minutes, with steady gaze listening to the sad song of his oppressed brethren as they left the spot, and reflecting still more on the miserable fate of the young mulatto freeman Lewis Grimes held by the slave-holder Dr. Johns of Texas, he with renewed energy, determined that nothing short of an interference by Divine Providence should stop his plans and progress. In soliloquy said Henry:

'Yes!

'If every foe stood martialed in the van,
I'd fight them single combat, man to man!'

and again he started with a manly will, as fixed and determined in his purpose as though no obstructions lay in his pathway.

From plantation to plantation did he go, sowing the seeds of future devastation and ruin to the master and redemption to the slave, an antecedent more terrible in its anticipation, than the warning voice of the destroying Angel, in commanding the slaughter of the first born of Egypt. Himself careworn, distressed and hungry, who just being supplied with nourishment for the system, Henry went forth a welcome messenger, casting his bread upon the turbid waters of oppression, in hopes of finding it after many days.

Holding but one seclusion on each plantation, his progress was consequently very rapid, in whatever direction he went.

With a bold stride from Louisiana, he went into Texas. Here he soon met with the man of his wishes. This presented in the person of Sampson, on the cotton place of proprietor Richardson. The master here though represented wealthy, with an accomplished and handsome young daughter, was a silly, stupid old dolt, an inordinate blabber and wine bibber. The number of his slaves was said to be great and he the owner of three plantations, one in Alabama, and the others in Texas.

Sampson was a black, tall, stoutly built, and manly, possessing much general intelligence, and a good looking person. His wife a neat, intelligent, handsome little woman, the complexion of himself, was the mother of a most interesting family of five pretty children, three boys and two girls. This family entered at once into the soul of his mission, seeming to have anticipated it.

With an ample supply of means, buried in a convenient well marked spot, he only awaited a favourable opportunity to effect his escape from slavery. With what anxiety did that wife gaze smilingly in his face, and a boy and girl cling tightly each to a knee, as this husband and father in whispers recounted his plans and determination of carrying them out. The scheme of Henry was at once committed to his confidence, and he requested to impart them wherever he went.

Richardson was a sportsman and Sampson his body servant,

they traveled through every part of the country, thus affording the greatest opportunity for propagating the measures of the secret organization. From Portland in Maine to Galveston in Texas, Sampson was as familiar as a civil engineer.

'Sampson, Sampson, stand by me! Stand by me my man; stand at your master's back!' was the language of this sottish old imbecile to his faithful manly attendant, whom he kept continually upon his feet for hours at a time when reveling at a gambling table, and who from excessive fatigue would sometimes squat or sit down upon the floor behind him. 'Sampson, Sampson! are you there? Stand by your master Sampson!' again would he exclaim, so soon as the tall commanding form of his black protector was missed from his sight.

Sampson and wife were both pious people, believing much in the providence of God, he, as he said having recently had it 'shown to' him—meaning a presentiment—that a messenger would come to him and reveal the plan of deliverance.

'I am glad to see that you have money,' said Henry; 'you are thereby well qualified for your mission. With money you may effect your escape almost at any time. Your most difficult point is an elevated obstruction, a mighty hill, a mountain; but through that hill there is a gap; and *money* is your passport through that *White Gap* to freedom. Mark that. It is the great range of *White* mountains and *White* river which are before you, and the *White* Gap that you must pass through to reach the haven of safety. Money alone will carry you through the White mountains or across the White river to liberty.'

'Brother my eyes is open, and my way clear!' responded Sampson to this advice.

'Then,' said Henry; 'you are ready to "rise and shine" for—'

'My light has come!' interrupted Sampson; 'but—'

'The glory of God is not yet shed abroad!' concluded Henry, who fell upon Sampson's neck with tears of joy in meeting unexpectedly one of his race so intelligent in that region of country.

Sampson and wife Dursie, taking Henry by the hand wept aloud, looking upon him as the messenger of deliverance foreshown to them.

Kneeling down a fervent prayer was offered by Sampson for

Henry's protection by the way, and final success in his 'mighty plans,' with many Amens and 'God grants,' by Dursie.

Partaking of a sumptuous fare on 'ash cake' and sweet milk—a dainty diet with many slaves—and bidding with a trembling voice and tearful eye a final 'Farewell!' in six hours he had left the state of Texas to the consequences of a deep laid scheme for a terrible insurrection.

XX. Advent Among the Indians

From Texas Henry went into the Indian Nation near Fort Towson, Arkansas.

'Make yourself at home sir!' invited Mr. Culver the intelligent old Chief of the United Nation; 'and Josephus will attend to you,' referring to his nephew Josephus Braser, an educated young chief and counsellor among his people.

'You are slaveholders I see Mr. Culver!' said Henry.

'We are sir, but not like the white men,' he replied.

'How many do you hold?'

'About two hundred on my two plantations.'

'I cant well understand how a man like you can reconcile your principles with the holding of slaves and—'

'We have had enough of that!' exclaimed Dr. Donald, with a tone of threatening authority.

'Hold your breath sir, else I'll stop it!' in a rage replied the young chief.

'Sir,' responded the Doctor; 'I was not speaking to you, but only speaking to that negro!'

'You're a fool!' roared Braser springing to his feet.

'Come, come, gentlemen!' admonished the old Chief; 'I think you are both going mad! I hope you'll behave something better.'

'Well uncle I cant endure him! he assumes so much authority!' replied he. 'He'll make the Indians slaves just now, then Negroes will have no friends.'

Donald was a white man, married among the Indians a sister of the old Chief and aunt to the young, for the sake of her wealth and a home. A physician without talents, was unable to make a business and unwilling to work.

'Mr. Bras—'

'I want nothing more of you,' interrupted Braser, 'and dont—'

'Josephus, Josephus!' interrupted the old chief; 'you will surely let the Doctor speak!'

Donald stood pale and trembling before the young Choctaw born to command, when receiving no favor he left the company muttering 'nigger!'

'Now you see,' said Mr. Culver as the Doctor left the room; 'the difference between a white man and Indian holding slaves. Indian work side by side with black man, eat with him, drink with him, rest with him and both lay down in shade together; white man even wont let you talk! In our Nation Indian and black all marry together. Indian like black man very much, ony he dont fight 'nough. Black man in Florida fight much, and Indian like 'im heap!'

'You make, sir, a slight mistake about my people. They would fight if in their own country they were united as the Indians here, and not scattered thousand of miles apart as they are. You should also remember, that the Africans have never permitted a subjugation of their country by foreigners as the Indians have theirs, and Africa to-day is still peopled by Africans, whilst America the home of the Indian who is fast passing away, is now possessed and ruled by foreigners.'

'True, true!' said the old Chief looking down reflectively; 'too true! I had not thought that way before. Do you think the white man couldn't take Africa if he wanted?'

'He might by a combination, and I still am doubtful whether then he could if the Africans were determined as formerly to keep him out. You will also remember, that the whites came in small numbers to America, and then drove the Indians from their own soil, whilst the blacks got in Africa as slaves, are taken by their own native conquerors, and sold to white men as prisoners of war.'

'That is true sir, true!' sighed the old chief; 'the Indian like game before the bow, is passing away before the gun of the white man!'

'What I now most wish to learn is, whether in case that the

blacks should rise, they may have hope or fear from the Indian?' asked Henry.

'I'm an old mouthpiece, been puffing out smoke and talk many seasons for the entertainment of the young and benefit of all who come among us. The squaws of the great men among the Indians in Florida were black women, and the squaws of the black men were Indian women. You see the vine that winds around and holds us together. Don't cut it, but let it grow till bimeby, it git so stout and strong, with many, very many little branches attached, that you can't separate them. I now reach to you the pipe of peace and hold out the olive-branch of hope! Go on young man, go on. If you want white man to love you, you must fight im!' concluded the intelligent old Choctaw.

'Then sir, I shall rest contented, and impart to you the object of my mission,' replied Henry.

'Ah hah!' exclaimed the old chief after an hour's seclusion with him, 'ah hah! Indian have something like that long-go. I wonder your people aint got it before! That what make Indian strong; that what make Indian and black man in Florida hold together. Go on young man, go on! may the Great Spirit make you brave!' exhorted Mr. Culver, when the parties retired for the evening, Henry rooming with the young warrior Braser.

By the aid of the young Chief and kindness of his uncle the venerable old brave, Henry was conducted quite through the nation on a pony placed at his service, affording to him an ample opportunity of examining into the condition of things. He left the settlement with the regrets of the people, being the only instance in which his seclusions were held with the master instead of the slave.

* * *

(Editor's note: In Chapter 21, after leaving the Indians, Henry Blake makes preparations for the rebellion in Arkansas.)

XXII. New Orleans

The season is the holidays, it is evening, and the night is beautiful. The moon, which in Louisiana is always an object of impressive interest, even to the slave as well as those of enlightened and scientific intelligence, the influence of whose soft and mellow light seems ever like the enchanting effect of some invisible being, to impart inspiration—now being shed from the crescent of the first day of the last quarter, appeared more interesting and charming than ever.

Though the cannon at the old fort in the Lower *Faubourg* had fired the significant warning, admonishing the slaves as well as free blacks to limit their movements, still there were passing to and fro with seeming indifference negroes, both free and slaves, as well as the whites and creole quadroons, fearlessly along the public highways, in seeming defiance of the established usage of negro limitation.

This was the evening of the day of *Maid digras,* and from long established and time-honored custom, the celebration which commenced in the morning was now being consummated by games, shows, exhibitions, theatrical performances, festivals, *masquerade* balls, and numerous entertainments and gatherings in the evening. It was on this account that the negroes had been allowed such unlimited privileges this evening.

Nor were they remiss to the utmost extent of its advantages.

The city which always at this season of the year is lively, and Chartier street gay and fashionable, at this time appeared more lively, gay and fashionable than usual. This fashionable thoroughfare, the pride of the city, was thronged with people, presenting complexions of every shade and color. Now could be seen and realized the expressive description in the popular song of the vocalist Cargill:

> 'I suppose you've heard how New Orleans
> Is famed for wealth and beauty;
> There's girls of every hue, it seems,
> From snowy white to sooty.'

The extensive shops and fancy stores presented the presence behind their counters as saleswomen in attendance of numerous females, black, white, mulatto and quadroon, politely bowing, courtesying, and rubbing their hands,—in accents of broken English inviting to purchase all who enter the threshold, or even look in at the door:

'Wat fa you want someting? Walk in, sire, I vill sell you one nice present fa one young lady.'

And so with many who stood or sat along the streets and at the store doors. Courtesying and smiling they give the civil banter:

'Come, sire, I sell you one pretty ting.'

The fancy stores and toy shops on this occasion were crowded seemingly to their greatest capacity. Here might be seen the fashionable young white lady of French or American extraction, and there the handsome, and frequently beautiful maiden of African origin, mulatto, quadroon, or sterling black, all fondly interchanging civilities, and receiving some memento or keepsake from the hand of an acquaintance. Many lively jests and impressive flings of delicate civility noted the greetings of the passers-by. Freedom seemed as though for once enshielded by her sacred robes and crowned with cap and wand in hand, to go forth untrammeled through the highways of the town. Along the private streets, sitting under the verandas, in the doors with half closed *jalousies,* or promenading unconcernedly the public ways, mournfully humming in solace or chanting in lively glee, could be seen and heard many a creole, male or female, black, white or mixed race, sometimes in reverential praise of—

Father, Son and Holy Ghost—
Madonna, and the Heavenly Host!

in sentimental reflection on some pleasant social relations, or the sad reminiscence of ill-treatment or loss by death of some loved one, or worse than death, the relentless and insatiable demands of slavery.

In the distance, on the levee or in the harbor among the steamers, the songs of the boatmen were incessant. Every few hours landing, loading and unloading, the glee of these men of sorrow was touchingly appropriate and impressive. Men of sorrow they are in reality; for if there be a class of men anywhere to be found, whose sentiments of song and words of lament are made to reach the sympathies of others, the black slave-boatmen on the Mississippi river is that class. Placed in positions the most favorable to witness the pleasures enjoyed by others, the tendency is only to augment their own wretchedness.

Fastened by the unyielding links of the iron cable of despotism, reconciling themselves to a life-long misery, they are seemingly contented by soothing their sorrows with songs and sentiments of apparently cheerful, but in reality wailing lamentations. The most attracting lament of the evening was sung to words, a stanza of which is presented in pathos of delicate tenderness, which is but a spray from the stream which gushed out in insuppressible jets from the agitated fountains of their souls, as if in unison with the restless current of the great river upon which they were compelled to toil, their troubled waters could not be quieted. In the capacity of leader, as is their custom, one poor fellow in pitiful tones lead off the song of the evening:

> 'Way down upon the Mobile river,
> Close to Mobile bay;
> There's where my thoughts is running ever,
> All through the livelong day:
> There I've a good and fond old mother,
> Though she is a slave;
> There I've a sister and a brother,
> Lying in their peaceful graves.

Then in chorus joined the whole company—

> 'O, could I somehow a'nother,
> Drive these tears away;
> When I think about my poor old mother,
> Down upon the Mobile bay.'

Standing in the midst of and contemplating such scenes as these, it was, that Henry determined to finish his mission in the city and leave it by the earliest conveyance over Pontchartrain for Alabama—Mobile being the point at which he aimed. Swiftly as the current of the fleeting Mississippi was time passing by, and many states lay in expanse before him, all of which, by the admonishing impulses of the dearest relations, he was compelled to pass over as a messenger of light and destruction.

Light, of necessity, had to be imparted to the darkened region of the obscure intellects of the slaves, to arouse them from their benighted condition to one of moral responsibility, to make them sensible that liberty was legitimately and essentially theirs, without which there was no distinction between them and the brute. Following as a necessary consequence would be the destruction of oppression and ignorance.

Alone and friendless, without a home, a fugitive from slavery, a child of misfortune and outcast upon the world, floating on the cold surface of chance, now in the midst of a great city of opulence, surrounded by the most despotic restrictions upon his race, with renewed determination Henry declared that nothing short of an unforeseen Providence should impede his progress in the spread of secret organization among the slaves. So aroused, he immediately started for a house in the Lower *Faubourg*.

'My frien', who yeh lookin' foh?' kindly enquired a cautious black man, standing concealed in the shrubbery near the door of a low, tile-covered house standing back in the yard.

'A friend,' replied Henry.

'Wat's 'is name?' continued the man.

'I do not rightly know.'

'Would yeh know it ef yeh heahed it, my fren'?'

'I think I would.'

'Is it Seth?'

'That's the very name!' said Henry.

'Wat yeh want wid 'm, my fren'?'

'I want to see him.'

'I spose yeh do, fren'; but dat ain' answer my questin' yet. Wat yeh want wid 'im?'

'I would rather see him, then I'll be better able to answer.'

'My fren',' replied the man, meaningly, 'ah see da is somethin' in yeh; come in!' giving a significant cough before placing his finger on the latch-string.

On entering, from the number and arrangement of the seats, there was evidence of an anticipated gathering; but the evening being that of the *Maid di gras,* there was nothing very remarkable in this. Out from another room came a sharp, observing, shrewd little dark brown-skin woman, called in that community a *griffe*. Bowing, sidling and courtesying, she smilingly came forward.

'Wat brotha dis, Seth?' enquired she.

'Ah don' o,' carelessly replied he with a signal of caution, which was not required in her case.

'Ah!' exclaimed Henry; 'this is Mr. Seth! I'm glad to see you.'

After a little conversation, in which freely participated Mrs. Seth, who evidently was deservingly the leading spirit of the evening, they soon become reconciled to the character and mission of their unexpected and self-invited guest.

'Phebe, go tell 'em,' said Seth; when lightly tripping away she entered the door of the other room, which after a few moments' delay was partially opened, and by a singular and peculiar signal, Seth and the stranger were invited in. Here sat in one of the most secret and romantic-looking rooms, a party of fifteen, the representatives of the heads of that many plantations, who that night had gathered for the portentious purpose of a final decision on the hour to strike the first blow. On entering, Henry stood a little in check.

'Trus' 'em!' said Seth; 'yeh fine 'em da right saut uh boys— true to deh own color! Da come fom fifteen diffent plantation.'

'They're the men for me!' replied Henry, looking around the room; 'is the house all safe?'

'Yes, brotha, all safe an' soun', an' a big dog in da yahd, so dat no one can come neah widout ouah knowin' it.'

'First, then, to prayer, and next to seclusion,' said Henry, looking at Seth to lead in prayer.

'Brotha, gib us wud a' prah,' said Seth to Henry, as the party on their knees bowed low their heads to the floor.

'I am not fit, brother, for a spiritual leader; my warfare is not Heavenly, but earthly; I have not to do with angels, but with men; not with righteousness, but wickedness. Call upon some brother who has more of the grace of God than I. If I ever were a Christian, slavery has made me a sinner; if I had been an angel, it would have made me a devil! I feel more like cursing than praying—may God forgive me! Pray for me, brethren!'

'Brotha Kits, gib us wud a prah, my brotha!' said Seth to an athletic, powerful black man.

'Its not fah ouah many wuds, noah long prah—ouah 'pinion uh

ouah self, nah sich like, dat Dou anseh us; but de 'cerity ob ouah hahts an ouah 'tentions. Bless de young man dat come 'mong us; make 'im fit fah 'is day, time, an' genration! Dou knows, Laud, dat fah wat we 'semble; anseh dis ouah 'tition, an' gib us token ob Dine 'probation!' petitioned Kits, slapping his hand at the conclusion down upon and splitting open a pine table before him.

'Amen' responded the gathering.

'Let da wud run an' be glorify!' exclaimed Nathan Seth.

The splitting of the table was regarded as omenous, but of doubtful signification, the major part considering it as rather unfavorable. Making no delay, lest a dispondency ensue through fear and superstition, Henry at once entered into seclusion, completing an organization.

'God sen' yeh had come along dis way befor'!' exclaimed Phebe Seth.

'God grant 'e had!' responded Nathan.

'My Laud! I feels like a Sampson! ah feels like gwine up to take de city mehself!' cried out Kits, standing erect in the floor, with fists clenched, muscles braced, eyes shut, and, head thrown back.

'Yes, yes!' exclaimed Phebe; 'blessed be God, brotha Kits, da King is in da camp!'

'Powah, powah!' responded Seth; 'da King is heah!'

'Praise 'Is name!' shouted Phebe clapping and rubbing her hands; 'fah wat I feels an' da knowledge I has receive dis night! I been all my days in darkness till now! I feels we shall be a people yit! Thang' God, thang God!' when she skipped over the floor from side to side, keeping time with a tune sung to the words—

We'll honor our Lord and Master;
We'll honor our Lord and King;
We'll honor our Lord and Master,
And bow at His command!

O! brothers, did you hear the news?
Lovely Jesus is coming!
If ever I get to the house of the Lord,
I'll never come back any more.'

'It's good to be heah!' shouted Seth.

'Ah! dat it is, brotha Seth!' responded Kits. 'Da Laud is nigh, dat 'e is! 'e promise whahsomeveh two-three 'semble, to be in da mids' an' dat to bless 'em, an' 'is promise not in vain, case 'e heah to-night!'

At the moment which Phebe took her seat, nearly exhausted with exercise, a loud rap at the door, preceded by the signal for the evening, alarmed the party.

'Come in, brotha Tib—come quick, if yeh comin!' bade Seth, in a low voice hastily, as he partially opened the door, peeping out into the other room.

'O, pshaw!' exclaimed Phebe, as he and her husband yet whispered; 'I wish he stay away. I sho nobody want 'im! he all'as half drunk anyhow. Good ev'nin', brotha Tib. How yeh been sense we see yeh early paut da night?'

'Reasable, sistah—reasable, thang God. Well, what yeh all 'cided on? I say dis night now au neveh!' said Tib, evidently bent on mischief.

'Foolishness, foolishness!' replied Phebe; 'it make me mad see people make fool uh demself! I wish 'e stay home an' not bothen heah!'

'Ah 'spose I got right to speak as well as da rest on yeh! Yeh all ain' dat high yit to keep body fom talkin', ah 'spose. Betta wait tell yeh git free fo' ye "temp" scrow oveh people dat way! I kin go out yeh house!' retorted the mischievous man, determined on distracting their plans.

'Nobody odeh yeh out, but I like see people have sense, specially befo' strangehs! an' know how behave demself!'

'I is gwine out yeh house,' gruffly replied the man.

'My friend,' said Henry, 'listen a moment to me. You are not yet ready for a strike; you not yet ready to do anything effective. You have barely taken the first step in the matter, and—'

'Strangeh!' interrupted the distracter; 'ah don'o yeh name, yeh strangeh to me—I see yeh talk bout "step;" how many step man got take fo' 'e kin walk? I likes to know dat! Tell me that fus, den yeh may ax me what yeh choose!'

'You must have all the necessary means, my brother,' persuasively resumed Henry, 'for the accomplishment of your ends. Intelligence among yourself on everything pertaining to your designs and project. You must know what, how, and when to do. Have all the instrumentalities necessary for an effective effort before making the attempt. Without this, you will fail, utterly fail!'

'Den ef we got wait all dat time, we neveh be free!' gruffly replied he. 'I goes in foh dis night! I say dis night! Who goes—'

'Shet yo' big mouth! Sit down! Now make a fool o' yo'self!' exclaimed several voices with impatience, which evidently only tended to increase the mischief.

'Dis night, dis night au neveh!' boisterously yelled the now infuriated man at the top of his voice; 'now's da time!' when he commenced shuffling about over the floor, stamping and singing at the top of his voice—

> 'Come all my brethren, let us take a rest,
> While the moon shines bright and clear;
> Old master died and left us all at last,
> And has gone at the bar to appear!
> Old master's dead and lying in his grave;
> And our blood will now cease to flow;
> He will no more tramp on the neck of the slave,
> For he's gone where slave-holders go!
> Hang up the shovel and the hoe—o—o—o!
> I don't care whether I work or no!
> Old master's gone to the slave-holders rest—
> He's gone where they all *ought* to go!'

pointing down and, concluding with an expression which indicated anything, but a religious feeling.

'Shame so it is dat he's lowed to do so! I wish I was man foh 'im, I'd make 'im fly!' said Phebe much alarmed, as she heard the great dog in the yard, which had been so trained as to know the family visitors, whining and manifesting an uneasiness unusual with him. On going to the back door, a person suddenly retreated into the shrubbery, jumping the fence, and disappearing.

Soon, however, there was an angry low heavy growling of the dog, with suppressed efforts to bark, apparently prevented by fear on the part of the animal. This was succeeded by cracking in the bushes, dull heavy footsteps, cautious whispering, and stillness.

'Hush! Listen!' admonished Phebe; 'what is dat? wy dont Tyger bark? I dont understan' it? Seth, go out and see, will you? Wy dont some you men make dat fool stop? I wish I was man, I'd break 'is neck, so I would!' during which the betrayer was shuffling, dancing, and singing at such a pitch as to attract attention from without.

Seth seizing him from behind by a firm grasp of the collar with both hands, Tib sprang forward, slipping easily out of it, leaving the overcoat suspended in his assailant's hands, displaying studded around his waist a formidable array of deathly weapons, when rushing out of the front door, he in terrible accents exclaimed:—

'Insurrection! Insurrection! Death to every white!'

With a sudden spring of their rattles, the *gens d'armes,* who in cloisters had surrounded the house, and by constant menacing gestures with their maces kept the great dog, which stood back in a corner, in a snarling position in fear, arrested the miscreant, taking him directly to the old fort *calaboose.* In the midst of the confusion which necessarily ensued, Henry, Seth, and Phebe, Kits and fellow-leaders from the fifteen plantations, immediately fled, all having passes for the day and evening, which fully protected them in any part of the city away from the scene of disturbance.

Intelligence soon reached all parts of the city, that an extensive plot for rebellion of the slaves had been timely detected. The place was at once thrown into a state of intense excitement, the military called into requisition, dragoons flying in every direction, cannon from the old fort sending forth hourly through the night, thundering peals to give assurance of their sufficiency, and the infantry on duty traversing the streets, stimulating with martial air with voluntary vocalists, who readily joined in chorus to the memorable citing words in the Southern States, of—

'Go tell Jack Coleman,
The Negroes are arising!'

Alarm and consternation succeeded pleasure and repose, sleep for the time seemed to have departed from the eyes of the inhabitants, men, women, and children ran every direction through the streets, seeming determined if they were to be massacred, that it should be done in the open highways rather than secretly in their own houses. The commotion thus continued till the morning, meanwhile editors, journalists, reporters, and correspondents, all were busily on the alert, digesting such information as would form an item of news for the press, or a standing reminiscence for historical reference in the future.

XXIII. The Rebel Blacks

For the remainder of the night secreting themselves in Conti and Burgundi streets, the rebel proprietors of the house in which was laid the plot for the destruction of the city were safe until the morning, their insurrectionary companions having effected a safe retreat to the respective plantations to which they belonged, that evening.

Jason and Phebe Seth were the hired slaves of their own time from a widower master, a wealthy retired attorney at Baton Rouge, whose only concern about them was to call every ninety days at the counter of the Canal Bank of New Orleans, and receive the price of their hire, which was there safely deposited to his credit by the industrious and faithful servants. The house in which the rebels met, had been hired for the occasion, being furnished rooms kept for transient accommodation.

On the earliest conveyance destined for the City of Mobile, Henry left, who, before he fled, admonished as his parting counsel, to 'stand still and see the salvation;' the next day being noted by General Ransom, as an incident in his history, to receive a formal visit of a fortnight's sojourn, in the person of his slaves Jason and Phebe Seth.

The inquisition held in the case of the betrayer Tib, developed fearful antecedence of extensive arrangements for the destruction of the city by fire and water, thereby compelling the white inhabitants, to take refuge in the swamps, whilst the blacks marched up the coast, sweeping the plantations as they went.

Suspicions were fixed upon many, among whom was an

unfortunate English school-teacher, who was arrested and imprisoned, when he died, to the last protesting his innocence. Mr. Farland was a good and brave hearted man, disdaining to appeal for redress to his country, lest it might be regarded as the result of cowardice.

Taking fresh alarm at this incident, the municipal regulations have been most rigid in a system of restriction and *espionage* toward negroes and mulattoes, almost destroying their self-respect and manhood, and certainly impairing their usefulness.

XXIV. A Flying Cloud

Safely in Mobile Henry landed without a question, having on the way purchased of a passenger who was deficient of means to bear expenses, a horse by which he made a daring entry into the place. Mounting the animal which was fully caparisoned, he boldly rode to the principal livery establishment, ordering for it the greatest care until his master's arrival.

Hastening into the country he readily found a friend and seclusion in the hut of Uncle Cesar, on the plantation of Gen. Audly. Making no delay, early next morning he returned to the city to effect a special object. Passing by the stable where the horse had been left, a voice loudly cried out;

'There's that negoo boy, now! Hallo, there, boy! didn't you leave a horse here?'

Heeding not the interrogation, but speedily turning the first corner, Henry hastened away and was soon lost among the inhabitants.

'How yeh do, me frien'?' saluted a black man whom he met in a by-street; 'ar' yeh strangeh?'

'Why?' inquired Henry.

'O, nothin'! on'y I hearn some wite men talkin' j's now, an' da say some strange nigga lef' a hoss dar, an'da blev 'e stole 'im, an' da gwine ketch an' put 'im in de jail.'

'If that's all, I live here. Good morning!' rejoined he who soon was making rapid strides in the direction of Georgia.

Every evening found him among the quarters of some plantations, safely secreted in the hut of some faithful, trustworthy slave, with attentive, anxious listeners, ready for an issue. So, on he went with flying haste, from plantation to plantation, till Alabama was left behind him.

In Georgia, though the laws were strict, the negroes were equally hopeful. Like the old stock of Maryland and Virginia blacks from whom they were descended, they manifested a high degree of intelligence for slaves. Receiving their messenger with open arms, the aim of his advent among them spread like fire in a stubble. Everywhere seclusions were held and organizations completed, till Georgia stands like a city at the base of a burning mountain, threatened with destruction by an overflow of the first outburst of lava from above. Clearing the State without an obstruction, he entered that which of all he most dreaded, the haughty South Carolina.

Here the most relentless hatred appears to exist against the negro, who seems to be regarded but as an animated thing of convenience or a domesticated animal, reared for the service of his master. The studied policy of the whites evidently is to keep the blacks in subjection and their spirits below a sentiment of self-respect. To impress the negro with a sense of his own inferiority is a leading precept of their social system; to be white is the only evidence necessary to establish a claim to superiority. To be a 'master' in South Carolina is to hold a position of rank and title, and he who approaches this the nearest is hightened at least in his own estimation.

These feelings engendered by the whites have been extensively incorporated with the elements of society among the colored people, giving rise to the 'Brown Society' an organized association of mulattos, created by the influence of the whites, for the purpose of preventing pure blooded negroes from entering the social circle, or holding intercourse with them.

Here intelligence and virtue are discarded and ignored, when not in conformity with these regulations. A man with the prowess of Memnon, or a woman with the purity of the 'black doves' of Ethiopia and charms of the 'black virgin' of Solomon, avails them nothing, if the blood of the oppressor, engendered by wrong, predominates not in their veins.

Oppression is the author of all this, and upon the heads of the white masters let the terrible responsibility of this miserable stupidity and ignorance of their mulatto children rest; since to them was left the plan of their social salvation, let upon their consciences rest the penalties cf their social damnation.

The transit of the runaway through this State was exceedingly difficult, as no fabrication of which he was capable could save him from the penalties of arrest. To assume freedom would be at once to consign himself to endless bondage, and to acknowledge himself a slave was at once to advertise for a master. His only course of safety was to sleep through the day and travel by night, always keeping the woods.

At a time just at the peep of day when making rapid strides the baying of hounds and soundings of horns were heard at a distance.

Understanding it to be the sport of the chase, Henry made a hasty retreat to the nearest hiding place which presented, in the hollow of a log. On attempting to creep in a snarl startled him, when out leaped the fox, having counterrun his track several times, and sheltered in a fallen sycamore. Using his remedy for distracting dogs, he succeeded the fox in the sycamore, resting in safety during the day without molestation, though the dogs bayed within thirty yards of him, taking a contrary course by the distraction of their scent.

For every night of sojourn in the State he had a gathering, not one of which was within a hut, so closely were the slaves watched by patrol, and sometimes by mulatto and black overseers. These gatherings were always held in the forest. Many of the confidants of the seclusions were the much dreaded runaways of the woods, a class of outlawed slaves, who continually seek the lives of their masters.

One day having again sought retreat in a hollow log where he lay sound asleep the day being chilly, he was awakened by a cold application to his face and neck, which proved to have been made by a rattlesnake of the largest size, having sought the warmth of his bosom. Henry made a hasty retreat, ever after declining the hollow of a tree. With rapid movements and hasty action, he like a wind cloud, flew through the State of South Carolina, who like 'a thief in the night' came when least expected.

Henry now entered Charleston, the metropolis, and head of the 'Brown Society,' the bane and dread of the blacks in the State, an organization formed through the instrumentality of the whites to keep the blacks and mulattos at variance. To such an extent is the error carried, that the members of the association, rather than their freedom would prefer to see the blacks remain in bondage. But many most excellent mulattos and quadroons condemn with execration this auxiliary of oppression. The eye of the intelligent world is on this 'Brown Society;' and its members when and wherever seen are scanned with suspicion and distrust. May they not be forgiven for their ignorance when proving by repentance their conviction of wrong?

Lying by till late next morning, he entered the city in daylight, having determined boldly to pass through the street, as he might not be known from any common negro. Coming to an extensive wood-yard, he learned by an old black man who sat at the gate that the proprietors were two colored men, one of whom he pointed out, saying:

'Dat is my mausta.'

Approaching a respectable looking mulatto gentleman standing in conversation with a white, his foot resting on a log:

'Do you wish to hire help, sir?' inquired Henry respectfully touching his cap.

'Take off your hat, boy!' ordered the mulatto gentleman. Obeying the order, he repeated the question:

'Who do you belong to?' inquired the gentleman.

'I am free, sir!' replied he.

'You a free boy! Are you not a stranger here?'

'Yes, sir.'

'Then you lie, sir!' replied the mulatto gentleman, 'as you know that no free negro is permitted to enter this State. You are a runaway, and I'll have you taken up!' at the same time walking through his office looking out at the front door as if for an officer.

Making a hasty retreat, in less than an hour he had left the city, having but a few minutes tarried in the hut of an old black family on the suburb, one of the remaining confidentials and adherents of the memorable South Carolina insurrection, when and to whom he imparted his fearful scheme.

'Ah!' said the old man, throwing his head in the lap of his old wife, with his hands around her neck, both of whom sat near the chimney with the tears coursing down their furrowed cheeks; 'dis many a day I been prayin' dat de Laud sen' a nudder Denmark 'mong us! De Laud now anseh my prar in dis young man! Go on, my son—go on—an' may God A'mighty bress yeh!'

North Carolina was traversed mainly in the night. When approaching the region of the Dismal Swamp, a number of the old confederates of the noted Nat Turner were met with, who hailed the daring young runaway as the harbinger of better days. Many of these are still long suffering, hard laboring slaves on the plantations; and some bold, courageous, and fearless adventurers, denizens of the mystical, antiquated, and almost fabulous Dismal Swamp, where for many years they have defied the approach of their pursuers.

Here Henry found himself surrounded by a different atmosphere, an entirely new element. Finding ample scope for undisturbed action, through the entire region of the Swamp, he continued to go scattering to the winds and sowing the seeds of a future crop, only to take root in the thick black waters which cover it, to be grown in devastation and reaped in a whirl-wind of ruin.

'I been lookin' fah yeh dis many years,' said old Gamby Gholar, a noted high conjurer and compeer of Nat Turner, who for more than thirty years has been secluded in the Swamp; 'an' been tellin' on 'em dat yeh 'ood come long, but da 'ooden' heah dat I tole 'em! Now da see! Dis many years I been seein' on yeh! Yes, 'ndeed, chile, dat I has!' and he took from a gourd of antiquated appearance which hung against the wall in his hut, many articles of a mysterious character, some resembling bits of woollen yarn, onionskins, oystershells, finger and toe nails, eggshells, and scales which he declared to be from very dangerous serpents, but which closely resembled, and were believed to be, those of innocent and harmless fish, with broken iron nails.

These he turned over and over again in his hands, closely inspecting them through a fragment of green bottle glass, which he claimed to be a mysterious and precious 'blue stone' got at a peculiar and unknown spot in the Swamp, whither by a special faith he was led—and ever after unable to find the same spot—putting them again into the gourd, the end of the neck being cut off so as to form a bottle, he rattled the 'goombah,' as he termed it, as if endeavoring to frighten his guest. This process ended, he whispered, then sighted into the neck, first with one eye, then with the other, then shook, and so alternately whispering, sighting and shaking, until apparently getting tired, again pouring them out, fumbling among them until finding a forked breast bone of a small bird, which, muttering to himself, he called the 'charm bone of a treefrog.'

'Ah,' exclaimed Gamby as he selected out the mystic symbol handing it to Henry: 'got yeh at las'. Take dis, meh son, an' so long as yeh keep it, da 'can' haum yeh, dat da cant. Dis woth money, meh son; da aint many sich like dat in de Swamp! Yeh never want for nothin' so long as yeh keep dat!'

In this fearful abode for years of some of Virginia and North Carolina's boldest black rebels, the names of Nat Turner, Denmark Veezie, and General Gabriel were held by them in sacred reverence; that of Gabriel as a talisman. With delight they recounted the many exploits of whom they conceived to be the greatest men who ever lived, the pretended deeds of whom were fabulous, some of the narrators claiming to have been patriots in the American Revolution.

'Yeh offen hearn on Maudy Ghamus,' said an old man stooped with age, having the appearance of a centenarian; 'dat am me—me heah!' continued he touching himself on the breast; 'I's de frien' on Gamby Gholar; an' I an' Gennel Gabel fit in de Malution wah, an' da want no sich fightin' dare as dat in Gabel wah!'

'You were then a soldier in the Revolutionary war for American Independence, father?' inquired Henry.

'Gau bress yeh hunny. Yes 'ndeed, chile, long 'for yeh baun; dat I did many long day go! Yes, chile, yes!'

'And General Gabriel, too, a soldier of the American Revolution?' replied Henry.

'Ah, chile, dat 'e did fit in de Molution wah, Gabel so, an' 'e fit like mad dog! Wen 'e sturt, chile, da cant stop 'im; da may as well let 'im go long, da cant do nuffin' wid 'im.'

Henry subscribed to his eminent qualifications as a warrior, assuring him that those were the kind of fighting men they then needed among the blacks. Maudy Ghamus to this assented, stating that the Swamp contained them in sufficient number to take the whole United States; the only difficulty in the way being that the slaves in the different States could not be convinced of their strength. He had himself for years been an emissary; also, Gamby Gholar, who had gone out among them with sufficient charms to accomplish all they desired, but could not induce the slaves to a general rising.

'Take plenty *goomba* an' *fongosa* 'long wid us, an' plant *mocasa* all along, an' da got nuffin' fah do but come, an' da 'ooden come!' despairingly declared Maudy Ghamus.

Gamby Gholar, Maudy Ghamus, and others were High Conjurers, who are ambassadors from the Swamp, were regularly sent out to create new conjurers, lay charms, take off 'spells' that could not be reached by Low Conjurers, and renew the art of all conjurors of seven years existence, at the expiration of which period the virtue was supposed to run out; holding their official position by fourteen years appointments. Through this means the revenue is obtained for keeping up an organized existence in this much dreaded morass—the Dismal Swamp.

Before Henry left they insisted upon, and anointed him a priest of the order of High Conjurers, and amusing enough it was to him who consented to satisfy the aged devotees of a time honored superstition among them. Their supreme executive body called the 'Head' consists in number of seven aged men, noted for their superior experience and wisdom. Their place of official meeting must be entirely secluded, either in the forest, a gully, secluded hut, an underground room, or a cave.

The seven old men who, with heightened spirits, hailed his advent among them, led Henry to the door of an ample cave—their hollow—at the door of which they were met by a large sluggish, lazy moving serpent, but so entirely tame and petted that it wagged its tail with fondness toward Maudy as he led the party. The old men suddenly stopping at the approach of the reptile, stepping back a pace, looked at each other mysteriously shaking their heads:

'Go back!' exclaimed Maudy waving his hand; 'go back, my chile! 'e in terrible rage! 'e got seben long toof, any on 'em kill yeh like flash!' tapping it slightly on the head with a twig of a grape vine which he carried in his hand.

Looking at the ugly beast, Henry had determined did it approach to harm, to slay it; but instead, it quietly coiled up and lay at the door as if asleep, which reminded him of queer and unmeaning sounds as they approached, uttered by Gholar,

which explained that the animal had been trained to approach
when called as any other pet. The 'Head' once in session, they
created him conjurer of the highest degree known to their art.
With this qualification he was licensed with unlimited power—a
power never before given any one—to go forth and do wonders.
The Head seemed, by the unlimited power given him, to place
greater reliance in the efforts of Henry for their deliverance,
than in their own seven heads together.

'Go, my son,' said they, 'an' may God A'mighty hole up yo'
han's an' grant us speedy 'liverence!'

Being now well refreshed—having rested without the fear of
detection—and in the estimation of Gholar, Ghamus and the
rest of the 'Heads,' well qualified to prosecute his project;
amidst the prayers, blessings, wishes, hopes, fears, pow-wows
and promises of a never failing conjuration, and tears of the
cloudy inhabitants of this great seclusion, among whom were
the frosty headed, bowed down old men of the Cave, Henry left
that region by his usual stealthy process, reaching Richmond,
Virginia, in safety.

* * *

(Editor's note: In Chapters 25 and 26, Henry Blake sets up a
revolutionary network as he travels from Richmond to Charleston to Nashville to Lexington and to Natchez.)

XXVII. A Night of Anxiety.

On Saturday evening, about half past seven, was it that Henry
dared again to approach the residence of Colonel Franks. The
family had not yet retired, as the lights still burnt briliantly in
the great house, when, secreted in the shrubbery contiguous to
the hut of Mammy Judy and Daddy Joe, he lie patiently
awaiting the withdrawal in the mansion.

'There's no use in talkin,' Andy, he's gittin' suspicious of us
all,' said Charles; 'as he threatens us all with the traders; an' if
Henry don't come soon, I'll have to leave anyhow! But the old
people, Andy, I can't think of leavin' them!'

'Do you think da would go if da had a chance, Chaules?'

'Go? yes 'ndeed, Andy, they'd go this night if they could git off. Since the sellin' of Maggie, and Henry's talkin to 'em, and his goin' and takin' little Joe, an' Ailsey, an' Cloe, an' Polly an' all clearin' out, they altered their notion about stayin' with ole Franks.'

'Wish we could know when Henry's comin' back! Wonder whar 'e is,' said Andy.

'Here!' was the reply in a voice so cautiously suppressed, and so familiarly distinct that they at once recognized it to be that of their long absent and most anxiously looked for friend. Rushing upon him, they mutually embraced, with tears of joy and anxiety.

'How have you been, anyhow, Henry?' exclaimed Charles in a suppressed tone. 'I's so glad to see yeh, dat I aint agwine to speak to yeh, so I aint!' added Andy.

'Come, brethren, to the woods!' said Henry; when the three went directly to the forest, two and a half miles from the city.

'Well now, Henry, tell us all about yourself. What you been doin'?' inquired Charles.

'I know of nothing about myself worth telling,' replied he.

'Oh, pshaw! wot saut a way is dat, Henry; yeh wont tell abody nothin'. Pshaw, dats no way,' grumbled Andy.

'Yes, Andy, I've much to tell you; but not of myself; 'tis about our poor oppressed people everywhere I've been; but we have not now time for that.'

'Why, cant you tell us nothin'?'

'Well, Andy, since you must have something, I'll tell you this much: I've been in the Dismal Swamp among the high conjurers, and saw the heads, old Maudy Ghamus and Gamby Gholar.'

'Hoop! now 'e's a talkin'! ef 'e wasn't I wouldn't tell yeh so! An' wat da sa to yeh, Henry?'

'They welcomed me as the messenger of their deliverance; and as a test of their gratitude, made me a high conjurer after their own order.'

'O pshaw, Henry! Da done what? Wy, ole feller, yeh is high sho 'nough!'

'What good does it do, Henry, to be a conjurer?' inquired Charles.

'It makes the more ignorant slaves have greater confidence in, and more respect for their headmen and leaders.'

'Oh yes, I see now! Because I couldn't see why you would submit to become a conjurer if it done no good.'

'That's it, Charles! as you know, I'll do anything not morally wrong, to gain our freedom; and to effect this, we must take the slaves, not as we wish them to be, but as we really find them to be.'

'You say it gives power, Henry; is there any reality in the art of conjuration?'

'It only makes the slaves afraid of you if you are called a 'conjurer,' that's all!'

'Oh, I understand it well enough now!' concluded Charles.

'I undehstood well 'nough fuss, but I want to know all I could, dat's all!' added Andy. 'Ole Maudy's a high feller, aint 'e, Henry?'

'Oh yes! he's the Head,' replied Charles.

'No,' explained Henry; 'he's not now 'Head,' but Gamby Gholar, who has for several years held that important position among them. Their Council consists of Seven, called the 'Heads,' and their Chief is called 'the Head.' Everything among them, in religion, medicine, laws, or politics, of a public character, is carried before the 'Head' in Council to be settled and disposed of.'

'Now we understan',' said Andy; 'but tell us, Henry, how yeh get 'long 'mong de folks whar yeh bin all dis time?'

'Very well everywhere, except Kentucky, and there you cant move them toward a strike!'

'Kentucky!' rejoined Andy; 'I all'as thought dat de slaves in dat State was de bes' treated uv any, an' dat da bin all 'long spectin' to be free.'

'That's the very mischief of it, Andy! 'Tis this confounded 'good treatment' and expectation of getting freed by their oppressors, that has been the curse of the slave. All shrewd masters, to keep their slaves in check, promise them their freedom at their, the master's death, as though they were certain to die first. This contents the slave, and makes him obedient and willing to serve and toil on, looking forward to the promised redemption. This is just the case precisely now in

Kentucky. It was my case. While Franks treated me well, and made promises of freedom to my wife'—and he gave a deep sigh—'I was satisfied, though a freeman, to remain with him and toil on hoping for the time of fulfilment of the promise. I would doubtless have been with him yet; but his bad treatment—his inhuman treatment of my wife—my poor, poor wife!—poor Maggie! was that which gave me courage, and made me determined to throw off the yoke, let it cost me what it would. Talk to me of a good master! A 'good master' is the very worst of masters. Were they all cruel and inhuman, or could the slaves be made to see their treatment aright, they would not endure their oppression for a single hour!'

'I sees it, I sees it!' replied Andy.

'An' so do I,' added Charles; 'who couldn't see that?'

'I tells yeh, Henry, it was mighty haud for me to make up my mine to leave ole Potteh; but ever sence you an' Chaules an' me made de vow togedder, I got mo' an' mo' to hate 'im. I could chop 'is head off sometime, I get so mad. I bleve I could chop off Miss Mary' head; an' I likes hur; she mighty good to we black folks.'

'Pshaw! yes 'ndeed; ole Frank's head would be nothin' for me to chop off; I could chop off mistess head, an' you know she's a good woman; but I mus' be mighty mad fus'!' said Charles.

'That's it, you see. There is no danger that a 'good master or mistress will ever be harmed by the slaves. There's neither of you, Andy, could muster up courage enough to injure a 'good master' or mistress. And even I now could not have the heart to injure Mrs. Franks,' said Henry.

'Nor me,' replied Charles.

'Yes, 'ndeed, dats a fac', case I knows I couldn' hurt Miss Mary Potteh. I bleve I'd almos' chop off anybody's head if I see 'em 'tempt to hurt 'e!' added Andy; when they heartily laughed at each other.

'Just so!' said Henry; 'a slave has no just conception of his own wrongs. Had I dealt with Franks as he deserved, for doing that for which he would have taken the life of any man had it been his case—tearing my wife from my bosom!—the most I could take courage directly to do, was to leave him, and take as many from him as I could induce to go. But maturer reflection drove me to the expedient of avenging the general wrongs of our people, by inducing the slave, in his might, to scatter red ruin throughout the region of the South. But still, I cannot find it in my heart to injure an individual, except in personal conflict.'

'An has yeh done it, Henry?' earnestly inquired Andy.

'Yes, Andy; yes, I have done it! and I thank God for it! I have taught the slave that mighty lesson: to strike for Liberty. 'Rather to die as freemen, than live as slaves!"'

'Thang God!' exclaimed Charles.

'Amen!' responded Andy.

'Now, boys, to the most important event of your lives!' said Henry.

'Wat's dat?' asked Andy.

'Why, get ready immediately to leave your oppressors to-night!' replied he.

'Glory to God!' cried Andy.

'Hallelujah!' responded Charles.

'Quietly! softly! easy, boys, easy!' admonished Henry, when the party in breathless silence, on tip-toe moved off from the thicket in which they were then seated, toward the city.

It was now one o'clock in the night, and Natchez shrouded in darkness and quiet, when the daring and fearless runaway with his companions, entered the enclosure of the great house grounds, and approached the door of the hut of Daddy Joe and Mammy Judy.

'Who dat! who dat, I say? Ole man, don' yeh hear some un knockin' at de doh?' with fright said Mammy Judy in a smothered tone, hustling and nudging the old man, who was in a deep sleep, when Henry rapped softly at the door.

'Wat a mautta, ole 'umin?' after a while inquired the old man, rubbing his eyes.

'Some un at de doh!' she replied.

'Who dar?' inquired daddy Joe.

'A friend!' replied Henry with suppressed voice.

'Ole man, open de doh quick! I bleve in me soul dat Henry! Open de doh!' said mammy.

On the door being opened, the surprise and joy of the old woman was only equalled by the emotion of her utterance.

'Dar! dar now, ole man! I tole 'em so, but da 'uden bleve me! I tole 'em 'e comin', but da 'uden lis'en to me! Did yeh git 'er, me son? Little Joe cum too? O Laud! whar's my po' chile! Whar's Margot?'

To evade further inquiry, Henry replied that they were all safe, and hoping to see her and the old man.

'How yeh bin my chile? I'se glad to see yeh, but mighty sorry yeh cum back; case de wite folks say, da once git der hands on yeh da neber let yeh go 'g'in! Potteh, Craig, Denny, and all on 'em, da tryin' to fine whar yeh is, hunny!'

'I am well mammy, and come now to see what is to be done with you old people,' said Henry.

'We 'ont be hear long, chile; da gwine sell us all to de traders!' replied mammy with a deep sigh.

'Yes chile,' added Daddy Joe; 'we all gwine to de soul driveh!'

'You'll go to no soul-drivers!' replied Henry, the flash of whose eyes startled mammy Judy.

'How yeh gwine help it, chile?' kindly asked daddy Joe.

'I'll show you. Come, come Mammy! You and daddy get ready, as I've come to take you away, and must be at the river before two o'clock,' said Henry, who with a single jerk of a board in the floor of the hut, had reached the hidden treasure of the old people.

'Who gwine wid us, chile?' inquired mammy Judy.

'Charles, Andy and his female friend, besides some we shall pick up by the way!' replied Henry.

'Now he's a talkin'!' jocosely said Charles, looking at Andy with a smile, at the mention of his female friend.

''E ain' doin' nothin' else!' replied Andy.

'Wat become o' po' little Tony! 'E sleep here to-night, case he not berry well. Po' chile!' sighed the old woman.

'We'll take him too, of course; and I would that I could take every slave in Natchez!' replied Henry. 'It is now half-past one,' said he, looking at his watch: 'and against two we must be at the river. Go Andy, and get your friend, and meet us at the old burnt sycamore stump above the ferry. Come mammy and daddy, not a word for your lives!' admonished Henry; when taking their package on his back, and little Tony by the hand, they left forever the great house premises of Col. Stephen Franks in Natchez.

On approaching the river a group was seen, which proved to consist of Andy, Clara (to whom his integrity was plighted), and the faithful old stump, their guide-post for the evening. Greeting each other with tears of joy and fearful hearts, they passed down to the water's edge, but a few hundred feet below.

The ferry boat in this instance was a light built yawl, commanded by a white man; the ferry one of many such selected along the shore, expressly for such occasions.

'Have you a pass?' demanded the boatman as a *ruse*, lest he might be watched by a concealed party; 'let me see it!'

'Here sir,' said Henry, presenting to him by the light of a match which he held in his hand for the purpose, the face of a half eagle.

'Here is seven of you, an' I cant do it for that!' in an humble undertone supplicating manner, said the man; 'I axes that for one!'

The weight of seven half eagles dropped into his hand, caused him eagerly to seize the oars, making the quickest possible time to the opposite side of the river.

XXVIII. Studying Head Work

'Now Henry,' said Andy, after finding themselves in a safe place some distance from the landing; 'you promise' w'en we stauted to show us de Noth star—which is it?' On looking up the sky was too much obscured with clouds.

'I cant show it to you now, but when we stop to refresh, I'll then explain it to you,' replied he.

'It high time now, chil'en, we had a mou'full to eat ef we got travel dis way!' suggested mammy Judy, breaking silence for the first time since they left the great house.

'Yes,' replied Andy; 'Clara and little Tony mus' wan' to eat, an' I knows wat dis chile wants!' touching himself on the breast.

The runaways stopped in the midst of an almost impenetrable thicket, kindled a fire to give them light, where to take their fare on cold meat, bread and butter, and cheese, of which the cellar and pantry of Franks, to which mammy Judy and Charles had access, afforded an ample supply.

Whilst the others were engaged in refreshing, Henry aside of a stump, was busily engaged with pencil and paper.

'Whar's Henry, dat 'e aint hear eatin?' inquired mammy Judy, looking about among the group.

'I sho ole 'umin, 'e's oveh dar by de stump,' replied daddy Joe.

'Wat dat boy doin' dar? Henry wat yeh doin'? Mus' be studyin' head-wuck, I reckon! Sho boy! betteh come 'long an' git a mou'full to eat. Yeh ain' hungry I reckon,' said the old woman.

'Henry, we dun eatin' now. You mos' ready to tell us 'bout de Noth star?' said Andy.

'Yes, I will show you,' said Henry, walking forward and seating himself in the center of the group. 'You see these seven stars which I've drawn on this piece of paper—numbered 1, 2, 3, 4, 5, 6, 7? From the peculiarity of the shape of their relative position to each other, the group is called the 'Dipper,' because to look at them, they look like a dipper or a vessel with a long handle.'

'I see it; dont you see dat, Chaules?' said Andy.

'Certainly, anybody could see that,' replied Charles.

'Ole umin,' said daddy Joe, 'don' yeh see it?'

'Sho' ole man! aint I lookin!' replied the old woman.

'You all see it then, do you?' inquired Henry.

'Yes, yes!' was the response.

'Now then,' continued Henry; 'for an explanation by which you can tell the North star, when or from whatever place you may see it. The two stars of the Dipper, numbered 6 and 7, are called the *pointers,* because they point directly to the North Star, a very small, bright star, far off from the pointers, generally seeming by itself, especially when the other stars are not very bright.

'The star numbered 8, above the pointer, a little to the left, is a dim, small star, which at first sight would seem to be in a direct line with it; but by drawing a line through 7 to 8, leaves a space as you see between the star 6 and lower part of the line; or forms an angle (as the "book men" call it, Andy) of ten degrees. The star number 9 in the distance, and a little to the right, would also seem to be directly opposite the pointers; but drawing a line through 7 to 9, there is still a space left between the lower end of the line and 6. Now trace the dotted line from 6 through the center of 7, and it leads directly to 10. This is the

North star, the slave's great Guide to Freedom! Do you all now understand it?'

'See it!' replied Andy; 'anybody can't see dat, ain' got sense 'nuff to run away, an' no call to be free, dat's all! I knows all about it. I reckon I almos' know it betteh dan you, Henry!'

'Dar, dar, I tole yeh so! I tole yeh dat boy studyin' head wuck, an' yeh 'uden bleve me! 'E run about yendeh so much, an' kick up 'e heel dat 'e talk so much gramma an' wot not, dat body haudly undehstan'! I knows dat 'e bin 'splainin do. Ole man, yeh understan'im?' said Mammy Judy.

'Ah, ole 'umin, dat I does! an' I' been gone forty years 'go, I' know'd dis much 'bout it!' replied daddy Joe.

'Above number 2 the second star of the handle of the Dipper, close to it, you will see by steadily looking, a very small star, which I call the knob or thumb-holt of the handle. You may always tell the Dipper by the knob of the handle; and the North star by the Dipper. The Dipper, during the night you will remember, continues to change its position in relation to the earth, so that it sometimes seems quite upside down.'

'See here, Henry, does you know all—'

'Stop, Andy, I've not done yet!' interrupted he.

'Uh, heh!' said Andy.

'When the North star cannot be seen,' continued Henry, 'you must depend alone upon nature for your guide. Feel, in the dark, around the trunks or bodies of trees, especially oak, and whenever you feel moss on the bark, that side on which the moss grows is always to the north. One more explanation and then we'll go. Do you see this little round metalic box? This is called a—'

'Wat dat you call 'talic, Henry? Sho, boy! yeh head so full ob gramma an' sich like dat yeh don' know how to talk!' interrupted mammy Judy.

'That only means iron or brass, or some hard thing like that, mammy,' explained he. 'The little box of which I was speaking, has in it what is called a compass. It has a face almost like a clock or watch, with one straight hand which reaches entirely across the face, and turns or shakes whenever you move the box. This hand or finger is a piece of metal called "loadstone" or "magnet," and termed the Needle of the compass; and this end with the little cross on it, always points in one direction, and that is to the north. See: it makes no difference which way it is moved, this point of the needle turns back and points that way.'

'An mus' ye al'as go de way it pints, Henry?' inquired Andy.

'No; not except you are running away from the South to Canada, or the Free States; because both of these places are in the north. But when you know which way the north is, you can easily find any other direction you wish. Notice this, all of you.

'When your face is to the north, your back is to the south; your right hand to the east, and your left to the west. Can you remember this?'

'O yes, easy!' replied Andy.

'Then you will always know which way to go, by the compass showing you which is north,' explained Henry.

'What does dese letters roun' hear mean, Henry?' farther inquired Andy.

'Only what I have already explained; meaning North, East, West, and South, with their intermediate—'

'Dar!' interrupted mammy Judy, ' 'e gone into big talk g'in! sho!'

'Intermediate, means between, mammy,' explained Henry.

'Den ef dat's it, I lis'en at yeh; case I want gwine bautheh my head wid yo' jography an' big talk like dat!' replied the old woman.

'What does a compass cost?' inquired Charles, who had been listening with intense interest and breathless silence at the information given by their much loved fellow bondman.

'One-half a dollar, or four bits, as we call it, so that every slave who will, may get one. Now, I've told you all that's necessary to guide you from a land of slavery and long suffering, to a land of liberty and future happiness. Are you now all satisfied with what you have learned?'

'Chauls, aint 'e high! See here, Henry, does yeh know all dat yeh tell us? Wy, ole feller, you is way up in de hoobanahs! Wy you is conjure sho 'nuff. Ef I on'y know'd dis befo', ole Potteh neveh keep me a day. O, pshaw! I bin gone long 'go!'

'He'll do!' replied Charles.

'Well, well, well!' apostrophised mammy Judy; 'dat beats all! Sence I was baun, I nebber hear de like! All along I been tellen on yeh, dat 'e got 'is head chuck cleanfull ob cumbustable, an' all dat, but yeh 'ud'n bleve me! Now yeh see!'

'Ole umin I 'fess dat's all head wuck! Dat beats Punton! dat boy's nigh up to Maudy Ghamus! Dat boy's gwine to be mighty!' with a deep sigh replied daddy Joe.

'Come, now, let's go!' said Henry.

On rising from where they had all been sitting with fixed attention upon their leader and his instruction, the sky was observed through the only break in the thicket above their heads, when suddenly they simultaneously exclaimed:

'There's the Dipper! there's the North star!' all pointing directly to the God-like beacon of liberty to the American slave.

Leaving Mammy Judy and Daddy Joe, Clara and little Tony, who had quite recovered from his indisposition the early part of the night, in charge of a friend who designedly met them on the Louisiana side of the river, with heightened spirits and a new impulse, Henry, Charles and Andy, started on their journey in the direction of their newly described guide, the North star.

> 'Star of the North thou art not bigger,
>   Than the diamond in my ring;
> Yet every black star-gazing nigger,
>   Looks up to thee as some great thing!'

was the apostrophe of an American writer to the sacred orb of Heaven, which in this case was fully verified.

During the remainder of the night and next day, being Sabbath, they continued their travel, only resting when overcome with fatigue. Continuing in Louisiana by night, and resting by day, Wednesday morning, before daybreak, brought them to the Arkansas river. At first they intended to ford, but like the rivers generally of the South, its depth and other contingencies made it necessary to seek some other means. After consultation in a canebreak, day beginning to dawn, walking boldly up to a man just loosening a skiff from its fastenings, they demanded a passage across the river. This the skiffman refused peremtorily on any pretext, rejecting the sight of a written pass.

'I want none of yer nigger passes!' angrily said he; 'they aint none uv 'em good 'or nothin', nohow! It's no use to show it to me, ye's cant git over!'

First looking meaningly and determinedly at Charles and Andy—biting his lips—then addressing himself to the man, Henry said:

'Then I have one that will pass us!' presenting the unmistaking evidence of a shining gold eagle, at the sight of which emblem of his country's liberty, the skiffman's patriotism was at once awakened, and their right to pass as American freemen indisputable.

A few energetic muscular exertions with the oars, and the sturdy boatman promptly landed his passengers on the other side of the river.

'Now gentlm'n, I done the clean thing, did'nt I, by jingo! Show me but half a chance an' I'll ack the man clean out. I dont go in for this slaveholding o' people in these Newnited States uv the South, nohow, so I dont. Dog gone it, let every feller have a fair shake!'

Dropping into his hand the ten dollar gold piece, the man bowed earnestly, uttering—

'I hope ye's good luck, gent'men! Ye'll al'as fine me ready when ye's come 'long this way!'

XXIX. The Fugitives

With much apprehension, Henry and comrades passed hastily through the State of Arkansas, he having previously traversed it partly, had learned sufficient to put him on his guard.

Traveling in the night, to avoid the day, the progress was not equal to the emergency. Though Henry carried a pocket compass, they kept in sight of the Mississippi river, to take their chance of the first steamer passing by.

The third night out, being Monday, at day-break in the morning, their rest for the day was made at a convenient point within the verge of a forest. Suddenly Charles gave vent to hearty laughter, at a time when all were supposed to be serious, having the evening past, been beset by a train of three negro dogs, which, having first been charmed, they slew at the instant; the dogs probably not having been sent on trail of them, but, after the custom of the state, baying on a general round to intimidate the slaves from clandestinely venturing out, and to attack such runaways as might by chance be found in their track.

'Wat's da mauttah Chauls?' enquired Andy.

'I was just thinking,' replied he, 'of the sight of three high conjurers, who if Ghamus and Gholar be true, can do anything they please, having to escape by night, and travel in the wild woods, to evade the pursuit of white men, who do not pretend to know anything about sich things.'

'Dat's a fack,' added Andy, 'an' little, scronny triflin' weak, white men at dat—any one uv us heah, ought to whip two or three uv 'em at once. Dares Hugh's a little bit a feller, I could take 'im in one han' an' throw 'im oveh my head, an' ole Pottah, for his paut, he so ole an' good foh nothin, I could whip wid one hand haf a dozen like 'im.'

'Now you see, boys,' said Henry, 'how much conjuration and such foolishness and stupidity is worth to the slaves in the South. All that it does, is to put money into the pockets of the pretended conjurer, give him power over others by making them afraid of him; and even old Gamby Gholar and Maudy Ghamus and the rest of the "Seven Heads," with all of the high conjurers in the Dismal Swamp, are depending more upon me to deliver them from their confinement as prisoners in the Swamp and runaway slaves, than all their combined efforts together. I made it a special part of my mission wherever I went, to enlighten them on this subject.'

'I wandah you didn't 'fend 'em,' replied Andy.

'No danger of that, since having so long, to no purpose, depended upon such persons and nonsense, they are sick at heart of them, and waiting willing and ready, for anything which may present for their aid, even to the destruction of their long cherished, silly nonsense of conjuration.'

'Thang God foh dat!' concluded Andy.

Charles having fallen asleep, Andy became the sentinel of the party, as it was the arrangement for each one alternately, every two hours during rest, to watch while the other two slept. Henry having next fallen into a doze, Andy heard a cracking among the bushes, when on looking around, two men approached them. Being fatigued, drowsy, and giddy, he became much alarmed, arousing his comrades, all springing to their feet. The men advanced, who, to their gratification proved to be Eli and Ambrose, two Arkansas slaves, who having promised to meet Henry on his return, had effected their escape immediately after first meeting him, lurking in the forest in the direction which he had laid out to take.

Eli was so fair as to be taken, when first seen to be a white man. Throwing their arms about Henry, they bestowed upon him their blessing and thanks, for his advent into the State, as the means of their escape.

While thus exchanging gratulations, the approach up stream of a steamer was heard, and at once Henry devised the expedient, and determined boldly to hail her and demand a passage. Putting Eli forward as the master, Ambrose carrying the *porte manteau* which belonged to the two, and the others with bundles in their hands, all rushed to the bank of the river on the verge of the thicket; Eli held up a handkerchief as a signal. The bell tolled, and the yawl immediately lowered, made for the shore. It was agreed that Eli should be known as 'Major Ely' of Arkansas.

Seeing that blacks were of the company, when the yawl approached, the mate stood upon her forecastle.

'What's the faction here?' cried out the sturdy mate.

'Where are you bound?' enquired Eli.

'For St. Louis.'

'Can I get a passage for myself and four negroes?'

'What's the name, sir?'

'Major Ely of Arkansas,' was the reply.

'Aye, aye, sir, come aboard,' said the mate; when, pulling away, the steamer was soon reached, the slaves going to the deck, and the master to the cabin.

On application for a state room, the clerk, on learning the name, desired to know his destination.

'The State of Missouri, sir,' said Eli, 'between the points of the mouth of the Ohio and St. Genevieve.'

'Ely,' repeated the clerk. 'I've heard that name before—it's a Missouri name—any relation to Dr. Ely, Major?'

'Yes, a brother's son,' was the prompt reply.

'Yes, yes, I thought I knew the name,' replied the clerk, 'but the old fellow wasn't quite of your way of thinking, concerning negroes, I believe?'

'No, he is one man, and I'm another, and he may go his way, and I'll go mine,' replied Eli.

'That's the right feeling, Major,' replied the clerk, 'and we would have a much healthier state of politics in the country, if men generally would only agree to act on that principle.'

'It has ever been my course,' said Eli.

'Peopling a new farm, I reckon major?'

'Yes sir.'

The master, keeping a close watch upon the slaves, was frequently upon deck among them, and requested that they might be supplied with more than common fare for slaves, he sparing no expense to make them comfortable. The slaves, on their part, appeared to be particularly attached to him, always smiling when he approached, apparently regretting when he left for the cabin.

Meanwhile, the steamer gracefully plowing up the current, making great headway, reached the point desired, when the master and slaves were safely transferred from the steamer to the shore of Missouri.

XXX. *The Pursuit*

The absence of mammy Judy, daddy Joe, Charles and little Tony, on the return early Monday morning, of Colonel Franks and lady from the country, unmistakably proved the escape of their slaves, and the farther proof of the exit of 'squire Potter's Andy and Beckwith's Clara, with the remembrance of the stampede a few months previously, required no farther confirmation of the fact, when the neighborhood again was excited to a ferment. The advisory committee was called into immediate council, and ways and means devised for the arrest of the recreant slaves recently left, and to prevent among them the recurrence of such things; a pursuit was at once commenced, which for the three succeeding days was carried in the wrong direction—towards Jackson, whither, it was supposed in the neighborhood, Henry had been lurking previous to the last sally upon their premises, as he had certainly been seen on Saturday evening, coming from the landing.

No traces being found in that direction, the course was changed, the swiftest steamer boarded in pursuit for the Ohio river. This point being reached but a few hours subsequent to that of the fugitives, when learning of their course, the pursuers proceeded toward the place of their destination, on the Mississippi river.

This point being the southern part of Missouri but a short distance above the confluence of the Ohio and Mississippi, the last named river had, of necessity, to be passed, being to the fugitives only practicable by means of a ferry. The ferryman in this instance commanded a horse-boat, he residing on the opposite side of the river. Stepping up to him—a tall, raw-boned, athletic, rough looking, bearded fellow—Eli saluted:

'We want to cross the river, sir!'

'Am yers free?' enquired the ferryman.

'Am *I* free! are *you* free?' rejoined Eli.

'Yes, I be's a *white* man!' replied the boatman.

'And so am I!' retorted Eli, 'and you dare not tell me I'm not.'

'I'll swong, stranger, yer mus' 'scuse me, as I didn' take notice on yez! but I like to know if them air black folks ye got wey yer am free, cause if they arn't, I be 'sponsible for 'em 'cording to the new law, called, I 'bleve the Nebrasky Complimize Fugintive Slave Act, made down at Californy, last year,' apologized and explained the somewhat confused ferryman.

'Yes,' replied Henry, 'we are free, and if we were not, I do'nt think it any part of your business to know. I thought you were here to carry people across the river.'

'But frien',' rejoined the man, 'yer don't understan' it. This are a law made by the Newnited States of Ameriky, an' I be 'bliged to fulfill it by ketchin' every fugintive that goes to cross this way, or I mus' pay a thousand dollars, and go to jail till the black folks is got, if that be's never. Yer see yez cant blame me, as I mus' 'bey the laws of Congress I'll swong it be's hardly a fair shake nuther, but I be 'bliged to 'bey the laws, yer know.'

'Well sir,' replied Henry, 'we want to cross the river.'

'Let me see yez papers frien'?' asked the ferryman.

'My friend,' said Henry, 'are you willing to make yourself a watch-dog for slaveholders, and do for them that which they would not do for themselves, catch runaway slaves? Don't you know that this is the work which they boast on having the poor white men at the North do for them? Have you not yet learned to attend to *your own interests* instead of theirs? Here are our free papers,' holding out his open hand, in which lay five half-eagle pieces.

'Jump aboard!' cried the ferryman. 'Quick, quick!' shouted he, as the swift feet of four horses were heard dashing up the road.

Scarcely had the boat moved from her fastenings, till they had arrived; the riders dismounted, who presenting revolvers, declared upon the boatman's life, instantly, if he did not change the direction of his boat and come back to the Missouri shore. Seizing a well-charged rifle belonging to the boatman, his comrades each with a well aimed six-barreled weapon.

'Shoot if you dare!' exclaimed Henry, the slaveholders declining their arms,—when, turning to the awe-stricken ferryman, handing him the twenty-five dollars, said, 'your cause is a just one, and your reward is sure; take this money, proceed and you are safe—refuse, and you instantly die!'

'Then I be to do right,' declared the boatman, 'if I die by it,' when applying the whip to the horses, in a few moments landed them on the Illinois shore.

This being the only ferry in the neighborhood, and fearing a bribe or coercion by the people on the Illinois side, or the temptation of a high reward from the slave catchers, Henry determined on eluding, if possible, every means of pursuit.

'What are your horses worth?' enquired he.

'They can't be no use to you frien' case they is both on 'em bline, an' couldn' travel twenty mile a day, on a stretch!'

'Have you any other horses?'

'They be all the horses I got; I gineraly feed a spell this side; I lives over here—this are my feedin' trip,' drawled the boatman.

'What will you take for them?'

'Well, frien' they arn't wuth much to buy, no how, but wuth good lock to me for drawin' the boat over, yer see.'

'What did they cost you in buying them?'

'Well, I o'ny gin six—seven dollars apiece, or sich a matter for 'em, when I got 'em, an' they cos me some two—three dollars, or sich a matter, more to get 'em in pullin' order, yer see.'

'Will you sell them to me?'

'I hadn't ort to part wey 'em frien', as I do good lock o' bisness hereabouts wey them air nags, bline as they be.'

'Here are thirty dollars for your horses,' said Henry, putting into his hand the money in gold pieces, when, unhitching them from their station, leading them out to the side of the boat, he shot them, pushing them over into the river.

'Farewell my friend,' saluted Henry, he and comrades leaving the astonished ferryman gazing after them, whilst the slaveholders on the other shore stood grinding their teeth, grimacing their faces, shaking their fists, with various gesticulations of threat, none of which were either heard, heeded or cared for by the fleeing party, or determined ferryman.

Taking a northeasterly course for Indiana, Andy being an accustomed singer, commenced, in lively glee and cheerful strains, singing to the expressive words:

> 'We are like a band of pilgrims,
>   In a strange and foreign land,
> With our knapsacks on our shoulders,
>   And our cudgels in our hands,
> We have many miles before us.
>   But it lessens not our joys,
> We will sing a merry chorus,
>   For we are the tramping boys.'

Then joined in chorus the whole party —

> 'We are all jogging,
> Jog, jog, jogging,
> And we're all jogging,
> We are going to the North!'

The Wabash river becoming the next point of obstruction, a ferry, as in the last case, had also to be crossed, the boatman residing on the Indiana side.

'Are you free?' enquired the boatman, as the party of blacks approached.

'We are,' was the reply of Henry.

'Where are you from?' continued he.

'We are from home, sir,' replied Charles, 'and the sooner you take us across the river, just so much sooner will we reach it.'

Still doubting their right to pass, he asked for their papers, but having by this time become so conversant with the patriotism and fidelity of these men to their country, Charles handing the Indianan a five dollar piece, who on seeing the out-stretched wings of the eagle, desired no farther evidence of their right to pass, conveying them into the State, contrary to the statutes of the Commonwealth.

On went the happy travelers without hinderance, or molestation, until the middle of the week next ensuing.

XXXI. The Attack, Resistance, Arrest

The travel for the last ten days had been pleasant, save the necessity in the more southern part of the State, of lying by through the day, and traveling at night—the fugitives cheerful and full of hope, nothing transpiring to mar their happiness, until approaching a village in the center of northern Indiana.

Supposing their proximity to the British Provinces made them safe, with an imprudence not before committed by the discreet runaways, when nearing a blacksmith's shop a mile and a half from the village, Andy in his usual manner, with stentorian voice, commenced the following song:

'I'm on my way to Canada,
　That cold and dreary land;
The dire effects of slavery,
　I can no longer stand.
My soul is vexed within me so,
　To think that I'm a slave,
I've now resolved to strike the blow,
　For Freedom or the grave.'

All uniting in the chorus,

'O, righteous Father
Wilt Thou not pity me,
And aid me on to Canada,
Where fugitives are free?
I heard old England plainly say,
If we would all forsake
Our native land of Slavery,
And come across the lake.'

'There, Ad'line! I golly, dont you hear that?' said Dave Starkweather, the blacksmith, to his wife, both of whom on hearing the unusual noise of singing, thrust their heads out of the door of a little log hut, stood patiently listening to the song, every word of which they distinctly caught; 'them's fugertive slaves, an' I'll have 'em tuck up; they might have passed, but for their singin' praise to that darned Queen! I cant stan' that no how!'

'No,' replied Adaline, 'I'm sure I don't see what they sing to her for; she's no 'Merican. We ain't under her now, am we Dave?'

'No, we ain't, Ad'line, not sence the battle o' Waterloo, an' I golly, we wouldn't be if we was. The 'Mericans could whip her a darned sight easier now than what they done when they fit her at Waterloo.'

'Lah me, Dave, you could whip 'er yourself, she ai'nt bigger nor tother wimin is she?' said Mrs. Starkweather.

'No she ain't, not a darn' bit!' replied he.

'Dave, ask 'em in the shop to rest,' suggested the wife in a hurried whisper, elbowing her husband as the party advanced, having ceased singing so soon as they saw the faces of white persons.

'Travlin' I reckon?' interrogated the blacksmith, 'little tired, I spose?'

'Yes sir, a little so,' replied Henry.

'Didn't come far, I 'spect?' continued he.

'Not very,' carelessly replied Henry.

'Take seat there, and rest ye little,' pointing to a smoothly-worn log, used by the visitors of the shop.

'Thank you,' said Henry, 'we will,' all seating themselves in a row.

'Take little somethin?' asked he; stepping back to a corner, taking out of a caddy in the wall, a rather corpulent green bottle, turning it up to his mouth, drenching himself almost to strangulation.

'We don't drink, sir,' replied the fugitives.

'Temperance, I reckon?' enquired the smith.

'Rather so,' replied Henry.

'Kind o' think we'll have a spell o' weather?'

'Yes,' said Andy, 'dat's certain; we'll have a spell a weatheh!'

On entering the shop, the person at the bellows, a tall, able-bodied young man, was observed to pass out at the back door, a number of persons of both sexes to come frequently look in, and depart, succeeded by others; no import being attached to this, supposing themselves to be an attraction, partly from their singing, and mainly from their color being a novelty in the neighborhood.

During conversation with the blacksmith, he after eying very closely the five strangers, was observed to walk behind the door, stand for some minutes looking as if reading, when resuming his place at the anvil, after which he went out at the back door. Curiosity now, with some anxiety induced Henry to look for the cause of it, when with no little alarm, he discovered a handbill fully descriptive of himself and comrades, having been issued in the town of St. Genevieve, offering a heavy reward, particularizing the scene at the Mississippi ferry, the killing of the horses as an aggravated offense, because depriving a poor man of his only means of livelihood, being designed to strengthen inducements to apprehend them, the bill being signed 'John Harris.'

Evening now ensuing, Henry and comrades, the more easily to pass through the village without attraction, had remained until this hour, resting in the blacksmith shop. Enquiring for some black family in the neighborhood, they were cited to one consisting of an old man and woman, Devan by name, residing on the other side, a short distance from the village.

'Ye'll fine ole Bill of the right stripe,' said the blacksmith knowingly, 'ye needn' be feard o' him. Ye'll fine him and ole Sally just what they say they is; I'll go bail for that. The first log hut ye come to after ye leave the village is thern; jist knock at the door, an' ye'll fine ole Bill an' Sally all right, blame if ye don't. Jis name me; tell 'em Dave Starkweather sent ye there, an' blamed if ye dont fine things at high water mark; I'm tellin' ye so, blamed if I ain't!' was the recomendation of the blacksmith.

'Thank you for your kindness,' replied Henry, politely bowing as they rose from the log, 'good bye sir!'

'Devilish decent lookin' black fellers,' said the man of the anvil, complimenting, designedly for them to hear, 'blamed if they ain't as free as we is—I golly they is!'

Without, as they thought, attracting attention, passing through the village a half mile or more, they came to a log hut on the right side of the way.

'How yeh do fren? How yeh come on?' saluted a short, rather corpulent wheezing old black man, 'come in. Hi! dahs good many on yeh; ole 'omin come, heah's some frens!' calling his wife Sally, an old woman, shorter in stature, but not less corpulent than he, sitting by a comfortable dry-stump fire.

'How is yeh, frens? How yeh do? come to da fiah, mighty cole!' said the old woman.

'Quite cool,' replied Andy, rubbing his hands, spreading them out, protecting his face from the heat.

'Yeh is travelin, I reckon, there is good many go 'long heah; we no call t' ask 'em whah da gwine, we knows who da is, case we come from dah. I an' ole man once slave in Faginny; mighty good country fah black folks.'

Sally set immediately about preparing something to give her guests a good meal. Henry admonished them against extra trouble, but they insisted on giving them a good supper.

Deeming it more prudent, the hut being on the highway, Henry requested to retire until summoned to supper, being shown to the loft attained by a ladder and simple hatchway, the door of which was shut down, and fastened on the lower side.

The floor consisting of rough, unjointed boards, containing great cracks through which the light and heat from below passed up, all could be both seen and heard, which transpired below.

Seeing the old man so frequently open and look out at the door, and being suspicious from the movements of the blacksmith and others, Henry affecting to be sleepy, requested Billy and his wife when ready, to awaken them, when after a few minutes, all were snoring as if fast asleep, Henry lying in such a position as through a knot-hole in the floor, to see every movement in all parts of the room. Directly above him in the rafter within his reach, hung a mowing scythe.

'Now's yeh time, ole man; da all fas' asleep! da snorin' good!' said old Sally, urging Billy to hasten, who immediately left the hut.

The hearts of the fugitives were at once 'in their mouths,' and with difficulty it was by silently reaching over and heavily pressing upon each of them, Henry succeeded in admonishing each to entire quietness and submission.

Presently entered a white man, who whispering with Sally left the room. Immediately in came old Bill, at the instant of which, Henry found his right hand above him, involuntarily grasped firmly on the snath of the scythe.

'Whah's da?' enquired old Bill, on entering the hut.

'Sho da whah yeh lef' 'em!' replied the old woman.

'Spose I kin bring 'em in now?' continued old Bill.

'Bring who in?'

'Da white folks; who else I gwine fetch in yeh 'spose?'

'Bettah let 'em 'tay whah da is, an' let de po' men lone, git sumpen t' eat, an' go 'long whah da gwine!' replied Sally, deceptiously.

'Huccum! yeh talk dat way? Sho yeh tole me go!' replied Billy.

'Didn' reckon yeh gwine bring 'em on da po' cretahs dis way, fo' da git moufful t' cat an' git way so.'

'How I gwine let 'em go now de white folks all out dah? Say Sally? Dat jis what make I tell yeh so!'

'Bettah let white folks 'lone, Willum! dat jis what I been tellin on yeh. Keep foolin' 'long wid white folks, byme by da show yeh! I no trus' white man, no how. Sho! da no fren' o' black folks. But spose body 'blige keep da right side on 'em long so.'

'Ole 'omin,' said Bill, 'yeh knows we make our livin' by da white folks, an' mus' do what da tell us, so whah's da use talkin' long so. 'Spose da come in now?'

'Sho, I tole yeh de man sleep! gwine bring white folks on 'em so! give po' cretahs no chance? Go long, do what yeh gwine do; yeh fine out one dese days!' concluded Sally.

Having stealthily risen to their feet, standing in a favorable position, Henry in whispers declared to his comrades that with that scythe he intended mowing his way into Canada.

Impatient for their entrance, throwing wide open the door of the hut, which being the signal, in rushed eleven white men, headed by Jud Shirly, constable, Dave Starkweather, the blacksmith, and Tom Overton as deputies; George Grove, a respectable well dressed villager, stood giving general orders.

With light and pistol in hand, Franey, mounting the stairway, commanded a surrender. Eli, standing behind the hatchway, struck the candle from his hand, when with a swing of the scythe, there was a screech, fall, and groan heard, then with a shout and leap, Henry in the lead, they cleared the stairs to the lower floor, the white men flying in consternation before them, making their way to the village, alarming the inhabitants.

The fugitives fled in great haste, continuing their flight for several miles, when becoming worn down with fatigue, retired under cover of a thicket a mile from a stage tavern kept by old Isaac Slusher of German descent.

The villagers following in quick pursuit, every horse which could be readily obtained being put on the chase, the slaves were overtaken, fired upon—a ball lodging in Charles' thigh—overpowered, and arrested. Deeming it, from the number of idlers about the place, and the condition of the stables, much the safest imprisonment, the captives were taken to the tavern of Slusher, to quarter for the night.

On arriving at this place, a shout of triumph rent the air, and a general cry 'take them into the bar room for inspection! hang them! burn them!' and much more.

Here the captives were derided, scoffed at and ridiculed, turned around, limbs examined, shoved about from side to side, then ordered to sit down on the floor, a non-compliance with which, having arranged themselves for the purpose, at a given signal, a single trip by an equal number of whites, brought the four poor prisoners suddenly to the floor on the broad of their backs, their heads striking with great force. At this abuse of helpless men, the shouts of laughter became deafening. It caused them to shun the risk of standing, and keep seated on the floor.

Charles having been wounded, affected inability to stand, but the injury being a flesh wound, was not serious.'

'We'll show ye yer places, ye black devils ye!' said Ned Bradly a rowdy, drawing back his foot to kick Henry in the face, as he sat upon the floor against the wall, giving him a slight kick in the side as he passed by him.

'Don't do that again sir!' sternly said Henry, with an expression full of meaning, looking him in the face.

Several feet in an instant were drawn back to kick, when Slusher interfering, said:

'Shendlemans! tem plack mans ish prishners! you tuz pring tem into mine horish, ant you shand puse tem dare!' when the rowdies ceased abusing them.

'Well, gentlemen,' said Tom Overton, a burly, bullying bar room person, 'we'd best git these blacks out of the way, if they's any fun up to night.'

'I cot plendy peds, shendlemans, I ondly vants to know who ish to bay me,' replied Slusher.

'I golly,' retorted Starkweather! 'you needn't give yourself no uneasiness about that, Slusher. I think me, and Shirly, and Grove is good for a night's lodging for five niggers, any how!'

'I'm in that snap, too!' hallooed out Overton.

'Golly! yes Tom, there's you we like to forgot, blamed if we didn't!' responded Starkweather.

'Dat ish all right nough zo far as te plack man's ish gonzern, put ten dare ish te housh vull o' peoples, vot vare must I gheep tem?'

'We four,' replied Grove, 'will see you paid, who else? Slusher, we want it understood, that we four stand responsible for all expenses incurred this night, in the taking of these negroes;' evidently expecting to receive as they claimed, the reward offered in the advertisement.

'Dat vill too ten,' replied Slusher. 'Vell, I ish ready to lit tese plack mans to ped.'

'No Slusher,' interrupted Grove, 'that's not the understanding, we don't pay for beds for niggers to sleep in!'

'No, by Molly!' replied Overton, 'dogged if that aint going a leetle too far! Slusher, you can't choke that down, no how you can fix in. If you do as you please with your own house, these niggers is in our custody, and we'll do as we please with them. We want you to know that we are white men, as well as you are, and cant pay for niggers to sleep in the same house with ourselves.'

'Gents,' said Ned Bradly, 'do you hear that?'

'What?' enquired several voices.

'Why, old Slusher wants to give the niggers a room up stairs with us!'

'With who?' shouted they.

'With us white men.'

'No, blamed if he does!' replied Starkweather.

'We won't stand that!' exclaimed several voices.

'Where's Slusher?' enquired Ben West a discharged stage driver, who hung about the premises, and now figured prominently.

'Here ish me, shendlemans!' answered Slusher, coming from the back part of the house, 'andt you may do as you blese midt tem plack mans, pud iv you dempt puse me, I vill pudt you all out mine housh!'

'The stable, the stable!' they all cried out, 'put the niggers in the stable, and we'll be satisfied!'

'Tare ish mine staple—you may pud tem vare you blese,' replied the old man, 'budt you shandt puse me!'

Securely binding them with cords, they were placed in a strongly built log stable closely weather-boarded, having but a door and window below, the latter being closely secured, and the door locked on the outside with a staple and padlock. The upper windows being well secured, the blacks thus locked in, were left to their fate, whilst their captors comfortably housed, were rioting in triumph through the night, over their misfortune, and blasted prospects for liberty.

XXXII. The Escape

This night the inmates of the tavern revelled with intoxication; all within the building, save the exemplary family of the stern old German, Slusher, who peremptorily refused from first to last, to take any part whatever with them, doubtless, being for the evening the victims of excessive indulgence in the beverage of ardent spirits. Now and again one and another of the numerous crowd gathered from the surrounding neighborhood, increasing as the intelligence spread, went alone to the stable to examine the door, reconnoiter the premises, and ascertain that the prisoners were secure. The company getting in such high glee that, fearing a neglect of duty, it became advisable to appoint for the evening a corps of sentinels whose special duty, according to their own arrangements, should be to watch and guard the captives. This special commission being one of pecuniary consideration, Jim Franey the township constable, the rowdy Ned Bradly, and Ben West the discharged stage-driver, who being about the premises, readily accepted the office, entering immediately on the line of duty.

The guard each alternately every fifteen minutes went out to examine the premises, when one and a half of the clock again brought around the period of Ben West's duty. Familiar with the premises and the arrangements of the stables, taking a lantern, West designed closely to inspect their pinions, that no lack of duty on his part might forfeit his claim to the promised compensation.

When placing them in the stable, lights then being in requisition, Henry discovered in a crevice between the wall and the end of the feed-trough, a common butcher knife used for the purpose of repairing harness. So soon as the parties left the stable, the captives lying with their heads resting on their bundles; Henry arising, took the knife, cutting loose himself and companions, but leaving the pinions still about their limbs as though fastened, resumed his position upon the bundle of straw. The scythe had been carelessly hung on a section of the worm fence adjoining the barn, near the door of the prison department, their weapons having been taken from them.

'Well, boys,' enquired West, holding up the lantern; 'you're all here, I see: do you want anything? Take some whiskey!' holding in his hand a quart bottle.

'The rope's too tight around my ankle!' complained Charles; 'its took all the feeling out of my leg.'

Dropping upon his knees to loosen the cord, at this moment, Henry standing erect brandishing the keen glistening blade of the knife before him—his companions having sprung to their feet—'Don't you breathe!' exclaimed the intrepid unfettered slave; 'or I'll bury the blade deep in your bosom! One hour I'll give you for silence, a breach of which will cost your life.' Taking a tin cup which West brought into the stable, pouring it full to the brim; 'Drink this!' said Henry, compelling the man who was already partially intoxicated, to drink as much as possible, which soon rendered him entirely insensible.

'Come, boys!' exclaimed he, locking the stable, putting the key into his pocket, leaving the intoxicated sentinel prostrated upon the bed of straw intended for them, and leaving the tavern house of the old German Slusher forever behind them.

The next period of watch, West being missed, Ned Bradly, on going to the stable, finding the door locked, reported favorably, supposing it to be still secure. Overton in turn did the same. When drawing near daylight—West still being missed—Franey advised that a search be made for him. The bedrooms, and such places into which he might most probably have retired, were repeatedly searched in vain, as calling at the stable elicited no answer, either from him nor the captives.

The sun was now more than two hours high, and word was received from the village to hasten the criminals in for examination before the magistrate. Determining to break open the door, which being done, Ben West was found outstretched upon the bed of straw, who, with difficulty, was aroused from his stupor. The surprise of the searchers on discovering his condition, was heightened on finding the escape of the fugitives. Disappointment and chagrin now succeeded high hopes and merriment, when a general reaction ran throughout the neighborhood; for the sensation at the escape even became greater than on the instance of the deed of resistance and success of the capture.

Of all the disappointments connected with this affair, there was none to be regretted save that of the old German tavern keeper, Isaac Slusher, who, being the only pecuniary sufferer, the entire crowd revelling at his expense.

'Gonvound dish bishnesh!' exclaimed Slusher with vexation; 'id alwaysh cosht more dan de ding ish wordt. Mine Got! afder dish I'll mindt mine own bishnesh. Iv tem Soudt Amerigans vill gheep niggersh de musht gedch dem demzelve. Mine ligger ish ghon, I losht mine resht, te niggersh rhun avay, un' I nod magk von zent!'

Immediate pursuit was sent out in search of the runaways but without success; for, dashing on, scythe in hand, with daring though peaceable strides through the remainder of the state and that of Michigan, the fugitives reached Detroit without further molestation or question from any source on the right of transit, the inhabitants mistaking them for resident blacks out from their homes in search of employment.

XXXIII. Happy Greeting

After their fortunate escape from the stables of Isaac Slusher in Indiana, Henry and comrades safely landed across the river in Windsor, Essex Co., Canada West, being accompanied by a mulatto gentleman, resident of Detroit, who from the abundance of his generous heart, with others there, ever stands ready and has proven himself an uncompromising, true and tried friend of his race, and every weary traveler on a fugitive slave pilgrimage, passing that way.

'Is dis Canada! is dis de good ole British soil we hear so much 'bout way down in Missierppi?' exclaimed Andy; 'Is dis free groun'? de lan' whar black folks is free! Thang God a mighty for dis privilege!' When he fell upon his hands and knees and kissed the earth.

Poor fellow! he little knew the unnatural feelings and course pursued toward his race by many Canadians, those too pretending to be Englishmen by birth, with some of whom the blacks had fought side by side in the memorable crusade made upon that fairest portion of Her Majesty's Colonial Possessions, by Americans in disguise, calling themselves 'Patriots.' He little knew that while according to fundamental British Law and constitutional rights, all persons are equal in the realm; yet by a systematic course of policy and artifice, his race with few exceptions in some parts, excepting the Eastern Province, is excluded from the enjoyment and practical exercise of every right, except mere suffrage-voting—even to those of sitting on a jury as its own peer, and the exercise of military duty. He little knew the facts, and as little expected to find such a state of things in the long talked of and much loved Canada by the slaves. He knew not that some of high intelligence and educational attainments of his race residing in many parts of the Provinces, were really excluded from and practically denied their rights, and that there was no authority known to the colony, to give redress and make restitution on the petition or application of these representative men of his race, which had frequently been done with the reply from the Canadian functionaries that they had no power to reach their case. It had never entered the mind of poor Andy, that in going to Canada in search of freedom, he was then in a country where privileges were denied him which are common to the slave in every Southern State—the right of going into the gallery of a public building—that a few of the most respectable colored ladies of a town in Kent County, desirous through reverence and respect, to see a British Lord Chief Justice on the Bench of Queen's Court, taking seats in the gallery of the court house assigned to females and other visitors, were ruthlessly taken hold of and shown down the stairway by a man and *officer* of the Court of Queen's Bench for that place. Sad would be to him the fact when he heard, that the construction given by authority to these grievances, when requested to remedy or remove them, was, that they were 'local contingencies to be reached alone by those who inflicted the injuries.' An emotion of unutterable indignation would swell the heart of the determined slave, and almost compel him to curse the country of his adoption. But Andy was free—being on British soil—from the bribes of slave-holding influences; where the unhallowed foot of the slave-catcher dare not tread; where no decrees of an American Congress sanctioned by a President, born and bred in a free state and himself once a poor apprentice boy in a village, could reach.

Thus far, Andy was happy; happy in the success of their escape, the enlarged hopes of future prospects in the industrial pursuits of life; and happy in the contemplation of meeting and seeing Clara.

There were other joys than those of Andy, and other hopes and anticipations to be realised. Charles, Ambrose, and Eli, who, though with hearts overflowing with gratitude, were silent in holy praise to heaven, claimed to have emotions equal to his, and conjugal expectations quite as sacred if not yet as binding.

'The first thing now to be done is to find our people!' said Henry with emotion, after the excess of Andy had ceased.

'Where are they?' inquired the mulatto gentleman; 'and what are their names?'

'Their names at home were Franks' Ailcey, Craig's Polly, and Little Joe, who left several months ago; and an old man and woman called daddy Joe and mammy Judy; a young woman called Clara Beckwith, and a little boy named Tony, who came on but a few days before us.'

'Come with me, and I'll lead you directly to him!' replied the mulatto gentlemen; when taking a vehicle, he drove them to the country a few miles from Windsor, where the parties under feelings such as never had been experienced by them before, fell into the embrace of each other.

'Dar now, dar! wat I tell you? Bless de laud, ef dar ain Chaules an' Henry!' exclaimed mammy Judy clapping her hands, giving vent to tears which stole in drops from the eyes of all. 'My po' chile! My po' Margot!' continued she in pitious tones as the bold and manly leader, pressed closely to his bosom his boy, who now was the image of his mother; 'My son did'n yeh hear nothing bout er? did'n yeh not bring my po' Margot?'

'No, mammy, no! I have not seen and did not bring her! No, mammy, no! But!' When Henry became choked with grief which found an audible response from the heart of every child of sorrow present.

Clara commenced, seconded by Andy and followed by all except him the pierce to whose manly heart had caused it, in tones the most affecting:

'Oh, when shall my sorrow subside!
And when shall my troubles be ended;
And when to the bosom of Christ be conveyed,
To the mansions of joy and bliss!
To the mansions of joy and bliss!'

Falling upon their knees, Andy uttered a most fervent prayer, invoking Heaven's blessings and aid.

'Amen!' responded Charles.

'Hallelujah!' cried Clara clapping her hands.

'Glory, glory, glory!' shouted Ailcey.

'Oh laud! w'en shall I get home!' mourned mammy Judy.

' 'Tis good to be here chilen! 'tis good to be here!' said daddy Joe, rubbing his hands quite wet with tears—when all rising to their feet met each other in the mutual embraces of christian affection, with heaving hearts of sadness.

'We have reason sir,' said Henry addressing himself to the mulatto gentleman who stood a tearful eye witness to the scenes; 'We have reason to thank God from the recesses of our hearts for the providential escape we've made from slavery!' which expression was answered only by trickles down the gentleman's cheeks.

The first care of Henry was to invest a portion of the old people's money by the purchase of fifty acres of land with improvements suitable, and provide for the schooling of the children until he should otherwise order. Charles by appointment in which Henry took part, was chosen leader of the runaway party, Andy being the second, Ambrose and Eli respectively the keepers of their money and accounts, Eli being a good penman.

'Now,' said Henry, after two days rest; 'the time has come and I must leave you! Polly, as you came as the mistress, you must now become the mother and nurse of my poor boy! Take good care of him—Mammy will attend to you. Charles, as you have all secured land close to, I want you to stand by the old people; Andy, you, Ambrose, and Eli, stand by Charles and the girls, and you must succeed, as nothing can separate you; your strength depending upon your remaining together.'

'Henry is yeh guine sho' nuff?' earnestly enquired Andy.

'Yes, I must go!'

'Wait little!' replied Andy, when after speaking aside with Eli and Ambrose, calling the girls they all whispered for sometime together; occasional evidence of seriousness, anxiety, and joy marking their expressions of countenance.

The Provincial regulations requiring a license, or three weeks report to a public congregation, and that many sabbaths from the altar of a place of worship to legalise a marriage, and there being now no time for either of these, the mulatto gentleman who was still with them, being a clergyman, declared, that in this case no such restrictions were binding; being originally intended for the whites and the free, and not for the panting runaway slave.

'Thank God, for that! That's good talk!' said Charles.

'Ef it aint dat, 'taint nothin! Dat's wat I calls good *black* talk!' replied Andy, causing the clergyman and all to look at each other with a smile.

The party gathered standing in a semicircle, the clergyman in the centre; a hymn being sung and prayer offered—rising to their feet, and an exhortation of comfort and encouragement being given, with the fatherly advice and instructions of their domestic guidance in after life by the aged man of God; the sacred and impressively novel words: 'I join you together in the bonds of matrimony!' gave Henry the pleasure before leaving of seeing upon the floor together, Charles and Polly, Andy and Clara, Eli and Ailcey, 'as man and wife forever.'

'Praise God!' exclaimed poor old mammy, whose heart was most tenderly touched by the scene before her, contrasting it by reflection, with the sad reminiscence of her own sorrowful and hopeless union with daddy Joe, with whom she had lived fifty years as happy as was possible for slaves to do.

'Bless de laud!' responded the old man.

The young wives all gave vent to sobs of sympathy and joy, when the parson as a solace sung in touching sentiments:

'Daughters of Zion! awake from thy sadness!
Awake for thy foes shall oppress thee no more.
Bright o'er the hills shines the day star of gladness
Arise! for the night of thy sorrow is o'er;
Daughters of Zion, awake from thy sadness!
Awake for thy foes shall oppress thee no more!'

'O glory!' exclaimed Mammy Judy, when the scene becoming most affecting; hugging his boy closely to his bosom, upon whose little cheeks and lips he impressed kisses long and affectionate, when laying him in the old woman's lap and kissing little Tony, turning to his friends with a voice the tone of which sent through them a thrill, he said:

'By the instincts of a husband, I'll have her if living! If dead, by the impulses of a Heaven inspired soul, I'll avenge her loss unto death! Farwell, farwell!' the tears streaming as he turned from his child and its grand parents; when but a few minutes found the runaway leader, seated in a car at the Windsor depot, from whence he reached the Suspension Bridge at Niagara *en route* for the Atlantic.

Part III
Violence in Fantasy:

THE FICTION OF WILLIAM WELLS BROWN

Men do not love those who remind them of their sins—unless they have a mind to repent—and the mulatto child's face is a standing accusation against him who is master and father to the child. What is still worse, perhaps, such a child is a constant offense to the wife. She hates its very presence, and when a slaveholding woman hates, she wants not means to give that hate telling effect.

Frederick Douglass, *My Bondage and My Freedom*

As I see it, it is through the process of making artistic forms—plays, poems, novels—out of one's experiences that one becomes a writer, and it is through this process, this struggle, that the writer helps give meaning to the experience of the group.

Ralph Ellison, *Shadow & Act*[1]

ART as William Wells Brown defined it for himself had little or no significance unless it was related to life and the struggle for black liberation. As he created his plays, short stories, and novels, Brown drew heavily from his experiences as a slave, protesting against the injustices and barbarities of the peculiar institution. Like Frederick Douglass' *The Heroic Slave* and Martin Delany's *Blake,* Brown's fiction had a definite political purpose. His abolitionism was quite obvious in his art. Commenting on Brown's novel *Clotel; or the President's Daughter* (1853), the Boston *Liberator* pointed out that there was much in it "calculated to intensify the moral indignation of the world against slavery." In a review of Brown's play *The Escape, or a Leap for Freedom* (1858), the Auburn (New York) *Daily Advertiser* praised the drama as "a masterly refutation of all apologies for slavery."[2] But Brown's creative expressions represented more than abolitionist tracts. In a crucial sense, his fiction was profoundly personal: It offered him a way to deal with the painful and vexing dilemmas he had experienced in his past and could not forget after his escape to the North. Thus his life and his fantasy graded into each other in his fiction, and this fusion served a need Brown deeply felt. In his imagination he was able to act out his rage and frustration as well as the violence he wished to bring down on his oppressors.

II

Slavery as William Wells Brown experienced it had a special anguish. His master, Dr. John Young, was his uncle. As a child William learned from his mother, a slave of "mixed blood" herself, that his father was a white man and his master's half brother. Dr. Young himself had admitted to young William that he was a relative and promised that he would not be sold to supply the New Orleans slave market. Consequently William was trained to be an office boy and medical assistant and lived in the big house of his master's plantation in Missouri.[3]

Life in the big house was quite distressing for young William because his mistress, Mrs. Young, hated him. His light skin was a constant and annoying reminder of his relationship to her husband, and his very presence in the household was a source of embarrassment and insult for her. On one occasion, for example, a Major Moore paid a visit during Dr. Young's absence and introduced himself to Mrs. Young. William was about ten years old at the time and was "as white as most white boys." Whenever visitors came to the house, William was required to wear a neat suit and stand behind the lady's chair in the living room. Thinking William was Dr. Young's son, Major Moore said to him: "How do you do, bub?" Then he turned to Mrs. Young and exclaimed: "Madam, I would have known your son if I had met him in Mexico; for he looks so much like his papa." Her face flushed, Mrs. Young replied: "That's one of the niggers, sir," and ordered William to go to the kitchen.4 Mrs. Young was undoubtedly responsible for changing William's name. A nephew named William had been taken into the Young family; thus there were two Williams and both of them were actually nephews. The slave William's name—a name he had had for twelve years—was changed to Sandford. "This, at the time," Brown recalled, "I thought to be one of the most cruel acts that could be committed upon my rights; and I received several very severe whippings for telling people that my name was William, after orders were given to change it." Clearly William was the object of his mistress' scorn. Humiliated at "the idea of having her husband's 'negro relations' in her sight," Mrs. Young often punished William for supposed offenses. Little wonder Brown in his *Narrative* described her as "very peevish and hard to please."5

As a mulatto, William encountered not only the hostility of Mrs. Young but also the resentment of his fellow black slaves. Hence, he was caught in a cross fire between his mistress and the blacks on the plantation. "The nearer a slave approaches an Anglo-Saxon complexion," explained Josephine Brown in her biography of her father, "the more he is abused by both owner and fellow-slaves. The owner flogs him to keep him 'in his place,' and the slaves hate him on account of his being whiter than themselves. Thus the complexion of the slave becomes a crime, and he is made to curse his father for the Anglo-Saxon blood that courses through his veins." Indeed, after he escaped North, Brown refused to take his father's name. "And as for my father," he bitterly declared, "I would rather have adopted the name of 'Friday,' and had been known as the servant of some Robinson Crusoe, than to have taken his name." Thus, grateful for the help he had received from the kind Quaker Wells Brown during his flight from slavery, he accepted as part of his own the name of his "first white friend" and "adopted father."6

The son of a slave mother and a white father, Brown was anxiously aware of the sexual exploitation of slave women. He saw that women in bondage were the defenseless victims of unrestrained white male sexuality and lust. He never forgot a distressing incident which occurred while he was working as a hired assistant for the slave trader James Walker. One day, while taking a gang of slaves to New Orleans on a steamboat, Walker ordered Brown to put a slave named Cynthia into a stateroom he had provided for her, apart from the other slaves. Cynthia was a quadroon and "one of the most beautiful women" Brown had ever seen, and he "had seen too much of the workings of slavery, not to know what this meant." Listening at the stateroom door, Brown heard Walker offer Cynthia a choice: to become his mistress at his farm in Missouri or to be sold as a field hand on the worst plantation in the Deep South. Afterward Brown tried to give Cynthia words of comfort and encouragement, but he "foresaw but too well what the result must be." She became Walker's mistress. Years later, after Brown had escaped to the North, he learned that Walker had married and "as a previous measure, sold poor Cynthia and her four children . . . into hopeless bondage."7

The degradation of Cynthia illustrated one of the dilemmas Brown faced as a slave. He felt he could do nothing to appease his pent-up rage and defend slave women like Cynthia against lascivious and brutal white men. He could only offer victimized black women mere words of comfort. Or he could withdraw into loneliness and tears, as he had done as a child after he had witnessed the overseer Cook whipping his mother. "I heard her voice," Brown recalled, "and knew it, and jumped out of my bunk, and went to the door." His mother was crying for mercy, "Oh! pray—Oh! pray—Oh! pray." "Though the field was some distance from the house, I could hear every crack of the whip, and every groan and cry of my poor mother. I remained at the door, not daring to venture any farther. The cold chills ran over me, and I wept aloud. After giving her ten lashes, the sound of the whip ceased, and I returned to my bed, and found no consolation but in my tears."8

Young William's fear of white men was reinforced by the breaking of Randall, a proud slave on the Young plantation. A tall and strong man, Randall had declared that "no white man should ever whip him—that he would die first." But Randall's defiant spirit was violently subdued. Overseer Cook with the help of three friends attacked Randall; they shot him, beat him with heavy clubs, and gave him more than a hundred lashes with a cowhide. Then they attached a ball and chain to his leg and forced him to work in the fields as hard as the other slaves.9 Clearly, William could see, the white oppressor had the will and power to inflict cruel and savage punishment on black men who tried to assert themselves or defend black women.

Brown had a cowardly fear of punishment, and on one occasion he used deception against a fellow black to avoid a whipping. He had been ordered to take a note and a dollar to the jailer, and suspecting something was wrong, he asked a sailor to read the note for him. The note instructed the jailer to whip Brown and accept the dollar as payment for the service. Brown knew he had to go to the jailer or suffer worse consequences. While wondering what to do, Brown saw a fellow black about his size and persuaded him to take the note to the jailer. "I told him I had a note to go into the jail, and get a trunk to carry to one of the steamboats; but was so busily engaged that I could not do it, although I had a dollar to pay for it." The black took the note and the dollar and went off to the jail to do the job; at the jail he had the money taken from him and was given twenty lashes. Afterward Brown, with tears running down his cheeks, returned to his master pretending he had been whipped severely.[10]

Brown's fear of punishment and his sense of powerlessness sharpened the frustration and anguish he felt as he saw his sister and mother taken away. Shortly after the incident involving Cynthia, Brown was shocked to learn that his sister had been sold and was to be taken to Mississippi. The moment of their separation was painful for him: It undoubtedly evoked anxious memories. "When I entered the room where she was, she was seated in one corner, alone. There were four other women in the same room, belonging to the same man. He had purchased them, he said, for his own use. . . . She said there was no hope for herself,—that she must live and die a slave." Brown gave his sister some encouragement, just as he had given Cynthia, and then he took a ring from his finger and placed it on hers. "I stood and looked at her. I could not protect her. I could not offer to protect her. I was a slave, and the only testimony that I could give her that I sympathised with her, was to allow the tears to flow freely down my cheeks. . . ."[11] Brown could only cry, as he had done as a terrified child hearing the whip cracking and his mother screaming.

Brown's separation from his mother was even more traumatic. Slavery as Brown experienced it did not destroy the deep and natural bond between mother and child. Sitting on his mother's knee, the child William had heard stories about how his mother had carried him on her back to the fields when he was an infant and how she had been whipped for leaving her work to nurse him. Years later, Brown resolved he would not leave the slave South without his mother. "I thought that to leave her in slavery, after she had undergone and suffered so much for me, would be proving recreant to the duty which I owed her." Thus, after his sister had been taken to Mississippi, Brown and his mother attempted to flee to Canada. After they had successfully crossed the river in a skiff to the Illinois shore, they imagined the happy prospects before them. They were eagerly talking about reaching Canada, earning some money, and buying a little farm, when three men came up on horseback and ordered them to stop. Both fugitives were returned to Missouri. As punishment for running away, Brown's mother was sent to the New Orleans slave market. Feelings of guilt swept over Brown when he saw her for the last time on the steamboat. "I thought myself to blame for her sad condition; for if I had not persuaded her to accompany me, she would not then have been in chains." He watched the boat until it was out of sight and then despondently returned home. "My thoughts were so absorbed in what I had witnessed, that I knew not what I was about half the time. Night came, but it brought no sleep to my eyes."[12]

This was the terrible past Brown carried with him as he made his way northward. The harshness of his white mistress, Mrs. Young, the barbarity of overseer Cook, the sexual passions of slave trader Walker, the cruel separation from his sister and mother remained vivid in his memory. "During the last night that I served in slavery," Brown wrote in his *Narrative,* "I did not close my eyes a single moment. When not thinking of the future, my mind dwelt on the past. . . . I imagined I saw my dear mother in the cotton-field, and no one to speak a consoling word to her! I beheld my dear sister in the hands of a slave-driver, and compelled to submit to his cruelty!"[13] Years after his escape Brown still thought about his past and still remembered his mother and sister in bondage as he wrote his antislavery fiction and worked out his bitterness, frustration, and guilt in his imagination.

III

Brown's need to remember and resolve in his fantasy the travail of his slavery may be seen in his play *The Escape, or a Leap for Freedom*. In this drama, slaves Glen and Melinda, in love with each other, are in a crisis. Slave master Dr. Gaines wants to exploit Melinda sexually, and Mrs. Gaines, aware of her husband's passion for slave women, despises Melinda and demands that her slave competitor be sold and sent away. The crisis has a simple resolution: Glen and Melinda escape to Canada. In *The Escape*, Brown used fiction not only to attack slavery and arouse Northern public opinion against the South but also to dramatize his old personal concerns—the lustfulness of white men, the viciousness of white women, and the powerlessness of black men.

Southern white men as Brown portrayed them in his play are lascivious pursuers of slave women. Evidence of their sexual exploitation of slave women is quite obvious: The mulatto children on the plantation resemble their masters. "Well, now, Squire," slave trader Walker exclaims in a conversation about a mulatto girl, "I thought that was your daughter; she looked mightily like you. She was your daughter, wasn't she? You need not be ashamed to own it to me, for I am mum upon such matters."[14]

But, while white men are "mum upon such matters," white women fully recognize the infidelity and perversity of their husbands, and this knowledge torments and deforms them. Thus, after her marriage, Mrs. Gaines is transformed from a woman of "sweet temper" into a hard and cruel tyrant. Like Mrs. Young, Brown's slaveholding mistress, Mrs. Gaines is embarrassed by the presence of a light-skinned slave child in her household. Sampey's complexion is so light, Brown describes him as "a white slave." On one occasion, a visitor notices Sampey and remarks to Mrs. Gaines: "Madame, I should have known that this was the Colonel's son, if I had met him in California; for he looks so much like his papa." And she quickly replies: "That is one of the niggers, sir." Later Dr. Gaines tells the visitor: "Ha, ha, ha. If you did call him my son, you didn't miss much." Jealous and angry over her husband's interest in Melinda, Mrs. Gaines takes out her hostility on her slaves, scolding and whipping them. Finally her fury and frustration explode as she attacks and attempts to murder Melinda.[15]

One of Brown's great anxieties as a slave was his inability to react violently against his oppressors and defend slave women against lascivious white men. In his play, however, Brown was able to imagine Glen boldly striking Melinda's oppressor, Dr. Gaines. Unlike Brown, Glen acts violently and expresses in his behavior and his words the anger Brown himself had felt as a slave. "I would have killed him," Glen declares. "Oh! there is a volcano pent up in the hearts of the slaves of these Southern states that will burst forth ere long. When that day comes, woe to those whom its unpitying fury may devour!" In order to make his escape to Canada, Glen knocks down the overseer. "I made the wine flow freely," he boasts to Melinda, "yes, I pounded his old skillet well for him, and then jumped out of the window. It was a leap for freedom."[16]

Actually Brown may have identified more closely with Cato than Glen. One of the parallels between Brown and Cato is superficial and explicit: Cato is Dr. Gaines' medical assistant. But the comparison has a deeper level. Cato is highly complicated. Like Brown, he feels his rage but represses it. In one scene, for example, Cato is upset over a tear in his coat and wants to be violent. "Oh, dear me! Oh, my coat—my coat is tore!" Cato screams. "Dat nigger has tore my coat. [*He gets angry, and rushes about the room frantic.*] Cuss dat nigger! Ef I could lay my hands on him, I'd tare him all to pieces,—dat I would." Cato's tantrum then focuses on Dr. Gaines. "An' de ole boss hit me wid his cane after dat nigger tore my coat. By golly I wants to fight somebody. Ef ole massa should come in now, I'd fight him." Dr. Gaines then enters the room and inquires about the noise. Quickly masking his real feelings, Cato meekly replies: "Nuffin', sir; only jess I is puttin' things to rights, as you tole me. I didn't hear any noise except de rats." Like Brown, Cato is trapped in a situation which allows him to have an extremely limited range of ways to behave. Cato knows he must behave submissively or be whipped; but at the same time he desperately wants to assert his true self: "Now, ef I could jess run away from ole massa, an' get to Canada . . . den I'd show 'em who I was." Cato manages to flee to the North, and his escape enables Cato to realize himself. "I wonder," he asks, "ef dis is me? By golly, I is free as a frog. . . . Cato, is dis you? Yes, seer. Well, now it is me, an' I em a free man."[17] His old slavish fears overcome and his docility gone, Cato fights Dr. Gaines in the final scene as he and his fellow fugitives slaves board a ferry departing for Canada.

The Escape, or a Leap for Freedom offered Brown a chance to do in a symbolic way what he had failed to do in his past. As a slave he had wanted to be a man and to protect Cynthia, his sister, and his mother; but at the same time he feared the terrible power of white men to punish and break slaves like Randall. The conflict between his desire to be a man and his desire to avoid punishment and possible death created frustration and guilt. Through Glen and Cato, existing in the fantasy of his fiction, Brown was able to assert his own manhood violently and to protect black women against libidinous white despoilers.

In his novel *Clotelle: A Tale of the Southern States* (the expanded 1864 version of the original work), Brown went far beyond *The Escape* in his effort to create fiction out of the experiences of his past and to construct in his imagination solutions to the predicaments of that past. Much of his novel reminds us of the play. But there is a crucial difference. In his novel, Brown gave greater attention to the anxieties of mulatto and quadroon slaves. Thus, while he merely alluded to Sampey in his play, he devoted most of his novel to Isabella and Clotelle.

Clearly Brown was thinking about Cynthia as he created Isabella. Isabella is a quadroon, and her skin is "as fair as most white women, her features as beautifully regular as any of her sex of pure Anglo-Saxon blood, her long black hair done up in a neat manner, her form tall and graceful, and her whole appearance indicating one superior to her condition."[18] Like Cynthia, Isabella is the victim of white male sexual manipulation: She is master Henry Linwood's mistress and the mother of his child Clotelle.

Due to the lightness of their skin, Isabella and Clotelle experience the torture Brown suffered as a mulatto. They encounter hatred and resentment from both white women and black slaves. Mrs. Miller, the mother-in-law of Henry Linwood, has many of the ugly qualities of Brown's former slaveholding mistress, Mrs. Young. "Mrs. Miller was a woman of little or no feeling, proud, peevish, and passionate, thus making everybody miserable that came near her; and when she disliked any one, her hatred knew no bounds." She is described as "a caged lioness" and "a hard-hearted woman."[19] The reason for her deformity is clear. She is bitter over the debauchery of Southern white men and the infidelity of her own husband, the father of seven mulatto children. Thus, when Mrs. Miller learns about Linwood s interest in Isabella, she is outraged. Clotelle becomes the special target of Mrs. Miller's fury, for the slave child has a very white complexion and resembles her father. To degrade Clotelle and to make her look like the pure-blooded slaves, Mrs. Miller has her servants cut the child's beautiful long hair and forces Clotelle to work in the hot sun in order to brown her skin. This hideous and barbaric process delights the black servants. They enthusiastically cut Clotelle's hair down to the scalp and shout: "Gins to look like a nigger, now." They seem to despise Clotelle and her whiteness almost as much as Mrs. Miller, and one of them declares: "I don't like dese merlatter niggers, no how."[20]

Ultimately, however, Clotelle is redeemed. Her persecutor, Mrs. Miller, becomes an alcoholic and "the most brutal creature that ever lived." "By some means" the bedding in her room catches fire, and she dies in her burning house.[21] Hers is the violent death that Brown may have wished upon his own mistress, Mrs. Young. Clotelle, on the other hand, grows up into a lovely woman, escapes to Europe, and marries Jerome. Her marriage to Jerome is crucial in her redemption. Jerome is "of pure African origin" and "perfectly black." Like Randall, he is proud and brave, determined no master should ever flog him; like Brown, he is enraged because his mother and sister had been torn away from him. Giving honest vent to his anger, he possesses none of the fear that had paralyzed Brown. To his white oppressors, Jerome announces defiantly: "If I mistake not, the day will come when the Negro will learn that he can get his freedom by fighting for it; and should that time arrive, the whites will be sorry that they have hated us so shamefully. I am free to say that, could I live my life over again, I would use all

the energies which God has given me to get up an insurrection."[22] Clotelle's marriage to Jerome implies an endorsement
of revolutionary violence to abolish slavery; moreover, their
union represents a disregard for color. Clotelle makes this clear
when she explains that she married him simply because she
loved him. "Why should the white man be esteemed as better
than the black? I find no difference in men on account of their
complexion. One of the cardinal principles of Christianity and
freedom is the equality and brotherhood of man."[23] Thus the
marriage between black Jerome and almost white Clotelle
signifies much more than a reconciliation between blacks and
mulattoes: Their love transcends the framework of color.

Clotelle's redemption is completed when she and Jerome
accidentally meet Henry Linwood in Europe. Driven close to
the point of madness by feelings of guilt over his daughter's
degradation, Linwood is overjoyed to discover Clotelle is alive
and well. He accepts her as his daughter but regrets she has
married Jerome, a man of such black complexion. But Clotelle's
sincere declaration of her love for Jerome as a person and
Linwood's own associations with Jerome convince the old white
Southerner that prejudice against color is the offspring of
slavery. Thus, in the end, Clotelle has what Brown himself could
not have—the punishment of her tormenter, the resolution of
conflict between blacks and mulattoes, and paternal love and
acceptance.

In his short story "A Thrilling Incident of the War" (1867),
Brown made an even less disguised attempt to resolve in his
fiction the problems of his slave past[24] Here Brown returned to
two of his most distressing concerns as a slave—his sense of
powerlessness and his separation from his sister and mother.

In this story the protagonist is a slave "whose complexion
showed plainly that other than Anglo-Saxon blood coursed
through his veins."[25] His mother is a slave and his father is his
master. Aware of his relationship to her husband and humiliated
by his existence, his slaveholding mistress often punishes him
severely; and his fellow slaves hate him because he is whiter
than themselves. Obviously this imaginary slave is Brown himself. But in the fictional world of "A Thrilling Incident of the
War," Brown imagined himself as a heroic and violent slave.
After the slave's mother is sold and taken away, he defends his

sister from the lustful slave driver. Unlike Brown in reality, the protagonist of the story does not cry when his sister appeals to him for protection. "My tears refused to flow: the fever in my brain dried them up. I could stand it no longer. I seized the wretch by the throat, and hurled him to the ground; and with this strong arm, I paid him for old and new."[26] But the fantasy becomes more involved. The slave runs away and finds refuge, as did Brown, in a home in Ohio and accepts as his own the name of his white friend. The fugitive then goes to Canada but returns to the United States to help suppress the Southern rebellion and fights under General Grant at the battle of Vicksburg. After the battle, as he moves among the newly liberated people, he meets an old woman; and during their conversation, she suddenly bursts out: "You don't mean to say dat you is William?"

IV

The Civil War was a time of great illusion. It gave Brown hope the redemption he had imagined in his fiction would happen in reality. The violence of black soldiers, he thought, assured the realization of this redemption. At Milliken's Bend, Fort Wagner, Port Hudson, and Honey Hill, black soldiers had proven their manhood and had given whites reason to abandon their old notions of black servility. The battle of Milliken's Bend "satisfied the slave masters of the South," Brown pointed out, "that their charm was gone; and that the negro, as a slave, was lost forever . . . no negro was ever found alive that was taken prisoner by the rebels in this fight." More important, black soldiers had fought for the freedom of their relatives still in bondage and had settled with the "ole boss" for a long score of cruelty.[28] Black soldiers were doing what Brown himself had not done as a slave: They were behaving like the imaginary Glen and Jerome, risking their lives, and fighting against their oppressors.

Surely Brown had reason for optimism. At a celebration of the first anniversary of the Emancipation Proclamation, he confidently claimed that the war marked the beginning of a new history for the race, the beginning of an assimilated America.

"This rebellion will extinguish slavery in our land, and the Negro is henceforth and forever to be part of the nation. His blood is to mingle with that of his former oppressor, and the two races blended in one will make a more peaceful, hardy, powerful, and intellectual race, than America has ever seen before." In his historical survey *The Rising Son; Or, The Antecedents and Advancements of the Colored Race* (1874), Brown echoed his earlier optimism about the future of the black in America. "The close of the Rebellion," he proclaimed, "opened to the Negro a new era in his history. The chains of slavery had been severed; and although he had not been clothed with all the powers of the citizen, the black man was, nevertheless, sure of all his rights being granted, for revolutions seldom go backward."[29]

But no real revolution had occurred, and redemption had taken place only in Brown's fantasy. Brown sensed this and in his final years he became profoundly discouraged and bitter. In *My Southern Home,* published four years before he died in 1884, he charged that whites were as vicious and violent as they had always been. They had forced blacks into peonage, kept them illiterate, and disfranchised them. The lynchings of hundreds of blacks symbolized the virulence of Southern racism. "The infliction of the death punishment, by 'Lynch Law,' on colored persons for the slightest offence," Brown protested, "proves that there is really no abatement in this hideous race prejudice that prevails throughout the South." He blamed the blacks themselves for much of their degradation: They had not been aggressive and violent enough in their resistance against oppression. "The efforts made by oppressed nations, or communities to throw off their chains, entitles them to, and gains for them the respect of mankind. This, the blacks never made, or what they did, was so feeble as scarcely to call for comment." Even the "good service" of black soldiers during the Civil War had limited significance, for "it would have been far better if they had commenced earlier, or had been under leaders of their own color." Convinced that blacks, if they remained in the South, would be doomed to a bleak and hopeless destiny, Brown cried out his final solution to the race problem: "Black men, emigrate."[30]

Unlike Brown's novel, reality did not have a happy ending.

There had been no reconstruction of white Southerners and no reunion between white fathers and their mulatto sons and daughters. The Clotelles and Jeromes of the real world did not experience the brotherhood and Christian spirit Brown had imagined. White Southerners of the postbellum years did not behave like Henry Linwood and did not give up their prejudices once the institution of slavery had been destroyed. The racial reconciliation in Brown's novel, like the amazing meeting between mother and son in "A Thrilling Incident of the War," remained fantasy.

The utter failure to make life resemble his art left Brown feeling dejected and depressed. Like Douglass and Delany, he had discovered in the writing of fiction a way to deal with the problems of oppression. But literary creativity had unique significance for Brown: He was an artist involved in political action, and his art was his primary political expression. Douglass and Delany, on the other hand, were political activists rather than artists: The writing of fiction was something momentary for them. Brown had invested his identity in art, but his fiction neither changed nor reflected racial power realities. Consequently his fiction, while affording him temporary psychic relief, led ultimately to greater despair. Sadly Brown realized that events did not happen the way he had wished or fantasized they would happen in his fiction as he withdrew into thoughts on emigration and as he reflected on the reality around him and the redemption impinging on but never entering into history.

FOOTNOTES

1. Frederick Douglass, *My Bondage and My Freedom* (New York, Dover, 1969), p. 59; Ralph Ellison, *Shadow & Act* (New York, New American Library, 1964), p. 150.
2. Boston *Liberator*, February 3, 1854; Auburn *Daily Advertiser*, quoted in Appendix, William Wells Brown, *The Escape, or a Leap for Freedom* (Boston, R. F. Wallcutt, 1858), p. 52.
3. William Wells Brown, *The American Fugitive in Europe . . . with a Memoir* (New York, Negro University Press, 1969), originally published in 1855, pp. 9-10; William Wells Brown, *Narrative of William Wells Brown*, republished in Gilbert Osofsky, *Puttin' On Ole Massa* (New York, Harper & Row, 1969), pp. 179, 180, 203, 208; William Wells Brown, *The Black Man, His Antecedents, His Genius, and His Achievement* (Boston, R. F. Wallcutt, 1865), p. 11; William Edward Farrison, *William Wells Brown, Author and Reformer* (Chicago, University of Chicago, 1969), pp. 5, 24; Josephine Brown, *Biography of an American Bondman, by His Daughter* (Boston, R. F. Wallcutt, 1856), p. 6.
4. William Wells Brown, *The Negro in the American Rebellion: His Heroism and His Fidelity* (New York, Johnson Reprint Corp., 1968), originally published in 1867, pp. 363-64.
5. Brown, *Narrative*, pp. 189, 190, 217; Josephine Brown, *Biography*, p. 10.
6. Josephine Brown, *Biography*, pp. 10-11; William Wells Brown, *Three Years in Europe* (London, Gilpin, 1852), pp. 274-75; Brown, *Narrative*, pp. 175, 218, 225.
7. Brown, *Narrative*, pp. 185, 194-95; see also Brown, in New York *National Anti-Slavery Standard*, May 26, 1860; Brown, *A Lecture delivered before the Female Anti-Slavery Society of Salem* (Boston, 1847), p. 6.
8. Brown, *Narrative*, p. 180.
9. *Ibid.*, p. 182.
10. *Ibid.*, pp. 198-200.
11. *Ibid.*, pp. 202-4; see also Brown, *Lecture . . . Female Anti-Slavery Society*, pp. 20-21.
12. Brown, *Narrative*, pp. 187-88, 204-15.
13. *Ibid.*, p. 215.
14. Brown, *The Escape, or A Leap for Freedom* (Boston, R. F. Wallcutt, 1858), pp. 18-19.
15. *Ibid.*, pp. 5, 31, 37.
16. *Ibid.*, p. 31.
17. *Ibid.*, pp. 10, 27, 44, 49.
18. Brown, *Clotelle*, text, p. 235.
19. *Ibid.*, p. 262.
20. *Ibid.*, pp. 271, 272.
21. *Ibid.*, p. 337.
22. *Ibid.*, p. 294.
23. *Ibid.*, p. 338.
24. Brown, "A Thrilling Incident of the War," in *The Negro in the American Rebellion*, pp. 283-90.
25. *Ibid.*, p. 284.
26. *Ibid.*, p. 258.
27. *Ibid.*, p. 289.
28. Brown, *The Negro in the American Rebellion*, pp. 137, 157.

29. Brown, quoted in Farrison, *William Wells Brown,* p. 385; Brown, *The Rising Son; Or, The Antecedents and Advancement of the Colored Race* (Boston, A. G. Brown & Co., 1874), pp. 381, 389, 413-14; Brown, in Boston *Liberator,* June 5, 1863.
30. Brown, *My Southern Home* (Boston, A. G. Brown, 1880), pp. 219-25, 243-48.

Clotelle: A Tale of the Southern States

BY W. W. BROWN

Chapter I

The Slave's Social Circle

With the growing population in the Southern States, the increase of mulattoes has been very great. Society does not frown upon the man who sits with his half-white child upon his knee whilst the mother stands, a slave, behind his chair. In nearly all the cities and towns of the Slave States, the real negro, or clear black, does not amount to more than one in four of the slave population. This fact is of itself the best evidence of the degraded and immoral condition of the relation of master and slave. Throughout the Southern States, there is a class of slaves who, in most of the towns, are permitted to hire their time from their owners, and who are always expected to pay a high price. This class is the mulatto women, distinguished for their fascinating beauty. The handsomest of these usually pay the greatest amount for their time. Many of these women are the favorites of men of property and standing, who furnish them with the means of compensating their owners, and not a few are dressed in the most extravagant manner.

When we take into consideration the fact that no safeguard is thrown around virtue, and no inducement held out to slave-women to be pure and chaste, we will not be surprised when told that immorality and vice pervade the cities and towns of the South to an extent unknown in the Northern States. Indeed, many of the slave-women have no higher aspiration than that of becoming the finely-dressed mistress of some white man. At negro balls and parties, this class of women usually make the most splendid appearance, and are eagerly sought after in the dance, or to entertain in the drawing-room or at the table.

A few years ago, among the many slave-women in Richmond, Virginia, who hired their time of their masters, was Agnes, a mulatto owned by John Graves, Esq., and who might be heard boasting that she was the daughter of an American Senator. Although nearly forty years of age at the time of which we write, Agnes was still exceedingly handsome. More than half white, with long black hair and deep blue eyes, no one felt like disputing with her when she urged her claim to her relationship with the Anglo-Saxon.

In her younger days, Agnes had been a housekeeper for a young slaveholder, and in sustaining this relation had become the mother of two daughters. After being cast aside by this young man, the slave-woman betook herself to the business of a laundress, and was considered to be the most tasteful woman in Richmond at her vocation.

Isabella and Marion, the two daughters of Agnes, resided with their mother, and gave her what aid they could in her business. The mother, however, was very choice of her daughters, and would allow them to perform no labor that would militate against their lady-like appearance. Agnes early resolved to bring up her daughters as ladies, as she termed it.

As the girls grew older, the mother had to pay a stipulated price for them per month. Her notoriety as a laundress of the first class enabled her to put an extra charge upon the linen that passed through her hands; and although she imposed little or no work upon her daughters, she was enabled to live in comparative luxury and have her daughters dressed to attract attention, especially at the negro balls and parties.

Although the term "negro ball" is applied to these gatherings, yet a large portion of the men who attend them are whites. Negro balls and parties in the Southern States, especially in the cities and towns, are usually made up of quadroon women, a few negro men, and any number of white gentlemen. These are gatherings of the most democratic character. Bankers, merchants, lawyers, doctors, and their clerks and students, all take part in these social assemblies upon terms of perfect equality. The father and son not unfrequently meet and dance *vis a vis* at a negro ball.

It was at one of these parties that Henry Linwood, the son of a wealthy and retired gentleman of Richmond, was first introduced to Isabella, the oldest daughter of Agnes. The young man had just returned from Harvard College, where he had spent the previous five years. Isabella was in her eighteenth year, and was admitted by all who knew her to be the handsomest girl, colored or white, in the city. On this occasion, she was attired in a sky-blue silk dress, with deep black lace flounces, and bertha of the same. On her well-moulded arms she wore massive gold bracelets, while her rich black hair was arranged at the back in broad basket plaits, ornamented with pearls, and the front in the French style (*a la Imperatrice*), which suited her classic face to perfection.

Marion was scarcely less richly dressed than her sister.

Henry Linwood paid great attention to Isabella, which was looked upon with gratification by her mother, and became a matter of general conversation with all present. Of course, the young man escorted the beautiful quadroon home that evening, and became the favorite visitor at the house of Agnes.

It was on a beautiful moonlight night in the month of August, when all who reside in tropical climates are eagerly gasping for a breath of fresh air, that Henry Linwood was in the garden which surrounded Agnes' cottage, with the young quadroon by his side. He drew from his pocket a newspaper wet from the press, and read the following advertisement:—

NOTICE.—Seventy-nine negroes will be offered for sale on Monday, September 10, at 12 o'clock, being the entire stock of the late John Graves. The negroes are in an excellent condition, and all warranted against the common vices. Among them are several mechanics, able-bodied field-hands, plough-boys, and women with children, some of them very prolific, affording a rare opportunity for any one who wishes to raise a strong and healthy lot of servants for their own use. Also several mulatto girls of rare personal qualities,—two of these very superior.

Among the above slaves advertised for sale were Agnes and her two daughters. Ere young Linwood left the quadroon that evening, he promised her that he would become her purchaser, and make her free and her own mistress.

Mr. Graves had long been considered not only an excellent and upright citizen of the first standing among the whites, but even the slaves regarded him as one of the kindest of masters. Having inherited his slaves with the rest of his property, he became possessed of them without any consultation or wish of his own. He would neither buy nor sell slaves, and was exceedingly careful, in letting them out, that they did not find oppressive and tyrannical masters. No slave speculator ever dared to cross the threshold of this planter of the Old Dominion. He was a constant attendant upon religious worship, and was noted for his general benevolence. The American Bible Society, the American Tract Society, and the cause of Foreign Missions, found in him a liberal friend. He was always anxious that his slaves should appear well on the Sabbath, and have an opportunity of hearing the word of God.

Chapter II

The Negro Sale

As might have been expected, the day of sale brought an unusually large number together to compete for the property to be sold. Farmers, who make a business of raising slaves for the market, were there, and slave-traders, who make a business of buying human beings in the slave-raising States and taking them to the far South, were also in attendance. Men and women, too, who wished to purchase for their own use, had found their way to the slave sale.

In the midst of the throng was one who felt a deeper interest in the result of the sale than any other of the bystanders. This was young Linwood. True to his promise, he was there with a blank bank-check in his pocket, awaiting with impatience to enter the list as a bidder for the beautiful slave.

It was indeed a heart-rending scene to witness the lamentations of these slaves, all of whom had grown up together on the old homestead of Mr. Graves, and who had been treated with great kindness by that gentleman, during his life. Now they were to be separated, and form new relations and companions. Such is the precarious condition of the slave. Even when with a good master, there is no certainty of his happiness in the future.

The less valuable slaves were first placed upon the auction-block, one after another, and sold to the highest bidder. Husbands and wives were separated with a degree of indifference that is unknown in any other relation in life. Brothers and sisters were torn from each other, and mothers saw their children for the last time on earth.

It was late in the day, and when the greatest number of persons were thought to be present, when Agnes and her daughters were brought out to the place of sale. The mother was first put upon the auction-block, and sold to a noted negro trader named Jennings. Marion was next ordered to ascend the stand, which she did with a trembling step, and was sold for $1200.

All eyes were now turned on Isabella, as she was led forward by the auctioneer. The appearance of the handsome quadroon caused a deep sensation among the crowd. There she stood, with a skin as fair as most white women, her features as beautifully regular as any of her sex of pure Anglo-Saxon blood, her long black hair done up in the neatest manner, her form tall and graceful, and her whole appearance indicating one superior to her condition.

The auctioneer commenced by saying that Miss Isabella was fit to deck the drawing-room of the finest mansion in Virginia.

"How much, gentlemen, for this real Albino!—fit fancy-girl for any one! She enjoys good health, and has a sweet temper. How much do you say?"

"Five hundred dollars."

"Only five hundred for such a girl as this? Gentlemen, she is worth a deal more than that sum. You certainly do not know the value of the article you are bidding on. Here, gentlemen, I hold in my hand a paper certifying that she has a good moral character."

"Seven hundred."

"Ah, gentlemen, that is something like. This paper also states that she is very intelligent."

"Eight hundred."

"She was first sprinkled, then immersed, and is now warranted to be a devoted Christian, and perfectly trustworthy."

"Nine hundred dollars."

"Nine hundred and fifty."

"One thousand."

"Eleven hundred."

Here the bidding came to a dead stand. The auctioneer stopped, looked around, and began in a rough manner to relate some anecdote connected with the sale of slaves, which he said had come under his own observation.

At this juncture the scene was indeed a most striking one. The laughing, joking, swearing, smoking, spitting, and talking, kept up a continual hum and confusion among the crowd, while the slave-girl stood with tearful eyes, looking alternately at her mother and sister and toward the young man whom she hoped would become her purchaser.

"The chastity of this girl," now continued the auctioneer, "is pure. She has never been from under her mother's care. She is virtuous, and as gentle as a dove."

The bids here took a fresh start, and went on until $1800 was reached. The auctioneer once more resorted to his jokes, and concluded by assuring the company that Isabella was not only pious, but that she could make an excellent prayer.

"Nineteen hundred dollars."

"Two thousand."

This was the last bid, and the quadroon girl was struck off, and became the property of Henry Linwood.

This was a Virginia slave-auction, at which the bones, sinews, blood, and nerves of a young girl of eighteen were sold for $500; her moral character for $200; her superior intellect for $100; the benefits supposed to accrue from her having been sprinkled and immersed, together with a warranty of her devoted Christianity, for $300; her ability to make a good prayer for $200; and her chastity for $700 more. This, too, in a city thronged with churches, whose tall spires look like so many signals pointing to heaven, but whose ministers preach that slavery is a God-ordained institution!

The slaves were speedily separated, and taken along by their respective masters. Jennings, the slave-speculator, who had purchased Agnes and her daughter Marion, with several of the other slaves, took them to the county prison, where he usually kept his human cattle after purchasing them, previous to starting for the New Orleans market.

Linwood had already provided a place for Isabella, to which she was taken. The most trying moment for her was when she took leave of her mother and sister. The "Good-by" of the slave is unlike that of any other class in the community. It is indeed a farewell forever. With tears streaming down their cheeks, they embraced and commended each other to God, who is no respecter of persons, and before whom master and slave must one day appear.

Chapter III

The Slave-Speculator

Dick Jennings the slave-speculator, was one of the few Northern men, who go to the South and throw aside their honest mode of obtaining a living and resort to trading in human beings. A more repulsive-looking person could scarcely be found in any community of bad looking men. Tall, lean and lank, with high cheek-bones, face much pitted with the small-pox, gray eyes with red eyebrows, and sandy whiskers, he indeed stood alone without mate or fellow in looks. Jennings prided himself upon what he called his goodness of heart, and was always speaking of his humanity. As many of the slaves whom he intended taking to the New Orleans market had been raised in Richmond, and had relations there, he determined to leave the city early in the morning, so as not to witness any of the scenes so common on the departure of a slave-gang to the far South. In this, he was most successful; for not even Isabella, who had called at the prison several times to see her mother and sister, was aware of the time that they were to leave.

The slave-trader started at early dawn, and was beyond the confines of the city long before the citizens were out of their beds. As a slave regards a life on the sugar, cotton, or rice plantation as even worse than death, they are ever on the watch for an opportunity to escape. The trader, aware of this, secures his victims in chains before he sets out on his journey. On this occasion, Jennings had the men chained in pairs, while the women were allowed to go unfastened, but were closely watched.

After a march of eight days, the company arrived on the banks of the Ohio River, where they took a steamer for the place of their destination. Jennings had already advertised in the New Orleans papers, that he would be there with a prime lot of able-bodied slaves, men and women, fit for field-service, with a few extra ones calculated for house-servants,—all between the ages of fifteen and twenty-five years; but like most men who make a business of speculating in human beings, he often bought many who were far advanced in years, and would try to pass them off for five or six years younger than they were. Few persons can arrive at anything approaching the real age of the negro, by mere observation, unless they are well acquainted with the race. Therefore, the slave-trader frequently carried out the deception with perfect impunity.

After the steamer had left the wharf and was fairly out on the bosom of the broad Mississippi, the speculator called his servant Pompey to him; and instructed him as to getting the negroes ready for market. Among the forty slaves that the trader had on this occasion, were some whose appearance indicated that they had seen some years and had gone through considerable service. Their gray hair and whiskers at once pronounced them to be above the ages set down in the trader's advertisement. Pompey had long been with Jennings, and understood his business well, and if he did not take delight in the discharge of his duty, he did it at least with a degree of alacrity, so that he might receive the approbation of his master.

Pomp, as he was usually called by the trader, was of real negro blood, and would often say, when alluding to himself, "Dis nigger am no counterfeit, he is de ginuine artikle. Dis chile is none of your haf-and-haf, dere is no bogus about him."

Pompey was of low stature, round face, and, like most of his race, had a set of teeth, which, for whiteness and beauty, could not be surpassed; his eyes were large, lips thick, and hair short and woolly. Pompey had been with Jennings so long, and had seen so much of buying and selling of his fellow-creatures, that he appeared perfectly indifferent to the heart-rending scenes which daily occurred in his presence. Such is the force of habit:—

> "Vice is a monster of such frightful mien,
> That to be hated, needs but to be seen;
> But seen too oft, familiar with its face,
> We first endure, then pity, then embrace."

It was on the second day of the steamer's voyage, that Pompey selected five of the oldest slaves, took them into a room by themselves, and commenced preparing them for the market.

"Now," said he, addressing himself to the company, "I is de chap dat is to get you ready for de Orleans market, so dat you will bring marser a good price. How old is you?" addressing himself to a man not less than forty.

"If I live to see next sweet-potato-digging time, I shall be either forty or forty-five, I don't know which."

"Dat may be," replied Pompey; "but now you is only thirty years old,—dat's what marser says you is to be."

"I know I is more den dat," responded the man.

"I can't help nuffin' about dat," returned Pompey; "but when you get into de market and any one ax you how old you is, and you tell um you is forty or forty-five, marser will tie you up and cut you all to pieces. But if you tell um dat you is only thirty, den he won't. Now remember dat you is thirty years old and no more."

"Well den, I guess I will only be thirty when dey ax me."

"What's your name?" said Pompey, addressing himself to another.

"Jeems."

"Oh! Uncle Jim, is it?"

"Yes."

"Den you must have all them gray whiskers shaved off, and all dem gray hairs plucked out of your head." This was all said by

Pompey in a manner which showed that he knew what he was about.

"How old is you?" asked Pompey of a tall, strong-looking man. "What's your name?"

"I am twenty-nine years old, and my name is Tobias, but they calls me Toby."

"Well, Toby, or Mr. Tobias, if dat will suit you better, you are now twenty-three years old; dat's all,—do you understand dat?"

"Yes," replied Toby.

Pompey now gave them all to understand how old they were to be when asked by persons who were likely to purchase, and then went and reported to his master that the old boys were all right.

"Be sure," said Jennings, "that the niggers don't forget what you have taught them, for our luck this time in the market depends upon their appearance. If any of them have so many gray hairs that you cannot pluck them out, take the blacking and brush, and go at them."

Chapter IV

The Boat-Race

At eight o'clock, on the evening of the third day of the passage, the lights of another steamer were seen in the distance, and apparently coming up very fast. This was the signal for a general commotion on board the Patriot, and everything indicated that a steamboat-race was at hand. Nothing can exceed the excitement attendant upon the racing of steamers on the Mississippi.

By the time the boats had reached Memphis they were side by side, and each exerting itself to get in advance of the other. The night was clear, the moon shining brightly, and the boats so near to each other that the passengers were within speaking distance. On board the Patriot the firemen were using oil, lard, butter, and even bacon, with wood, for the purpose of raising the steam to its highest pitch. The blaze mingled with the black smoke that issued from the pipes of the other boat, which showed that she also was burning something more combustible than wood.

The firemen of both boats, who were slaves, were singing songs such as can only be heard on board a Southern steamer. The boats now came abreast of each other, and nearer and nearer, until they were locked so that men could pass from one to the other. The wildest excitement prevailed among the men employed on the steamers, in which the passengers freely participated.

The Patriot now stopped to take in passengers, but still no steam was permitted to escape. On the starting of the boat again, cold water was forced into the boilers by the feed-pumps, and, as might have been expected, one of the boilers exploded with terrific force, carrying away the boiler-deck and tearing to pieces much of the machinery. One dense fog of steam filled every part of the vessel, while shrieks, groans, and cries were heard on every side. Men were running hither and thither looking for their wives, and women were flying about in the wildest confusion seeking for their husbands. Dismay appeared on every countenance.

The saloons and cabins soon looked more like hospitals than anything else; but by this time the Patriot had drifted to the shore, and the other steamer had come alongside to render assistance to the disabled boat. The killed and wounded (nineteen in number) were put on shore, and the Patriot, taken in tow by the Washington, was once more on her journey.

It was half-past twelve, and the passengers, instead of retiring to their berths, once more assembled at the gambling-tables. The practice of gambling on the western waters has long been a source of annoyance to the more moral persons who travel on our great rivers. Thousands of dollars often change owners during a passage from St. Louis or Louisville to New Orleans, on a Mississippi steamer. Many men are completely ruined on such occasions, and duels are often the consequence.

"Go call my boy, steward," said Mr. Jones, as he took his cards one by one from the table.

In a few minutes a fine-looking, bright-eyed mulatto boy, apparently about sixteen years of age, was standing by his master's side at the table.

"I am broke, all but my boy," said Jones, as he ran his fingers through his cards; "but he is worth a thousand dollars, and I will bet the half of him."

"I will call you," said Thompson, as he laid five hundred dollars at the feet of the boy, who was standing on the table, and at the same time throwing down his cards before his adversary.

"You have beaten me," said Jones; and a roar of laughter followed from the other gentleman as poor Joe stepped down from the table.

"Well, I suppose I owe you half the nigger," said Thompson, as he took hold of Joe and began examining his limbs.

"Yes," replied Jones, "he is half yours. Let me have five hundred dollars, and I will give you a bill of sale of the boy."

"Go back to your bed," said Thompson to his chattel, "and remember that you now belong to me."

The poor slave wiped the tears from his eyes, as, in obedience, he turned to leave the table.

"My father gave me that boy," said Jones, as he took the money, "and I hope, Mr. Thompson, that you will allow me to redeem him."

"Most certainly, sir," replied Thompson. "Whenever you hand over the cool thousand the negro is yours."

Next morning, as the passengers were assembling in the cabin and on deck, and while the slaves were running about waiting on or looking for their masters, poor Joe was seen entering his new master's stateroom, boots in hand.

"Who do you belong to?" inquired a gentleman of an old negro, who passed along leading a fine Newfoundland dog which he had been feeding.

"When I went to sleep las' night," replied the slave, "I 'longed to Massa Carr; but he bin gamblin' all night, an' I don't know who I 'longs to dis mornin'."

Such is the uncertainty of a slave's life. He goes to bed at night the pampered servant of his young master, with whom he has played in childhood, and who would not see his slave abused under any consideration, and gets up in the morning the property of a man whom he has never before seen.

To behold five or six tables in the saloon of a steamer, with half a dozen men playing cards at each, with money, pistols, and bowie-knives spread in splendid confusion before them, is an ordinary thing on the Mississippi River.

Chapter V

The Young Mother

On the fourth morning, the Patriot landed at Grand Gulf, a beautiful town on the left bank of the Mississippi. Among the numerous passengers who came on board at Rodney was another slave-trader, with nine human chattels which he was conveying to the Southern market. The passengers, both ladies and gentlemen, were startled at seeing among the new lot of slaves a woman so white as not to be distinguishable from the other white women on board. She had in her arms a child so white that no one would suppose a drop of African blood flowed through its blue veins.

No one could behold that mother with her helpless babe, without feeling that God would punish the oppressor. There she sat, with an expressive and intellectual forehead, and a countenance full of dignity and heroism, her dark golden locks rolled back from her almost snow-white forehead and floating over her swelling bosom. The tears that stood in her mild blue eyes showed that she was brooding over sorrows and wrongs that filled her bleeding heart.

The hearts of the passers-by grew softer, while gazing upon that young mother as she pressed sweet kisses on the sad, smiling lips of the infant that lay in her lap. The small, dimpled hands of the innocent creature were slyly hid in the warm bosom on which the little one nestled. The blood of some proud Southerner, no doubt, flowed through the veins of that child.

When the boat arrived at Natchez, a rather good-looking, genteel-appearing man came on board to purchase a servant. This individual introduced himself to Jennings as the Rev. James Wilson. The slave-trader conducted the preacher to the deck-cabin, where he kept his slaves, and the man of God, after having some questions answered, selected Agnes as the one best suited to his service.

It seemed as if poor Marion's heart would break when she found that she was to be separated from her mother. The preacher, however, appeared to be but little moved by their sorrow, and took his newly-purchased victim on shore. Agnes begged him to buy her daughter, but he refused, on the ground that he had no use for her.

During the remainder of the passage, Marion wept bitterly.

After a run of a few hours, the boat stopped at Baton Rouge, where an additional number of passengers were taken on board, among whom were a number of persons who had been attending the races at that place. Gambling and drinking were now the order of the day.

The next morning, at ten o'clock, the boat arrived at New Orleans, where the passengers went to their hotels and homes, and the negroes to the slave-pens.

Lizzie, the white slave-mother, of whom we have already spoken, created as much of a sensation by the fairness of her complexion and the alabaster whiteness of her child, when being conveyed on shore at New Orleans, as she had done when brought on board at Grand Gulf. Every one that saw her felt that slavery in the Southern States was not confined to the negro. Many had been taught to think that slavery was a benefit rather than an injury, and those who were not opposed to the institution before, now felt that if whites were to become its victims, it was time at least that some security should be thrown around the Anglo-Saxon to save him from this servile and degraded position.

Chapter VI

The Slave-Market

Nor far from Canal Street, in the city of New Orleans, stands a large two-story, flat building, surrounded by a stone wall some twelve feet high, the top of which is covered with bits of glass, and so constructed as to prevent even the possibility of any one's passing over it without sustaining great injury. Many of the rooms in this building resemble the cells of a prison, and in a small apartment near the "office" are to be seen any number of iron collars, hobbles, handcuffs, thumbscrews, cowhides, chains, gags, and yokes.

A back-yard, enclosed by a high wall, looks something like the playground attached to one of our large New England schools, in which are rows of benches and swings. Attached to the back premises is a good-sized kitchen, where, at the time of which we write, two old negresses were at work, stewing, boiling, and baking, and occasionally wiping the perspiration from their furrowed and swarthy brows.

The slave-trader, Jennings, on his arrival at New Orleans, took up his quarters here with his gang of human cattle, and the morning after, at 10 o'clock, they were exhibited for sale. First of all came the beautiful Marion, whose pale countenance and dejected look told how many sad hours she had passed since parting with her mother at Natchez. There, too, was a poor woman who had been separated from her husband; and another woman, whose looks and manners were expressive of deep anguish, sat by her side. There was "Uncle Jeems," with his whiskers off, his face shaven clean, and the gray hairs plucked out, ready to be sold for ten years younger than he was. Toby was also there, with his face shaven and greased, ready for inspection.

The examination commenced, and was carried on in such a manner as to shock the feelings of any one not entirely devoid of the milk of human kindness.

"What are you wiping your eyes for?" inquired a fat, red-faced man, with a white hat set on one side of his head and a cigar in his mouth, of a woman who sat on one of the benches.

"Because I left my man behind."

"Oh, if I buy you, I will furnish you with a better man than you left. I've got lots of young bucks on my farm."

"I don't want and never will have another man," replied the woman.

"What's your name?" asked a man in a straw hat of a tall negro who stood with his arms folded across his breast, leaning against the wall.

"My name is Aaron, sar."

"How old are you?"

"Twenty-five."

"Where were you raised?"

"In ole Virginny, sar."

"How many men have owned you?"

"Four."

"Do you enjoy good health?"

"Yes, sar."

"How long did you live with your first owner?"

"Twenty years."

"Did you ever run away?"

"No, sar."

"Did you ever strike your master?"

"No, sar."

"Were you ever whipped much?"

"No, sar; I s'pose I didn't desarve it, sar."

"How long did you live with your second master?"

"Ten years, sar."

"Have you a good appetite?"

"Yes, sar."

"Can you eat your allowance?"

"Yes, sar,—when I can get it."

"Where were you employed in Virginia?"

"I worked de tobacker fiel'."

"In the tobacco field, eh?"

"Yes, sar."

"How old did you say you was?"

"Twenty-five, sar, nex' sweet-'tater-diggin' time."

"I am a cotton-planter, and if I buy you, you will have to work in the cotton-field. My men pick one hundred and fifty pounds a day, and the women one hundred and forty pounds; and those who fail to perform their task receive five stripes for each pound that is wanting. Now, do you think you could keep up with the rest of the hands?"

"I don't know, sar, but I 'specs I'd have to."

"How long did you live with your third master?"

"Three years, sar."

"Why, that makes you thirty-three. I thought you told me you were only twenty-five?"

Aaron now looked first at the planter, then at the trader, and seemed perfectly bewildered. He had forgotten the lesson given him by Pompey relative to his age; and the planter's circuitous questions—doubtless to find out the slave's real age—had thrown the negro off his guard.

"I must see your back, so as to know how much you have been whipped, before I think of buying."

Pompey, who had been standing by during the examination, thought that his services were now required, and, stepping forth with a degree of officiousness, said to Aaron,—

"Don't you hear de gemman tell you he wants to 'zamin you. Cum, unharness yo'seff, ole boy, and don't be standin' dar."

Aaron was soon examined, and pronounced "sound;" yet the conflicting statement about his age was not satisfactory.

Fortunately for Marion, she was spared the pain of undergoing such an examination. Mr. Cardney, a teller in one of the banks, had just been married, and wanted a maid-servant for his wife, and, passing through the market in the early part of the day, was pleased with the young slave's appearance, and his dwelling the quadroon found a much better home than often falls to the lot of a slave sold in the New Orleans market.

Chapter VII

The Slave-Holding Parson

The Rev. James Wilson was a native of the State of Connecticut, where he was educated for the ministry in the Methodist persuasion. His father was a strict follower of John Wesley, and spared no pains in his son's education, with the hope that he would one day be as renowned as the leader of his sect. James had scarcely finished his education at New Haven, when he was invited by an uncle, then on a visit to his father, to spend a few months at Natchez in Mississippi. Young Wilson accepted his uncle's invitation, and accompanied him to the South. Few young men, and especially clergymen, going fresh from college to the South, but are looked upon as geniuses in a small way, and who are not invited to all the parties in the neighborhood. Mr. Wilson was not an exception to this rule. The society into which he was thrown, on his arrival at Natchez, was too brilliant for him not to be captivated by it, and, as might have been expected, he succeeded in captivating a plantation with seventy slaves if not the heart of the lady to whom it belonged.

Added to this, he became a popular preacher, and had a large congregation with a snug salary. Like other planters, Mr. Wilson confided the care of his farm to Ned Huckelby, an overseer of high reputation in his way.

The Poplar Farm, as it was called, was situated in a beautiful valley, nine miles from Natchez, and near the Mississippi River. The once unshorn face of nature had given way, and the farm now blossomed with a splendid harvest. The neat cottage stood in a grove, where Lombardy poplars lift their tops almost to prop the skies, where the willow, locust, and horse-chestnut trees spread forth their branches, and flowers never ceased to blossom.

This was the parson's country residence, where the family spent only two months during the year. His town residence was a fine villa, seated on the brow of a hill, at the edge of the city.

It was in the kitchen of this house that Agnes found her new home. Mr. Wilson was every inch a democrat, and early resolved that "his people," as he called his slaves, should be well-fed and not over-worked, and therefore laid down the law and gospel to the overseer as well as to the slaves. "It is my wish," said he to Mr. Carlingham, an old school-fellow who was spending a few days with him,—"It is my wish that a new system be adopted on the plantations in this State. I believe that the sons of Ham should have the gospel, and I intend that mine shall have it. The gospel is calculated to make mankind better and none should be without it."

"What say you," said Carlingham, "about the right of man to his liberty?"

"Now, Carlingham, you have begun to harp again about men's rights. I really wish that you could see this matter as I do."

"I regret that I cannot see eye to eye with you," said Carlingham. "I am a disciple of Rousseau, and have for years made the rights of man my study, and I must confess to you that I see no difference between white and black, as it regards liberty."

"Now, my dear Carlingham, would you really have the negroes enjoy the same rights as ourselves?"

"I would most certainly. Look at our great Declaration of Independence! look even at the Constitution of our own Connecticut, and see what is said in these about liberty."

"I regard all this talk about rights as mere humbug. The Bible is older than the Declaration of Independence, and there I take my stand."

A long discussion followed, in which both gentlemen put forth their peculiar ideas with much warmth of feeling.

During this conversation, there was another person in the room, seated by the window, who, although at work, embroidering a fine collar, paid minute attention to what was said. This was Georgiana, the only daughter of the parson, who had but just returned from Connecticut, where she had finished her education. She had had the opportunity of contrasting the spirit of Christianity and liberty in New England with that of slavery in her native State, and had learned to feel deeply for the injured negro.

Georgiana was in her nineteenth year, and had been much benefited by her residence of five years at the North. Her form was tall and graceful, her features regular and well-defined, and her complexion was illuminated by the freshness of youth, beauty, and health.

The daughter differed from both the father and visitor upon the subject which they had been discussing; and as soon as an opportunity offered, she gave it as her opinion that the Bible was both the bulwark of Christianity and of liberty. With a smile she said,—

"Of course, papa will overlook my difference with him, for although I am a native of the South, I am by education and sympathy a Northerner."

Mr. Wilson laughed, appearing rather pleased than otherwise at the manner in which his daughter had expressed herself. From this Georgiana took courage and continued,—

" 'Thou shalt love thy neighbor as thyself.' This single passage of Scripture should cause us to have respect for the rights of the slave. True Christian love is of an enlarged and disinterested nature. It loves all who love the Lord Jesus Christ in sincerity, without regard to color or condition."

"Georgiana, my dear, you are an abolitionist,—your talk is

fanaticism!" said Mr. Wilson, in rather a sharp tone; but the subdued look of the girl and the presence of Carlingham caused him to soften his language.

Mr. Wilson having lost his wife by consumption, and Georgiana being his only child, he loved her too dearly to say more, even if he felt disposed. A silence followed this exhortation from the young Christian, but her remarks had done a noble work. The father's heart was touched, and the sceptic, for the first time, was viewing Christianity in its true light.

Chapter VIII

A Night in the Parson's Kitchen

Besides Agnes, whom Mr. Wilson had purchased from the slave-trader, Jennings, he kept a number of house-servants. The chief one of these was Sam, who must be regarded as second only to the parson himself. If a dinner-party was in contemplation, or any company was to be invited, after all the arrangements had been talked over by the minister and his daughter, Sam was sure to be consulted on the subject by "Miss Georgy," as Miss Wilson was called by all the servants. If furniture, crockery, or anything was to be purchased, Sam felt that he had been slighted if his opinion was not asked. As to the marketing, he did it all. He sat at the head of the servants' table in the kitchen, and was master of the ceremonies. A single look from him was enough to silence any conversation or noise among the servants in the kitchen or in any other part of the premises.

There is in the Southern States a great amount of prejudice in regard to color, even among the negroes themselves. The nearer the negro or mulatto approaches to the white, the more he seems to feel his superiority over those of a darker hue. This is no doubt the result of the prejudice that exists on the part of the whites against both the mulattoes and the blacks.

Sam was originally from Kentucky, and through the instrumentality of one of his young masters, whom he had to take to school, he had learned to read so as to be well understood, and, owing to that fact, was considered a prodigy, not only among his own master's slaves, but also among those of the town who knew him. Sam had a great wish to follow in the footsteps of his master and be a poet, and was therefore often heard singing doggerels of his own composition.

But there was one drawback to Sam, and that was his color. He was one of the blackest of his race. This he evidently regarded as a great misfortune; but he endeavored to make up for it in dress. Mr. Wilson kept his house-servants well dressed, and as for Sam, he was seldom seen except in a ruffled shirt. Indeed, the washerwoman feared him more than any one else in the house.

Agnes had been inaugurated chief of the kitchen department, and had a general supervision of the household affairs. Alfred, the coachman, Peter, and Hetty made up the remainder of the house-servants. Besides these, Mr. Wilson owned eight slaves who were masons. These worked in the city. Being mechanics, they were let out to greater advantage than to keep them on the farm.

Every Sunday evening, Mr. Wilson's servants, including the brick-layers, assembled in the kitchen, where the events of the week were fully discussed and commented upon. It was on a Sunday evening, in the month of June, that there was a party at Mr. Wilson's house, and, according to custom in the Southern States, the ladies had their maid-servants with them. Tea had been served in "the house," and the servants, including the strangers, had taken their seats at the table in the kitchen. Sam, being a "single gentleman," was unusually attentive to the "ladies" on this occasion. He seldom let a day pass without spending an hour or two in combing and brushing his "har." He had an idea that fresh butter was better for his hair than any other kind of grease, and therefore on churning days half a pound of butter had always to be taken out before it was salted. When he wished to appear to great advantage, he would grease his face to make it "shiny." Therefore, on the evening of the party, when all the servants were at the table, Sam cut a big figure. There he sat, with his wool well combed and buttered, face nicely greased, and his ruffles extending five or six inches from his bosom. The parson in his drawing-room did not make a more imposing appearance than did his servant on this occasion.

"I jis bin had my fortune tole last Sunday night," said Sam, while helping one of the girls.

"Indeed!" cried half a dozen voices.

"Yes," continued he; "Aunt Winny tole me I's to hab de prettiest yallah gal in de town, and dat I's to be free!"

All eyes were immediately turned toward Sally Johnson, who was seated near Sam.

"I 'specs I see somebody blush at dat remark," said Alfred.

"Pass dem pancakes an' 'lasses up dis way, Mr. Alf., and none ob your 'sinuwashuns here," rejoined Sam.

"Dat reminds me," said Agnes, "dat Dorcas Simpson is gwine to git married."

"Who to, I want to know?" inquired Peter.

"To one of Mr. Darby's field-hands," answered Agnes.

"I should tink dat gal wouldn't frow herseff away in dat ar way," said Sally. "She's good lookin' 'nough to git a house-servant, and not hab to put up wid a field-nigger."

"Yes," said Sam, "dat's a werry unsensible remark ob yourn, Miss Sally. I admires your judgment werry much, I 'sures you. Dar's plenty ob susceptible an' well-dressed house-serbants dat a gal ob her looks can git widout takin' up wid dem common darkies."

The evening's entertainment concluded by Sam's relating a little of his own experience while with his first master, in old Kentucky. This master was a doctor, and had a large practice among his neighbors, doctoring both masters and slaves. When Sam was about fifteen years old, his master set him to grinding up ointment and making pills. As the young student grew older and became more practised in his profession, his services were of more importance to the doctor. The physician having a good business, and a large number of his patients being slaves,—the most of whom had to call on the doctor when ill,—he put Sam to bleeding, pulling teeth, and administering medicine to the slaves. Sam soon acquired the name among the slaves of the "Black Doctor." With this appellation he was delighted; and no regular physician could have put on more airs than did the black doctor when his services were required. In bleeding, he must have more bandages, and would rub and smack the arm more than the doctor would have thought of.

Sam was once seen taking out a tooth for one of his patients, and nothing appeared more amusing. He got the poor fellow down on his back, and then getting astride of his chest, he applied the turnkeys and pulled away for dear life. Unfortunately, he had got hold of the wrong tooth, and the poor man screamed as loud as he could; but it was to no purpose, for Sam had him fast, and after a pretty severe tussle out came the sound grinder. The young doctor now saw his mistake, but consoled himself with the thought that as the wrong tooth was out of the way, there was more room to get at the right one.

Bleeding and a dose of calomel were always considered indispensable by the "old boss," and as a matter of course, Sam followed in his footsteps.

On one occasion the old doctor was ill himself, so as to be unable to attend to his patients. A slave, with pass in hand, called to receive medical advice, and the master told Sam to examine him and see what he wanted. This delighted him beyond measure, for although he had been acting his part in the way of giving out medicine as the master ordered it, he had never been called upon by the latter to examine a patient, and this seemed to convince him after all that he was no sham doctor. As might have been expected, he cut a rare figure in his first examination. Placing himself directly opposite his patient, and folding his arms across his breast, looking very knowingly, he began,—

"What's de matter wid you?"

"I is sick."

"Where is you sick?"

"Here," replied the man, putting his hand upon his stomach.

"Put out your tongue," continued the doctor.

The man ran out his tongue at full length.

"Let me feel your pulse;" at the same time taking his patient's hand in his, and placing his fingers upon his pulse, he said,—

"Ah! your case is a bad one; ef I don't do something for you, and dat pretty quick, you'll be a gone coon, and dat's sartin."

At this the man appeared frightened, and inquired what was the matter with him, in answer to which Sam said,—

"I done told dat your case is a bad one, and dat's enuff."

On Sam's returning to his master's bedside, the latter said,—

"Well, Sam, what do you think is the matter with him?"

"His stomach is out ob order, sar," he replied.

"What do you think had better be done for him?"

"I tink I'd better bleed him and gib him a dose ob calomel," returned Sam.

So, to the latter's gratification, the master let him have his own way.

On one occasion, when making pills and ointment, Sam made a great mistake. He got the preparations for both mixed together, so that he could not legitimately make either. But fearing that if he threw the stuff away, his master would flog him, and being afraid to inform his superior of the mistake, he resolved to make the whole batch of pill and ointment stuff into pills. He well knew that the powder over the pills would hide the inside, and the fact that most persons shut their eyes when taking such medicine led the young doctor to feel that all would be right in the end. Therefore Sam made his pills, boxed them up, put on the labels, and placed them in a conspicuous position on one of the shelves.

Sam felt a degree of anxiety about his pills, however. It was a strange mixture, and he was not certain whether it would kill or cure; but he was willing that it should be tried. At last the young doctor had his vanity gratified. Col. Tallen, one of Dr. Saxondale's patients, drove up one morning, and Sam as usual ran out to the gate to hold the colonel's horse.

"Call your master," said the colonel; "I will not get out."

The doctor was soon beside the carriage, and inquired about the health of his patient. After a little consultation, the doctor returned to his office, took down a box of Sam's new pills, and returned to the carriage.

"Take two of these every morning and night," said the doctor, "and if you don't feel relieved, double the dose."

"Good gracious," exclaimed Sam in an undertone, when he heard his master tell the colonel how to take the pills.

It was several days before Sam could learn the result of his new medicine. One afternoon, about a fortnight after the colonel's visit, Sam saw his master's patient riding up to the gate on horseback. The doctor happened to be in the yard, and met the colonel and said,—

"How are you now?"

"I am entirely recovered," replied the patient. "Those pills of yours put me on my feet the next day."

"I knew they would, " rejoined the doctor.

Sam was near enough to hear the conversation, and was delighted beyond description. The negro immediately ran into the kitchen, amongst his companions, and commenced dancing.

"What de matter wid you?" inquired the cook.

"I is de greatest doctor in dis country," replied Sam. "Ef you ever get sick, call on me. No matter what ails you, I is de man dat can cure you in no time. If you do hab de backache, de rheumatics, de headache, de coller morbus, fits, er any ting else, Sam is de gentleman dat can put you on your feet wid his pills."

For a long time after, Sam did little else than boast of his skill as a doctor.

We have said that the "black doctor" was full of wit and good sense. Indeed, in that respect, he had scarcely an equal in the neighborhood. Although his master resided some little distance out of the city, Sam was always the first man in all the negro balls and parties in town. When his master could give him a pass, he went, and when he did not give him one, he would steal away after his master had retired, and run the risk of being taken up by the night-watch. Of course, the master never knew anything of the absence of the servant at night without permission. As the negroes at these parties tried to excel each other in the way of dress, Sam was often at a loss to make that appearance that his heart desired, but his ready wit ever helped him in this. When his master had retired to bed at night, it was the duty of Sam to put out the lights, and take out with him his master's clothes and boots, and leave them in the office until morning, and then black the boots, brush the clothes, and return them to his master's room.

Having resolved to attend a dress-ball one night, without his master's permission, and being perplexed for suitable garments, Sam determined to take his master's. So, dressing himself in the doctor's clothes, even to his boots and hat, off the negro started for the city. Being well acquainted with the usual walk of the patrols he found no difficulty in keeping out of their way. As might have been expected, Sam was the great gun with the ladies that night.

The next morning, Sam was back home long before his master's time for rising, and the clothes were put in their accustomed place. For a long time Sam had no difficulty in attiring himself for parties; but the old proverb that "It is a long lane that has no turning," was verified in the negro's case. One stormy night, when the rain was descending in torrents, the doctor heard a rap at his door. It was customary with him, when called up at night to visit a patient, to ring for Sam. But this time, the servant was nowhere to be found. The doctor struck a light and looked for clothes; they, too, were gone. It was twelve o'clock, and the doctor's clothes, hat, boots, and even his watch, were nowhere to be found. Here was a pretty dilemma for a doctor to be in. It was some time before the physician could fit himself out so as to make the visit. At last, however, he started with one of the farm-horses, for Sam had taken the doctor's best saddle-horse. The doctor felt sure that the negro had robbed him, and was on his way to Canada; but in this he was mistaken. Sam had gone to the city to attend a ball, and had decked himself out in his master's best suit. The physician returned before morning, and again retired to bed but with little hope of sleep, for his thoughts were with his servant and horse. At six o'clock, in walked Sam with his master's clothes, and the boots neatly blacked. The watch was placed on the shelf, and the hat in its place. Sam had not met any of the servants, and was therefore entirely ignorant of what had occurred during his absence.

"What have you been about, sir, and where was you last night when I was called?" said the doctor.

"I don't know, sir. I 'spose I was asleep," replied Sam.

But the doctor was not to be so easily satisfied, after having been put to so much trouble in hunting up another suit without the aid of Sam. After breakfast, Sam was taken into the barn, tied up, and severely flogged with the cat, which brought from him the truth concerning his absence the previous night. This forever put an end to his fine appearance at the negro parties. Had not the doctor been one of the most indulgent of masters, he would not have escaped with merely a severe whipping.

As a matter of course, Sam had to relate to his companions that evening in Mr. Wilson's kitchen all his adventures as a physician while with his old master.

Chapter IX

The Man of Honor

Augustine Cardinay, the purchaser of Marion, was from the Green Mountains of Vermont, and his feelings were opposed to the holding of slaves; but his young wife persuaded him into the idea that it was no worse to own a slave than to hire one and pay the money to another. Hence it was that he had been induced to purchase Marion.

Adolphus Morton, a young physician from the same State, and who had just commenced the practice of his profession in New Orleans, was boarding with Cardinay when Marion was brought home. The young physician had been in New Orleans but a very few weeks, and had seen but little of slavery. In his own mountain-home, he had been taught that the slaves of the Southern States were negroes, and if not from the coast of Africa, the descendants of those who had been imported. He was unprepared to behold with composure a beautiful white girl of sixteen in the degraded position of a chattel slave.

The blood chilled in his young heart as he heard Cardinay tell how, by bantering with the trader, he had bought her two hundred dollars less than he first asked. His very looks showed that she had the deepest sympathies of his heart.

Marion had been brought up by her mother to look after the domestic concerns of her cottage in Virginia, and well knew how to perform the duties imposed upon her. Mrs. Cardinay was much pleased with her new servant, and often mentioned her good qualities in the presence of Mr. Morton.

After eight months acquaintance with Marion, Morton's sympathies ripened into love, which was most cordially reciprocated by the friendless and inured child of sorrow. There was but one course which the young man could honorably pursue, and that was to purchase Marion and make her his lawful wife; and this he did immediately, for he found Mr. and Mrs. Cardinay willing to second his liberal intentions.

The young man, after purchasing Marion from Cardinay, and marrying her, took lodgings in another part of the city. A private teacher was called in, and the young wife was taught some of those accomplishments so necessary for one taking a high position in good society.

Dr. Morton soon obtained a large and influential practice in his profession, and with it increased in wealth; but with all his wealth he never owned a slave. Probably the fact that he had raised his wife from that condition kept the hydra-headed system continually before him. To the credit of Marion be it said, she used every means to obtain the freedom of her mother, who had been sold to Parson Wilson, at Natchez. Her efforts, however, had come too late; for Agnes had died of a fever before the arrival of Dr. Morton's agent.

Marion found in Adolphus Morton a kind and affectionate husband; and his wish to purchase her mother, although unsuccessful, had doubly endeared him to her. Ere a year had elapsed from the time of their marriage, Mrs. Morton presented her husband with a lovely daughter, who seemed to knit their hearts still closer together. This child they named Jane; and before the expiration of the second year, they were blessed with another daughter, whom they named Adrika.

These children grew up to the ages of ten and eleven, and were then sent to the North to finish their education, and receive that refinement which young ladies cannot obtain in the Slave States.

Chapter X

The Quadroon's Home

A few miles out of Richmond is a pleasant place, with here and there a beautiful cottage surrounded by trees so as scarcely to be seen. Among these was one far retired from the public roads, and almost hidden among the trees. This was the spot that Henry Linwood had selected for Isabella, the eldest daughter of Agnes. The young man hired the house, furnished it, and placed his mistress there, and for many months no one in his father's family knew where he spent his leisure hours.

When Henry was not with her, Isabella employed herself in looking after her little garden and the flowers that grew in front of her cottage. The passion-flower, peony, dahlia, laburnum, and other plants, so abundant in warm climates, under the tasteful hand of Isabella, lavished their beauty upon this retired spot, and miniature paradise.

Although Isabella had been assured by Henry that she should be free and that he would always consider her as his wife, she nevertheless felt that she ought to be married and acknowledged by him. But this was an impossibility under the State laws, even had the young man been disposed to do what was right in the matter. Related as he was, however, to one of the first families in Virginia, he would not have dared to marry a woman of so low an origin, even had the laws been favorable.

Here, in this secluded grove, unvisited by any other except her lover, Isabella lived for years. She had become the mother of a lovely daughter, which its father named Clotelle. The complexion of the child was still fairer than that of its mother. Indeed, she was not darker than other white children, and as she grew older she more and more resembled her father.

As time passed away, Henry became negligent of Isabella and his child, so much so, that days and even weeks passed without their seeing him, or knowing where he was. Becoming more acquainted with the world, and moving continually in the society of young women of his own station, the young man felt that Isabella was a burden to him, and having as some would say, "outgrown his love," he longed to free himself of the responsibility; yet every time he saw the child, he felt that he owed it his fatherly care.

Henry had now entered into political life, and been elected to a seat in the legislature of his native State; and in his intercourse with his friends had become acquainted with Gertrude Miller, the daughter of a wealthy gentleman living near Richmond. Both Henry and Gertrude were very good-looking, and a mutual attachment sprang up between them.

Instead of finding fault with the unfrequent visits of Henry, Isabella always met him with a smile, and tried to make both him and herself believe that business was the cause of his negligence. When he was with her, she devoted every moment of her time to him, and never failed to speak of the growth and increasing intelligence of Clotelle.

The child had grown so large as to be able to follow its father on his departure out to the road. But the impression made on

Henry's feelings by the devoted woman and her child was momentary. His heart had grown hard, and his acts were guided by no fixed principle. Henry and Gertrude had been married nearly two years before Isabella knew anything of the event, and it was merely by accident that she became acquainted with the facts.

One beautiful afternoon, when Isabella and Clotelle were picking wild strawberries some two miles from their home, and near the road-side, they observed a one-horse chaise driving past. The mother turned her face from the carriage not wishing to be seen by strangers, little dreaming that the chaise contained Henry and his wife. The child, however, watched the chaise, and startled her mother by screaming out at the top of her voice, "Papa! papa!" and clapped her little hands for joy. The mother turned in haste to look at the strangers, and her eyes encountered those of Henry's pale and dejected countenance. Gertrude's eyes were on the child. The swiftness with which Henry drove by could not hide from his wife the striking resemblance of the child to himself. The young wife had heard the child exclaim "Papa! papa!" and she immediately saw by the quivering of his lips and the agitation depicted in his countenance, that all was not right.

"Who is that woman? and why did that child call you papa?" she inquired, with a trembling voice.

Henry was silent; he knew not what to say, and without another word passing between them, they drove home.

On reaching her room, Gertrude buried her face in her handkerchief and wept. She loved Henry, and when she had heard from the lips of her companions how their husbands had proved false, she felt that he was an exception, and fervently thanked God that she had been so blessed.

When Gertrude retired to her bed that night, the sad scene of the day followed her. The beauty of Isabella, with her flowing curls, and the look of the child, so much resembling the man whom she so dearly loved, could not be forgotten; and little Clotelle's exclamation of "Papa! papa!" rang in her ears during the whole night.

The return of Henry at twelve o'clock did not increase her happiness. Feeling his guilt, he had absented himself from the house since his return from the ride.

Chapter XI

To-day a Mistress, To-morrow a Slave

The night was dark, the rain descended in torrents from the black and overhanging clouds, and the thunder, accompanied with vivid flashes of lightning, resounded fearfully, as Henry Linwood stepped from his chaise and entered Isabella's cottage.

More than a fortnight had elapsed since the accidental meeting, and Isabella was in doubt as to who the lady was that Henry was with in the carriage. Little, however, did she think that it was his wife. With a smile, Isabella met the young man as he entered her little dwelling. Clotelle had already gone to bed, but her father's voice aroused her from her sleep, and she was soon sitting on his knee.

The pale and agitated countenance of Henry betrayed his uneasiness, but Isabella's mild and laughing allusion to the incident of their meeting him on the day of his pleasure-drive, and her saying, "I presume, dear Henry, that the lady was one of your relatives," led him to believe that she was still in ignorance of his marriage. She was, in fact, ignorant who the lady was who accompanied the man she loved on that eventful day He, aware of this, now acted more like himself, and passed the thing off as a joke. At heart, however, Isabella felt uneasy, and this uneasiness would at times show itself to the young man. At last, and with a great effort, she said,—

"Now, dear Henry, if I am in the way of your future happiness, say so, and I will release you from any promises that you have made me. I know there is no law by which I can hold you, and if there was, I would not resort to it. You are as dear to me as ever, and my thoughts shall always be devoted to you. It would be a great sacrifice for me to give you up to another, but if it be your desire, as great as the sacrifice is, I will make it. Send me and your child into a Free State if we are in your way."

Again and again Linwood assured her that no woman possessed his love but her. Oh, what falsehood and deceit man can put on when dealing with woman's love!

The unabated storm kept Henry from returning home until after the clock had struck two, and as he drew near his residence he saw his wife standing at the window. Giving his horse in charge of the servant who was waiting, he entered the house, and found his wife in tears. Although he had never satisfied Gertrude as to who the quadroon woman and child were, he had kept her comparatively easy by his close attention to her, and by telling her that she was mistaken in regard to the child's calling him "papa." His absence that night, however, without any apparent cause, had again aroused the jealousy of Gertrude; but Henry told her that he had been caught in the rain while out, which prevented his sooner returning, and she, anxious to believe him, received the story as satisfactory.

Somewhat heated with brandy, and wearied with much loss of sleep, Linwood fell into a sound slumber as soon as he retired. Not so with Gertrude. That faithfulness which has ever distinguished her sex, and the anxiety with which she watched all his movements, kept the wife awake while the husband slept. His sleep, though apparently sound, was nevertheless uneasy. Again and again she heard him pronounce the name of Isabella, and more than once she heard him say, "I am not married; I will never marry while you live." Then he would speak the name of Clotelle and say, "My dear child, how I love you!"

After a sleepless night, Gertrude arose from her couch, resolved that she would reveal the whole matter to her mother. Mrs. Miller was a woman of little or no feeling, proud, peevish, and passionate, thus making everybody miserable that came near her; and when she disliked any one, her hatred knew no bounds. This Gertrude knew; and had she not considered it her duty, she would have kept the secret locked in her own heart.

During the day, Mrs. Linwood visited her mother and told her all that had happened. The mother scolded the daughter for not having informed her sooner, and immediately determined to find out who the woman and child were that Gertrude had met on the day of her ride. Three days were spent by Mrs. Miller in this endeavor, but without success.

Four weeks had elapsed, and the storm of the old lady's temper had somewhat subsided, when, one evening, as she was approaching her daughter's residence, she saw Henry walking in the direction of where the quadroon was supposed to reside. Being satisfied that the young man had not seen her, the old woman at once resolved to follow him. Linwood's boots squeaked so loudly that Mrs. Miller had no difficulty in following him without being herself observed.

After a walk of about two miles, the young man turned into a narrow and unfrequented road, and soon entered the cottage occupied by Isabella. It was a fine starlight night, and the moon was just rising when they got to their journey's end. As usual, Isabella met Henry with a smile, and expressed her fears regarding his health.

Hours passed, and still old Mrs. Miller remained near the house, determined to know who lived there. When she undertook to ferret out anything, she bent her whole energies to it. As Michael Angelo, who subjected all things to his pursuit and the idea he had formed of it, painted the crucifixion by the side of a writhing slave and would have broken up the true cross for pencils, so Mrs. Miller would have entered the sepulchre, if she could have done it, in search of an object she wished to find.

The full moon had risen, and was pouring its beams upon surrounding objects as Henry stepped from Isabella's door, and looking at his watch, said,—

"I must go, dear; it is now half-past ten."

Had little Clotelle been awake, she too would have been at the door. As Henry walked to the gate, Isabella followed with her left hand locked in his. Again he looked at his watch, and said,—

"I must go."

"It is more than a year since you staid all night," murmured Isabella, as he folded her convulsively in his arms, and pressed upon her beautiful lips a parting kiss.

He was nearly out of sight when, with bitter sobs, the quadroon retraced her steps to the door of the cottage. Clotelle had in the mean time awoke, and now inquired of her mother how long her father had been gone. At that instant, a knock was heard at the door, and supposing that it was Henry returning for something he had forgotten, as he frequently did, Isabella flew to let him in. To her amazement, however, a strange woman stood in the door.

"Who are you that comes here at this late hour?" demanded the half-frightened Isabella.

Without making any reply, Mrs. Miller pushed the quadroon aside, and entered the house.

"What do you want here?" again demanded Isabella.

"I am in search of you," thundered the maddened Mrs. Miller; but thinking that her object would be better served by seeming to be kind, she assumed a different tone of voice, and began talking in a pleasing manner.

In this way, she succeeded in finding out the connection existing between Linwood and Isabella, and after getting all she could out of the unsuspecting woman, she informed her that the man she so fondly loved had been married for more than two years. Seized with dizziness, the poor, heart-broken woman fainted and fell upon the floor. How long she remained there she could not tell; but when she returned to consciousness, the strange woman was gone, and her child was standing by her side. When she was so far recovered as to regain her feet, Isabella went to the door, and even into the yard, to see if the old woman was not somewhere about.

As she stood there, the full moon cast its bright rays over her whole person, giving her an angelic appearance and imparting to her flowing hair a still more golden hue. Suddenly another change came over her features, and her full red lips trembled as with suppressed emotion. The muscles around her faultless mouth became convulsed, she gasped for breath, and exclaiming, "Is it possible that man can be so false!" again fainted.

Clotelle stood and bathed her mother's temples with cold water until she once more revived.

Although the laws of Virginia forbid the education of slaves, Agnes had nevertheless employed an old free negro to teach her two daughters to read and write. After being separated from her mother and sister, Isabella turned her attention to the subject of Christianity, and received that consolation from the Bible which is never denied to the children of God. This was now her last hope, for her heart was torn with grief and filled with all the bitterness of disappointment.

The night passed away, but without sleep to poor Isabella. At the dawn of day, she tried to make herself believe that the whole of the past night was a dream, and determined to be satisfied with the explanation which Henry should give on his next visit.

Chapter XII

The Mother-in-law

When Henry returned home, he found his wife seated at the window, awaiting his approach. Secret grief was gnawing at her heart. Her sad, pale cheeks and swollen eyes showed too well that agony, far deeper than her speech portrayed, filled her heart. A dull and death-like silence prevailed on his entrance. His pale face and brow, dishevelled hair, and the feeling that he manifested on finding Gertrude still up, told Henry in plainer words than she could have used that his wife was aware that her love had never been held sacred by him. The window-blinds were still unclosed, and the full-orbed moon shed her soft refulgence over the unrivalled scene, and gave it a silvery lustre which sweetly harmonized with the silence of the night. The clock's iron tongue, in a neighboring belfry, proclaimed the hour of twelve, as the truant and unfaithful husband seated himself by the side of his devoted and loving wife, and inquired if she was not well.

"I am, dear Henry," replied Gertrude; "but I fear *you* are not. If well in body, I fear you are not at peace in mind."

"Why?" inquired he.

"Because," she replied, "you are so pale and have such a wild look in your eyes."

Again he protested his innocence, and vowed she was the only woman who had any claim upon his heart. To behold one thus playing upon the feelings of two lovely women is enough to make us feel that evil must at last bring its own punishment.

Henry and Gertrude had scarcely risen from the breakfast-table next morning ere old Mrs. Miller made her appearance. She immediately took her daughter aside, and informed her of her previous night's experience, telling her how she had followed Henry to Isabella's cottage, detailing the interview with the quadroon, and her late return home alone. The old woman urged her daughter to demand that the quadroon and her child be at once sold to the negro speculators and taken out of the State, or that Gertrude herself should separate from Henry.

"Assert your rights, my dear. Let no one share a heart that justly belongs to you," said Mrs. Miller, with her eyes flashing fire. "Don't sleep this night, my child, until that wench has been removed from that cottage; and as for the child, hand that over to me,—I saw at once that it was Henry's."

During these remarks, the old lady was walking up and down the room like a caged lioness. She had learned from Isabella that she had been purchased by Henry, and the innocence of the injured quadroon caused her to acknowledge that he was the father of her child. Few women could have taken such a matter in hand and carried it through with more determination and success than old Mrs. Miller. Completely inured in all the crimes and atrocities connected with the institution of slavery, she was also aware that, to a greater or less extent, the slave women shared with their mistress the affections of their master. This caused her to look with a suspicious eye on every good-looking negro woman that she saw.

While the old woman was thus lecturing her daughter upon her rights and duties, Henry, unaware of what was transpiring, had left the house and gone to his office. As soon as the old woman found that he was gone, she said,—

"I will venture anything that he is on his way to see that wench again. I'll lay my life on it."

The entrance, however, of little Marcus, or Mark, as he was familiarly called, asking for Massa Linwood's blue bag, satisfied her that her son-in-law was at his office. Before the old lady returned home, it was agreed that Gertrude should come to her mother's to tea that evening, and Henry with her, and that Mrs. Miller should there charge the young husband with inconstancy to her daughter, and demand the removal of Isabella.

With this understanding, the old woman retraced her steps to her own dwelling.

Had Mrs. Miller been of a different character and not surrounded by slavery, she could scarcely have been unhappy in such a home as hers. Just at the edge of the city, and sheltered by large poplar-trees was the old homestead in which she resided. There was a splendid orchard in the rear of the house, and the old weather-beaten sweep, with "the moss-covered bucket" at its end, swung majestically over the deep well. The garden was scarcely to be equalled. Its grounds were laid out in excellent taste, and rare exotics in the greenhouse made it still more lovely.

It was a sweet autumn evening, when the air breathed through the fragrant sheaves of grain, and the setting sun, with his golden kisses, burnished the rich clusters of purple grapes, that Henry and Gertrude were seen approaching the house on foot; it was nothing more than a pleasant walk. Oh, how Gertrude's heart beat as she seated herself, on their arrival!

The beautiful parlor, surrounded on all sides with luxury and taste, with the sun creeping through the damask curtains, added a charm to the scene. It was in this room that Gertrude had been introduced to Henry, and the pleasant hours that she had spent there with him rushed unbidden on her memory. It was here that, in former days, her beautiful countenance had made her appearance as fascinating and as lovely as that of Cleopatra's. Her sweet, musical voice might have been heard in every part of the house, occasionally thrilling you with an unexpected touch. How changed the scene! Her pale and wasted features could not be lighted up by any thoughts of the past, and she was sorrowful at heart.

As usual, the servants in the kitchen were in ecstasies at the announcement that "Miss Gerty," as they called their young mistress, was in the house, for they loved her sincerely. Gertrude had saved them from many a flogging, by interceding for them, when her mother was in one of her uncontrollable passions. Dinah, the cook, always expected Miss Gerty to visit the kitchen as soon as she came, and was not a little displeased, on this occasion, at what she considered her young mistress's neglect. Uncle Tony, too, looked regularly for Miss Gerty to visit the green house, and congratulate him on his superiority as a gardener.

When tea was over, Mrs. Miller dismissed the servants from the room, then told her son-in-law what she had witnessed the previous night, and demanded for her daughter that Isabella should be immediately sent out of the State, and to be sure that the thing would be done, she wanted him to give her the power to make such disposition of the woman and child as she should think best. Gertrude was Mrs. Miller's only child, and Henry felt little like displeasing a family upon whose friendship he so much depended, and, no doubt, long wishing to free himself from Isabella, he at once yielded to the demands of his mother-in-law. Mr. Miller was a mere cipher about his premises.

If any one came on business connected with the farm, he would invariably say, "Wait till I see my wife," and the wife's opinion was sure to be law in every case. Bankrupt in character, and debauched in body and mind, with seven mulatto children who claimed him as their father, he was badly prepared to find fault with his son-in-law. It was settled that Mrs. Miller should use her own discretion in removing Isabella from her little cottage, and her future disposition. With this understanding Henry and Gertrude returned home. In the deep recesses of his heart the young man felt that he would like to see his child and its mother once more; but fearing the wrath of his mother-in-law, he did not dare to gratify his inclination. He had not the slightest idea of what would become of them; but he well knew that the old woman would have no mercy on them.

Chapter XIII

A Hard-hearted Woman

With no one but her dear little Clotelle, Isabella passed her weary hours without partaking of either food or drink, hoping that Henry would soon return, and that the strange meeting with the old woman would be cleared up.

While seated in her neat little bedroom with her fevered face buried in her handkerchief, the child ran in and told its mother that a carriage had stopped in front of the house. With a palpitating heart she arose from her seat and went to the door, hoping that it was Henry; but, to her great consternation, the old lady who had paid her such an unceremonious visit on the evening that she had last seen Henry, stepped out of the carriage, accompanied by the slave-trader, Jennings.

Isabella had seen the trader when he purchased her mother and sister, and immediately recognized him. What could these persons want there? thought she. Without any parleying or word of explanation, the two entered the house, leaving the carriage in charge of a servant.

Clotelle ran to her mother, and clung to her dress as if frightened by the strangers.

"She's a fine-looking wench," said the speculator, as he seated himself, unasked, in the rocking-chair; "yet I don't think she is worth the money you ask for her."

"What do you want here?" inquired Isabella, with a quivering voice.

"None of your insolence to me," bawled out the old woman, at the top of her voice; "if you do, I will give you what you deserve so much, my lady,—a good whipping."

In an agony of grief, pale, trembling, and ready to sink to the floor, Isabella was only sustained by the hope that she would be able to save her child. At last, regaining her self-possession, she ordered them both to leave the house. Feeling herself insulted, the old woman seized the tongs that stood by the fire-place, and raised them to strike the quadroon down; but the slave-trader immediately jumped between the women, exclaiming,—

"I won't buy her, Mrs. Miller, if you injure her."

Poor little Clotelle screamed as she saw the strange woman raise the tongs at her mother. With the exception of old Aunt Nancy, a free colored woman, whom Isabella sometimes employed to work for her, the child had never before seen a strange face in her mother's dwelling. Fearing that Isabella would offer some resistance, Mrs. Miller had ordered the overseer of her own farm to follow her; and, just as Jennings had stepped between the two women, Mull, the negro-driver, walked into the room.

"Seize that impudent hussy," said Mrs. Miller to the overseer, "and tie her up this minute, that I may teach her a lesson she won't forget in a hurry."

As she spoke, the old woman's eyes rolled, her lips quivered, and she looked like a very fury.

"I will have nothing to do with her, if you whip her, Mrs. Miller," said the slave-trader. "Niggers ain't worth half so much in the market with their backs newly scarred," continued he, as the overseer commenced his preparations for executing Mrs. Miller's orders.

Clotelle here took her father's walking-stick, which was lying on the back of the sofa where he had left it, and, raising it, said,—

"If you bad people touch my mother, I will strike you."

They looked at the child with astonishment; and her extreme youth, wonderful beauty, and uncommon courage, seemed for a moment to shake their purpose. The manner and language of this child were alike beyond her years, and under other circumstances would have gained for her the approbation of those present.

"Oh, Henry, Henry!" exclaimed Isabella, wringing her hands.

"You need not call on him, hussy; you will never see him again," said Mrs. Miller.

"What! is he dead?" inquired the heart-stricken woman.

It was then that she forgot her own situation, thinking only of the man she loved. Never having been called to endure any kind of abusive treatment, Isabella was not fitted to sustain herself against the brutality of Mrs. Miller, much less the combined ferociousness of the old woman and the overseer too. Suffice it to say, that instead of whipping Isabella, Mrs. Miller transferred her to the negro-speculator, who took her immediately to his slave-pen. The unfeeling old woman would not permit Isabella to take more than a single change of her clothing, remarking to Jennings,—

"I sold you the wench, you know,—not her clothes."

The injured, friendless, and unprotected Isabella fainted as she saw her child struggling to release herself from the arms of old Mrs. Miller, and as the wretch boxed the poor child's ears.

After leaving directions as to how Isabella's furniture and other effects should be disposed of, Mrs. Miller took Clotelle into her carriage and drove home. There was not even color enough about the child to make it appear that a single drop of African blood flowed through its blue veins.

Considerable sensation was created in the kitchen among the servants when the carriage drove up, and Clotelle entered the house.

"Jes' like Massa Henry fur all de worl'," said Dinah, as she caught a glimpse of the child through the window.

"Wondah whose brat dat ar' dat missis bringin' home wid her?" said Jane, as she put the ice in the pitchers for dinner. "I warrant it's some poor white nigger somebody bin givin' her."

The child was white. What should be done to make it look like other negroes, was the question which Mrs. Miller asked herself. The callous-hearted old woman bit her nether lip, as she viewed that child, standing before her, with her long, dark ringlets clustering over her alabaster brow and neck.

"Take this little nigger and cut her hair close to her head," said the mistress to Jane, as the latter answered the bell.

Clotelle screamed, as she felt the scissors grating over her head, and saw those curls that her mother thought so much of falling upon the floor.

A roar of laughter burst from the servants, as Jane led the child through the kitchen, with the hair cut so short that the naked scalp could be plainly seen.

" 'Gins to look like nigger, now," said Dinah, with her mouth upon a grin.

The mistress smiled, as the shorn child reentered the room; but there was something more needed. The child was white, and that was a great objection. However, she hit upon a plan to remedy this which seemed feasible. The day was excessively warm. Not a single cloud floated over the blue vault of heaven; not a breath of wind seemed moving, and the earth was parched by the broiling sun. Even the bees had stopped humming, and the butterflies had hid themselves under the broad leaves of the burdock. Without a morsel of dinner, the poor child was put in the garden, and set to weeding it, her arms, neck, and head completely bare. Unaccustomed to toil, Clotelle wept as she exerted herself in pulling up the weeds. Old Dinah, the cook, was as unfeeling as her mistress, and she was pleased to see the child made to work in the hot sun.

"Dat white nigger'll soon be brack enuff if missis keeps her workin' out dar," she said, as she wiped the perspiration from her sooty brow.

Dinah was the mother of thirteen children, all of whom had been taken from her when young; and this, no doubt, did much to harden her feelings, and make her hate all white persons.

The burning sun poured its rays on the face of the friendless child until she sank down in the corner of the garden, and was actually broiled to sleep.

"Dat little nigger ain't workin' a bit, missus," said Dinah to Mrs. Miller, as the latter entered the kitchen.

"She's lying in the sun seasoning; she will work the better by and by," replied the mistress.

"Dese white niggers always tink dey seff good as white folks," said the cook.

"Yes; but we will teach them better, won't we, Dinah?" rejoined Mrs. Miller.

"Yes, missus," replied Dinah; "I don't like dese merlatter niggers, no how. Dey always want to set dey seff up for sumfin' big." With this remark the old cook gave one of her coarse laughs, and continued: "Missis understands human nature, don't she? Ah! ef she ain't a whole team and de ole gray mare to boot, den Dinah don't know nuffin'.''

Of course, the mistress was out of the kitchen before these last remarks were made.

It was with the deepest humiliation that Henry learned from one of his own slaves the treatment which his child was receiving at the hands of his relentless mother-in-law.

The scorching sun had the desired effect; for in less than a fortnight, Clotelle could scarcely have been recognized as the same child. Often was she seen to weep, and heard to call on her mother.

Mrs. Miller, when at church on Sabbath, usually, on warm days, took Nancy, one of her servants, in her pew, and this girl had to fan her mistress during service. Unaccustomed to such a soft and pleasant seat, the servant would very soon become sleepy and begin to nod. Sometimes she would go fast asleep, which annoyed the mistress exceedingly. But Mrs. Miller had nimble fingers, and on them sharp nails, and, with an energetic pinch upon the bare arms of the poor girl, she would arouse the daughter of Africa from her pleasant dreams. But there was no one of Mrs. Miller's servants who received so much punishment as old Uncle Tony.

Fond of her greenhouse, and often in the garden, she was ever at the old gardener's heels. Uncle Tony was very religious, and, whenever his mistress flogged him, he invariably gave her a religious exhortation. Although unable to read, he, nevertheless, had on his tongue's end portions of Scripture which he could use at any moment. In one end of the greenhouse was Uncle

Tony's sleeping room, and those who happened in that vicinity, between nine and ten at night, could hear the old man offering up his thanksgiving to God for his protection during the day. Uncle Tony, however, took great pride, when he thought that any of the whites were within hearing, to dwell, in his prayer, on his own goodness and the unfitness of others to die. Often was he heard to say, "O Lord, thou knowest that the white folks are not Christians, but the black people are God's own children." But if Tony thought that his old mistress was within the sound of his voice, he launched out into deeper water.

It was, therefore, on a sweet night, when the bright stars were looking out with a joyous sheen, that Mark and two of the other boys passed the greenhouse, and heard Uncle Tony in his devotions.

"Let's have a little fun," said the mischievous Marcus to his young companions. "I will make Uncle Tony believe that I am old mistress, and he'll give us an extra touch in his prayer." Mark immediately commenced talking in a strain of voice resembling, as well as he could, Mrs. Miller, and at once Tony was heard to say in a loud voice, "O Lord, thou knowest that the white people are not fit to die; but, as for old Tony, whenever the angel of the Lord comes, he's ready." At that moment, Mark tapped lightly on the door. "Who's dar?" thundered old Tony. Mark made no reply. The old man commenced and went through with the same remarks addressed to the Lord, when Mark again knocked at the door. "Who dat dar?" asked Uncle Tony, with a somewhat agitated countenance and trembling voice. Still Mark would not reply. Again Tony took up the thread of his discourse, and said, "O Lord, thou knowest as well as I do that dese white folks are not prepared to die, but here is old Tony, when de angel of de Lord comes, he's ready to go to heaven." Mark once more knocked on the door. "Who dat dar?" thundered Tony at the top of his voice.

"De angel of de Lord," replied Mark, in a somewhat suppressed and sepulchral voice.

"What de angel of de Lord want here?" inquired Tony, as if much frightened.

"He's come for poor old Tony, to take him out of the world," replied Mark, in the same strange voice.

"Dat nigger ain't here; he die tree weeks ago," responded

Tony, in a still more agitated and frightened tone. Mark and his companions made the welkin ring with their shouts at the old man's answer. Uncle Tony hearing them, and finding that he had been imposed upon, opened his door, came out with stick in hand, and said, "Is dat you, Mr. Mark? you imp, if I can get to you I'll larn you how to come here wid your nonsense."

Mark and his companions left the garden, feeling satisfied that Uncle Tony was not as ready to go with "de angel of de Lord" as he would have others believe.

Chapter XIV

The Prison

While poor little Clotelle was being kicked about by Mrs. Miller, on account of her relationship to her son-in-law, Isabella was passing lonely hours in the county jail, the place to which Jennings had removed her for safe-keeping, after purchasing her from Mrs. Miller. Incarcerated in one of the iron-barred rooms of that dismal place, those dark, glowing eyes, lofty brow, and graceful form wilted down like a plucked rose under a noonday sun, while deep in her heart's ambrosial cells was the most anguishing distress.

Vulgar curiosity is always in search of its victims, and Jennings' boast that he had such a ladylike and beautiful woman in his possession brought numbers to the prison who begged of the jailer the privilege of seeing the slave-trader's prize. Many who saw her were melted to tears at the pitiful sight, and were struck with admiration at her intelligence; and, when she spoke of her child, they must have been convinced that a mother's sorrow can be conceived by none but a mother's heart. The warbling of birds in the green bowers of bliss, which she occasionally heard, brought no tidings of gladness to her. Their joy fell cold upon her heart, and seemed like bitter mockery. They reminded her of her own cottage, where, with her beloved child, she had spent so many happy days.

The speculator had kept close watch over his valuable piece of property, for fear that it might damage itself. This, however, there was no danger of, for Isabella still hoped and believed that

Henry would come to her rescue. She could not bring herself to believe that he would allow her to be sent away without at least seeing her, and the trader did all he could to keep this idea alive in her.

While Isabella, with a weary heart, was passing sleepless nights thinking only of her daughter and Henry, the latter was seeking relief in that insidious enemy of the human race, the intoxicating cup. His wife did all in her power to make his life a pleasant and a happy one, for Gertrude was devotedly attached to him; but a weary heart gets no gladness out of sunshine. The secret remorse that rankled in his bosom caused him to see all the world blood-shot. He had not visited his mother-in-law since the evening he had given her liberty to use her own discretion as to how Isabella and her child should be disposed of. He feared even to go near the house, for he did not wish to see his child. Gertrude felt this every time he declined accompanying her to her mother's. Possessed of a tender and confiding heart, entirely unlike her mother, she sympathized deeply with her husband. She well knew that all young men in the South, to a greater or less extent, became enamored of the slave-women, and she fancied that his case was only one of the many, and if he had now forsaken all others for her she did not wish for him to be punished; but she dared not let her mother know that such were her feelings. Again and again had she noticed the great resemblance between Clotelle and Henry, and she wished the child in better hands than those of her cruel mother.

At last Gertrude determined to mention the matter to her husband. Consequently, the next morning, when they were seated on the back piazza, and the sun was pouring its splendid rays upon everything around, changing the red tints on the lofty hills in the distance into streaks of purest gold, and nature seeming by her smiles to favor the object, she said,—

"What, dear Henry, do you intend to do with Clotelle?"

A paleness that overspread his countenance, the tears that trickled down his cheeks, the deep emotion that was visible in his face, and the trembling of his voice, showed at once that she had touched a tender chord. Without a single word, he buried his face in his handkerchief, and burst into tears.

This made Gertrude still more unhappy, for she feared that he had misunderstood her; and she immediately expressed her regret that she had mentioned the subject. Becoming satisfied from this that his wife sympathized with him in his unhappy situation, Henry told her of the agony that filled his soul, and Gertrude agreed to intercede for him with her mother for the removal of the child to a boarding-school in one of the Free States.

In the afternoon, when Henry returned from his office, his wife met him with tearful eyes, and informed him that her mother was filled with rage at the mere mention of the removal of Clotelle from her premises.

In the mean time, the slave-trader, Jennings, had started for the South with his gang of human cattle, of whom Isabella was one. Most quadroon women who are taken to the South are either sold to gentlemen for their own use or disposed of as house-servants or waiting-maids. Fortunately for Isabella, she was sold for the latter purpose. Jennings found a purchaser for her in the person of Mr. James French.

Mrs. French was a severe mistress. All who lived with her, though well-dressed, were scantily fed and over-worked. Isabella found her new situation far different from her Virginia cottage-life. She had frequently heard Vicksburg spoken of as a cruel place for slaves, and now she was in a position to test the truthfulness of the assertion.

A few weeks after her arrival, Mrs. French began to show to Isabella that she was anything but a pleasant and agreeable mistress. What social virtues are possible in a society of which injustice is a primary characteristic,—in a society which is divided into two classes, masters and slaves? Every married woman at the South looks upon her husband as unfaithful, and regards every negro woman as a rival.

Isabella had been with her new mistress but a short time when she was ordered to cut off her long and beautiful hair. The negro is naturally fond of dress and outward display. He who has short woolly hair combs and oils it to death; he who has long hair would sooner have his teeth drawn than to part with it. But, however painful it was to Isabella, she was soon seen with her hair cut short, and the sleeves of her dress altered to fit tight to her arms. Even with her hair short and with her ill-looking dress, Isabella was still handsome. Her life had been a secluded one, and though now twenty-eight years of age, her beauty had only assumed a quieter tone. The other servants only laughed at Isabella's misfortune in losing her beautiful hair.

"Miss 'Bell needn't strut so big; she got short nappy har's well's I," said Nell, with a broad grin that showed her teeth.

"She tink she white when she cum here, wid dat long har ob hers," replied Mill.

"Yes," continued Nell, "missus make her take down her wool, so she no put it up to-day."

The fairness of Isabella's complexion was regarded with envy by the servants as well as by the mistress herself. This is one of the hard features of slavery. To-day a woman is mistress of her own cottage; to-morrow she is sold to one who aims to make her life as intolerable as possible. And let it be remembered that the house-servant has the best situation a slave can occupy.

But the degradation and harsh treatment Isabella experienced in her new home was nothing compared to the grief she underwent at being separated from her dear child. Taken from her with scarcely a moment's warning, she knew not what had become of her.

This deep and heartfelt grief of Isabella was soon perceived by her owners, and fearing that her refusal to take proper food would cause her death, they resolved to sell her. Mr. French found no difficulty in securing a purchaser for the quadroon woman, for such are usually the most marketable kind of property. Isabella was sold at private sale to a young man for a housekeeper; but even he had missed his aim.

Mr. Gordon, the new master, was a man of pleasure. He was the owner of a large sugar plantation, which he had left under the charge of an overseer, and was now giving himself up to the pleasures of a city life. At first Mr. Gordon sought to win Isabella's favor by flattery and presents, knowing that whatever he gave her he could take from her again. The poor innocent creature dreaded every moment lest the scene should change. At every interview with Gordon she stoutly maintained that she had left a husband in Virginia, and could never think of taking another. In this she considered that she was truthful, for she had ever regarded Henry as her husband. The gold watch and chain and other glittering presents which Gordon gave to her were all kept unused.

In the same house with Isabella was a man-servant who had

from time to time hired himself from his master. His name was William. He could feel for Isabella, for he, like her, had been separated from near and dear relatives, and he often tried to console the poor woman. One day Isabella observed to him that her hair was growing out again.

"Yes," replied William; "you look a good deal like a man with your short hair."

"Oh," rejoined she, "I have often been told that I would make a better looking man than woman, and if I had the money I might avail myself of it to bid farewell to this place."

In a moment afterwards, Isabella feared that she had said too much, and laughingly observed, "I am always talking some nonsense; you must not heed me."

William was a tall, full-blooded African, whose countenance beamed with intelligence. Being a mechanic, he had by industry earned more money than he had paid to his owner for his time, and this he had laid aside, with the hope that he might some day get enough to purchase his freedom. He had in his chest about a hundred and fifty dollars. His was a heart that felt for others, and he had again and again wiped the tears from his eyes while listening to Isabella's story.

"If she can get free with a little money, why not give her what I have?" thought he, and then resolved to do it.

An hour after, he entered the quadroon's room, and, laying the money in her lap, said,—

"There, Miss Isabella, you said just now that if you had the means you would leave this place. There is money enough to take you to England, where you will be free. You are much fairer than many of the white women of the South, and can easily pass for a free white woman."

At first Isabella thought it was a plan by which the negro wished to try her fidelity to her owner; but she was soon convinced, by his earnest manner and the deep feeling he manifested, that he was entirely sincere.

"I will take the money," said she, "only on one condition, and that is that I effect your escape, as well as my own."

"How can that be done?" he inquired, eagerly.

"I will assume the disguise of a gentleman, and you that of a servant, and we will thus take passage in a steamer to Cincinnati, and from thence to Canada."

With full confidence in Isabella's judgment, William consented at once to the proposition. The clothes were purchased; everything was arranged, and the next night, while Mr. Gordon was on one of his sprees, Isabella, under the assumed name of Mr. Smith, with William in attendance as a servant, took passage for Cincinnati in the steamer Heroine.

With a pair of green glasses over her eyes, in addition to her other disguise, Isabella made quite a gentlemanly appearance. To avoid conversation, however, she kept closely to her state-room, under the plea of illness.

Meanwhile, William was playing his part well with the servants. He was loudly talking of his master's wealth, and nothing on the boat appeared so good as in his master's fine mansion.

"I don't like dese steamboats, no how," said he; "I hope when massa goes on anoder journey, he take de carriage and de hosses."

After a nine-days' passage, the Heroine landed at Cincinnati, and Mr. Smith and his servant walked on shore.

"William, you are now a free man, and can go on to Canada," said Isabella; "I shall go to Virginia, in search of my daughter."

This sudden announcement fell heavily upon William's ears, and with tears he besought her not to jeopardize her liberty in such a manner; but Isabella had made up her mind to rescue her child if possible.

Taking a boat for Wheeling, Isabella was soon on her way to her native State. Several months had elapsed since she left Richmond, and all her thoughts were centred on the fate of her dear Clotelle. It was with a palpitating heart that this injured woman entered the stage-coach at Wheeling and set out for Richmond.

Chapter XV

The Arrest

It was late in the evening when the coach arrived at Richmond, and Isabella once more alighted in her native city. She had intended to seek lodgings somewhere in the outskirts of the town, but the lateness of the hour compelled her to stop at one of the principal hotels for the night. She had scarcely entered the inn before she recognized among the numerous black servants one to whom she was well known, and her only hope was that her disguise would keep her from being discovered. The imperturbable calm and entire forgetfulness of self which induced Isabella to visit a place from which she could scarcely hope to escape, to attempt the rescue of a beloved child, demonstrate that over-willingness of woman to carry out the promptings of the finer feelings of the heart. True to woman's nature, she had risked her own liberty for another's. She remained in the hotel during the night, and the next morning, under the plea of illness, took her breakfast alone.

That day the fugitive slave paid a visit to the suburbs of the town, and once more beheld the cottage in which she had spent so many happy hours. It was winter, and the clematis and passion-flower were not there; but there were the same walks her feet had so often pressed, and the same trees which had so often shaded her as she passed through the garden at the back of the house. Old remembrances rushed upon her memory and caused her to shed tears freely. Isabella was now in her native town, and near her daughter; but how could she communicate with her? how could she see her? To have made herself known would have been a suicidal act; betrayal would have followed, and she arrested. Three days passed away, and still she remained in the hotel at which she had first put up, and yet she got no tidings of her child.

Unfortunately for Isabella, a disturbance had just broken out among the slave population in the State of Virginia, and all strangers were treated with suspicion.

The insurrection to which we now refer was headed by a full-blooded negro, who had been born and brought up a slave. He had heard the crack of the driver's whip, and seen the warm blood streaming from the negro's body. He had witnessed the separation of parents from children, and was made aware, by too many proofs, that the slave could expect no justice from the hands of the slave-owner. The name of this man was Nat Turner. He was a preacher amongst the negroes, distinguished for his eloquence, respected by the whites, loved and venerated by the negroes. On the discovery of the plan for the outbreak, Turner fled to the swamps, followed by those who had joined in the insurrection. Here the revolted negroes numbered some hundreds, and for a time bade defiance to their oppressors. The Dismal Swamps cover many thousand acres of wild land, and a dense forest, with wild animals and insects such as are unknown in any other part of Virginia. Here runaway negroes usually seek a hiding-place, and some have been known to reside here for years. The revolters were joined by one of these. He was a large, tall, full-blooded negro, with a stern and savage countenance; the marks on his face showed that he was from one of the barbarous tribes in Africa, and claimed that country as his native land. His only covering was a girdle around his loins, made of skins of wild beasts which he had killed. His only token of authority among those that he led was a pair of epaulettes, made of the tail of a fox, and tied to his shoulder by a cord. Brought from the coast of Africa, when only fifteen years of age, to the island of Cuba, he was smuggled from thence into Virginia. He had been two years in the swamps, and considered it his future home. He had met a negro woman, who was also a runaway, and, after the fashion of his native land, had gone through the process of oiling her, as the marriage ceremony. They had built a cave on a rising mound in the swamp, and this was their home. This man's name was Picquilo. His only weapon was a sword made from a scythe which he had stolen from a neighboring plantation. His dress, his character, his manners, and his mode of fighting were all in keeping with the early training he had received in the land of his birth. He moved about with the activity of a cat, and neither the thickness of the trees nor the depth of the water could stop him. His was a bold, turbulent spirit; and, from motives of revenge, he imbrued his hands in the blood of all the whites he could meet. Hunger, thirst, and loss of sleep, he seemed made to endure, as if by peculiarity of constitution. His air was fierce, his step oblique, his look sanguinary.

Such was the character of one of the negroes in the Southampton Insurrection. All negroes were arrested who were found beyond their master's threshold, and all white strangers were looked upon with suspicion.

Such was the position in which Isabella found affairs when she returned to Virginia in search of her child. Had not the slave-owners been watchful of strangers, owing to the outbreak, the fugitive could not have escaped the vigilance of the police; for advertisements announcing her escape, and offering a large reward for her arrest, had been received in the city previous to her arrival, and officers were therefore on the lookout for her.

It was on the third day after her arrival in Richmond, as the quadroon was seated in her room at the hotel, still in the disguise of a gentleman, that two of the city officers entered the apartment and informed her that they were authorized to examine all strangers, to assure the authorities that they were not in league with the revolted negroes.

With trembling heart the fugitive handed the key of her trunk to the officers. To their surprise they found nothing but female apparel in the trunk, which raised their curiosity, and caused a further investigation that resulted in the arrest of Isabella as a fugitive slave. She was immediately conveyed to prison, there to await the orders of her master.

For many days, uncheered by the voice of kindness, alone, hopeless, desolate, she waited for the time to arrive when the chains should be placed on her limbs, and she returned to her inhuman and unfeeling owner.

The arrest of the fugitive was announced in all the newspapers, but created little or no sensation. The inhabitants were too much engaged in putting down the revolt among the slaves; and, although all the odds were against the insurgents, the whites found it no easy matter, with all their caution. Every day brought news of fresh outbreaks. Without scruple and without pity, the whites massacred all blacks found beyond the limits of their owners' plantations. The negroes, in return, set fire to houses, and put to death those who attempted to escape from the flames. Thus carnage was added to carnage, and the blood of the whites flowed to avenge the blood of the blacks.

These were the ravages of slavery. No graves were dug for the negroes, but their bodies became food for dogs and vultures; and their bones, partly calcined by the sun, remained scattered about, as if to mark the mournful fury of servitude and lust of power. When the slaves were subdued, except a few in the swamps, bloodhounds were employed to hunt out the remaining revolters.

Chapter XVI

Death is Freedom

On receiving intelligence of the arrest of Isabella, Mr. Gordon authorized the sheriff to sell her to the highest bidder. She was, therefore, sold; the purchaser being the noted negro-trader, Hope H. Slater, who at once placed her in prison. Here the fugitive saw none but slaves like herself, brought in and taken out to be placed in ships, and sent away to some part of the country to which she herself would soon be compelled to go. She had seen or heard nothing of her daughter while in Richmond, and all hopes of seeing her had now fled.

At the dusk of the evening previous to the day when she was to be sent off, as the old prison was being closed for the night, Isabella suddenly darted past the keeper, and ran for her life. It was not a great distance from the prison to the long bridge which passes from the lower part of the city across the Potomac to the extensive forests and woodlands of the celebrated Arlington Heights, then occupied by that distinguished relative and descendant of the immortal Washington, Mr. Geo. W. Custis. Thither the poor fugitive directed her flight. So unexpected was her escape that she had gained several rods the start before the keeper had secured the other prisoners, and rallied his assistants to aid in the pursuit. It was at an hour, and in a part of the city where horses could not easily be obtained for the chase; no bloodhounds were at hand to run down the flying woman, and for once it seemed as if there was to be a fair trial of speed and endurance between the slave and the slave-catchers.

The keeper and his force raised the hue-and-cry on her path as they followed close behind; but so rapid was the flight along the wide avenue that the astonished citizens, as they poured forth from their dwellings to learn the cause of alarm, were only able to comprehend the nature of the case in time to fall in with the motley throng in pursuit, or raise an anxious prayer to heaven as they refused to join in the chase (as many a one did that night) that the panting fugitive might escape, and the merciless soul-dealer for once be disappointed of his prey. And now, with the speed of an arrow, having passed the avenue, with the distance between her and her pursuers constantly increasing, this poor, hunted female gained the "Long Bridge," as it is called, where interruption seemed improbable. Already her heart began to beat high with the hope of success. She had only to pass three-quarters of a mile across the bridge, when she could bury herself in a vast forest, just at the time when the curtain of night would close around her, and protect her from the pursuit of her enemies.

But God, by his providence, had otherwise determined. He had ordained that an appalling tragedy should be enacted that night within plain sight of the President's house, and the Capitol of the Union, which would be an evidence wherever it should be known of the unconquerable love of liberty which the human heart may inherit, as well as a fresh admonition to the slave-dealer of the cruelty and enormity of his crimes.

Just as the pursuers passed the high draw, soon after entering upon the bridge, they beheld three men slowly approaching from the Virginia side. They immediately called to them to arrest the fugitive, proclaiming her a runaway slave. True to their Virginia instincts, as she came near, they formed a line across the narrow bridge to intercept her. Seeing that escape was impossible in that quarter, she stopped suddenly, and turned upon her pursuers.

On came the profane and ribald crew faster than ever, already exulting in her capture, and threatening punishment for her flight. For a moment she looked wildly and anxiously around to see if there was no hope of escape. On either hand, far down below, rolled the deep, foaming waters of the Potomac, and before and behind were the rapidly approaching steps and noisy voices of her pursuers. Seeing how vain would be any further effort to escape, her resolution was instantly taken. She clasped her hands convulsively together, raised her tearful and imploring eyes toward heaven, and begged for the mercy and compassion there which was unjustly denied her on earth; then, exclaiming, "Henry, Clotelle, I die for thee!" with a single bound, vaulted over the railing of the bridge, and sank forever beneath the angry and foaming waters of the river!

Such was the life, and such the death, of a woman whose virtues and goodness of heart would have done honor to one in a higher station of life, and who, had she been born in any other land but that of slavery, would have been respected and beloved. What would have been her feelings if she could have known that the child for whose rescue she had sacrificed herself would one day be free, honored, and loved in another land?

Chapter XVII

Clotelle

The curtain rises seven years after the death of Isabella. During that interval, Henry, finding that nothing could induce his mother-in-law to relinquish her hold on poor little Clotelle, and not liking to contend with one on whom a future fortune depended, gradually lost all interest in the child, and left her to her fate.

Although Mrs. Miller treated Clotelle with a degree of harshness scarcely equalled, when applied to one so tender in years, still the child grew every day more beautiful, and her hair, though kept closely cut, seemed to have improved in its soft, silk-like appearance. Now twelve years of age, and more than usually well-developed, her harsh old mistress began to view her with a jealous eye.

Henry and Gertrude had just returned from Washington, where the husband had been on his duties as a member of Congress, and where he had remained during the preceding three years without returning home. It was on a beautiful evening, just at twilight, while seated at his parlor window, that Henry saw a young woman pass by and go into the kitchen. Not aware of ever having seen the person before, he made an errand into the cook's department to see who the girl was. He, however, met her in the hall, as she was about going out.

"Whom did you wish to see?" he inquired.

"Miss Gertrude," was the reply.

"What did you want to see her for?" he again asked.

"My mistress told me to give her and Master Henry her compliments, and ask them to come over and spend the evening."

"Who is your mistress?" he eagerly inquired.

"Mrs. Miller, sir," responded the girl.

"And what's your name?" asked Henry, with a trembling voice.

"Clotelle, sir," was the reply.

The astonished father stood completely amazed, looking at the now womanly form of her who, in his happier days, he had taken on his knee with so much fondness and alacrity. It was then that he saw his own and Isabella's features combined in the beautiful face that he was then beholding. It was then that he was carried back to the days when with a woman's devotion, poor Isabella hung about his neck and told him how lonely were the hours in his absence. He could stand it no longer. Tears rushed to his eyes, and turning upon his heel, he went back to his own room. It was then that Isabella was revenged; and she no doubt looked smilingly down from her home in the spirit-land on the scene below.

On Gertrude's return from her shopping tour, she found Henry in a melancholy mood, and soon learned its cause. As Gertrude had borne him no children, it was but natural, that he should now feel his love centering in Clotelle, and he now intimated to his wife his determination to remove his daughter from the hands of his mother-in-law.

When this news reached Mrs. Miller, through her daughter, she became furious with rage, and calling Clotelle into her room, stripped her shoulders bare and flogged her in the presence of Gertrude.

It was nearly a week after the poor girl had been so severely whipped and for no cause whatever, that her father learned of the circumstance through one of the servants. With a degree of boldness unusual for him, he immediately went to his mother-in-law and demanded his child. But it was too late,—she was gone. To what place she had been sent no one could tell, and Mrs. Miller refused to give any information whatever relative to the girl.

It was then that Linwood felt deepest the evil of the institution under which he was living; for he knew that his daughter would be exposed to all the vices prevalent in that part of the country where marriage is not recognized in connection with that class.

Chapter XVIII

A Slave-hunting Parson

It was a delightful evening after a cloudless day, with the setting sun reflecting his golden rays on the surrounding hills which were covered with a beautiful greensward, and the luxuriant verdure that forms the constant garb of the tropics, that the steamer Columbia ran into the dock at Natchez, and began unloading the cargo, taking in passengers and making ready to proceed on her voyage to New Orleans. The plank connecting the boat with the shore had scarcely been secured in its place, when a good-looking man about fifty years of age, with a white neck-tie, and a pair of gold-rimmed glasses on, was seen hurrying on board the vessel. Just at that moment could be seen a stout man with his face pitted with the small-pox, making his way up to the above-mentioned gentleman.

"How do you do. my dear sir? this is Mr. Wilson, I believe," said the short man, at the same time taking from his mouth a large chew of tobacco, and throwing it down on the ship's deck.

"You have the advantage of me, sir," replied the tall man.

"Why, don't you know me? My name is Jennings; I sold you a splendid negro woman some years ago."

"Yes, yes," answered the Natchez man. "I remember you now, for the woman died in a few months, and I never got the worth of my money out of her."

"I could not help that," returned the slave-trader, "she was as sound as a roach when I sold her to you."

"Oh, yes," replied the parson, "I know she was; but now I want a young girl, fit for house use,—one that will do to wait on a lady."

"I am your man," said Jennings, "just follow me," continued he, "and I will show you the fairest little critter you ever saw." And the two passed to the stern of the boat to where the trader had between fifty and sixty slaves, the greater portion being women.

"There," said Jennings, as a beautiful young woman shrunk back with modesty. "There, sir, is the very gal that was made for you. If she had been made to your order, she could not have suited you better."

"Indeed, sir, is not that young woman white?" inquired the parson.

"Oh, no, sir; she is no whiter than you see!"

"But is she a slave?" asked the preacher.

"Yes," said the trader, "I bought her in Richmond, and she comes from an excellent family. She was raised by Squire Miller, and her mistress was one of the most pious ladies in that city, I may say; she was the salt of the earth, as the ministers say."

"But she resembles in some respect Agnes, the woman I bought from you," said Mr. Wilson. As he said the name of Agnes, the young woman started as if she had been struck. Her pulse seemed to quicken, but her face alternately flushed and turned pale, and tears trembled upon her eyelids. It was a name she had heard her mother mention, and it brought to her memory those days,—those happy days, when she was so loved and caressed. This young woman was Clotelle, the grand-daughter of Agnes. The preacher, on learning the fact, pur-chased her, and took her home, feeling that his daughter Georgiana would prize her very highly. Clotelle found in Georgiana more a sister than a mistress, who, unknown to her father, taught the slave-girl how to read, and did much toward improving and refining Clotelle's manners, for her own sake. Like her mother fond of flowers, the "Virginia Maid," as she was sometimes called, spent many of her leisure hours in the garden. Beside the flowers which sprang up from the fertility of soil unplanted and unattended, there was the heliotrope, sweet-pea, and cup-rose, transplanted from the island of Cuba. In her new home Clotelle found herself saluted on all sides by the fragrance of the magnolia. When she went with her young mistress to the Poplar Farm, as she sometimes did, nature's wild luxuriance greeted her, wherever she cast her eyes.

The rustling citron, lime, and orange, shady mango with its fruits of gold, and the palmetto's umbrageous beauty, all welcomed the child of sorrow. When at the farm, Huckelby, the overseer, kept his eye on Clotelle if within sight of her, for he knew she was a slave, and no doubt hoped that she might some day fall into his hands. But she shrank from his looks as she would have done from the charm of the rattlesnake. The negro-driver always tried to insinuate himself into the good opinion of Georgiana and the company that she brought. Knowing that Miss Wilson at heart hated slavery, he was ever trying to show that the slaves under his charge were happy and contented. One day, when Georgiana and some of her Connecticut friends were there, the overseer called all the slaves up to the "great house," and set some of the young ones to dancing. After awhile whiskey was brought in and a dram given to each slave, in return for which they were expected to give a toast, or sing a short piece of his own composition; when it came to Jack's turn he said,—

"The big bee flies high, the little bee makes the honey: the black folks make the cotton, and the white folks gets the money."

Of course, the overseer was not at all elated with the sentiment contained in Jack's toast. Mr. Wilson had lately purchased a young man to assist about the house and to act as coachman. This slave, whose name was Jerome, was of pure African origin, was perfectly black, very fine-looking, tall, slim, and erect as any one could possibly be. His features were not bad, lips thin, nose prominent, hands and feet small. His brilliant black eyes lighted up his whole countenance. His hair which was nearly straight, hung in curls upon his lofty brow. George Combe or Fowler would have selected his head for a model. He was brave and daring, strong in person, fiery in spirit, yet kind and true in his affections, earnest in his doctrines. Clotelle had been at the parson's but a few weeks when it was observed that a mutual feeling had grown up between her and Jerome. As time rolled on, they became more and more attached to each other. After satisfying herself that these two really loved, Georgiana advised their marriage. But Jerome contemplated his escape at some future day, and therefore feared that if married it might militate against it. He hoped, also, to be able to get Clotelle away too, and it was this hope that kept him from trying to escape by himself. Dante did not more love his Beatrice, Swift his Stella, Waller his Saccharissa, Goldsmith his Jessamy bride, or Burns his Mary, than did Jerome his Clotelle. Unknown to her father, Miss Wilson could permit these two slaves to enjoy more privileges than any of the other servants. The young mistress taught Clotelle, and the latter imparted her instructions to her lover, until both could read so as to be well understood. Jerome felt his superiority, and always declared that no master should ever flog him. Aware of his high spirit and determination, Clotelle was in constant fear lest some difficulty might arise between her lover and his master.

One day Mr. Wilson, being somewhat out of temper and irritated at what he was pleased to call Jerome's insolence, ordered him to follow him to the barn to be flogged. The young slave obeyed his master, but those who saw him at the moment felt that he would not submit to be whipped.

"No, sir," replied Jerome, as his master told him to take off his coat: "I will serve you, Master Wilson, I will labor for you day and night, if you demand it, but I will not be whipped."

This was too much for a white man to stand from a negro, and the preacher seized his slave by the throat, intending to choke him. But for once he found his match. Jerome knocked him down, and then escaped through the back-yard to the street, and from thence to the woods.

Recovering somewhat from the effect of his fall, the parson regained his feet and started in pursuit of the fugitive. Finding, however, that the slave was beyond his reach, he at once resolved to put the dogs on his track. Tabor, the negro-catcher, was sent for, and in less than an hour, eight or ten men, including the parson, were in the woods with hounds, trying the trails. These dogs will attack a negro at their master's bidding; and cling to him as the bull-dog will cling to a beast. Many are the speculations as to whether the negro will be secured alive or dead, when these dogs once get on his track. Whenever there is to be a negro hunt, there is no lack of participants. Many go to enjoy the fun which it is said they derive from these scenes.

The company had been in the woods but a short time ere they got on the track of two fugitives, one of whom was Jerome. The slaves immediately bent their steps toward the swamp, with the hope that the dogs, when put upon their scent would be unable to follow them through the water.

The slaves then took a straight course for the Baton Rouge and Bayou Sara road, about four miles distant. Nearer and nearer the whimpering pack pressed on; their delusion begins to dispel. All at once the truth flashes upon the minds of the fugitives like a glare of light,—'tis Tabor with his dogs!

The scent becomes warmer and warmer, and what was at first an irregular cry now deepens into one ceaseless roar, as the relentless pack presses on after its human prey.

They at last reach the river, and in the negroes plunge, followed by the catch-dog. Jerome is caught and is once more in the hands of his master, while the other poor fellow finds a watery grave. They return, and the preacher sends his slave to jail.

Chapter XIX

The True Heroine

In vain did Georgiana try to console Clotelle, when the latter heard, through one of the other slaves, that Mr. Wilson had started with the dogs in pursuit of Jerome. The poor girl well knew that he would be caught, and that severe punishment, if not death, would be the result of his capture. It was therefore with a heart filled with the deepest grief that the slave-girl heard the footsteps of her master on his return from the chase. The dogged and stern manner of the preacher forbade even his daughter inquiring as to the success of his pursuit. Georgiana secretly hoped that the fugitive had not been caught; she wished it for the sake of the slave, and more especially for her maid-servant, whom she regarded more as a companion than a menial. But the news of the capture of Jerome soon spread through the parson's household, and found its way to the ears of the weeping and heart-stricken Clotelle.

The reverend gentleman had not been home more than an hour ere some of his parishioners called to know if they should not take the negro from the prison and execute *Lynch law* upon him.

"No negro should be permitted to live after striking a white man; let us take him and hang him at once," remarked an elderly-looking man, whose gray hairs thinly covered the crown of his head.

"I think the deacon is right," said another of the company; "if our slaves are allowed to set the will of their masters at defiance, there will be no getting along with them,—an insurrection will be the next thing we hear of."

"No, no," said the preacher; "I am willing to let the law take its course, as it provides for the punishment of a slave with death if he strikes his master. We had better let the court decide the question. Moreover, as a Christian and God-fearing people, we ought to submit to the dictates of justice. Should we take this man's life by force, an Allwise Providence would hold us responsible for the act."

The company then quietly withdrew, showing that the preacher had some influence with his people.

"This," said Mr. Wilson, when left alone with his daughter,— "this, my dear Georgiana, is the result of your kindness to the negroes. You have spoiled every one about the house. I can't whip one of them, without being in danger of having my life taken."

"I am sure, papa," replied the young lady,—"I am sure I never did any thing intentionally to induce any of the servants to disobey your orders."

"No, my dear," said Mr. Wilson, "but you are too kind to them. Now, there is Clotelle,—that girl is completely spoiled. She walks about the house with as dignified an air as if she was mistress of the premises. By and by you will be sorry for this foolishness of yours."

"But," answered Georgiana, "Clotelle has a superior mind, and God intended her to hold a higher position in life than that of a servant."

"Yes, my dear, and it was your letting her know that she was intended for a better station in society that is spoiling her. Always keep a negro in ignorance of what you conceive to be his abilities," returned the parson.

It was late on the Saturday afternoon, following the capture of Jerome that, while Mr. Wilson was seated in his study preparing his sermon for the next day, Georgiana entered the room and asked in an excited tone if it were true that Jerome was to be hanged on the following Thursday.

The minister informed her that such was the decision of the court.

"Then," said she, "Clotelle will die of grief."

"What business has she to die of grief?" returned the father, his eyes at the moment flashing fire.

"She has neither eaten nor slept since he was captured," replied Georgiana; "and I am certain that she will not live through this."

"I cannot be disturbed now," said the parson; "I must get my sermon ready for to-morrow. I expect to have some strangers to preach to, and must, therefore, prepare a sermon that will do me credit."

While the man of God spoke, he seemed to say to himself,—

> "With devotion's visage, and pious actions,
> We do sugar over the devil himself."

Georgiana did all in her power to soothe the feelings of Clotelle, and to induce her to put her trust in God. Unknown to her father, she allowed the poor girl to go every evening to the jail to see Jerome, and during these visits, despite her own grief, Clotelle would try to comfort her lover with the hope that justice would be meted out to him in the spirit-land.

Thus the time passed on, and the day was fast approaching when the slave was to die. Having heard that some secret meeting had been held by the negroes, previous to the attempt of Mr. Wilson to flog his slave, it occurred to a magistrate that Jerome might know something of the intended revolt. He accordingly visited the prison to see if he could learn anything from him, but all to no purpose. Having given up all hopes of escape, Jerome had resolved to die like a brave man. When questioned as to whether he knew anything of a conspiracy among the slaves against their masters, he replied,—

"Do you suppose that I would tell you if I did?"

"But if you know anything," remarked the magistrate, "and will tell us, you may possibly have your life spared."

"Life," answered the doomed man, "is worth nought to a slave. What right has a slave to himself, his wife, or his children? We are kept in heathenish darkness, by laws especially enacted to make our instruction a criminal offence; and our bones, sinews, blood, and nerves are exposed in the market for sale.

"My liberty is of as much consequence to me as Mr. Wilson's

is to him. I am as sensitive to feeling as he. If I mistake not, the day will come when the negro will learn that he can get his freedom by fighting for it; and should that time arrive, the whites will be sorry that they have hated us so shamefully. I am free to say that, could I live my life over again, I would use all the energies which God has given me to get up an insurrection."

Every one present seemed startled and amazed at the intelligence with which this descendant of Africa spoke.

"He's a very dangerous man," remarked one.

"Yes," said another, "he got some book-learning somewhere, and that has spoiled him."

An effort was then made to learn from Jerome where he had learned to read, but the black refused to give any information on the subject.

The sun was just going down behind the trees as Clotelle entered the prison to see Jerome for the last time. He was to die on the next day. Her face was bent upon her hands, and the gushing tears were forcing their way through her fingers. With beating heart and trembling hands, evincing the deepest emotion, she threw her arms around her lover's neck and embraced him. But, prompted by her heart's unchanging love, she had in her own mind a plan by which she hoped to effect the escape of him to whom she had pledged her heart and hand. While the overcharged clouds which had hung over the city during the day broke, and the rain fell in torrents, amid the most terrific thunder and lightning, Clotelle revealed to Jerome her plan for his escape.

"Dress yourself in my clothes," said she, "and you can easily pass the jailer."

This Jerome at first declined doing. He did not wish to place a confiding girl in a position where, in all probability, she would have to suffer; but being assured by the young girl that her life would not be in danger, he resolved to make the attempt. Clotelle being very tall, it was not probable that the jailer would discover any difference in them.

At this moment, she took from her pocket a bunch of keys and unfastened the padlock, and freed him from the floor.

"Come, girl, it is time for you to go," said the jailer, as Jerome was holding the almost fainting girl by the hand.

Being already attired in Clotelle's clothes, the disguised man embraced the weeping girl, put his handkerchief to his face, and passed out of the jail, without the keeper's knowing that his prisoner was escaping in a disguise and under cover of the night.

Chapter XX

The Hero of Many Adventures

Jerome had scarcely passed the prison-gates, ere he reproached himself for having taken such a step. There seemed to him no hope of escape out of the State, and what was a few hours or days at most, of life to him, when, by obtaining it, another had been sacrificed. He was on the eve of returning, when he thought of the last words uttered by Clotelle. "Be brave and determined, and you will still be free." The words sounded like a charm in his ears and he went boldly forward.

Clotelle had provided a suit of men's clothes and had placed them where her lover could get them, if he should succeed in getting out.

Returning to Mr. Wilson's barn, the fugitive changed his apparel, and again retraced his steps into the street. To reach the Free States by travelling by night and lying by during the day, from a State so far south as Mississippi, no one would think for a moment of attempting to escape. To remain in the city would be a suicidal step. The deep sound of the escape of steam from a boat, which was at that moment ascending the river, broke upon the ears of the slave. "If that boat is going up the river," said he, "why not I conceal myself on board, and try to escape?" He went at once to the steamboat landing, where the boat was just coming in. "Bound for Louisville," said the captain, to one who was making inquiries. As the passengers were rushing on board, Jerome followed them, and proceeding to where some of the hands were stowing away bales of goods, he took hold and aided them.

"Jump down into the hold, there, and help the men," said the mate to the fugitive, supposing that, like many persons, he was working his way up the river. Once in the hull among the boxes, the slave concealed himself. Weary hours, and at last days, passed without either water or food with the hidden slave. More than once did he resolve to let his case be known; but the knowledge that he would be sent back to Natchez kept him from doing so. At last, with lips parched and fevered to a crisp, the poor man crawled out into the freight-room, and began wandering about. The hatches were on, and the room dark. There happened to be on board a wedding party, and a box, containing some of the bridal cake, with several bottles of port wine, was near Jerome. He found the box, opened it, and helped himself. In eight days, the boat tied up at the wharf at the place of her destination. It was late night; the boat's crew, with the single exception of the man on watch, were on shore. The hatches were off, and the fugitive quietly made his way on deck and jumped on shore. The man saw the fugitive, but too late to seize him.

Still in a Slave State, Jerome was at a loss to know how he should proceed. He had with him a few dollars, enough to pay his way to Canada, if he could find a conveyance. The fugitive procured such food as he wanted from one of the many eating-houses, and then, following the direction of the North Star, he passed out of the city, and took the road leading to Covington. Keeping near the Ohio River, Jerome soon found an opportunity to cross over into the State of Indiana. But liberty was a mere name in the latter State, and the fugitive learned, from some colored persons that he met, that it was not safe to travel by daylight. While making his way one night, with nothing to cheer him but the prospect of freedom in the future, he was pounced upon by three men who were lying in wait for another fugitive, an advertisement of whom they had received through the mail. In vain did Jerome tell them that he was not a slave. True, they had not caught the man they expected; but, if they could make this slave tell from what place he had escaped, they knew that a good price would be paid them for the negro's arrest.

Tortured by the slave-catchers, to make him reveal the name of his master and the place from whence he had escaped, Jerome gave them a fictitious name in Virginia, and said that his master would give a large reward, and manifested a willingness to return to his "old boss." By this misrepresentation, the fugitive hoped to have another chance of getting away. Allured with the prospect of a large sum of the needful, the slave-catchers started back with their victim. Stopping on the second night at an inn, on the banks of the Ohio River, the kidnappers, in lieu of a suitable place in which to confine their prize during the night, chained him to the bed-post of their sleeping-chamber. The white men were late in retiring to rest, after an evening spent in drinking. At dead of night, when all was still, the slave arose from the floor, upon which he had been lying, looked around and saw that Morpheus had possession of his captors. For once, thought he, the brandy bottle has done a noble work. With palpitating heart and trembling limbs, he viewed his position. The door was fast, but the warm weather had compelled them to leave the window open. If he could but get his chains off, he might escape through the window to the piazza. The sleepers' clothes hung upon chairs by the bedside. The slave thought of the padlock-key, examined the pockets, and found it. The chains were soon off, and the negro stealthily making his way to the window. He stopped, and said to himself, "These men are villains; they are enemies to all who, like me, are trying to be free. Then why not I teach them a lesson?" He then dressed himself in the best suit, hung his own worn-out and tattered garments on the same chair, and silently passed through the window to the piazza, and let himself down by one of the pillars, and started once more for the North.

Daylight came upon the fugitive before he had selected a hiding-place for the day, and he was walking at a rapid rate, in hopes of soon reaching some woodland or forest. The sun had just begun to show itself, when the fugitive was astounded at seeing behind him, in the distance, two men upon horseback. Taking a road to the right, the slave saw before him a farmhouse, and so near was he to it that he observed two men in front of it looking at him. It was too late to turn back. The kidnappers were behind him—strange men before him. Those in the rear he knew to be enemies, while he had no idea of what principles were the farmers. The latter also saw the white men coming, and called to the fugitive to come that way. The broad-brimmed hats that the farmers wore told the slave that they were Quakers.

Jerome had seen some of these people passing up and down the river, when employed on a steamer between Natchez and New Orleans, and had heard that they disliked slavery. He, therefore, hastened toward the drab-coated men, who, on his approach, opened the barn-door, and told him to "run in."

When Jerome entered the barn, the two farmers closed the door, remaining outside themselves, to confront the slave-catchers, who now came up and demanded admission, feeling that they had their prey secure.

"Thee can't enter my premises," said one of the Friends, in rather a musical voice.

The negro-catchers urged their claim to the slave, and intimated that, unless they were allowed to secure him, they would force their way in. By this time, several other Quakers had gathered around the barn-door. Unfortunately for the kidnappers, and most fortunately for the fugitive, the Friends had just been holding a quarterly meeting in the neighborhood, and a number of them had not yet returned to their homes.

After some talk, the men in drab promised to admit the hunters, provided they procured an officer and a search-warrant from a justice of the peace. One of the slave-catchers was left to see that the fugitive did not get away, while the other went in pursuit of an officer. In the mean time, the owner of the barn sent for a hammer and nails, and began nailing up the barn-door.

After an hour in search of the man of the law, they returned with an officer and a warrant. The Quaker demanded to see the paper, and, after looking at it for some time, called to his son to go into the house for his glasses. It was a long time before Aunt Ruth found the leather case, and when she did, the glasses wanted wiping before they could be used. After comfortably adjusting them on his nose, he read the warrant over leisurely.

"Come, Mr. Dugdale, we can't wait all day," said the officer.

"Well, will thee read it for me?" returned the Quaker.

The officer complied, and the man in drab said,—

"Yes, thee may go in, now. I am inclined to throw no obstacles in the way of the execution of the law of the land."

On approaching the door, the men found some forty or fifty nails in it, in the way of their progress.

"Lend me your hammer and a chisel, if you please, Mr. Dugdale," said the officer.

"Please read that paper over again, will thee?" asked the Quaker.

The officer once more read the warrant.

"I see nothing there which says I must furnish thee with tools to open my door. If thee wants a hammer, thee must go elsewhere for it; I tell thee plainly, thee can't have mine."

The implements for opening the door are at length obtained, and, after another half-hour, the slave-catchers are in the barn. Three hours is a long time for a slave to be in the hands of Quakers. The hay is turned over, and the barn is visited in every part; but still the runaway is not found. Uncle Joseph has a glow upon his countenance; Ephraim shakes his head knowingly; little Elijah is a perfect know-nothing, and, if you look toward the house, you will see Aunt Ruth's smiling face, ready to announce that breakfast is ready.

"The nigger is not in this barn," said the officer.

"I know he is not," quietly answered the Quaker.

"What were you nailing up your door for, then, as if you were afraid we would enter?" inquired one of the kidnappers.

"I can do what I please with my own door, can't I," said the Quaker.

The secret was out; the fugitive had gone in at the front door and out at the back; and the reading of the warrant, nailing up of the door, and other preliminaries of the Quaker, was to give the fugitive time and opportunity to escape.

It was now late in the morning, and the slave-catchers were a long way from home, and the horses were jaded by the rapid manner in which they had travelled. The Friends, in high glee, returned to the house for breakfast; the man of the law, after taking his fee, went home, and the kidnappers turned back, muttering, "Better luck next time."

Chapter XXI

Self-Sacrifice

Now in her seventeenth year, Clotelle's personal appearance presented a great contrast to the time when she lived with old Mrs. Miller. Her tall and well-developed figure; her long, silky black hair, falling in curls down her swan-like neck; her bright, black eyes lighting up her olive-tinted face, and a set of teeth that a Tuscarora might envy, she was a picture of tropical-ripened beauty. At times, there was a heavenly smile upon her countenance, which would have warmed the heart of an anchorite. Such was the personal appearance of the girl who was now in prison by her own act to save the life of another. Would she be hanged in his stead, or would she receive a different kind of punishment? These questions Clotelle did not ask herself. Open, frank, free, and generous to a fault, she always thought of others, never of her own welfare.

The long stay of Clotelle caused some uneasiness to Miss Wilson; yet she dared not tell her father, for he had forbidden the slave-girl's going to the prison to see her lover. While the clock on the church nearby was striking eleven, Georgiana called Sam, and sent him to the prison in search of Clotelle.

"The girl went away from here at eight o'clock," was the jailer's answer to the servant's inquiries.

The return of Sam without having found the girl saddened the heart of the young mistress. "Sure, then," said she, "the poor, heart-broken thing has made way with herself."

Still, she waited till morning before breaking the news of Clotelle's absence to her father.

The jailer discovered, the next morning, to his utter astonishment, that his prisoner was white instead of black, and his first impression was that the change of complexion had taken place during the night, through fear of death. But this conjecture was soon dissipated; for the dark, glowing eyes, the sable curls upon the lofty brow, and the mild, sweet voice that answered his questions, informed him that the prisoner before him was another being.

On learning, in the morning, that Clotelle was in jail dressed in male attire, Miss Wilson immediately sent clothes to her to make a change in her attire. News of the heroic and daring act of the slave-girl spread through the city with electric speed.

"I will sell every nigger on the place," said the parson, at the breakfast-table,—"I will sell them all, and get a new lot, and whip them every day."

Poor Georgiana wept for the safety of Clotelle, while she felt glad that Jerome had escaped. In vain did they try to extort from the girl the whereabouts of the man whose escape she had effected. She was not aware that he had fled on a steamer, and when questioned, she replied,—

"I don't know; and if I did I would not tell you. I care not what you do with me, if Jerome but escapes."

The smile with which she uttered these words finely illustrated the poet's meaning, when he says,—

> "A fearful gift upon thy heart is laid,
> Woman—the power to suffer and to love."

Her sweet simplicity seemed to dare them to lay their rough hands amid her trembling curls.

Three days did the heroic young woman remain in prison, to be gazed at by an unfeeling crowd, drawn there out of curiosity. The intelligence came to her at last that the court had decided to spare her life, on condition that she should be whipped, sold, and sent out of the State within twenty-four hours.

This order of the court she would have cared but little for, had she not been sincerely attached to her young mistress.

"Do try and sell her to some one who will use her well," said Georgiana to her father, as he was about taking his hat to leave the house.

"I shall not trouble myself to do any such thing," replied the hard-hearted parson. "I leave the finding of a master for her with the slave-dealer."

Bathed in tears, Miss Wilson paced her room in the absence of her father. For many months Georgiana had been in a decline, and any little trouble would lay her on a sick bed for days. She was, therefore, poorly able to bear the loss of this companion, whom she so dearly loved.

Mr. Wilson had informed his daughter that Clotelle was to be flogged; and when Felice came in and informed her mistress that the poor girl had just received fifty lashes on her bare person, the young lady fainted and fell on the floor. The servants placed their mistress on the sofa, and went in pursuit of their master. Little did the preacher think, on returning to his daughter, that he should soon be bereft of her; yet such was to be his lot. A blood-vessel had been ruptured, and the three physicians who were called in told the father that he must prepare to lose his child. That moral courage and calmness, which was her great characteristic, did not forsake Georgiana in her hour of death. She had ever been kind to the slaves under her charge, and they loved and respected her. At her request, the servants were all brought into her room, and took a last farewell of their mistress. Seldom, if ever, was there witnessed a more touching scene than this. There lay the young woman, pale and feeble, with death stamped upon her countenance, surrounded by the sons and daughters of Africa, some of whom had been separated from every earthly tie, and the most of whose persons had been torn and gashed by the negro-whip. Some were upon their knees at the bedside, others standing around, and all weeping.

Death is a leveler; and neither age, sex, wealth, nor condition, can avert when he is permitted to strike. The most beautiful flowers must soon fade and droop and die. So, also, with man; his days are as uncertain as the passing breeze. This hour he glows in the blush of health and vigor, but the next, he may be counted with the number no more known on earth. Oh, what a silence pervaded the house when this young flower was gone! In the midst of the buoyancy of youth, this cherished one had drooped and died. Deep were the sounds of grief and mourning heard in that stately dwelling when the stricken friends, whose office it had been to nurse and soothe the weary sufferer, beheld her pale and motionless in the sleep of death.

Who can imagine the feeling with which poor Clotelle received the intelligence of her kind friend's death? The deep gashes of the cruel whip had prostrated the lovely form of the quadroon, and she lay upon her bed of straw in the dark cell. The speculator had bought her, but had postponed her removal till she should recover. Her benefactress was dead, and—

"Hope withering fled, and mercy sighed farewell."

"Is Jerome safe?" she would ask herself continually. If her lover could have but known of the sufferings of that sweet flower,—that polyanthus over which he had so often been in his dreams,—he would then have learned that she was worthy of his love.

It was more than a fortnight before the slave-trader could take his prize to more comfortable quarters. Like Alcibiades, who defaced the images of the gods and expected to be pardoned on the ground of eccentricity, so men who abuse God's image hope to escape the vengeance of his wrath under the plea that the law sanctions their atrocious deeds.

Chapter XXII

Love at First Sight and What Followed

It was a beautiful Sunday in September, with a cloudless sky, and the rays of the sun parching the already thirsty earth, that Clotelle stood at an upper window in Slater's slave-pen in New Orleans, gasping for a breath of fresh air. The bells of thirty churches were calling the people to the different places of worship. Crowds were seen wending their way to the houses of God; one followed by a negro boy carrying his master's Bible; another followed by her maid-servant holding the mistress' fan; a third supporting an umbrella over his master's head to shield him from the burning sun. Baptists immersed, Presbyterians sprinkled, Methodists shouted, and Episcopalians read their prayers, while ministers of the various sects preached that Christ died for all. The chiming of the bells seemed to mock the sighs and deep groans of the forty human beings then incarcerated in the slave-pen. These imprisoned children of God were many of them Methodists, some Baptists, and others claiming to believe in the faith of the Presbyterians and Episcopalians.

Oh, with what anxiety did these creatures await the close of that Sabbath, and the dawn of another day, that should deliver them from those dismal and close cells. Slowly the day passed away, and once more the evening breeze found its way through the barred windows of the prison that contained these injured sons and daughters of America. The clock on the calaboose had just struck nine on Monday morning, when hundreds of persons were seen threading the gates and doors of the negro-pen. It was the same gang that had the day previous been stepping to the tune and keeping time with the musical church bells. Their Bibles were not with them, their prayer-books were left at home, and even their long and solemn faces had been laid aside for the week. They had come to the man-market to make their purchases. Methodists were in search of their brethren. Baptists were looking for those that had been immersed, while Presbyterians were willing to buy fellow-Christians, whether sprinkled or not. The crowd was soon gazing at and feasting their eyes upon the lovely features of Clotelle.

"She is handsomer," muttered one to himself, "than the lady that sat in the pew next to me yesterday."

"I would that my daughter was half so pretty," thinks a second.

Groups are seen talking in every part of the vast building, and the topic on 'Change, is the "beautiful quadroon." By and by, a tall young man with a foreign face, the curling mustache protruding from under a finely-chiseled nose, and having the air of a gentleman, passes by. His dark hazel eye is fastened on the maid, and he stops for a moment; the stranger walks away, but soon returns—he looks, he sees the young woman wipe away the silent tear that steals down her alabaster cheek; he feels ashamed that he should gaze so unmanly on the blushing face of the woman. As he turns upon his heel he takes out his white hankerchief and wipes his eyes. It may be that he has lost a sister, a mother, or some dear one to whom he was betrothed. Again he comes, and the quadroon hides her face. She has heard that foreigners make bad masters, and she shuns his piercing gaze. Again he goes away and then returns. He takes a last look and then walks hurriedly off.

The day wears away, but long before the time of closing the sale the tall young man once more enters the slave-pen. He looks in every direction for the beautiful slave, but she is not there—she has been sold! He goes to the trader and inquires, but he is too late, and he therefore returns to his hotel.

Having entered a military school in Paris when quite young, and soon after been sent with the French army to India, Antoine Devenant had never dabbled in matters of love. He viewed all women from the same stand-point—respected them for their virtues, and often spoke of the goodness of heart of the sex, but never dreamed of taking to himself a wife. The unequalled beauty of Clotelle had dazzled his eyes, and every look that she gave was a dagger that went to his heart. He felt a shortness of breath, his heart palpitated, his head grew dizzy, and his limbs trembled; but he knew not its cause. This was the first stage of "love at first sight."

He who bows to the shrine of beauty when beckoned by this mysterious agent seldom regrets it. Devenant reproached himself for not having made inquiries concerning the girl before he left the market in the morning. His stay in the city was to be short, and the yellow fever was raging, which caused him to feel like making a still earlier departure. The disease appeared in a form unusually severe and repulsive. It seized its victims from amongst the most healthy of the citizens. The disorder began in the brain by oppressive pain accompanied or followed by fever. Fiery veins streaked the eye, the face was inflamed and dyed of a dark dull red color; the ears from time to time rang painfully. Now mucous secretions surcharged the tongue and took away the power of speech; now the sick one spoke, but in speaking had foresight of death. When the violence of the disease approached the heart, the gums were blackened. The sleep broken, troubled by convulsions, or by frightful visions, was worse than the waking hours; and when the reason sank under a delirium which had its seat in the brain, repose utterly forsook the patient's couch. The progress of the fever within was marked by yellowish spots, which spread over the surface of the body. If then, a happy crisis came not, all hope was gone. Soon the breath infected the air with a fetid odor, the lips were glazed, despair painted itself in the eyes, and sobs, with long intervals of silence, formed the only language. From each side of the mouth, spread foam tinged with black and burnt blood. Blue streaks mingled with the yellow all over the frame. All remedies were useless. This was the yellow fever. The disorder spread alarm and confusion throughout the city. On an average more than four hundred died daily. In the midst of disorder and confusion, death heaped victims on victims. Friend followed friend in quick succession. The sick were avoided from the fear of contagion, and for the same reason the dead were left unburied. Nearly two thousand dead bodies lay uncovered in the burial-ground, with only here and there a little lime thrown over them, to prevent the air becoming infected. The negro, whose home is in a hot climate, was not proof against the disease. Many plantations had to suspend their work for want of slaves to take the places of those who had been taken off by the fever.

Chapter XXIII

Meeting of the Cousins

The clock in the hall had scarcely finished striking three when Mr. Taylor entered his own dwelling, a fine residence in Camp Street, New Orleans, followed by the slave-girl whom he had just purchased at the negro-pen. Clotelle looked around wildly as she passed through the hall into the presence of her new mistress. Mrs. Taylor was much pleased with her servant's appearance, and congratulated her husband on his judicious choice.

"But," said Mrs. Taylor, after Clotelle had gone into the kitchen, "how much she looks like Miss Jane Morton."

"Indeed," replied the husband, "I thought, the moment I saw her that she looked like the Mortons."

"I am sure I never saw two faces more alike in my life, than that girl's and Jane Morton's," continued Mrs. Taylor.

Dr. Morton, the purchaser of Marion, the youngest daughter of Agnes, and sister to Isabella, had resided in Camp Street, near the Taylors, for more than eight years, and the families were on very intimate terms, and visited each other frequently. Every one spoke of Clotelle's close resemblance to the Mortons, and especially to the eldest daughter. Indeed, two sisters could hardly have been more alike. The large, dark eyes, black, silk-like hair, tall, graceful figure, and mould of the face, were the same.

The morning following Clotelle's arrival in her new home, Mrs. Taylor was conversing in a low tone with her husband, and both with their eyes following Clotelle as she passed through the room.

"She is far above the station of a slave," remarked the lady. "I saw her, last night, when removing some books, open one and stand over it a moment as if she was reading; and she is as white as I am. I am almost sorry you bought her."

At this juncture the front door-bell rang, and Clotelle hurried through the room to answer it.

"Miss Morton," said the servant as she returned to the mistress' room.

"Ask her to walk in," responded the mistress.

"Now, my dear," said Mrs. Taylor to her husband, "just look and see if you do not notice a marked resemblance between the countenances of Jane and Clotelle."

Miss Morton entered the room just as Mrs. Taylor ceased speaking.

"Have you heard that the Jamisons are down with the fever?" inquired the young lady, after asking about the health of the Taylors.

"No, I had not; I was in hopes it would not get into our street," replied Mrs. Taylor.

All this while Mr. and Mrs. Taylor were keenly scrutinizing their visitor and Clotelle and even the two young women seemed to be conscious that they were in some way the objects of more than usual attention.

Miss Morton had scarcely departed before Mrs. Taylor began questioning Clotelle concerning her early childhood, and became more than ever satisfied that the slave-girl was in some way connected with the Mortons.

Every hour brought fresh news of the ravages of the fever, and the Taylors commenced preparing to leave town. As Mr. Taylor could not go at once, it was determined that his wife should leave without him, accompanied by her new maid-servant. Just as Mrs. Taylor and Clotelle were stepping into the carriage, they were informed that Dr. Morton was down with the epidemic.

It was a beautiful day, with a fine breeze for the time of year, that Mrs. Taylor and her servant found themselves in the cabin of the splendid new steamer "Walk-in-the-Water," bound from New Orleans to Mobile. Every berth in the boat was occupied by persons fleeing from the fearful contagion that was carrying off its hundreds daily.

Late in the day, as Clotelle was standing at one of the windows of the ladies' saloon, she was astonished to see near her, and with eyes fixed intently upon her, the tall young stranger whom she had observed in the slave-market a few days before. She turned hastily away, but the heated cabin and the want of fresh air soon drove her again to the window. The young gentleman again appeared, and coming to the end of the saloon, spoke to the slave-girl in broken English. This confirmed her in her previous opinion that he was a foreigner, and she rejoiced that she had not fallen into his hands.

"I want to talk with you," said the stranger.

"What do you want with me?" she inquired.

"I am your friend," he answered. "I saw you in the slave-market last week, and regretted that I did not speak to you then. I returned in the evening, but you was gone."

Clotelle looked indignantly at the stranger, and was about leaving the window again when the quivering of his lips and the trembling of his voice struck her attention and caused her to remain.

"I intended to buy you and make you free and happy, but I was too late," continued he.

"Why do you wish to make me free?" inquired the girl.

"Because I once had an only and lovely sister, who died three years ago in France, and you are so much like her that had I not known of her death I should certainly have taken you for her."

"However much I may resemble your sister, you are aware that I am not she; why, then, take so much interest in one whom you have never seen before and may never see again?"

"The love," said he, "which I had for my sister is transferred to you."

Clotelle had all along suspected that the man was a knave, and this profession of love at once confirmed her in that belief. She therefore immediately turned away and left him.

Hours elapsed. Twilight was just "letting down her curtain and pinning it with a star," as the slave-girl seated herself on a sofa by the window, and began meditating upon her eventful history, meanwhile watching the white waves as they seemed to sport with each other in the wake of the noble vessel, with the rising moon reflecting its silver rays upon the splendid scene, when the foreigner once more appeared near the window. Although agitated for fear her mistress would see her talking to a stranger, and be angry, Clotelle still thought she saw something in the countenance of the young man that told her he was sincere, and she did not wish to hurt his feelings.

"Why persist in your wish to talk with me?" she said, as he again advanced and spoke to her.

"I wish to purchase you and make you happy," returned he.

"But I am not for sale now," she replied. "My present mistress will not sell me, and if you wished to do so ever so much you could not."

"Then," said he, "if I cannot buy you, when the steamer reaches Mobile, fly with me, and you shall be free."

"I cannot do it," said Clotelle; and she was just leaving the stranger when he took from his pocket a piece of paper and thrust it into her hand.

After returning to her room, she unfolded the paper, and found, to her utter astonishment that it contained a one hundred dollar note on the Bank of the United States. The first impulse of the girl was to return the paper and its contents immediately to the giver, but examining the paper more closely, she saw in faint pencil-marks, "Remember this is from one who loves you." Another thought was to give it to her mistress, and she returned to the saloon for that purpose; but on finding Mrs. Taylor engaged in conversation with some ladies, she did not deem it proper to interrupt her.

Again, therefore, Clotelle seated herself by the window, and again the stranger presented himself. She immediately took the paper from her pocket, and handed it to him; but he declined taking it, saying,—

"No keep it; it may be of some service to you when I am far away."

"Would that I could understand you," said the slave.

"Believe that I am sincere, and then you will understand me," returned the young man. "Would you rather be a slave than be free?" inquired he, with tears that glistened in the rays of the moon.

"No," said she, "I want my freedom, but I must live a virtuous life."

"Then, if you would be free and happy, go with me. We shall be in Mobile in two hours, and when the passengers are going on shore, you take my arm. Have your face covered with a veil, and you will not be observed. We will take passage immediately for France; you can pass as my sister, and I pledge you my honor that I will marry you as soon as we arrive in France."

This solemn promise, coupled with what had previously been said, gave Clotelle confidence in the man, and she instantly determined to go with him. "But then," thought she, "what if I should be detected? I would be forever ruined, for I would be sold, and in all probability have to end my days on a cotton, rice, or sugar plantation." However, the thought of freedom in the future outweighed this danger, and her resolve was taken.

Dressing herself in some of her best clothes, and placing her veiled bonnet where she could get it without the knowledge of her mistress, Clotelle awaited with a heart filled with the deepest emotions and anxiety the moment when she was to take a step which seemed so rash, and which would either make or ruin her forever.

The ships which leave Mobile for Europe lie about thirty miles down the bay, and passengers are taken down from the city in small vessels. The "Walk-in-the-Water" had just made her lines fast, and the passengers were hurrying on shore, when a tall gentleman with a lady at his side descended the stage-plank, and stepped on the wharf. This was Antoine Devenant and Clotelle.

Chapter XXIV

The Law And Its Victim

The death of Dr. Morton, on the third day of his illness, came like a shock upon his wife and daughters. The corpse had scarcely been committed to its mother earth before new and unforeseen difficulties appeared to them. By the laws of the Slave States, the children follow the condition of their mother. If the mother is free, the children are free; if a slave, the children are slaves. Being unacquainted with the Southern code, and no one presuming that Marion had any negro blood in her veins, Dr. Morton had not given the subject a single thought. The woman whom he loved and regarded as his wife was, after all, nothing more than a slave by the laws of the State. What would have been his feelings had he known that at his death his wife and children would be considered as his property? Yet such was the case. Like most men of means at that time, Dr.

Morton was deeply engaged in speculation, and though generally considered wealthy, was very much involved in his business
affairs.

After the disease with which Dr. Morton had so suddenly died
had to some extent subsided, Mr. James Morton, a brother of
the deceased, went to New Orleans to settle up the estate. On
his arrival there, he was pleased with and felt proud of his
nieces, and invited them to return with him to Vermont, little
dreaming that his brother had married a slave, and that his
widow and daughters would be claimed as such. The girls
themselves had never heard that their mother had been a slave,
and therefore knew nothing of the danger hanging over their
heads.

An inventory of the property of the deceased was made out
by Mr. Morton, and placed in the hands of the creditors. These
preliminaries being arranged, the ladies, with their relative,
concluded to leave the city and reside for a few days on the
banks of Lake Ponchartrain, where they could enjoy a fresh air
that the city did not afford. As they were about taking the cars,
however, an officer arrested the whole party—the ladies as
slaves, and the gentleman upon the charge of attempting to
conceal the property of his deceased brother. Mr. Morton was
overwhelmed with horror at the idea of his nieces being claimed
as slaves, and asked for time, that he might save them from such
a fate. He even offered to mortgage his little farm in Vermont
for the amount which young slave-women of their ages would
fetch. But the creditors pleaded that they were an "extra
article," and would sell for more than common slaves, and must
therefore be sold at auction.

The uncle was therefore compelled to give them up to the
officers of the law, and they were separated from him. Jane, the
oldest of the girls, as we have before mentioned, was very
handsome, bearing a close resemblance to her cousin Clotelle.
Alreka, though not as handsome as her sister, was nevertheless a
beautiful girl, and both had all the accomplishments that wealth
and station could procure.

Though only in her fifteenth year, Alreka had become
strongly attached to Volney Lapie, a young Frenchman, a
student in her father's office. This attachment was reciprocated,

although the poverty of the young man and the extreme youth of the girl had caused their feelings to be kept from the young lady's parents.

The day of sale came, and Mr. Morton attended, with the hope that either the magnanimity of the creditors or his own little farm in Vermont might save his nieces from the fate that awaited them. His hope, however, was in vain. The feelings of all present seemed to be lost in the general wish to become the possessor of the young ladies, who stood trembling, blushing, and weeping as the numerous throng gazed at them, or as the intended purchaser examined the graceful proportions of their fair and beautiful frames. Neither the presence of the uncle nor young Lapie could at all lessen the gross language of the officers, or stay the rude hands of those who wished to examine the property thus offered for sale. After a fierce contest between the bidders, the girls were sold, one for two thousand three hundred, and the other for two thousand three hundred and fifty dollars. Had these girls been bought for servants only, they would in all probability have brought not more than nine hundred or a thousand dollars each. Here were two beautiful young girls, accustomed to the fondest indulgence, surrounded by all the refinements of life, and with the timidity and gentleness which such a life would naturally produce, bartered away like cattle in the markets of Smithfield or New York.

The mother, who was also to have been sold, happily followed her husband to the grave, and was spared the pangs of a broken heart.

The purchaser of the young ladies left the market in triumph, and the uncle, with a heavy heart, started for his New England home, with no earthly prospect of ever beholding his nieces again.

The seizure of the young ladies as slaves was the result of the administrator's having found among Dr. Morton's papers the bill-of-sale of Marion which he had taken when he purchased her. He had doubtless intended to liberate her when he married her, but had neglected from time to time to have the proper papers made out. Sad was the result of this negligence.

Chapter XXV

The Flight

On once gaining the wharf, Devenant and Clotelle found no difficulty in securing an immediate passage to France. The fine packet-ship Utica lay down the bay, and only awaited the return of the lighter that night to complete her cargo and list of passengers, ere she departed. The young Frenchman therefore took his prize on board, and started for the ship.

Daylight was just making its appearance the next morning when the Utica weighed anchor and turned her prow toward the sea. In the course of three hours, the vessel, with outspread sails, was rapidly flying from land. Everything appeared to be auspicious. The skies were beautifully clear, and the sea calm, with a sun that dazzled the whole scene. But clouds soon began to chase each other through the heavens, and the sea became rough. It was then that Clotelle felt that there was hope of escaping. She had hitherto kept in the cabin, but now she expressed a wish to come on deck. The hanging clouds were narrowing the horizon to a span, and gloomily mingling with the rising surges. The old and grave-looking seamen shook their weather-wise heads as if foretelling a storm.

As Clotelle came on deck, she strained her eyes in vain to catch a farewell view of her native land. With a smile on her countenance, but with her eyes filled with tears, she said,—

"Farewell, farewell to the land of my birth, and welcome, welcome, ye dark blue waves. I care not where I go, so it is

'Where a tyrant never trod,
    Where a slave was never known,
But where nature worships God,
    If in the wilderness alone.'"

Devenant stood by her side, seeming proud of his future wife, with his face in a glow at his success, while over his noble brow clustering locks of glossy black hair were hanging in careless ringlets. His finely-cut, classic features wore the aspect of one possessed with a large and noble heart.

Once more the beautiful Clotelle whispered in the ear of her lover,—

> "Away, away, o'er land and sea,
> America is now no home for me."

The winds increased with nightfall, and impenetrable gloom surrounded the ship. The prospect was too uncheering, even to persons in love. The attention which Devenant paid to Clotelle, although she had been registered on the ship's passenger list as his sister, caused more than one to look upon his as an agreeable travelling companion. His tall, slender figure and fine countenance bespoke for him at first sight one's confidence. That he was sincerely and deeply enamored of Clotelle all could see.

The weather became still more squally. The wind rushed through the white, foaming waves, and the ship groaned with its own wild and ungovernable labors, while nothing could be seen but the wild waste of waters. The scene was indeed one of fearful sublimity.

Day came and went without any abatement of the storm. Despair was now on every countenance. Occasionally a vivid flash of lightning would break forth and illuminate the black and boiling surges that surrounded the vessel, which was now scudding before the blast under bare poles.

After five days of most intensely stormy weather, the sea settled down into a dead calm, and the passengers flocked on deck. During the last three days of the storm, Clotelle had been so unwell as to be unable to raise her head. Her pale face and quivering lips and languid appearance made her look as if every pulsation had ceased. Her magnificent large and soft eyes, fringed with lashes as dark as night, gave her an angelic appearance. The unreserved attention of Devenant, even when sea-sick himself, did much to increase the little love that the at first distrustful girl had placed in him. The heart must always have some object on which to centre its affections, and Clotelle having lost all hope of ever again seeing Jerome, it was but natural that she should now transfer her love to one who was so greatly befriending her. At first she respected Devenant for the love he manifested for her, and for his apparent willingness to make any sacrifice for her welfare. True, this was an adventure upon which she had risked her all, and should her heart be foiled in this search for hidden treasures, her affections would be shipwrecked forever. She felt under great obligations to the man who had thus effected her escape, and that noble act alone would entitle him to her love.

Each day became more pleasant as the noble ship sped onward amid the rippled spray. The whistling of the breeze through the rigging was music to the ear, and brought gladness to the heart of every one on board. At last, the long suspense was broken by the appearance of land, at which all hearts leaped for joy. It was a beautiful morning in October. The sun had just risen, and sky and earth were still bathed in his soft, rosy glow, when the Utica hauled into the dock at Bordeaux. The splendid streets, beautiful bridges, glittering equipages, and smiling countenances of the people, gave everything a happy appearance, after a voyage of twenty-nine days on the deep, deep sea.

After getting their baggage cleared from the custom-house and going to a hotel, Devenant made immediate arrangements for the marriage. Clotelle, on arriving at the church where the ceremony was to take place, was completely overwhelmed at the spectacle. She had never beheld a scene so gorgeous as this. The magnificent dresses of the priests and choristers, the deep and solemn voices, the elevated crucifix, the burning tapers, the splendidly decorated altar, the sweet-smelling incense, made the occasion truly an imposing one. At the conclusion of the ceremony, the loud and solemn peals of the organ's swelling anthem were lost to all in the contemplation of the interesting scene.

The happy couple set out at once for Dunkirk, the residence of the bridegroom's parents. But their stay there was short, for they had scarcely commenced visiting the numerous friends of the husband ere orders came for him to proceed to India to join that portion of the French army then stationed there.

In due course of time they left for India, passing through Paris and Lyons, taking ship at Marseilles. In the metropolis of France, they spent a week, where the husband took delight in introducing his wife to his brother officers in the French army, and where the newly-married couple were introduced to Louis Philippe, then King of France. In all of these positions, Clotelle sustained herself in a most ladylike manner.

At Lyons, they visited the vast factories and other public works, and all was pleasure with them. The voyage from Marseilles to Calcutta was very pleasant, as the weather was exceedingly fine. On arriving in India, Captain Devenant and lady were received with honors—the former for his heroic bravery in more than one battle, and the latter for her fascinating beauty and pleasing manners, and the fact that she was connected with one who was a general favorite with all who had his acquaintance. This was indeed a great change for Clotelle. Six months had not elapsed since her exposure in the slave-market of New Orleans. This life is a stage, and we are indeed all actors.

Chapter XXVI

The Hero of a Night

Mounted on a fast horse, with the Quaker's son for a guide, Jerome pressed forward while Uncle Joseph was detaining the slave-catchers at the barn-door, through which the fugitive had just escaped. When out of present danger, fearing that suspicion might be aroused if he continued on the road in open day, Jerome buried himself in a thick, dark forest until nightfall. With a yearning heart, he saw the splendor of the setting sun lingering on the hills, as if loath to fade away and be lost in the more sombre hues of twilight, which, rising from the east, was slowly stealing over the expanse of heaven, bearing silence and repose, which should cover his flight from a neighborhood to him so full of dangers.

Wearily and alone, with nothing but the hope of safety before him to cheer him on his way, the poor fugitive urged his tired and trembling limbs forward for several nights. The new suit of clothes with which he had provided himself when he made his escape from his captors, and the twenty dollars which the young Quaker had slipped into his hand, when bidding him "Fare thee well," would enable him to appear genteelly as soon as he dared to travel by daylight, and would thus facilitate his progress toward freedom.

It was late in the evening when the fugitive slave arrived at a small town on the banks of Lake Erie, where he was to remain over night. How strange were his feelings! While his heart throbbed for that freedom and safety which Canada alone could furnish to the whip-scarred slave, on the American continent, his thoughts were with Clotelle. Was she still in prison, and if so, what would be her punishment for aiding him to escape from prison? Would he ever behold her again? These were the thoughts that followed him to his pillow, haunted him in his dreams, and awakened him from his slumbers.

The alarm of fire aroused the inmates of the hotel in which Jerome had sought shelter for the night from the deep sleep into which they had fallen. The whole village was buried in slumber, and the building was half consumed before the frightened inhabitants had reached the scene of the conflagration. The wind was high, and the burning embers were wafted like so many rockets through the sky. The whole town was lighted up, and the cries of women and children in the streets made the scene a terrific one. Jerome heard the alarm, and hastily dressing himself, he went forth and hastened toward the burning building.

"There,—there in that room in the second story, is my child!" exclaimed a woman, wringing her hands, and imploring some one to go to the rescue of her little one.

The broad sheets of fire were flying in the direction of the chamber in which the child was sleeping, and all hope of its being saved seemed gone. Occasionally the wind would lift the pall of smoke, and show that the work of destruction was not yet complete. At last a long ladder was brought, and one end placed under the window of the room. A moment more and a bystander mounted the ladder and ascended in haste to the window. The smoke met him as he raised the sash, and he cried out, "All is lost!" and returned to the ground without entering the room.

Another sweep of the wind showed that the destroying element had not yet made its final visit to that part of the doomed building. The mother, seeing that all hope of again meeting her child in this world was gone, wrung her hands and seemed inconsolable with grief.

At this juncture, a man was seen to mount the ladder, and ascend with great rapidity. All eyes were instantly turned to the figure of this unknown individual as it disappeared in the cloud of smoke escaping from the window. Those who a moment before had been removing furniture, as well as the idlers who had congregated at the ringing of the bells, assembled at the foot of the ladder, and awaited with breathless silence the reappearance of the stranger, who, regardless of his own safety, had thus risked his life to save another's. Three cheers broke the stillness that had fallen on the company, as the brave man was seen coming through the window and slowly descending to the ground, holding under one arm the inanimate form of the child. Another cheer, and then another, made the welkin ring, as the stranger, with hair burned and eyebrows closely singed, fainted at the foot of the ladder. But the child was saved.

The stranger was Jerome. As soon as he revived, he shrunk from every eye, as if he feared they would take from him the freedom which he had gone through so much to obtain.

The next day, the fugitive took a vessel, and the following morning found himself standing on the free soil of Canada. As his foot pressed the shore, he threw himself upon his face, kissed the earth, and exclaimed, "O God! I thank thee that I am a free man."

Chapter XXVII

True Freedom

The history of the African race is God's illuminated clock, set in the dark steeple of time. The negro has been made the hewer of wood and the drawer of water for nearly all other nations. The people of the United States, however, will have an account to settle with God, owing to their treatment of the negro, which will far surpass the rest of mankind.

Jerome, on reaching Canada, felt for the first time that personal freedom which God intended that all who bore his image should enjoy. That same forgetfulness of self which had always characterized him now caused him to think of others. The thoughts of dear ones in slavery were continually in his mind, and above all others, Clotelle occupied his thoughts. Now that he was free, he could better appreciate her condition as a slave. Although Jerome met, on his arrival in Canada, numbers who had escaped from the Southern States, he nevertheless shrank from all society, particularly that of females. The soft, silver-gray tints on the leaves of the trees, with their snow-spotted trunks, and a biting air, warned the new-born freeman that he was in another climate. Jerome sought work, and soon found it; and arranged with his employer that the latter should go to Natchez in search of Clotelle. The good Scotchman, for whom the fugitive was laboring, freely offered to go down and purchase the girl, if she could be bought, and let Jerome pay him in work. With such a prospect of future happiness in view, this injured descendant of outraged and bleeding Africa went daily to his toil with an energy hitherto unknown to him. But oh, how vain are the hopes of man!

Chapter XXVIII

Farewell to America

Three months had elapsed, from the time the fugitive commenced work for Mr. Streeter, when that gentleman returned from his Southern research, and informed Jerome that Parson Wilson had sold Clotelle, and that she had been sent to the New Orleans slave-market.

This intelligence fell with crushing weight upon the heart of Jerome, and he now felt that the last chain which bound him to his native land was severed. He therefore determined to leave America forever. His nearest and dearest friends had often been flogged in his very presence, and he had seen his mother sold to the negro-trader. An only sister had been torn from him by the soul-driver; he had himself been sold and resold, and been compelled to submit to the most degrading and humiliating insults; and now that the woman upon whom his heart doted, and without whom life was a burden, had been taken away forever, he felt it a duty to hate all mankind.

If there is one thing more than another calculated to make one hate and detest American slavery, it is to witness the meetings between fugitives and their friends in Canada. Jerome had beheld some of these scenes. The wife who, after years of separation, had escaped from her prison-house and followed her husband had told her story to him. He had seen the newly-arrived wife rush into the arms of the husband, whose dark face she had not looked upon for long, weary years. Some told of how a sister had been ill-used by the overseer; others of a husband's being whipped to death for having attempted to protect his wife. He had sat in the little log-hut, by the fireside, and heard tales that caused his heart to bleed; and his bosom swelled with just indignation when he thought that there was no remedy for such atrocious acts. It was with such feelings that he informed his employer that he should leave him at the expiration of a month.

In vain did Mr. Streeter try to persuade Jerome to remain with him; and late in the month of February, the latter found himself on board a small vessel loaded with pine-lumber, descending the St. Lawrence, bound for Liverpool. The bark, though an old one, was, nevertheless, considered seaworthy, and the fugitive was working his way out. As the vessel left the river and gained the open sea, the black man appeared to rejoice at the prospect of leaving a country in which his right to manhood had been denied him, and his happiness destroyed.

The wind was proudly swelling the white sails, and the little craft plunging into the foaming waves, with the land fast receding in the distance, when Jerome mounted a pile of lumber to take a last farewell of his native land. With tears glistening in his eyes, and with quivering lips, he turned his gaze toward the shores that were fast fading in the dim distance, and said,—

"Though forced from my native land by the tyrants of the South, I hope I shall some day be able to return. With all her faults, I love my country still."

Chapter XXIX

A Stranger in a Strange Land

The rain was falling on the dirty pavements of Liverpool as Jerome left the vessel after her arrival. Passing the custom-house, he took a cab, and proceeded to Brown's Hotel, Clayton Square.

Finding no employment in Liverpool, Jerome determined to go into the interior and seek for work. He, therefore, called for his bill, and made ready for his departure. Although but four days at the Albion, he found the hotel charges larger than he expected; but a stranger generally counts on being "fleeced" in travelling through the Old World, and especially in Great Britain. After paying his bill, he was about leaving the room, when one of the servants presented himself with a low bow, and said,—

"Something for the waiter, sir?"

"I thought I had paid my bill," replied the man, somewhat surprised at this polite dun.

"I am the waiter, sir, and gets only what strangers see fit to give me."

Taking from his pocket his nearly empty purse, Jerome handed the man a half-crown; but he had hardly restored it to his pocket, before his eye fell on another man in the waiting costume.

"What do you want?" he asked.

"Whatever your honor sees fit to give me, sir. I am the tother waiter."

The purse was again taken from the pocket, and another half-crown handed out. Stepping out into the hall, he saw standing there a good-looking woman, in a white apron, who made a very pretty courtesy.

"What's your business?" he inquired.

"I am the chambermaid, sir, and looks after the gentlemen's beds."

Out came the purse again, and was relieved of another half-crown; whereupon another girl, with a fascinating smile, took the place of the one who had just received her fee.

"What do you want?" demanded the now half-angry Jerome.

"Please, sir, I am the tother chambermaid."

Finding it easier to give shillings than half-crowns, Jerome handed the woman a shilling, and again restored his purse to his pocket, glad that another woman was not to be seen.

Scarcely had he commenced congratulating himself, however, before three men made their appearance, one after another.

"What have *you* done for me?" he asked of the first.

"I am the boots, sir."

The purse came out once more, and a shilling was deposited in the servant's hand.

"What do I owe you?" he inquired of the second.

"I took your honor's letter to the post, yesterday, sir."

Another shilling left the purse.

"In the name of the Lord, what am I indebted to you for?" demanded Jerome, now entirely out of patience, turning to the last of the trio.

"I told yer vership vot time it vas, this morning."

"Well!" exclaimed the indignant man, "ask here what o'clock it is, and you have got to pay for it."

He paid this last demand with a sixpence, regretting that he had not commenced with sixpences instead of half-crowns.

Having cleared off all demands in the house, he started for the railway station; but had scarcely reached the street, before he was accosted by an old man with a broom in his hand, who, with an exceedingly low bow, said,—

"I is here, yer lordship."

"I did not send for you; what is your business?" demanded Jerome.

"I is the man what opened your lordship's cab-door, when your lordship came to the house on Monday last, and I know your honor won't allow a poor man to starve."

Putting a sixpence in the old man's hand, Jerome once more started for the depot. Having obtained letters of introduction to persons in Manchester, he found no difficulty in getting a situation in a large manufacturing house there. Although the salary was small, yet the situation was a much better one than he had hoped to obtain. His compensation as out-door clerk enabled him to employ a man to teach him at night, and, by continued study and attention to business, he was soon promoted.

After three years in his new home, Jerome was placed in a still higher position, where his salary amounted to fifteen hundred dollars a year. The drinking, smoking, and other expensive habits, which the clerks usually indulged in, he carefully avoided.

Being fond of poetry, he turned his attention to literature. Johnson's "Lives of the Poets," the writings of Dryden, Addison, Pope, Clarendon, and other authors of celebrity, he read with attention. The knowledge which he thus picked up during his leisure hours gave him a great advantage over the other clerks, and caused his employers to respect him far more than any other in their establishment. So eager was he to improve the time that he determined to see how much he could read during the unemployed time of night and morning, and his success was beyond his expectations.

Chapter XXX

New Friends

Broken down in health, after ten years of close confinement in his situation, Jerome resolved to give it up, and thereby release himself from an employment which seemed calculated to send him to a premature grave.

It was on a beautiful morning in summer that he started for Scotland, having made up his mind to travel for his health. After visiting Edinburgh and Glasgow, he concluded to spend a few days in the old town of Perth, with a friend whose acquaintance he had made in Manchester. During the second day of his stay in Perth, while crossing the main street, Jerome saw a pony-chaise coming toward him with great speed. A lady, who appeared to be the only occupant of the vehicle, was using her utmost strength to stop the frightened horses. The footman, in his fright, had leaped from behind the carriage, and was following with the crowd. With that self-forgetfulness which was one of his chief characteristics, Jerome threw himself before the horses to stop them; and, seizing the high-spirited animals by the bit, as they dashed by him, he was dragged several rods before their speed was checked, which was not accomplished until one of the horses had fallen to the ground, with the heroic man struggling beneath him.

All present were satisfied that this daring act alone had saved the lady's life, for the chaise must inevitably have been dashed in pieces, had the horses not been thus suddenly checked in their mad career.

On the morning following this perilous adventure, Col. G — called at Jerome's temporary residence, and, after expressing his admiration for his noble daring, and thanking him for having saved his daughter's life, invited him to visit him at his country residence. This invitation was promptly accepted in the spirit in which it was given; and three days after, Jerome found himself at the princely residence of the father of the lady for whose safety he had risked his own life. The house was surrounded by fine trees, and a sweet little stream ran murmuring at the foot, while beds of flowers on every hand shed their odors on the summer air. It was, indeed, a pleasant place to spend the warm weather, and the colonel and his family gave Jerome a most cordial welcome. Miss G. showed especial attention to the stranger. He had not intended remaining longer than the following day; but the family insisted on his taking part in a fox-hunt that was to come off on the morning of the third day. Wishing to witness a scene as interesting as the chase usually proves to be, he decided to remain.

Fifteen persons, five of whom were ladies, were on the ground at the appointed hour. Miss G. was, of course, one of the party. In vain Jerome endeavored to excuse himself from joining in the chase. His plea of ill-health was only met by smiles from the young ladies, and the reply that a ride would effect a cure.

Dressed in a scarlet coat and high boots, with the low, round cap worn in the chase, Jerome mounted a high-spirited horse, whip in hand, and made himself one of the party. In America, riding is a necessity; in England, it is a pleasure. Young men and women attend riding-school in our fatherland, and consider that they are studying a science. Jerome was no rider. He had not been on horseback for more than ten years, and as soon as he mounted, every one saw that he was a novice, and a smile was on the countenance of each member of the company.

The blowing of the horn, and assembling of the hounds, and finally the release of the fox from his close prison, were the signals for the chase to commence. The first half-mile the little animal took his course over a beautiful field where there was neither hedge nor ditch. Thus far the chase was enjoyed by all, even by the American rider, who was better fitted to witness the scene than to take part in it.

We left Jerome in our last reluctantly engaged in the chase; and though the first mile or so of the pursuit, which was over smooth meadow-land, had had an exhilarating effect upon his mind, and tended somewhat to relieve him of the embarrassment consequent upon his position, he nevertheless still felt that he was far from being in his proper element. Besides, the fox had now made for a dense forest which lay before, and he saw difficulties in that direction which to him appeared insurmountable.

Away went the huntsmen, over stone walls, high fences, and deep ditches. Jerome saw the ladies even leading the gentlemen, but this could not inspire him. They cleared the fences, four and five feet high with perfect ease, showing they were quite at home in the saddle. But alas for the poor American! As his fine steed came up to the first fence, and was about to make the leap, Jerome pulled at the bridle, and cried at the top of his voice, "Whoa! whoa! whoa!" the horse at the same time capering about, and appearing determined to keep up with the other animals.

Away dashed the huntsmen, following the hounds, and all were soon lost to the view of their colored companion. Jerome rode up and down the field looking for a gate or bars, that he might get through without risking his neck. Finding, however, that all hope of again catching up with the party was out of the question, he determined to return to the house, under a plea of sudden illness, and back he accordingly went.

"I hope no accident has happened to your honor," said the groom, as he met our hero at the gate.

"A slight dizziness," was the answer.

One of the servants, without being ordered, went at once for the family physician. Ashamed to own that his return was owing to his inability to ride, Jerome resolved to feign sickness. The doctor came, felt his pulse, examined his tongue, and pronounced him a sick man. He immediately ordered a tepid bath, and sent for a couple of leeches.

Seeing things taking such a serious turn, the American began to regret the part he was playing; for there was no fun in being rubbed and leeched when one was in perfect health. He had gone too far to recede, however, and so submitted quietly to the directions of the doctor; and, after following the injunctions given by that learned Esculapius, was put to bed.

Shortly after, the sound of the horns and the yelp of the hounds announced that the poor fox had taken the back track, and was repassing near the house. Even the pleasure of witnessing the beautiful sight from the window was denied to our hero; for the physician had ordered that he must be kept in perfect quiet.

The chase was at last over, and the huntsmen all in, sympathizing with their lost companion. After nine days of sweating, blistering, and leeching, Jerome left his bed convalescent, but much reduced in flesh and strength. This was his first and last attempt to follow the fox and hounds.

During his fortnight's stay at Colonel G.'s, Jerome spent most of his time in the magnificent library. Claude did not watch with more interest every color of the skies, the trees, the grass, and the water, to learn from nature, than did this son of a despised race search books to obtain that knowledge which his early life as a slave had denied him.

Chapter XXXI

The Mysterious Meeting

After more than a fortnight spent in the highlands of Scotland, Jerome passed hastily through London on his way to the continent.

It was toward sunset, on a warm day in October, shortly after his arrival in France, that, after strolling some distance from the Hotel de Leon, in the old and picturesque town of Dunkirk, he entered a burial-ground—such places being always favorite walks with him—and wandered around among the silent dead. All nature around was hushed in silence, and seemed to partake of the general melancholy that hung over the quiet resting-place of the departed. Even the birds seemed imbued with the spirit of the place, for they were silent, either flying noiselessly over the graves, or jumping about in the tall grass. After tracing the various inscriptions that told the characters and conditions of the deceased, and viewing the mounds beneath which the dust of mortality slumbered, he arrived at a secluded spot near where an aged weeping willow bowed its thick foliage to the ground, as though anxious to hide from the scrutinizing gaze of curiosity the grave beneath it. Jerome seated himself on a marble tombstone, and commenced reading from a book which he had carried under his arm. It was now twilight, and he had read but a few minutes when he observed a lady, attired in deep black, and leading a boy, apparently some five or six years old, coming up one of the beautiful, winding paths. As the lady's veil was drawn closely over her face, he felt somewhat at liberty to see her more closely. While thus engaged, the lady gave a slight scream, and seemed suddenly to have fallen into a fainting condition. Jerome sprang from his seat, and caught her in time to save her from falling to the ground.

At this moment an elderly gentleman, also dressed in black, was seen approaching with a hurried step, which seemed to indicate that he was in some way connected with the lady. The old man came up, and in rather a confused manner inquired what had happened, and Jerome explained matters as well as he was able to do so. After taking up the vinaigrette, which had fallen from her hand, and holding the bottle a short time to her face, the lady began to revive. During all this time, the veil had still partly covered the face of the fair one, so that Jerome had scarcely seen it. When she had so far recovered as to be able to look around her, she raised herself slightly, and again screamed and swooned. The old man now feeling satisfied that Jerome's dark complexion was the immediate cause of the catastrophe, said in a somewhat petulant tone,—

"I will be glad, sir, if you will leave us alone."

The little boy at this juncture set up a loud cry, and amid the general confusion, Jerome left the ground and returned to his hotel.

While seated at the window of his room looking out upon the crowded street, with every now and then the strange scene in the graveyard vividly before him, Jerome suddenly thought of the book he had been reading, and, remembering that he had left it on the tombstone, where he dropped it when called to the lady's assistance, he determined to return for it at once.

After a walk of some twenty minutes, he found himself again in the burial-ground and on the spot where he had been an hour before. The pensive moon was already up, and its soft light was sleeping on the little pond at the back of the grounds, while the stars seemed smiling at their own sparkling rays gleaming up from the beautiful sheet of water.

Jerome searched in vain for his book; it was nowhere to be found. Nothing, save the bouquet that the lady had dropped, and which lay half-buried in the grass, from having been trodden upon, indicated that any one had been there that evening. The stillness of death reigned over the place; even the little birds, that had before been twittering and flying about, had retired for the night.

Taking up the bunch of flowers, Jerome returned to his hotel. "What can this mean?" he would ask himself; "and why should they take my book?" These questions he put to himself again and again during his walk. His sleep was broken more than once that night, and he welcomed the early dawn as it made its appearance.

Chapter XXXII

The Happy Meeting

After passing a sleepless night, and hearing the clock strike six, Jerome took from his table a book, and thus endeavored to pass away the hours before breakfast-time. While thus engaged, a servant entered and handed him a note. Hastily tearing it open, Jerome read as follows:—

"SIR,—I owe you an apology for the abrupt manner in which I addressed you last evening, and the inconvenience to which you were subjected by some of my household. If you will honor us with your presence to-day at four o'clock, I shall be most happy to give you due satisfaction. My servant will be waiting with the carriage at half-past three.

I am, sir, yours, &c.,   J. DEVENANT.
JEROME FLETCHER, Esq.

Who this gentleman was, and how he had found out his name and the hotel at which he was stopping, were alike mysteries to Jerome. And this note seemed to his puzzled brain like a challenge. "Satisfaction?" He had not asked for satisfaction. However, he resolved to accept the invitation, and, if need be, meet the worst. At any rate, this most mysterious and complicated affair would be explained.

The clock on a neighboring church had scarcely finished striking three when a servant announced to Jerome that a carriage had called for him. In a few minutes, he was seated in a sumptuous barouche, drawn by a pair of beautiful iron-grays, and rolling over a splendid gravel road entirely shaded by trees, which appeared to have been the accumulated growth of many centuries. The carriage soon stopped at a low villa, which was completely embowered in trees.

Jerome alighted, and was shown into a superb room, with the walls finely decorated with splendid tapestry, and the ceilings exquisitely frescoed. The walls were hung with fine specimens from the hands of the great Italian masters, and one by a German artist, representing a beautiful monkish legend connected with the "Holy Catharine," an illustrious lady of Alexandria. High-backed chairs stood around the room, rich curtains of crimson damask hung in folds on either side of the window, and a beautiful, rich, Turkey carpet covered the floor. In the centre of the room stood a table covered with books, in the midst of which was a vase of fresh flowers, loading the atmosphere with their odors. A faint light, together with the quiet of the hour, gave beauty beyond description to the whole scene. A half-open door showed a fine marble floor to an adjoining room, with pictures, statues, and antiquated sofas, and flower-pots filled with rare plants of every kind and description.

Jerome had scarcely run his eyes over the beauties of the room when the elderly gentleman whom he had met on the previous evening made his appearance, followed by the little boy, and introduced himself as Mr. Devenant. A moment more and a lady, a beautiful brunette, dressed in black, with long black curls hanging over her shoulders, entered the room. Her dark, bright eyes flashed as she caught the first sight of Jerome. The gentleman immediately arose on the entrance of the lady, and Mr. Devenant was in the act of introducing the stranger when he observed that Jerome had sunk back upon the sofa, in a faint voice exclaiming,—

"It is she!"

After this, all was dark and dreary. How long he remained in this condition, it was for others to tell. The lady knelt by his side and wept; and when he came to, he found himself stretched upon the sofa with his boots off and his head resting upon a pillow. By his side sat the old man, with the smelling-bottle in one hand and a glass of water in the other, while the little boy stood at the foot of the sofa. As soon as Jerome had so far recovered as to be able to speak, he said,—

"Where am I, and what does all this mean?"

"Wait awhile," replied the old man, "and I will tell you all."

After the lapse of some ten minutes, Jerome arose from the sofa, adjusted his apparel, and said,—

"I am now ready to hear anything you have to say."

"You were born in America?" said the old man.

"I was," he replied.

"And you knew a girl named Clotelle," continued the old man.

"Yes, and I loved her as I can love none other."

"The lady whom you met so mysteriously last evening was she," said Mr. Devenant.

Jerome was silent, but the fountain of mingled grief and joy stole out from beneath his eyelashes, and glistened like pearls upon his ebony cheeks.

At this juncture, the lady again entered the room. With an enthusiasm that can be better imagined than described, Jerome sprang from the sofa, and they rushed into each other's arms, to the great surprise of the old gentleman and little Antoine, and to the amusement of the servants who had crept up, one by one and were hid behind the doors or loitering in the hall. When they had given vent to their feelings and sufficiently recovered their presence of mind, they resumed their seats.

"How did you find out my name and address?" inquired Jerome.

"After you had left the grave-yard," replied Clotelle, "our little boy said, 'Oh, mamma! if there ain't a book!' I opened the book, and saw your name written in it, and also found a card of the Hotel de Leon. Papa wished to leave the book, and said it was only a fancy of mine that I had ever seen you before; but I was perfectly convinced that you were my own dear Jerome."

As she uttered the last words, tears—the sweet bright tears that love alone can bring forth—bedewed her cheeks.

"Are you married?" now inquired Clotelle, with a palpitating heart and trembling voice.

"No, I am not, and never have been," was Jerome's reply.

"Then, thank God!" she exclaimed, in broken accents.

It was then that hope gleamed up amid the crushed and broken flowers of her heart, and a bright flash darted forth like a sunbeam.

"Are you single now?" asked Jerome.

"Yes, I am," was the answer.

"Then you will be mine after all?" said he with a smile.

Her dark, rich hair had partly come down, and hung still more loosely over her shoulders than when she first appeared; and her eyes, now full of animation and vivacity, and her sweet, harmonious, and well-modulated voice, together with her modesty, self-possession, and engaging manners, made Clotelle appear lovely beyond description. Although past the age when men ought to think of matrimony, yet the scene before Mr. Devenant brought vividly to his mind the time when he was young and had a loving bosom companion living, and tears were wiped from the old man's eyes. A new world seemed to unfold itself before the eyes of the happy lovers, and they were completely absorbed in contemplating the future. Furnished by nature with a disposition to study, and a memory so retentive that all who knew her were surprised at the ease with which she acquired her education and general information, Clotelle might now be termed a most accomplished lady. After her marriage with young Devenant, they proceeded to India, where the husband's regiment was stationed. Soon after their arrival, however, a battle was fought with the natives, in which several officers fell, among whom was Captain Devenant. The father of the young captain being there at the time, took his daughter-in-law and brought her back to France, where they took up their abode at the old homestead.

Old Mr. Devenant was possessed of a large fortune, all of which he intended for his daughter-in-law and her only child.

Although Clotelle had married young Devenant, she had not forgotten her first love, and her father-in-law now willingly gave his consent to her marriage with Jerome. Jerome felt that to possess the woman of his love, even at that late hour, was compensation enough for the years that he had been separated from her, and Clotelle wanted no better evidence of his love for her than the fact of his having remained so long unmarried. It was indeed a rare instance of devotion and constancy in a man, and the young widow gratefully appreciated it.

It was late in the evening when Jerome led his intended bride to the window, and the magnificent moonlight illuminated the countenance of the lovely Clotelle, while inward sunshine, emanating from a mind at ease, and her own virtuous thoughts, gave brightness to her eyes and made her appear a very angel. This was the first evening that Jerome had been in her company since the night when, to effect his escape from prison, she disguised herself in male attire. How different the scene now. Free instead of slaves, wealthy instead of poor, and on the eve of an event that seemed likely to result in a life of happiness to both.

Chapter XXXIII

The Happy Day

It was a bright day in the latter part of October that Jerome and Clotelle set out for the church, where the marriage ceremony was to be performed. The clear, bracing air added buoyancy to every movement, and the sun poured its brilliant rays through the deeply-stained windows, as the happy couple entered the sanctuary, followed by old Mr. Devenant, whose form, bowed down with age, attracted almost as much attention from the assembly as did the couple more particularly interested.

As the ceremonies were finished and the priest pronounced the benediction on the newly-married pair, Clotelle whispered in the ear of Jerome,—

" 'No power in death shall tear our names apart,
    As none in life could rend thee from my heart.' "

A smile beamed on every face as the wedding-party left the church and entered their carriage. What a happy day, after ten years' separation, when, both hearts having been blighted for a time, they are brought together by the hand of a beneficient and kind Providence, and united in holy wedlock.

Everything being arranged for a wedding tour extending up the Rhine, the party set out the same day for Antwerp. There are many rivers of greater length and width than the Rhine. Our Mississippi would swallow up half a dozen Rhines. The Hudson is grander, the Tiber, the Po, and the Mincio more classic; the Thames and Seine bear upon their waters greater amounts of wealth and commerce; the Nile and the Euphrates have a greater antiquity; but for a combination of interesting historical incidents and natural scenery, the Rhine surpasses them all. Nature has so ordained it that those who travel in the valley of the Rhine shall see the river, for there never will be a railroad upon its banks. So mountainous is the land that it would have to be one series of tunnels. Every three or four miles from the time you enter this glorious river, hills, dales, castles, and crags present themselves as the steamer glides onward.

Their first resting-place for any length of time was at Coblentz, at the mouth of the "Blue Moselle," the most interesting place on the river. From Coblentz they went to Brussels, where they had the greatest attention paid them. Besides being provided with letters of introduction, Jerome's complexion secured for him more deference than is usually awarded to travellers.

Having letters of introduction to M. Deceptiax, the great lace manufacturer, that gentleman received them with distinguished honors, and gave them a splendid *soiree,* at which the *elite* of the city were assembled. The sumptuously-furnished mansion was lavishly decorated for the occasion, and every preparation made that could add to the novelty or interest of the event.

Jerome, with his beautiful bride, next visited Cologne, the largest and wealthiest city on the banks of the Rhine. The Cathedral of Cologne is the most splendid structure of the kind in Europe, and Jerome and Clotelle viewed with interest the beautiful arches and columns of this stupendous building, which strikes with awe the beholder, as he gazes at its unequalled splendor, surrounded, as it is, by villas, cottages, and palace-like mansions, with the enchanting Rhine winding through the vine-covered hills.

After strolling over miles and miles of classic ground, and

visiting castles, whose legends and traditions have given them an enduring fame, our delighted travellers started for Geneva, bidding the picturesque banks of the Rhine a regretful farewell. Being much interested in literature, and aware that Geneva was noted for having been the city of refuge to the victims of religious and political persecution, Jerome arranged to stay here for some days. He was provided with a letter of introduction to M. de Stee, who had been a fellow-soldier of Mr. Devenant in the East India wars, and they were invited to make his house their home during their sojourn. On the side of a noble mountain, whose base is kissed by the waves of Lake Geneva, and whose slopes are decked with verdure to the utmost peak of its rocky crown, is situated the delightful country-residence of this wealthy, retired French officer. A winding road, with frequent climbs and brakes, leads from the valley to this enchanting spot, the air and scenery of which cannot be surpassed in the world.

Chapter XXXIV

Clotelle Meets Her Father

The clouds that had skirted the sky during the day broke at last, and the rain fell in torrents, as Jerome and Clotelle retired for the night, in the little town of Ferney, on the borders of Lake Leman. The peals of thunder, and flashes of vivid lightning, which seemed to leap from mountain to mountain and from crag to crag, reverberating among the surrounding hills, foretold a heavy storm.

"I would we were back at Geneva," said Clotelle, as she heard groans issuing from an adjoining room. The sounds, at first faint, grew louder and louder, plainly indicating that some person was suffering extreme pain.

"I did not like this hotel, much, when we came in," said Jerome, relighting the lamp, which had been accidentally extinguished.

"Nor I," returned Clotelle.

The shrieks increased, and an occasional "She's dead!" "I

killed her!" "No, she is not dead!" and such-like expressions, would be heard from the person, who seemed to be deranged.

The thunder grew louder, and the flashes of lightning more vivid, while the noise from the sick-room seemed to increase.

As Jerome opened the door, to learn, if possible, the cause of the cries and groans, he could distinguish the words, "She's dead! yes, she's dead! but I did not kill her. She was my child! my own daughter. I loved her, and yet I did not protect her."

"Whoever he is," said Jerome, "he's crack-brained; some robber, probably, from the mountains."

The storm continued to rage, and the loud peals of thunder and sharp flashes of lightning, together with the shrieks and moans of the maniac in the adjoining room, made the night a fearful one. The long hours wore slowly away, but neither Jerome nor his wife could sleep, and they arose at an early hour in the morning, ordered breakfast, and resolved to return to Geneva.

"I am sorry, sir, that you were so much disturbed by the sick man last night," said the landlord, as he handed Jerome his bill. "I should be glad if he would get able to go away, or die, for he's a deal of trouble to me. Several persons have left my house on his account."

"Where is he from?" inquired Jerome.

"He's from the United States, and has been here a week to-day, and has been crazy ever since."

"Has he no friends with him?" asked the guest.

"No, he is alone," was the reply.

Jerome related to his wife what he had learned from the landlord, respecting the sick man, and the intelligence impressed her so strongly, that she requested him to make further inquiries concerning the stranger.

He therefore consulted the book in which guests usually register their names, and, to his great surprise, found that the American's name was Henry Linwood, and that he was from Richmond, Va.

It was with feelings of trepidation that Clotelle heard these particulars from the lips of her husband.

"We must see this poor man, whoever he is," said she, as Jerome finished the sentence.

The landlord was glad to hear that his guests felt some interest in the sick man, and promised that the invalid's room should be got ready for their reception.

The clock in the hall was just striking ten, as Jerome passed through and entered the sick man's chamber. Stretched upon a mattress, with both hands tightly bound to the bedstead, the friendless stranger was indeed a pitiful sight. His dark, dishevelled hair prematurely gray, his long, unshaven beard, and the wildness of the eyes which glanced upon them as they opened the door and entered, caused the faint hope which had so suddenly risen in Clotelle's heart, to sink, and she felt that this man could claim no kindred with her. Certainly, he bore no resemblance to the man whom she had called her father, and who had fondly dandled her on his knee in those happy days of childhood.

"Help!" cried the poor man, as Jerome and his wife walked into the room. His eyes glared, and shriek after shriek broke forth from his parched and fevered lips.

"No, I did not kill my daughter!—I did not! she is not dead! Yes, she is dead! but I did not kill her—poor girl! Look! that is she! No, it cannot be! she cannot come here! it cannot be my poor Clotelle."

At the sound of her own name, coming from the maniac's lips, Clotelle gasped for breath, and her husband saw that she had grown deadly pale. It seemed evident to him that the man was either guilty of some terrible act, or imagined himself to be. His eyeballs rolled in their sockets, and his features showed that he was undergoing "the tortures of that inward hell," which seemed to set his whole brain on fire.

After recovering her self-possession and strength, Clotelle approached the bedside, and laid her soft hand upon the stranger's hot and fevered brow.

One long, loud shriek rang out on the air, and a piercing cry, "It is she!—Yes, it is she! I see, I see! Ah! no, it is not my daughter! She would not come to me if she could!" broke forth from him.

"I am your daughter," said Clotelle, as she pressed her handkerchief to her face, and sobbed aloud.

Like balls of fire, the poor man's eyes rolled and glared upon the company, while large drops of perspiration ran down his pale and emaciated face. Strange as the scene appeared, all present saw that it was indeed a meeting between a father and his long-lost daughter. Jerome now ordered all present to leave the room, except the nurse, and every effort was at once made to quiet the sufferer. When calm, a joyous smile would illuminate the sick man's face, and a strange light beam in his eyes, as he seemed to realize that she who stood before him was indeed his child.

For two long days and nights did Clotelle watch at the bedside of her father before he could speak to her intelligently. Sometimes, in his insane fits, he would rave in the most frightful manner, and then, in a few moments, would be as easily governed as a child. At last, however, after a long and apparently refreshing sleep, he awoke suddenly to a full consciousness that it was indeed his daughter who was watching so patiently by his side.

The presence of his long absent child had a soothing effect upon Mr. Linwood, and he now recovered rapidly from the sad and almost hopeless condition in which she had found him. When able to converse, without danger of a relapse, he told Clotelle of his fruitless efforts to obtain a clew to her whereabouts after old Mrs. Miller had sold her to the slave-trader. In answer to his daughter's inquiries about his family affairs up to the time that he left America, he said,—

"I blamed my wife for your being sold and sent away, for I thought she and her mother were acting in collusion; But I afterwards found that I had blamed her wrongfully. Poor woman! she knew that I loved your mother, and feeling herself forsaken, she grew melancholy and died in a decline three years ago."

Here both father and daughter wept at the thought of other days. When they had recovered their composure, Mr. Linwood went on again:

"Old Mrs. Miller," said he, "after the death of Gertrude, aware that she had contributed much toward her unhappiness, took to the free use of intoxicating drinks, and became the most brutal creature that ever lived. She whipped her slaves without the slightest provocation, and seemed to take delight in inventing new tortures with which to punish them. One night last winter, after having flogged one of her slaves nearly to death, she returned to her room, and by some means the bedding took fire, and the house was in flames before any one was awakened. There was no one in the building at the time but the old woman and the slaves, and although the latter might have saved their mistress, they made no attempt to do so. Thus, after a frightful career of many years, this hard-hearted woman died a most miserable death, unlamented by a single person."

Clotelle wiped the tears from her eyes, as her father finished this story, for, although Mrs. Miller had been her greatest enemy, she regretted to learn that her end had been such a sad one.

"My peace of mind destroyed," resumed the father, "and broken down in health, my physician advised me to travel, with the hope of recruiting myself, and I sailed from New York two months ago."

Being brought up in America, and having all the prejudice against color which characterizes his white fellow-countrymen, Mr. Linwood very much regretted that his daughter, although herself tinctured with African blood, should have married a black man, and he did not fail to express to her his dislike of her husband's complexion.

"I married him," said Clotelle, "because I loved him. Why should the white man be esteemed as better than the black? I find no difference in men on account of their complexion. One of the cardinal principles of Christianity and freedom is the equality and brotherhood of man."

Every day Mr. Linwood became more and more familiar with Jerome, and eventually they were on the most intimate terms.

Fifteen days from the time that Clotelle was introduced into her father's room, they left Ferney for Geneva. Many were the excursions Clotelle made under the shadows of Mont Blanc, and with her husband and father for companions; she was now in the enjoyment of pleasures hitherto unknown.

Chapter XXXV

The Father's Resolve

Aware that her father was still a slave-owner, Clotelle determined to use all her persuasive power to induce him to set them free, and in this effort she found a substantial supporter in her husband.

"I have always treated my slaves well," said Mr. Linwood to Jerome, as the latter expressed his abhorrence of the system; "and my neighbors, too, are generally good men; for slavery in Virginia is not like slavery in the other States," continued the proud son of the Old Dominion.

"Their right to be free, Mr. Linwood," said Jerome, "is taken from them, and they have no security for their comfort, but the humanity and generosity of men, who have been trained to regard them not as brethren, but as mere property. Humanity and generosity are, at best, but poor guaranties for the protection of those who cannot assert their rights, and over whom law throws no protection."

It was with pleasure that Clotelle obtained from her father a promise that he would liberate all his slaves on his return to Richmond. In a beautiful little villa, situated in a pleasant spot, fringed with hoary rocks and thick dark woods, within sight of the deep blue waters of Lake Leman, Mr. Linwood, his daughter, and her husband, took up their residence for a short time. For more than three weeks, this little party spent their time in visiting the birth-place of Rousseau, and the former abodes of Byron, Gibbon, Voltaire, De Stael, Shelley, and other literary characters.

We can scarcely contemplate a visit to a more historic and interesting place than Geneva and its vicinity. Here, Calvin, that great luminary in the Church, lived and ruled for years; here, Voltaire, the mighty genius, who laid the foundation of the French Revolution, and who boasted, "When I shake my wig, I powder the whole republic," governed in the higher walks of life.

Fame is generally the recompense, not of the living, but of the dead,—not always do they reap and gather in the harvest who sow the seed; the flame of its altar is too often kindled from the ashes of the great. A distinguished critic has beautifully said, "The sound which the stream of high thought, carried down to future ages, makes, as it flows—deep, distant, murmuring ever more, like the waters of the mighty ocean." No reputation can be called great that will not endure this test. The distinguished men who had lived in Geneva transfused their spirit, by their writings, into the spirit of other lovers of literature and everything that treated of great authors. Jerome and Clotelle lingered long in and about the haunts of Geneva and Lake Leman.

An autumn sun sent down her bright rays, and bathed every object in her glorious light, as Clotelle, accompanied by her husband and father set out one fine morning on her return home to France. Throughout the whole route, Mr. Linwood saw by the deference paid to Jerome, whose black complexion excited astonishment in those who met him, that there was no hatred to the man in Europe, on account of his color; that what is called prejudice against color is the offspring of the institution of slavery; and he felt ashamed of his own countrymen, when he thought of the complexion as distinctions, made in the United States, and resolved to dedicate the remainder of his life to the eradication of this unrepublican and unchristian feeling from the land of his birth, on his return home.

After a stay of four weeks at Dunkirk, the home of the Fletchers, Mr. Linwood set out for America, with the full determination of freeing his slaves, and settling them in one of the Northern States, and then to return to France to end his days in the society of his beloved daughter.

THE END.

Bibliographical Essay

One of the most provocative books on slavery is William Styron's *The Confessions of Nat Turner* (New York, Random House, 1967). For the controversy over the novel, see Martin Duberman, "Historical Fictions," *New York Times Book Review*, August 11, 1968; C. Van Woodward, "Confessions of a Rebel: 1831," *New Republic*, CLVII (October 7, 1967), pp. 25-28; Herbert Aptheker, "Styron-Turner and Nat Turner: Myth and Truth," *Political Affairs*, XLVI (October, 1967), pp. 40-50; Marc L. Ratner, "Styron's Rebel," *American Quarterly*, XXI (Fall, 1969), No. 3, pp. 595 608; Stanley Kauffman, "Styron's Unwritten Novel," *Hudson Review*, XX (Winter, 1967-68), pp. 675-80; William E. Akin, "Toward an Impressionistic History: Pitfalls and Possibilities in William Styron's Meditation on History," *American Quarterly*, XXI (Winter, 1969), No. 4, pp. 805-12; Curtis Harnack, "The Quiddities of Detail," *Kenyon Review* II (Issue 1, 1968), pp. 125-32; John Henrik Clarke, ed., *William Styron's Nat Turner: Ten Black Writers Respond* (Boston, Beacon, 1968); Eugene Genovese, "The Nat Turner Case—A Review of *William Styron's Nat Turner: Ten Black Writers Respond*," *New York Review of Books*, September 12, 1968; "An Exchange on 'Nat Turner,' " *New York Review of Books*, November 7, 1968. For some of Styron's observations and comments, see Styron, "This Quiet Dist," *Harper's Magazine*, Vol. 230 (April, 1965), pp. 135-46; "Truth & Nat Turner: An Exchange between Herbert Aptheker and

William Styron," *Nation,* April 22, 1968, pp. 543-47; Styron, "Overcome," *New York Review of Books,* September 26, 1963; "Two Writers Talk It Over," *Esquire,* LX (July, 1963), pp. 57-58; Page Stegner and Robert Conzoneri, "An Interview with William Styron," *Per/Se* (Summer, 1966), pp. 37-44; "Into the Mind of Nat Turner," *Newsweek,* LXX (October 16, 1967), pp. 65-69. For a black novelist's interpretation of the slave rebel Gabriel Prosser, see Arna Bontemps, *Black Thunder: Gabriel's Revolt: Virginia: 1800* (Boston, Beacon, 1968; originally published in 1936). Unfortunately the debate over Styron's novel has not shed much light on the meaning of the vision of the mysterious white marble temple which Styron's Turner beheld with terrible awe and puzzlement.

The controversy over Styron's novel has focused on crucial questions about black thought in antebellum slave society: What did it mean to be black in white America, and what and how did black slaves feel and think about themselves and whites? These questions have concerned historians and anthropologists for a long time. U. B. Phillips devoted much of his lifetime to a study of *American Negro Slavery* (Gloucester, Massachusetts, Peter Smith, 1959, originally published in 1918). His emphasis on slave docility has been challenged by Raymond A. Bauer and Alice H. Bauer, "Day to Day Resistance to Slavery," *Journal of Negro History,* XXVII (October, 1942), No. 4, pp. 388-419; Richard Hofstadter, "U. B. Phillips and the Plantation Legend," *Journal of Negro History,* XIX (April, 1944), No. 2, pp. 109-24; Herbert Aptheker, *American Negro Slave Revolts* (New York, Columbia University Press, 1943); Harvey Wish, "American Slave Insurrections before 1861," *Journal of Negro History,* XXII (July, 1937); Marion D. de B. Kilson, "Towards Freedom: An Analysis of Slave Revolts in the United States," *Phylon,* XXV (Summer, 1964); Kenneth Stampp, "The Historian and Southern Negro Slavery," *American Historical Review* LVII (April, 1956), pp. 613-24; Stampp, *The Peculiar Institution: Slavery in the Ante-Bellum South* (New York, Knopf, 1956); Vincent Harding, "Religion and Resistance Among Antebellum Negroes, 1800-1860," in August Meier and Elliot Rudwick, eds., *The Making of Black America* (New York, Atheneum, 1969), Vol. I.

Stanley Elkins, *Slavery: A Problem in American Institutional and Intellectual Life* (Chicago, University of Chicago, 1959), offers a sociopsychological explanation of Sambo. The discussions contained in his footnotes and appendix show that Elkins has a more sophisticated understanding of slave personality than his text would indicate. For responses to Elkins' study, see "The Question of 'Sambo,' " *The Newberry Library Bulletin*, V (December, 1958); Earl E. Thorpe, "Chattel Slavery and Concentration Camps," *Negro History Bulletin*, XXV (May, 1962), pp. 171-76; Sidney W. Mintz, "Review of *Slavery* by Stanley Elkins," *American Anthropologist*, Vol. 63 (June, 1961), No. 3, pp. 579-87; George M. Frederickson and Christopher Lasch, "Resistance to Slavery," *Civil War History*, XIII (December, 1967), No. 4, pp. 315-29; Eugene D. Genovese, "Rebelliousness and Docility in the Negro Slave: A Critique of the Elkins Thesis," *Civil War History*, XIII (December, 1967), No. 4, pp. 293-314.

Studies of urban slavery in the Old South have also given attention to questions concerning slave docility and rebelliousness. See Richard C. Wade, *Slavery in the Cities; the South: 1820-1860* (New York, Oxford University Press, 1964); Alan Dowty, "Urban Slavery in Pro-Southern Fiction of the 1850's," *Journal of Southern History*, XXXII, pp. 25-41; Robert S. Starobin, *Industrial Slavery in the Old South* (New York, Oxford University Press, 1970). Various aspects of slave thought are explored in Jessie W. Parkhurst, "The Role of the Black Mammy in the Plantation Household," *Journal of Negro History*, XXIII (July, 1938), No. 3; Bell I. Wiley, *Southern Negroes, 1861-1865* (New Haven, Yale, 1938); Melville J. Herskovits, *The Myth of the Negro Past* (Boston, Beacon, 1967); Eugene Genovese, "The Legacy of Slavery and the Roots of Black Nationalism," *Studies on the Left*, Vol. 6 (1966), No. 6, pp. 3-26; and Genovese, "American Slaves and Their History," *New York Review of Books* (December 3, 1970). Indispensable are slave narratives and songs. See Robin W. Winks, *et al.*, eds., *Four Fugitive Slave Narratives* (Reading, Massachusetts, Addison-Wesley, 1969); Gilbert Osofsky, *Puttin' On Ole Massa: The Slave Narratives of Henry Bibb, William Wells Brown, and Solomon Northup* (New York, Harper, 1969); and William Francis Allen, *et al.*, eds., *Slave Songs of the United States* (New York, Peter Smith, 1929, copyright 1867). Two of the most suggestive articles on the free black in the South are by E. Horace Fitchett, "The Traditions of the Free Negro in Charleston, South Carolina," *Journal of Negro History*, XXV (April, 1940), No. 2, pp. 139-51; "The Origin and Growth of the Free Negro Populations of Charleston, South Carolina," *Journal of Negro History* (October, 1941), No. 4, pp. 421-37.

The standard work on the black in the North is Leon Litwack, *North of Slavery: The Negro in the Free States, 1790-1860* (Chicago, University of Chicago, 1961). Eugene H. Berwanger, *The Frontier Against Slavery: Western Anti-Negro Prejudice and the Slavery Extension Controversy* (Urbana, University of Illinois, 1967), documents the ubiquity and virulence of racism in the Western territories and states. Useful state and local studies are Louis Ruchames, "Race and Education in Massachusetts," *Negro History Bulletin*, XIII (December, 1949), pp. 53-59, 71; Ruchames, "Jim Crow Railroads in Massachusetts," *American Quarterly*, VIII (1956), pp. 61-75; Charles H. Wesley, "The Negroes of New York in the Emancipation Movement," *Journal of Negro History*, XXIV (January, 1939); Robert Ernst, "The Economic Status of New York City Negroes, 1850-63," *Negro History Bulletin*, XII (March, 1949), pp. 131-32, 139-43; Leo H. Hirsch, Jr., "The Negro in New York, 1783-1865," *Journal of Negro History*, XV (1931); Dixon Ryan Fox, "The Negro Vote in Old New York," *Political Science Quarterly*, XXXII (June, 1917), p. 252-75; Edward R. Turner, *The Negro in Pennsylvania: Slavery, Servitude, Freedom, 1639-1861* (Washington, 1911); Emma Lou Thornbrough, *The Negro in Indiana* (Indianapolis, 1957); Charles T. Hickok, *The Negro in Ohio, 1802-70* (Cleveland, 1896); Carter G. Woodson, "The Negroes of Cincinnati Prior to the Civil War," *Journal of Negro History*, I (1916), pp. 1-22; Richard C. Wade, "The Negro in Cincinnati, 1800-1830," *Journal of Negro History*, XXXIX (1954), pp. 43-57. E. Franklin Frazier offers a fascinating and controversial interpretation of the *Black Bourgeoisie* (New York, 1957).

For the black abolitionists, see Benjamin Quarles, *Black Abolitionists* (New York, Oxford, 1969); Carleton Mabee, *Black Freedom: The Nonviolent Abolitionists from 1830 through the Civil War* (New York, Macmillan, 1970); Martin Duberman, ed., *The Antislavery Vanguard* (Princeton, Princeton, 1965); August

Meier, "The Emergence of Negro Nationalism: A Study in Ideologies," *Midwest Journal*, IV (Winter, 1951-52), pp. 96-104, and (Summer, 1952) pp. 95-111; Howard H. Bell, *A Survey of the Negro Convention Movement, 1830-1861* (New York, Arno, 1969); Charles H. Wesley, "The Participation of Negroes in Anti-Slavery Political Parties," *Journal of Negro History*, XXIX (January, 1944); Wesley, "The Negro in the Organization of Abolition," *Phylon*, II (Third quarter, 1941), pp. 223-35; William H. and Jane H. Pease, "Antislavery Ambivalence: Immediatism, Expediency, Race," *American Quarterly*, XVII (Winter, 1965); Larry Gara, *The Liberty Line* (Lexington, University of Kentucky, 1961); William M. Brewer, "John B. Russwurm," *Journal of Negro History* (1928), pp. 413-22; William M. Brewer, "Henry Highland Garnet," *Journal of Negro History*, XIII (1928), pp. 36-52; Henry N. Sherwood, "Paul Cuffee," *Journal of Negro History*, VIII (1923), pp. 153-229; Charles H. Wesley, *Richard Allen* (Washington, 1935), Earl Conrad, *Harriet Tubman* (New York, Eriksson, 1969).

Important black abolitionist documents may be found in the Boston *Liberator*, the New York *Anti-Slavery Standard*, the Rochester *North Star, Frederick Douglass' Paper, Frederick Douglass' Monthly*, the New York *Anglo-African Magazine*, the New York *Weekly Anglo-African*, the *Annual Reports of the American and Foreign Anti-Slavery Society*, Carter G. Woodson, *The Mind of the Negro as Reflected in Letters during the Crisis, 1800-1860*. See also David Walker, *Appeal to the Colored Citizens of the World* (New York, Hill and Wang, 1965); Henry Highland Garnet, "An Address to the Slaves of the United States of America," reprinted in Garnet, *A Memorial Discourse* (Philadelphia, Wilson, 1865); Garnet, *The Past and the Present Condition, and the Destiny of the Colored Race* (Troy, Kneeland, 1848).

Documents related to Frederick Douglass are abundant. Private letters may be found in the Anti-Slavery Collection of the Boston Public Library; the Douglass MSS, Anacostia Heights, Washington, D.C.; the Douglass MSS, Syracuse University Library; the S. D. Porter Papers, University of Rochester Library. Philip Foner's *The Life and Writings of Frederick Douglass* (New York, International, 1955), 4 vols., is a magnificent collection. Very useful are Douglass' autobiographies: *Narrative of the Life of Frederick Douglass, an American Slave*.

Written by himself. (New York, New American Library, 1968, originally published in 1845); *My Bondage and My Freedom* (New York, Arno, 1968, originally published in 1855); *Life and Times of Frederick Douglass* (New York, Collier, 1962, originally published in 1884). Also indispensable are *The Heroic Slave*, republished here, and his Rochester *North Star, Frederick Douglass' Paper,* and *Frederick Douglass' Monthly.* See also Theodore Stanton, "Frederick Douglass in Paris," *Open Court,* I, (April 28, 1887), p. 151; F. B. Sanborn, *Life and Letters of John Brown* (Concord, Sanborn, 1910); Lillie Buffum Chace and Arthur Crawford Wyman, *Elizabeth Buffum Chace and Her Environment* (Boston, Clark, 1914); Jane Marsh Parker, "Reminiscences of Frederick Douglass," *Outlook,* 51 (April 6, 1895), pp. 552-55; Rosetta Douglass Sprague, "My Mother as I Recall Her," *Journal of Negro History,* VIII (January, 1923); Francis J. Grimke, "The Second Marriage of Frederick Douglass," *Journal of Negro History,* XIX (July, 1934). Benjamin Quarles' biography of *Frederick Douglass* (New York, Atheneum, 1968, copyright 1948) is a solid piece of scholarship. For some provocative thoughts on violence see Willie Lee Rose, "Killing for Freedom," *New York Review of Books,* December 3, 1970.

Unpublished documents related to Martin Delany are scarce, but some of them may be found in the Boston Public Library and the Countway Library of the Harvard Medical School. Delany's most important writings are *The Condition, Elevation, Emigration and Destiny of the Colored People of the United States* (New York, Arno, 1969, originally published in 1852); "Political Destiny of the Colored Race on the American Continent," in Appendix, Frank A. Rollin, *Life and Public Services of Martin R. Delany* (Boston, Lee and Shepard, 1883); *Blake; or, the Huts of America,* in the New York *Anglo-African Magazine,* January-July, 1859; the New York *Weekly Anglo-African,* November, 1861-May, 1862 (republished recently by Beacon Press, 1970); *Official Report of the Niger Valley Exploring Party,* republished in Howard H. Bell, *Search for a Place* (Ann Arbor, University of Michigan, 1969); *Principia of Ethnology: The Origin of Races and Color* (Philadelphia, Harper, 1879). Delany's essays published in the *North Star,* 1848-49, contain his observations on the despair of black life in

Northern society and reveal his increasing alienation from America.

Early studies of Delany are Rollin's *Delany, op. cit.,* and William J. Simmons, *Men of Mark: Eminent, Progressive and Rising* (Cleveland, Revell, 1887). Recent helpful studies are W. Montague Cobb, "Martin Robinson Delany, 1812-1885," *Journal of the National Medical Association,* XLIV (May, 1952), pp. 232-38; Theodore Draper, "The Father of American Black Nationalism," *New York Review of Books,* March 12, 1970; Dorothy Sterling, *The Making of an Afro-American: Martin Robinson Delany, 1812-1885* (Garden City, Doubleday, 1971); Victor Ullman, *Martin R. Delany: The Beginnings of Black Nationalism* (Boston, Beacon Press, 1971). For information on black emigrationism, see Hollis Lynch, *Edward W. Blyden: Pan-Negro Patriot* (New York, Oxford, 1970); Lynch, "Pan-Negro Nationalism in the New World, Before 1862," in Meier and Rudwick, *The Making of Black America, op. cit.*; William Lloyd Garrison, *Thoughts on African Colonization* (New York, Arno, 1968); Robert Campbell, *A Pilgrimage to My Motherland: An Account of a Journey among the Egbas and Yorubas of Central Africa,* in Bell, *Search for a Place*; Bell, "The Negro Emigration Movement, 1849-1854: A Phase of Negro Nationalism," *Phylon,* XX (1959), No. 2, pp. 132-42; Bell, "Expressions of Negro Militancy in the North, 1840-1860," *Journal of Negro History,* XLV (January, 1960), No. 1, pp. 11-20, Louis R. Mehlinger, "The Attitude of the Free Negro Toward Colonization," *Journal of Negro History,* I (1916), pp. 276-301.

The most important (and virtually the only) study of William Wells Brown is William Edward Farrison, *William Wells Brown: Author and Reformer* (Chicago, University of Chicago, 1970), an informative narrative biography. Josephine Brown published a brief *Biography of an American Bondman, by His Daughter* (Boston, Wallcutt, 1856). For Brown's life as a slave, see *Narrative of William Wells Brown,* republished in Osofsky, *op. cit.* Brown was a very prolific writer and left behind a little library of publications for the historian to examine: *A Lecture delivered before the Female Anti-Slavery Society of Salem* (Boston, Massachusetts Anti-Slavery Society, 1847); *Three Years in Europe* (London, Gilpin, 1852); *Clotel: or, The President's Daughter* (London, 1853), later published in revised form as *Clotelle: A Tale of the Southern States* (Boston, Redpath, 1864); *The American Fugitive in Europe* (New York, Negro University Press, 1969, originally published in 1855); *St. Domingo: Its Revolutions and its Patriots* (Boston, Bela March, 1855); *The Escape, or A Leap for Freedom* (Boston, Wallcutt, 1858); *The Black Man, His Antecedents, His Genius, and His Achievements* (New York, Hamilton, 1863); *The Negro in the American Rebellion: His Heroism and His Fidelity* (Boston, Lee and Shepard, 1867); *The Rising Sun, or the History of the Colored Race* (Boston, Brown, 1874); *My Southern Home: or, The South and Its People* (Boston, Brown, 1880).

Insightful and thought-provoking analyses of violence may be found in Richard Wright, *Native Son* (New York, Harper & Row, 1940); Frantz Fanon, *Wretched of the Earth* (New York, Grove, 1966); Martin Luther King, Jr., *Where Do We Go From Here: Chaos Or Community?* (New York, Harper & Row, 1967); and Theodore Roszak, "The Hard and the Soft: The Force of Feminism in Modern Times," in Roszaks, eds., *Masculine/Feminine: Readings in Sexual Mythology and the Liberation of Women* (New York, Harper & Row, 1969).